RICHARD BALLANTINE first fell in love with cycling when his father gave him a classic single-speed, balloon-tyre paper-boy bike to help him get over a case of measles. In the 40 years since he has churned along on anything with wheels and pedals, including antique high bicycles and ultra-modern, streamlined human powered vehicles.

Richard's gift for sharing his cycling enthusiasms surfaced with RICHARD'S BICYCLE BOOK, originally published in 1972 and now, with over one million copies printed, the best-selling bicycle book of all time. In 1981 he founded Britain's first glossy colour monthly, *Bicycle Magazine*. In 1985 he launched the annual *Bicycle Buyer's Bible* and in 1987 launched the RICHARD'S BICYCLE BOOK SERIES.

Richard lives with his family, an ever-growing collection of bikes, and several animals, including a dog, in a north London house that he plans to equip with London's first bikeport.

RICHARD'S

New Bicycle Book

New Bicycle Book

by Richard Ballantine

Illustrations by
John Batchelor and Peter Williams

Pan Books
London, Sydney and Auckland

This book is dedicated to
Samuel Joseph Melville,
Hero.

First published as Richard's Bicycle Book in 1975 by Pan Books Ltd, Cavaye Place, London SW10 9PG

This edition published 1990

9 8 7 6 5 4 3 2

ISBN 0 330 31315 0

Printed and bound in Great Britain by Richard Clay Ltd, Bungay, Suffolk

Series created by Richard Grant and Richard Ballantine

Designed by Richard Grant

Produced by Tamshield Limited, London.

Cover bike and equipment courtesy of F.W. Evans Ltd., 77 The Cut, London SE1

BOOK ONE

BOOK TWO

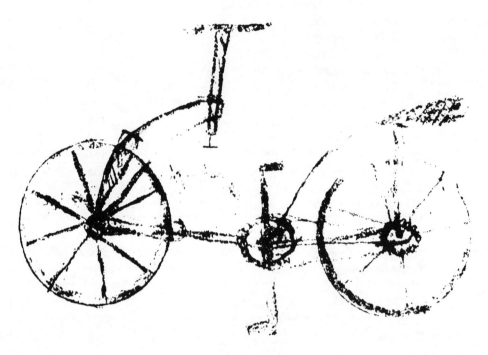

Leonardo's bicycle
Design for a bicycle from the studio of Leonardo da Vinci

Bike!

'Get a bicycle.
You will not regret it if you live.'
—Mark Twain

It is almost impossible to make a bicycle that will not work. Yet so far as is known, not one of the ancient and classical civilizations that established culture and society, built the pyramids, conquered the known world, or otherwise epically marked the course of history ever came up with the idea of a bicycle. The first evidence of the concept comes from the late fifteenth century studio of Leonardo da Vinci, where a student or students made a rough sketch of what is essentially a modern bicycle with pedals and a chain drive. Renaissance technology was capable of building such a machine, but the context of the sketch—alongside pornographic drawings and a caricature of one of da Vinci's pupils—suggests that even then the idea must have appeared fanciful and absurd.

The practical beginning of the bicycle took place over 300 years later, with the invention by Baron Karl von Drais in 1817 of a running-machine. Popularly known as a hobby-horse, the vehicle consisted of a body set above two wheels, and was powered by the rider pushing his feet alternately against the ground. The front wheel could be steered, and the discovery that such a vehicle would stay upright was a fundamental breakthrough. The hobby-horse was crude

Hobby-horse

and severely uncomfortable, but it was the fastest road-going vehicle of the day. In one celebrated race, a hobby-horse rider beat a four-horse coach from London to Brighton.

A number of subsequent inventors made the logical next step of creating two-wheel machines with pedal-drive transmissions, but it was not until the late 1860s that bicycles with pedals were manufactured in quantity in France, Britain, and America. Based on the velocipede launched by Pierre Michaux of Paris in 1861, and known as 'boneshakers' in Britain, the machines had pedals and cranks attached directly to the front wheel. The design had the advantage of being easy to manufacture, but made speed while pedalling a function of wheel size; the larger the diameter of the driving wheel, the faster the machine could go. Rider

Boneshaker

leg length determined maximum possible wheel size and since in terms of power the best riding position was almost straight above the wheel, through the 1870s the boneshaker literally grew into the famous high-wheel bicycle popularly known as a penny-farthing, a machine that often stood as tall as a man.

A high centre of gravity made the penny-farthing extremely unstable and virtually impossible to brake, and a riding position some five feet above the ground made falls—which were inevitable—horrendous. Cycling in the latter part of the nineteenth century was a highly athletic and adventurous activity largely confined to young, middle-class sporting bloods, and, as such, often sat poorly with the mainstream public. Cyclists tended to band together in quasi-military clubs that required uniforms and strict riding rules, partly as a means for satisfying and expressing self-esteem, but more practically, for group protection against the frequent abuse, sticks, and stones hurled at them when on club runs.

Penny-farthing

Two inventions made bicycles into a practical form of personal transport. The first was the chain-drive rear wheel, the key feature of the Rover Safety bicycle designed by John Kemp Starley and launched in 1885. There were earlier chain-drive bicycles, but it was the Rover that succeeded in commercial production and, as advertised, truly 'set the fashion for the world'. The use of a chain enabled gearing and hence wheels of a reasonable size, resulting in a stable machine that could utilize brakes. The smaller wheels reacted more harshly to bumps and holes, but this problem was solved by the second invention critical to the development of cycling: the pneumatic tyre patented by John Boyd Dunlop in 1888. The air-filled inner tube provided a cushion against road shock and vibration, and also dramatically reduced rolling resistance. The chain-drive bicycle was already far swifter than the direct-drive high bicycle; shod with pneumatic tyres it became the fastest, most energy-efficient personal vehicle on earth—for the rider, truly like sprouting wings.

The bicycle gave individual freedom and mobility, and in the period 1890-1910, its development and spread throughout the world was incandescent. The scale of usefulness for what Stuart S. Wilson of Oxford University describes as the most important modern invention was vast, and ranged through all walks of life: at once, bicycles were instrumental in liberating house-bound women from skirts and dom-

ELLIMAN'S 1/1½
UNIVERSAL EMBROCATION

STIFFNESS ACHES SPRAINS BRUISES

estic servitude, and in exploring and opening up rugged wilderness areas such as the Australian Outback and the Canadian North-West Territories. Sport, service trades, postal deliveries, gold prospecting, courting—bicycles were used in almost every sphere of life. Transport for the people had arrived.

In the twentieth century the development of cycling was affected by two world wars, and profoundly influenced by the rise of the automobile. The wars were not so bad—in fact, during the 1914-18 and 1939-45 conflicts, when both petrol and mass transportation were scarce, bicycles proved more useful than ever. The effect of the automobile, which has killed more people than both world wars combined, was another story.

In America, the passion for automobiles simply swept away the bicycle. After World War I enclaves of cycle sport persisted in a few places, but with the onset of the Great Depression of the 1930s the American bicycle industry came to a virtual standstill. Only 194,000 bicycles were sold in 1932. In 1933 Arnold, Schwinn, and Company introduced a new range of bicycles with low-pressure, 2.125-inch tyres. The bikes were styled like motorcycles and were sturdy but cumbersome. Equipped with massive cowhorn handlebars, a single pedal-operated coaster brake, and one low, slow gear, these 'balloon-tyre bombers' hit the scales at up to 70 lb plus and were used primarily by youngsters not old enough to drive, and by people who had no other alternative.

The story in Britain was quite different. In the years between the wars the popularity of cycling, both as a recreational activity and as a general means of transport, expanded enormously; the year 1935 saw a record 1.6 million bikes sold. The basic bicycle design established by 1910 had been subject to a long evolutionary series of minor improvements. Most mass-produced bicycles were middleweights with lightened frames, roller lever rim brakes, and 1.5-inch tyres, while fancier, even lighter models had calliper cable-actuated rim brakes, hub gears, and 1.25- or 1.5-inch tyres. Tipping the scales at 45-50 lb, they were dubbed 'English Racers' by the Americans because of their startlingly better performance over the domestic product. In Britain, they were just the ordinary ride-around bike for local use, to and from work, postal delivery, police work, window cleaning, light touring, and the like. True lightweight racing bikes with handmade frames and derailleur gears were the provenance of individual framebuilders, and old-time riders and cycle dealers say that nearly every village had a builder, and associated coterie of club riders.

It was a great time. People had a love of cycling. In the late 1930s there were over 9 million regular cyclists—bakers, racers, entire families—on the roads. The end was also at hand; in 1936, a relatively few 2.5 million motorists killed 1,496 cyclists and injured 71,193 more. Of all road casualties in that year, 31 per cent were cyclists. There was a hue and cry, but no effective remedial action from either cyclists or the government, and the problem was soon supplanted by the life-and-death global conflict of World War II.

In the post-war period 1945-55 the number of cars in Britain tripled. The motoring boom was on; cycling was ignored or even actively discouraged. Britain went car-crazy, and roads, car parks, petrol stations, and cars, cars, cars proliferated, transforming towns and villages into mazes of one-way motordromes and elevating Britain to a world leader in numbers of cars per mile of road. The bicycle went the way of the dodo. Sales dropped to less than 500,000 a year. The only people who cycled were keepers of the classic faith, or those who could afford no better.

Back in America, however, samples of English Racers and other lightweight European machines brought home by returning soldiers provided the impetus for the development of cycling as an adult activity. Where the balloon-tyre bomber needed King Kong on the pedals to get anywhere, the English Racer was a realistic proposition as transportation. Moreover, it was fun! In the late 1950s and early 1960s stores devoted mainly to the sale and rental of bicycles developed steadily. Americans began spending more of their increased free time on afternoon rides in the countryside or parks. Bikes appeared in force on university campuses, and hardier souls began using them as all-around transportation.

In the 1960s came the 10- and 15-speed derailleur-gear, drop-handlebar racing and touring bikes. Just as there was no comparison in performance between a balloon-tyre bomber and an English Racer, the new lightweight '10-speed' bikes moved far faster and more easily than ordinary bikes. The first models in America came from Europe and short supply made them very expensive. But the new adult customers had the economic clout to buy what they wanted—bikes!

The Great American Bike Boom is a chapter in history now. It was wonderful fun while it lasted. People bought anything that rolled on two wheels, so long as it had drop handlebars, chromed fork blades, quick-release hubs, and derailleur gears. Small factories in Europe and Asia produced crude machines for the U.S. by the container load, with no thought for servicing or availability of spare parts. Trading in the bicycle business was like being first in line at the 1849 California gold rush; individual fortunes were made overnight. Annual sales took a decade to double from 4.4 million in 1960 to 8.9 million in 1971, but only two years to nearly double again at 15.8 million in 1973, with a final crest in 1974-5 at nearly 17 million.

The ebb of the boom saw annual sales drop to 8-9 million, and then recover: 10.4 million in 1984, 11.4 million in 1985, and now, over 13 million.

In Great Britain the Bike Boom had a later start, but was no less spectacular: in just eight years, annual sales went from 700,000 in 1972 to 1.6 million in 1980, a match for the halcyon record set in 1935. The bike was back—and thriving. Sales reached 1.85 million in 1982, and peaked at an astonishing 2.15 million in 1983. Volume in 1984 at 2.05 million was nearly as good, but then fell sharply to 1.5 million in 1985 and 1.3 million in 1986. The market has now stabilized, and current annual sales are in the region of 1.9 million. Altogether, there are some 15 million operational bikes in Britain.

Behind the figures are fundamental changes in the nature of cycling, both as an activity and as an industry. Where once the majority of bikes sold were for children, adult models now account for around 80 per cent of all bikes sold. Of these, more than half are sport bikes. Across Britain during the growth years between 1974 and 1984, cycle mileage rose by 56 per cent while motor vehicle traffic grew by 31 per cent. This reflects the return of the bike as adult, day-to-day transport; of cycling trips, 29 per cent are to and from work, 26 per cent are for shopping, 11 per cent are to and from education, and 25 per cent are recreational.

The rise in popularity of cycling—annual global production of bikes is over 100 million a year—has been accompanied by the development of new bike designs, manufacturing technologies, and materials. Handmade bicycles are a continuing tradition, but fine, high-quality bikes are now mass-produced in the millions and millions. Today, you can buy better bikes, for less money, than ever before. And the menu of technical choice is incredibly varied: anything from simple, cheerful single-speed cruisers through to bikes—yes, bikes—that can break the national speed limit.

The original impetus for the Bike Boom came from European cycle technology and ideas, but cycling is now a world-wide activity and industry. The latest and possibly most significant development in cycling is an American invention—the mountain bike, a machine that mates the robust construction and go-anywhere nature of the original balloon-tyre bomber with the light weight and multiple gears of a road racer. It's a bike that can go where there are no roads, clambering up and down mountains, or traversing deserts, which is also perfect for charging through rough, potholed urban streets.

There are many different kinds of bikes, and a multitude of reasons for owning a bike, or bikes. Some people cycle when they need to, like opening an umbrella when it rains. They need to go somewhere, they get on a bike. Other people practically live on their machines. They look for places to go and for excuses to ride. They race, tour, explore, or whatever. Each to his or her own. Many are the ways. Bikes are tools and are what you make of them. But as tools, and sources of satisfaction and joy, bikes have some fundamental characteristics worth thinking about.

Economics

Can you afford not to own a bike? With even moderate use it will pay for itself.

Over a year, using a bike instead of public transportation to get to work and back will save £300-400—more than enough for a good bike. If you've been using a car, then switching to a bike will save £800-1000 annually—enough for the latest in super-bikes, plus plenty of spare change as well. As a commuting vehicle, a bike usually recovers the cost of purchase within a few months. Thereafter, you are money in pocket, and over a year or two the amount is enough to make a real difference—equipment for other sports, the holiday of a lifetime, an addition to the house, a nice boat . . . take your pick.

Commuting to and from work is just the start. Bikes are great for general moving around: nipping to the shops, visiting friends, going to the theatre, and so on. You save money every time, and again, the cumulative total can be substantial. In times past people who rode bikes were thought to be poor. These days, using a bike marks a lifestyle interested in making the most of resources. In this case, at least, less is more.

Bikes are highly economic—it's cheaper to cycle than to walk—but the bottom line is that they are fun. A bike easily 'pays for itself' in pleasure rides. And as an item of sports or leisure equipment, the cost of a first-class bike is very competitive with the cost of equipment for outdoor sports such as skiing, SCUBA diving, wind-surfing, and hiking and camping.

Incidentally, if you are a car owner try this exercise: total all your car-related expenses for the year. (Average annual costs by engine displacement are: 1 litre, £3,000; 1-1.5 litres, £3,500; 1.5-2 litres, £4,200; and 2-3 litres, £6,900.) Add in the total annual expenditure on all other transport.

Next, add up the costs of: bikes and accessories for each family member (say, £400 per person); renting cars for weekends, holidays, and so on; and all other transport, including a sizeable allowance for taxi-cabs.

Unless you drive many miles a year, or have a very large family, using bikes and renting cars when required will probably show money in pocket within a year, two years at most—and you still have a car or taxi-cab whenever required. Try it out. For many people it is both cheaper and more convenient not to own a car.

Take charge

In metropolitan areas for a distance up to 5 miles, a bike is faster than a train, bus, or car. In heavy traffic you can expect to average 10 mph, and in lighter traffic 12-15 mph. In London, I regularly ride 7 miles between Primrose Hill and London Bridge in 25 minutes. If it's a cool, clear night with little traffic, and I'm running the Speedy (a machine I'll tell you more about later), the time is sometimes under 20 minutes. The same journey by tube takes around 40 minutes if all goes well, and an hour or more if beset with delays—which are chronic. In New York City I regularly rode 2½ miles to mid-town Manhattan from an apartment on the lower East Side in 15 minutes, usually less. The bus took at least 30-40 minutes, the train about 25-35. The story is the same everywhere. There have been bike versus bus, train, and car contests in many cities, and in each case I know about, the bike has always won.

One reason a bike is so fast is that it wiggle through the traffic jams that now typify cities and towns. A car or bus may have a higher peak speed, but is often completely immobile. A bike can just keep on moving, posting a higher average speed. Another factor is that a bike is door to door. If you use a bus or train you've got to walk to the local stop, wait around for the thing to show up, travel (possibly with a transfer and another wait), and then walk again to your destination. If you use a car you've got to find a parking space, a rarely easy task that also usually involves a walk. With a bike you simply step out the door and take off. No waiting, no parking problems.

A bike is freedom. You can go where you want, when you want. Things like bus and train schedules, awareness of periods peak traffic congestion, or worries about money for transport or whether the car will start are simply not part of your consciousness. If you feel like going to a film, trying out a new restuarant, or dashing off to buy a kite, you go. Bing. There's nothing to think about except doing it. What's more, you'll always be able to get back. Taxi-cabs, trains, and buses have early bedtimes, but a bike is always ready to go when you are. In fact, late at night is one of the nicest times to ride a bike. In cities, the streets are quiet and calm, the air is cleaner, and you glide along with smooth grace. In the country, you are a part of the night under the moon and stars. Reliability? No problem. A bike kept in decent condition is going to work. Any problem that does arise can usually be solved in minutes. With a bike your life is under your direct control. If you want to be (or leave) someplace, you do it. It does not take much experience to make the timing of most journeys predictable within a minute or two. With a bike there is no 'perhaps'. You are mobile.

Health and Fitness

Riding a bike makes you feel better. When you do physical work you take in oxygen and use it to burn the fuel stored in your body. Efficiency in respiration, and in delivering oxygen to the body tissues while simultaneously clearing away the by-products of muscle activity, is the important measure of fitness. Exercise increases your fitness and makes all your other activities—from gardening to washing the dishes to thinking through a chess problem—easier to do. Riding a bike is ideal exercise. Your lungs, heart, and general blood circulation system are exercised at the pace that suits you best. There's no stress to joints—just a nice, general work-out that leaves you in better shape. How better? Put it this way: if you are fairly sedentary and take up riding a bike with reasonable regularity, your life span will increase by about five years! The reason is that by exercising your heart and lungs you make them more efficient and keep them cleaned out, so they work better, and for longer.

In a little more detail, the cardiovascular problems that account for over 50 per cent of all deaths each year are basically due to one form or another of clogging. When you are quiet, your heart pumps 5 quarts of blood per minute. When you exercise, the rate reaches up to 30 quarts per minute. The heart is a muscle. Periodically giving it some real work to do makes it stronger. Your veins, arteries, and other blood circulation mechanisms are essentially tubes. If the flow of blood is slow, the walls of the system calcify and harden. Fatty deposits accumulate. The bores of the tubes decrease, and ability to carry blood is reduced. To cope, the heart pumps harder—higher blood pressure, and in turn, greater risk of stoke or rupture of brain blood vessels. Or, one of those fatty deposits gets stuck at a critical point like the heart or brain—brain stroke or heart attack. Exercise stimulates the blood flow, thereby reducing the rate of calcification (arteriosclerosis) and helping to prevent fatty deposits (atherosclerosis).

Cycling is a complete exercise. The legs, the body's largest accessory blood pumping mechanism, are used extensively, but arm, shoulder, back, abdominal, and diaphragm muscles are also put to use. Critically, you set the pace. This is perhaps one of the very best features of using a bike for exercise. If you want to get really fit—biking fit—then at times you're going to have to hit it hard enough so that it hurts at least a little bit. But we've all got good days and bad days. Sometimes when you ride, the buzz is on, and you whirl along out on the edge with all systems go. Other times, you are happy to ride well within capacity and enjoy the scenery. On average, you'll still improve. Cycling has natural bite: the more you do it, the better you become, and so the more inclined you are to do it. Naturally.

Cycling is fairly unique in that you can combine exercise and things you have to do anyhow, like commuting to and from work. It's lots of fun to do things like skiing, swimming, tennis, fishing, and a zillion other outdoor activities. But swimming to the bank would be a fair trick. Cycling is something you can mix into regular daily routines. The importance of this feature depends on your circumstances and on how you like to live. Some people have heavily physical lifestyles and are already very fit, while others only move fast when racing to the cinema. But most of us need more exercise—lots more—and with it, live happier and longer.

Riding a bike also clears the mind. What happens is up to you. At one level, this is because riding a bike is physical. At a deeper level, how you ride reflects your feelings and thoughts. You are with yourself. It's your moment. I reckon that this is the most precious and valuable thing about riding a bike.

A word about weight control. Cycling or other exercise will help your body's tone and figure, but a brisk ride does not entitle you to apple pie and ice cream. Cycling burns off anywhere from 300 to 800 calories per hour, depending on the speed and extent of effort. Your body uses up about 150 calories per hour just hanging around, which means that in regular cycling the extra burn is only about 150 calories per hour. At 3,600 calories per pound, it would take 24 hours of riding to lose this amount. There are easier ways.

Of course, nutrition and health are more than a matter of calories. Exercise has a great effect on how the body uses food. You need both to exercise and to eat foods that burn cleanly in your system. If you are overweight because of poor eating habits then cycling may help to change your metabolic balance and restore normal automatic appetite control, so that you eat no more than you actually need.

Ecology

In Britain, air pollution is a major problem. Cars are the source of up to 85 per cent of all air pollution in cities, and of an especially noxious quality. The effluents from petrol engines hang in the air and chemically interact with other substances and sunlight to form even deadlier poisons. Living in a major city is the same thing as smoking two packs of cigarettes a day—dangerous to your health.

All city transportation contributes to pollution. Trains run on electricity generated in plants fired by fossil fuels or deadly atomic reactors. But as anyone who has been lucky enough to live through a taxi-cab strike or vehicle ban knows, cars and buses are the real problem. I shall never forget a winter long ago when a friend and I came driving into New York City late at night after a vacation in Canada. To my amazement, the air was perfectly clear. The lights of the city shone like jewels and each building was clear and distinct. Looking across the Hudson River from the west bank I could for the first (and perhaps only) time in my life see Manhattan and the Bronx in perfect detail from beginning to end, and even beyond to Brooklyn and her bridges. As we crossed the George Washington Bridge the air was clean and fresh, and the city, usually an object of horror and revulsion, was astoundingly beautiful and iridescent. The explanation was simple: enough snow had fallen to effectively eliminate vehicle traffic for a couple of days. No vehicles, no junk in the air. A better world.

Arguments against motorized transport are usually dismissed as idealistic and impractical and on the grounds that the time-saving characteristics of such vehicles are essential. Bilge. Even pedestrians often drone past urban traffic, and bicycles of course do even better. Cars perhaps offer a saving in physical effort, but few of us are healthy enough to need this, or to dismiss the damage caused by inhaling the poisons that petrol engines produce. Nor do we need to waste time and energy.

In Britain, transport accounts for over 25 per cent of all energy consumed, and for over 50 per cent of petroleum used for all purposes. There are three people for each car (as against 22,535 persons per vehicle in China) and yet, 74 per cent of all journeys are under 5 miles, and a staggering 86 per cent are under 10 miles. We tend to think of cars in association with motorways and 70 mph speeds, but in fact, the majority of motor journeys are short and local, use up a lot of petrol, take a long time, and smell bad. Walking, roller-skating, or cycling is an efficient use of energy and reduces wastage. It's generally reckoned that a cyclist can do 1,600 miles on the food energy equivalent of a gallon of petrol, which will move a car only some 10 to 30 miles.

Facts and figures be as they may, utilizing a 100-horsepower, 3,000- pound behemoth to move one single 150-pound person a few miles is like using an atomic bomb to kill a canary. Great Britain runs neck and neck with the U.S. in its ability to consume and waste, and in relation to the size of her population, utilizes a disproportionate amount of the world's resources. Doing well through enterprise and industry is one thing; ripping people off because they have no power to resist is quite another. For example, Britain imports fish meal as feed for beef herds, and most of it come from African countries where people are starving. Or: in South America the forests are being burnt away to make room for beef herds. Never mind that the ecology of the planet is being irreversibly damaged. Do the people down there—also starving—get to eat the beef? Nope, it's sent to America, Britain, and elsewhere, to make fast service hamburgers. Anyone in Africa or South America who objects gets zapped. And we wonder why they don't like us. Using a bicycle is using less, an initial antidote to the horrors of consumerism.

Which brings us to the most positive series of reasons for trying to use bicycles at every opportunity. Basically, this is that it will enhance your life, bringing to it an increase in quality of experience which will find its reflection in everything you do.

Well! You have to expect that I would believe cycling is a good idea, but how do I get off expressing the notion that it is philosophically and morally sound? Because it is something *you do*, not something that is done to you. Need I chronicle the oft-cited concept of increasing alienation in our lives? The mechanization of work and daily activities, the hardships our industrial society places in the way of loving and fulfilling relationships and family life, the tremendous difficulties individuals experience trying to influence political and economic decisions which affect them and others?

What are real values? Some people say that they like things the way they are. They find trains really interesting, or insist on their 'right' to charge around in high-performance automobiles. But facts are facts. Trains are crowded, noisy, dirty, and increasingly dangerous, and nearly all cars are ego-structured, worthless junk.

The most important negative effect of mechanical contraptions is that they defeat consciousness. Consciousness, self-awareness, and development are the prerequisites for a life worth living. Now look at what happens to you on a bicycle. It's immediate and direct. *You* pedal. *You* make decisions. *You* experience the tang of the air and the surge of power as you bite into the road. You're vitalized. As you hum along you fully and gloriously experience the day, the sunshine, the clouds, the breezes. You're alive! You are going someplace, and it is *you* who is doing it. Awareness increases, and each day becomes a little more important to you. With increased awareness you see and notice more, and this further reinforces awareness.

Each time you insert *you* into a situation, each time *you* experience, you fight against alienation and impersonality, you build consciousness and identity. You try to understand things in the ways that are important to you. And these qualities carry over into everything you do.

An increased value on one's own life is the first step in social consciousness and politics. Because to you life is dear and important and fun, it is much easier to understand why this is also true for others, wherever they live, and whatever their colour, language, and culture. Believe it. The salvation of the world is the development of personality and identity for everybody in it. Much work, many lifetimes. But a good start for you is to *get a bicycle!*

Bike Genealogy

What kind of bike for you? This chapter gives an overview of the types of cycles and main points in selecting a machine. Read also the chapters on bike selection, bike anatomy, riding, fitting, touring, mountain biking, commuting, HPVs, and racing for additional information on the capabilities of various types of cycles and what your particular needs may be before arriving at a final choice.

What's a Bicycle?

Conventional full-size bicycles are called 'safety' bicycles, and owe the term to an unendearing characteristic of an earlier design, the high bicycle or penny-farthing.

Singer 'Xtraordinary

'Coming a cropper'

The high bicycle had pedals and cranks attached directly to the front wheel, and the only way to make such a machine go faster was to increase the diameter of the front wheel—in extreme cases, up to 60 inches. The rider, perched above the wheel just abaft the centre of gravity, was lofted up to between 4½ and 5½ feet off the ground. The view was great and the high bicycle was magnificent, elegant, and even rather fast, but any slight impediment to forward progress, such as the then oft-encountered stone, would cause the bike to cartwheel and catapult the rider over the handlebars to 'come a cropper'.

American Star Machine

To move the rider's weight back toward the rear wheel and thereby improve stability, some designers utilized a treadle drive, as in the Singer 'Xtraordinary. A different tactic was employed by the famous American Star Machine, which placed the small 'rear' wheel at the front. There were many other design variations, but the route to go was chain drive and gearing, and the first such machine to gain widespread attention was the Lawson Bicyclette of 1879.

'Here, indeed, is safety guaranteed,' wrote the *Cyclist* on 21 April 1880 of the Lawson Bicyclette, 'and the cyclist may ride rough-shod over hedges, ditches and similar

The Lawson Bicyclette—also known as 'The Crocodile'

obstacles without fear of going over the handles.' Such machines were advertised as 'safety bicycles', and the conventional high wheeler came to be called an 'Ord-

The Rover Safety bicycle—1884

inary'. Although the latter had firm adherents, the safety offered incomparably better handling, braking, and speed, and the type flourished rapidly; by 1885, with the advent of the second model Rover Safety, the bicycle was recognizably in the form we know today.

Now the applecart is being upset yet again by a new generation of low-slung cycles called recumbents. In these, the rider is positioned as if in a lounge chair, with legs and feet pointing forward and back reclined. Some racing models have the rider fully supine, as when in bed. Lowering the rider reduces the frontal area and hence aerodynamic drag. Maintaining a constant 20 mph on a safety bike takes 200 Watts, or slightly over one-quarter horsepower, with some 85 per cent of the energy used just to overcome air resistance. A low-slung recumbent has 25 per cent less aerodynamic drag than a safety bike, which reduces the energy requirement for 20 mph to 160 Watts, or one-fifth horsepower. The really

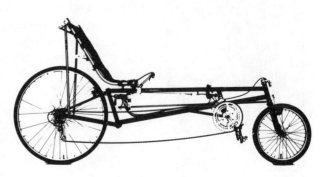

Avatar 2000 recumbent bicycle

fast machines use streamlined body shells to cut air resistance to the minimum, and are called human powered vehicles, or HPVs for short. They need but 90-odd Watts, or one-eighth horsepower for 20 mph, and at full stretch some can break 60 mph.

Technically, any vehicle with pedals is an HPV. Well, technically safeties and Ordinaries are bicycles. In terms of both design and performance there is a world of difference between the two. When thinking of modern bicycles it makes sense to differentiate between the broad design categories: safety, recumbent, and streamlined HPV.

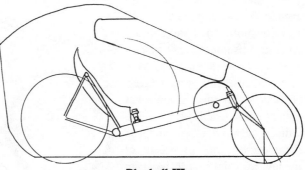

Bluebell III

As in the early days of the safety bicycle, the development of recumbent cycles and HPVs is at an embryonic stage and commercial production is limited to individual builders and small firms. There is little doubt that these designs will gain in popularity, and their substantial benefits are discussed in a later chapter. But recumbents and HPVs complement rather than supersede the safety bicycle; each type has advantages and disadvantages. Unlike the Ordinary, the safety bicycle will keep on rolling for millenaries to come.

Safety Bicycles

Bicycles are designed according to the job, or jobs, they are built to do. Some designs are specific, such as track racing bikes without gears or brakes. Others overlap, such as touring and sport touring bikes. In the following quick run-through of categories some of the distinctions and terminology may be confusing. Hang on. Next comes bike anatomy, to explain what makes a bike tick, whatever it is called.

Beach cruiser. A modern reincarnation of the classic American 'paper-boy' bike, a.k.a. the balloon-tyre bomber. Built entirely of steel, with a heavy, robust frame, 26-inch wheels with hefty 2-inch wide tyres, and a 1- or 2-speed hub with a pedal-operated coaster brake, these are simple, laidback, comfortable machines for casual fun with little or no mechanical care. Beach cruisers are about style rather than per-

Beach cruiser

formance. They're usually done up in bright, cheerful colours, and are fine for promenading along a flat boardwalk or boulevard, or splashing through surf. They'll also do as rugged, dependable local transportation, so long as you don't mind taking your time; at a weight of around 50 lb or more they roll fast downhill, but uphill, you'll have to dismount and push.

Some beach cruiser models are available with alloy wheels, an option that greatly improves riding ease and enjoyment. Others feature 5- or 6-speed derailleur gears, a waste of money as you'll still have to push them uphill.

BMX cruiser

BMX cruiser. Derived from BMX dirt track racing bikes, generally fitted with 24-inch wheels and wide, knobby tyres, single speed gear, and BMX-style straight front forks with welded plates to provide mounting holes for the front wheel axle (beach cruisers use conventional curved forks). BMX cruiser bikes are basically BMX for bigger boys and girls. They're OK for fun charging around a dirt track, and not a lot else.

'Old Faithful'

Heavy roadster. As seen in 1920. Made entirely of steel, with 26- or 28-inch wheels and 1.5-inch wide tyres, roller lever rim brakes, and 1- or 3-speed gears. Weight about 50 lb. This is the European version of the balloon-tyre bomber, and is sometimes called an 'Africa' model because of its popularity in developing countries for transporting heavy loads across deserts, through jungles, and the like. They were used extensively and very successfully by the North Vietnamese for transporting supplies during their last war with the Americans. In China, they are the backbone of a national transport system based on pedal power.

In Britain, many 'Old Faithfuls' are still trundling out decades of service, and new machines continue to be produced by a few manufacturers. Heavy roadsters imported from the Netherlands or from China also are available from time to time. The bikes are well made and pretty, with a lot of rustic charm, and they ride steadily and gracefully—so long as the terrain is flat. Pedalling them where there is any kind of hill is hard work. The bikes are not cheap either; for the same money you can have a lighter bike that is a lot easier to ride.

Light roadster. Also called tourist model or English Racer. Lighter weight steel frame and mudguards, 26-inch wheels with 1.375-inch wide tyres, calliper rim brakes, and 1- or 3-speed hub gears. Weight around 35 lb. Lighter and more sprightly than the heavy roadster and more for personal transportation than carrying things: local errands, shopping, lots of stop-and-go riding, and short trips. Good durability with minimal maintenance.

Light roadster

Commuter. A hybrid: flat handlebars and a wide saddle give the familiar upright roadster riding position, but the bike itself is a true lightweight with 27-inch wheels and 1.25-inch wide tyres,

Commuter or town bike

alloy components, and derailleur gears. Weight 25-30 lb. A nice bike for beginners, with pleasantly brisk performance, that can essay day rides and light touring (25-35 miles) as well as regular commuting.

Sports bike. Often called a 10-speed. Lightweight frame, steel or alloy components depending on model, 27-inch wheels with 1.25-inch wide tyres, calliper rim brakes, derailleur gears, narrow saddle, and drop handlebars. Weight 30 lb or more.

Sports bikes vary a lot in quality. At one end of the spectrum, the machine may be an ordinary roadster fitted with derailleur gears and drop handlebars for a peppy appearance. At the other end, the machine may be a genuine lightweight with fairly lively performance. In general, though, better machines are

Sports bike

functionally more specific: fast touring, triathlon, racing and so on. Sports bikes have modest performance and easy, predictable handling, with good directional stability and a comfortable ride over rough surfaces. They're quicker than light roadsters, and good for general riding, commuting, light touring (35-50 miles), and moderately hilly terrain.

Touring. A touring bike will follow the general outlines of the sports bike above, but is particularly designed for a comfortable ride and predictable handling when carrying heavy loads. There is provision for fitting mudguards and carrier racks for panniers, the gearing is wide-range, with low ratios for easier hill climbing, and

the brakes are stout and strong. Machines of this description are of course excellent for general use and commuting, but their proper activity is daily touring in the 50-100 mile range. Some models are claimed to weigh as little as 24 lb, but 27-32 lb is more likely.

Touring bike

Fast touring. Often called sport touring. A touring bike tweaked with narrow 1- or 1.125-inch wide tyres, and stiffer frame geometry. The result is a machine that is quick, but able to manage light touring loads. This 'best of both worlds' approach is popular with urban riders who want a brisk bike for general riding and commuting, and a mount that will serve for weekend and holiday touring. There is provision for mounting mudguards, and often carrier racks as well. Weight 23-28 lb.

Sport touring bike

Fast road/training bike. Fast touring bikes can be very quick, but are rooted in touring and carrying things. Fast road or training bikes are derived from racing

bikes, and the main emphasis is on performance. There is usually no facility for mounting mudguards or carrier racks. The frame is designed for quick handling and rapid translation of pedalling effort into forward motion and, shod with narrow-profile 1- or 1.125-inch wide tyres, has a stiff ride over rough surfaces. Fast road bikes

Road racer

weigh 21-26 lb and while intended primarily for sport, are also used by experienced riders for very fast, exciting general transportation.

Triathlon. A category created by the great popularity of triathlon (swimming-running-cycling) events. Most of the bikes are simply fast road models fitted with an abundance of water bottles. If the bike is specifically designed for tri events, then the back end will be tight, for quick response to pedal input, but the front end will be somewhat relaxed, to help guide tired riders through the bends. Weight 21-26 lb.

Road racing. The business. Strong, tight frame for taut responsiveness and crisp, quick handling. Close-ratio gears, and sew-up tubular tyres—narrow, fast, and more fragile than the conventional wire-on type. Road racing in a pack of riders is often tough and rough, and the bikes are made to be light but strong and reliable. Weight is

Low-profile track bike

usually 20-22 lb, but can go down to 18 lb. With tubular tyres a racing bike is strictly for competition. But it is common, and very easy, to substitute wheels with more durable wire-on tyres for training and general road riding. A bike set up this way can be motion and bliss incarnate on a smooth, fast road, but painful in a city with jagged, debris-strewn streets. (There are ways and means of coping with this problem, of which more later.)

Track. Made for racing on wooden tracks, these are utterly stark greyhounds with a single fixed gear (the wheels turn when the cranks turn and vice versa), no brakes, and a weight of 16-17 lb. Only the most expert of riders can use these in traffic.

Mountain bikes. Made for off-road riding and usually fit-

Mountain bike

ted with wide, knobby tyres, mountain bikes superficially resemble cruiser bikes. This is like comparing a lightning bolt to a candle. Cruisers weigh around 50 lb, mountain bikes are 25-30 lb, and a really hot-shot competition model can be as light as 22 lb.

Mountain bikes started out in life as the cycling equivalents of Land Rovers and four-wheel-drive vehicles. In just a few years they have evolved into distinct genres that are very similar to the subdivisions for road bikes. There are mountain bikes for touring, for sport, for competition, for town riding, and for trials. With modern tyres some of these machines are as at home on the street as on dirt. In fact, for general cycling, mountain bikes are the greatest shot in the arm since the invention of derailleur gears.

The virtues of mountain bikes are worth a book, and a good one is *Richard's Mountain Bike Book*, by Charles Kelly and Nick Crane (Oxford Illustrated Press, Sparkford). Basically, mountain bikes are light, tough, strong, and powerful. They've got plenty of gears, and mega-powerful brakes are standard equipment. The wheels are typically 26-inch, with tyre widths from 1.375- to 2.125-inch. For the most part, they are equipped with wide, flat handlebars for good handling control, and padded

Sport mountain bike

anatomic or semi-mattress saddles. Can a mountain bike blow off a road racing bike? On an open, clear road, of course not. But in transportation riding (to and from work, the cinema, the hideout), conditions and circumstances are often more important than the distance. A mountain bike is about confidence and the ability to pull through, no matter what. That really counts. The other fantastic thing about a mountain bike is, it doesn't need a road. You can go where you like. It opens up the outdoors, and it also opens up the back alley. A mountain bike is a kind of freedom that is unique.

Summary

Very, very broadly, there are four basic types of safety bikes:

1. Heavy, wide-tyre cruiser bikes, with coaster (pedal-operated) brakes, flat handlebars, and wide saddles.

2. Roadster bikes with medium-weight tyres, hub gears, calliper brakes, flat handlebars, and mattress saddles.

3. Lightweight, narrow-tyre road bikes, with derailleur gears, calliper brakes, drop or flat handlebars, and narrow or semi-mattress saddles. These can be general use machines (sports bikes), or more refined racing and touring models.

4. Mountain bikes with medium to wide tyres, derailleur gears, strong calliper or hub brakes, flat handlebars, and saddles to choice.

Whippet Spring-Frame Dwarf Safety Roadster

COVENTRY MACHINISTS' COMPANY, LIMITED.

THE "CLUB" SEMI-RACER.

H. SWAINE

THIS Machine has been designed for those requiring a Bicycle of stouter build than the Racer, but lighter than the "Special Club." It is well adapted for racing on grass, or for making fast times on good roads. Being built with our new deep section hollow felloe, it has very great rigidity, and makes an unequalled Roadster for light riders. Having had numerous enquiries for the tangent spokes, we build the "Club" Semi-Racer with either tangent or direct spokes, at the option of the purchaser.

SPECIFICATION.—Very easy Sliding Spring with Rubber Cushion in front.—Plain Hollow Steel Front and Back Forks.—Elliptical Steel Backbone.—Stanley Head with improved Long Centres.—Deep Neck.—Improved Adjustable Single Ball Bearings to Front and Back Wheels.—Improved New Deep Section Hollow Felloes—⅞in. Best Rubber Tyres.—Steel Hubs with Direct or Tangent Spokes.—24in. or 26in. Bent Handle Bars.—Painted or Enamelled Plain Black.—Head, Hubs, Handle-bar and Cranks Plated.

Weight of 56in. Machine, about 30 lbs.

PRICES :

48in., £17.   50in., £17 10s.   52in., £18.   54in., £18 10s.   56in., £19.

Odd sizes, or any size above 56in., made to order, at an extra charge of 10s. for every one or two inches.

Complete with Rubber or Rat-trap Cone Pedals, Patent Suspension Saddle, Plated Spanners, and Oilcan.

EXTRAS.—Nickelling, No. 2, all over except felloes, £3 10s.; ditto, No. 3, all over, £4 10s.; ball pedals, £1; gold lines, 10s. 6d.; gold lines to felloes only, 5s.; ⅝in. and ¾in. tyres, 17s. 6d.; lined on enamel, 7s. 6d.

Selection
Part I

Selecting the right bike or bikes for you is a journey through an elaborate spectrum of possibilities. The process may be simple and quick, or complex and long. It depends on what you already know, your nature, and specific needs. This chapter discusses the fundamentals of weight, gearing systems, and road or off-road design. The next chapter, Bike Anatomy, is a whopper that goes into a fair bit of mechanical detail. It's useful stuff to know when messing around with bikes of whatever kind, but if you find your eyes starting to glaze over, then skim on ahead to Chapter 5, Selection - Part II, returning back for more information as you need it.

Weight

Bike weight is fundamental. If a machine is heavy, it just cannot be made to go. The limiting factor is the human power plant. Gifted athletes are able to churn out one and one-half horsepower or even more, but only for a few seconds. Thereafter, output rarely exceeds one-half horsepower. Ordinary people make do with much less: one-eighth to one-quarter horsepower on a steady basis.

Power-to-weight ratio is the summary determinant of performance. The effect of bike weight is most evident when accelerating or climbing, and the demarcation line is 30 lb: bikes at 35 lb are hard work to move, while bikes at 25 lb seem to go down the road by themselves. Good quality, general use lightweight bikes are 28-30 lb and similar grade no-frills sports machines are 24-26 lb. Really fine racing bikes weigh 21-22 lb and are joy incarnate.

Bike weight is a function of the materials from which the bike is made. It comes down to money. A heavy material like mild steel is cheap, and is easily managed by simple, high-volume mass production machines; lightweight materials like alloy steel and aluminium cost more, and working them into bicycles requires sophisticated manufacturing techniques and equipment. Beach cruisers and mountain bikes look much alike, but the former are usually made of mild steel and weigh around 50 lb, while the latter are usually made of alloy steel or aluminium and weigh under 30 lb.

Some people think that spending money on a bike is frivolous; the whole point is that the thing should be cheap. A bike they can hardly pick up is wonderful because after all, hard work is good for you. This downbeat reasoning misleads them into feeling happier with a rust-frozen old hulk than a nice new bike that works. A change of heart is typically very swift: usually, the first time a lightweight sweeps on by going up a hill. Slogging away at a heavy bike wears you out while doing little to make you more fit. Would you run better with concrete blocks on your feet? For getting anywhere by bike, and for quality exercise, you need a lightweight machine that moves when you do. My advice is to save money by buying a decent, proper lightweight bike in the first place. You get the most fun and turn-on for your money, and you get it right away.

What about durability? Cruiser bikes and heavy roadsters are very sturdy, but for flat-out, bomb-proof toughness it's hard to beat a mountain bike—at half the weight of a heavy roadster. Ultra-lightweight road racing bikes also have extraordinary strength and resilience, but can be damaged by casual abuse or rough off-road riding. As for light roadsters with hub gears, sad to say, most modern models are cheaply constructed and flimsy.

Rider sense and skill also affect durability. Someone who just sits on the saddle like a sack of oats when the bike hits a bump needs a machine that can absorb punishment. A rider who actively moves with the bike, allowing it to pivot underneath him or her over the bumps, can use a lighter and more responsive machine. But this is a classic chicken-and-egg proposition. Because heavy bikes are slow to respond, they encourage an inert style of riding—'sit up and beg'. In contrast, the quickness and vitality of lightweight bikes stimulates active riding. It's a partnership: the bike goes, you go; you go, the bike goes.

Bike weight is also a big factor when you are off the bike and have to handle it, for example up and down stairs at home or at work, on and off a car, or aboard a train. Carrying a 35-40 lb heavyweight can be a real chore, but handling a 25 lb lightweight is a breeze. Better yet if the bike is 21-22 lb. It may be hard to believe that a mere 10-15 lb makes such a difference, but it does, it does.

Gears

Gears convert energy input at the pedals into power. There are two broad types of transmissions: internal hub gears and external derailleur gears. Basically, hub gears are simple, reliable, and a bit slow, while in comparison, derailleur gears are more complex, need more frequent servicing, and are extremely efficient—fast. In years past, derailleur gears needed more skill to operate than hub gears, but most of the popular modern derailleur systems are now indexed—push or pull the shift lever one notch, keep pedalling, and the rest of a gear ratio change takes care of itself. Even a traditional, non-indexed system is easy enough to use once you get the knack.

A choice between hub or derailleur gears depends on the kind of person you are and what you want from a bike. Derailleur gears are the route to go if: you're interested in cycling as a sporting, dynamic activity; you need to go places at an appreciable velocity, or for long distances; or hills of any kind are involved. Hub gears are the thing to consider if: you're not terribly interested in cycling and just want something you can use once a month or so; you, or the prospective rider, are not at all mechanically inclined and never will be; or you just want the most worry-free machine possible. There is nothing degenerate about this last state of affairs. A no-think bike is fun: you can leave it wherever,

Sturmey-Archer 3-speed hub, 1936

bash it around, loan it to casual friends, and in general never give it a thought.

If the business is cycling, however, consider this: Professor David Gordon Wilson of the Massachusetts Institute of Technology has calculated that the energy requirement for maintaining an even 12 mph on a lightweight sports bike is half that for the same speed on a hub gear roadster. Half. This is more than just a matter of the gears of course, but the basic idea holds: one machine is a lump, the other can move. And over the long haul, the derailleur-gear lightweight is so much better, so much more rewarding, that it will surely overcome any diffidence you feel about cycling and make you an enthusiast.

Cyclo derailleur, 1936

For frequency of repair, hub gears have it all over derailleur gears. All a hub gear will need for years, perhaps even a lifetime, is a monthly shot of lubricant. It's a complex piece of business, so if it does go—which is not often—the usual course is to replace it rather than attempt a mend. Derailleur gears want reasonably frequent cleaning, lubrication, and adjustment. However, because the parts are all fairly simple and out in the open where they are readily to hand, maintenance is easy. In fact, maintenance is part of the fun of riding. You come to enjoy fine-tuning the transmission, and keeping the bike sharp and smooth. What it all comes down to on just about any count other than expense (an item we'll come back to) is, a lightweight with derailleur gears.

Road or Dirt

Which leaves road, or off-road. Broadly, road bikes are for going on roads with maximum efficiency, and mountain bikes are for going no matter what. A choice between the two types should not be made at the drop of a hat, however, because many possible permutations and combinations are possible. Road bikes can be set up to be durable, mountain bikes can be tweaked to be swift. To really understand the options you need to know more about how bikes are designed and built.

Bike Anatomy

In order of importance a bike consists of:
- the frame;
- wheels (hubs, spokes, rims, tyres);
- transmission (pedals, chainset, gear changers, chain, freewheel);
- brakes;
- stem, handlebars, and saddle.

The frame carries the maker's brand name—Raleigh, Fisher, Saracen, Cannondale, Condor, or whatever—and the rest of the components are known as the *specification*. Some manufacturers make their own frames, others buy frames from outside builders, and many do both. Components are supplied by specialist companies, and are made in various grades of quality. Some manufacturers produce particular components such as cranksets or brakes; others produce ranges of *group sets*, with each group set containing all the components of a complete specification. 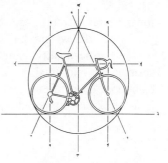 Group sets are identified by a name or model number, as in Campagnolo Chorus or Shimano 105, and are ranked by design and quality or, more simply, cost. Depending on grade of frame and specification, bikes range in price from under £50 for discount store specials with crude steel parts to well beyond £1,000 for fancy superbikes with handmade frames and finely finished alloy components.

Small bike manufacturers generally concentrate on a few models in one or two categories, while large manufacturers with large distribution networks to satisfy tend to offer models in every category and price range. As a result, comparable models from different brand name 'manufacturers' can and often do have exactly the same specification. If the frames have been bought in as well (common with low-price bikes), it is quite possible for two 'different' bikes to be absolutely identical!

When assessing a frame and/or components the three main factors to consider are design, materials, and quality of building. The interface of these elements determines the usefulness, quality, and value of a product. For example, a racing frame built with heavy, inert mild steel is pointless, because the material does not have the performance to fulfil the design. Equally, making a roadster out of ultra-light carbon fibre would be a waste of performance potential—and money. Good bikes are balanced throughout: design and materials for both frame and specification are in harmony with the bike's intended purpose and price range. Quality of construction and assembly is also vital: a plain bike that works is infinitely superior to a more glamorous model that does not.

Frame

The frame is the heart and soul of a bicycle. It translates pedal effort into forward motion, guides the wheels in the direction you select, and helps absorb road shock.

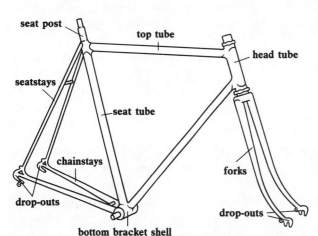

How well the frame does these various jobs is determined by the materials from which it is built, the design, or geometry used, and the method of construction. There is no way to work around a cheap frame. The specification can be modified or changed with relative ease, but the frame endures, and it should be the first focus of your attention when considering a prospective bike.

Weight in a bike is pretty well everything, and the most fundamental factor in this department is the frame. Very simply, the better the frame the lighter the weight for the same or even greater strength. Closely related to weight is a dynamic quality known as resiliency, twang, or flex, which gives better bikes springiness and vitality. Frames low in resiliency are wooden and unresponsive—bath-tubs. The difference is identical to that between heavy, unyielding cast iron and light, flexible tempered steel.

Materials

Steel and aluminium are the mainstream materials for bike frames. In years past there were two extremes: low-price bikes made in heavy steels by mass production machines, and expensive bikes made in refined alloy steels by individual artisans. The fine metals were strong but required sensitive building techniques beyond the capabilities of machine assembly. Nowadays great advances have been made in the development of alloy steels that are lightweight and resilient, and yet compatible with mass production machines, and this has done wonders for the quality and availability of middle-price bikes. There's been a similar evolution in aluminium metal technologies, and for value-for-money performance, aluminium bikes are now in the front rank. Very advanced bikes are made using titanium, carbon fibre, Kevlar, and other exotic metals and composites. For a keen enthusiast or professional cyclist the lightness, performance, and comfort qualities of frames made from these high-tech materials are often well worth the cost—which is considerable.

There's a good bit to sort out with frame materials, and the starting point is the label on the bike. If the materials are worth mentioning there will be a maker's transfer or sticker, usually on the seat tube just below the saddle. If there is no transfer the chances are that the bike is something very rare, something resprayed, or a bath-tub made of low-carbon mild steel.

Mild steel is heavy and inert, and when arranged in the shape of a bicycle makes a passable small boat anchor. The economic justification for using mild steel to build bikes has been surpassed by modern inexpensive alloy steels, which cost only a tiny bit more. These days, few if any bicycle buying guides even bother to list bikes made with mild steel.

'High-tensile' and 'high-tension' are terms for alloy steels with more carbon and minute quantities of nickel. Frames made from genuine high-tensile steels are lighter and livelier than those made from mild steels. However, manufacturers of cheap bikes are particularly prone to describe mild steel frames as high-tensile, slapping on racy stickers such as 'Hi-Ti', 'Hi-Ten', etc., and so unfortunately these terms have little practical meaning.

The first grade of quality alloy steels worth spending money on have frame stickers identifying the tubes as Columbus Aelle, Fuji Valite, Ishiwata Mangy-X, Reynolds 453, Tange Mangaloy, or Vitus 181 or 888. The stickers are, or should be, quite specific in the information they provide. Thus, if it says 'Reynolds 453 main tubes' then the seat, down, and top tubes are Reynolds 453, and the forks and stays are probably high-tensile steel. If it says 'Reynolds 453 main tubes, forks, and stays' then the frame is uniform in quality throughout.

There are two types of frame tubing: straight- or plain-gauge, and double-butted. Plain-gauge tubing is uniform in wall thickness, or external and internal diameters.

Double-butted tubing is uniform in external diameter, but on the inside is thinner in the middle sections and thicker at the ends, for greater strength at the joins. On average, double-butted tubing in place of plain-gauge tubing reduces frame weight by 1 lb. Double-butted tubing is also more resilient.

There are two types of double-butted tubing: seamed and seamless. Seamed double-butted tubing is made by roll-

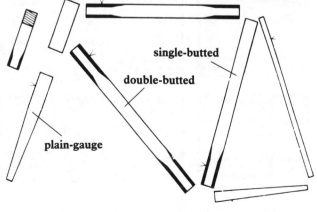

single-butted

double-butted

plain-gauge

ing a flat strip of steel and welding the edges together. In quality it is about one notch below seamless double-butted tubing, but at much less cost. It's often used

Selection of frame stickers. Each indicates the quality of the tubing used.

for mid-range price bikes: Reynolds 501, Ishiwata EXO and EX, Columbus Tenax, and Tange 900, 1000 and Infinity are common brands.

Seamless double-butted tubings in manganese-molybdenum (Reynolds 753 and Reynolds 531) and chrome-molybdenum (Columbus, Tange Champion, True Temper, and Ishiwata) steels are the top of the range. At this quality level the design and construction of tubing sets is specific to the intended use, as in Reynolds 531 Special

THE RUDGE TRIPLET TANDEM QUADRICYCLE DIRECT STEERING ROADSTER.

Tourist (touring bikes) and Reynolds 531 All Terrain (mountain bikes). Some distinctions are fine but nonetheless real, as in Reynolds 531 Professional (road racing) and Reynolds 531 Competition (fractionally stouter, for road racing, time trials, cyclo-cross, and track). The categories are not gospel: for example, Reynolds 531 Competition tubing is often used for touring bikes. As ever, much depends on the rider. A lightweight frame that is flexible for a 200 lb rider may be very stiff for a 140 lb rider.

Keep a wary eye on plain-gauge chrome-molybdenum (chrome-moly, or just cro-mo) tubing, which can vary in quality from equivalent to seamed double-butted tubing down to little better than good high-tensile tubing. Like the term high-tensile, cro-mo is a bandwagon label that all too many manufacturers use as a matter of course. If the label says 'Cro-mo' and nothing else, be sure to compare the bike (or frameset) with others of known pedigree.

Some bikes use quality tubing for the main frame (top, seat, and down) tubes, and more ordinary tubing for stays and forks. It's usually better if the frame is consistent in quality throughout. The forks are particularly important to bike performance. A frame that is Reynolds 501 throughout, or a good cro-mo with Reynolds

531 forks, is likely to be better than a bike with Reynolds 531 main tubes and high-tensile steel forks and stays. The little transfers on the tubes give all the information; be sure to read them carefully. Manufacturers' leaflets with an abundance of technical data are also available in most good bike shops.

Aluminium frame bikes are rapidly gaining in popularity. Aluminium has advantages in lightness, flex characteristics, and ability to soak up road shock. Very broadly, there are two types of aluminium frames. Many American builders in aluminium use 'oversize' tubing—that is, larger in diameter than standard alloy steel tubing. Frames of this type are noticeably stiffer than their alloy steel equivalents. Most European builders, on the other hand, use aluminium tubes of about the same diameter as conventional steel tubes. Frames of this type are usually very flexible. Likes and dislikes in this area depend a lot on the kind of rider, the conditions of use, and the particular aluminium bike in question.

Big, strong racers frequently dislike aluminium frames with narrow tubes, because in sprints the frame 'whips'—flexes back and forth—reducing the rider's control of the bike. (It's often claimed that frame whip reduces speed by absorbing energy that would otherwise go directly to the rear wheel and immediate forward motion. If this were true, then very stiff frames would consistently win races. They don't.) However, in a long race or when there is a lot of climbing, the lightness of an aluminium frame is a considerable advantage. Aluminium frames are also better at absorbing road shock than steel frames, and their ability to reduce rider fatigue often greatly improves the overall performance of the rider.

Once the business of snapping away in a sprint as fast as possible is eliminated, a narrow-tube aluminium frame has an awful lot of advantages. Lightness and a smooth ride are always welcome assets. People light in body weight obtain the greatest benefit from narrow-tube aluminium bikes. Most of them do not have enough peak power to start bending things over-much. Their advantage is in power-to-weight ratio; relative to heavier riders, lighter riders gain more from reduced bike weight.

The heavyweight, hairy-chested, pedal-stomper brigade, and those who favour touring with heavy loads, want to look at aluminium frames with large-diameter tubes. Briefly, these do not bend at all. Some makers have even secured patents for the degree of stiffness that can be obtained with aluminium. And yet, the nature of aluminium is such that even these extremely rigid frames excel at soaking up road shock.

On the downbeat side, aluminium is subject to fatigue. It wears out. Fatigue is not a significant factor for large-tube frames, but narrow-tube frames can noticeably degrade in vitality over a single season of hard riding. This applies only to frames used by professional, working riders spending many hours in the saddle (15,000-20,000 miles/year)—exactly the people who most value performance and comfort and least begrudge the cost of proper equipment. In fact, one testimonial for narrow-tube aluminium frames is their outstanding popularity with pro riders. Average riders (2,000-3,000 miles/year) will take a long time to wear out a narrow-tube aluminium frame—and enjoy every moment!

Top of the materials tree and priced accordingly are frames and components made from carbon fibre, which is light but incredibly strong. It is capable of brilliant performance and a level of comfort that ecstatic testers describe as 'too good to be true'. This leading edge of frame technology of course has question mark areas. In common with aluminium, fatigue is a potential problem. Manufacturers claim that in tests, carbon fibre frames last as long as steel frames, or well-nigh infinitely. Probably so, but real world confirmation will take time. One unique problem with carbon fibre is delamination of the fibres from the binding resin. The material simply loses cohesion and becomes soft. No-one knows just how much of a problem this may, or may not, be. Fah. You only live once. A state-of-the-art carbon fibre bike is one of the most fun things around. If the performance and price tag suit you, then give this kind of bike a try.

The most recent high-tech material for frames is titanium, which is ultra-lightweight, corrosion- and fatigue-free, and very strong—at least as strong as steel. Titanium frames do not whip, and yet like aluminium frames, they excel at soaking up road shock. Ideal—but for cost. Titanium itself is very expensive, and fabricating it is extremely difficult; the cost of tooling (making machines to work it) can be blinding. At this writing, the first production titanium framesets are costing about £1,000 each, and complete bikes are at the £2,000 mark. Again, if state-of-the-art-plus suits you, and money is not a problem, then have a look—if you buy, you'll be among the first few of what may become many.

Construction

A major element of frame quality is construction, which varies in method for different materials. Mild steel frames are usually just stuck together and welded by machine, leaving a smooth join. Better quality steels with a high carbon content become brittle and subject to fatigue when heated to high temperatures. Frames of this material are brazed, a joining method that uses lower temperatures than welding. As an aid to accurate assembly, lugs are used to position the tubes. Strictly speaking, lugs do not need to be neat and tidy for a strong join. However, clean lugwork is a sign of care and thoroughness that bodes well for the rest of the bike. There's a type of lug, by the way, which is internal and therefore invisible.

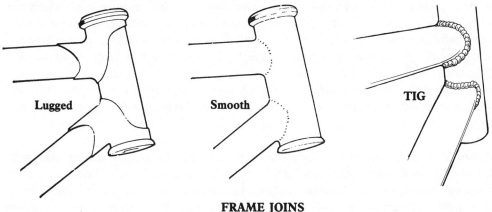

FRAME JOINS

Tandems, mountain bikes, recumbents, and other machines with odd size tubing or special requirements in frame geometry often cannot use lugs, and have bronze welded (filleted) joints. Many conventional bikes are also made this way. One great advantage of the method is that everything is out in the open, where you can see it.

A decade ago, when frame steels were divided sharply into crude or fine grades, lugs were the indication of a quality bike. The development and widespread use of high grade steels that can safely be machine brazed or welded at higher temperatures has eliminated this easy distinction. By and large, conventional design frames in standard tubings continue to use lugs. To some extent this is a prejudice in favour of tradition, and you'll sometimes hear people decry lugless, TIG (tungsten inert gas) welded frames as crude and somehow less worthy than lugged frames. Pooh. TIG welded joints are strong and the appearance—stippled, like the decorative frosting on a birthday cake—is pleasing. Moreover, you can see for yourself if the frame is properly joined together. I've had more than one disappointment with frames where the lugs concealed inept brazing. A visible check is especially useful in the case of mid-range production bikes, where value for money is a great attraction, but pedigree is usually anonymous.

What's the likelihood of problems with steel frames? Very, very slight. Failures do occur—fractures, split tubing, hairline cracks, and other joys. Every bike shop has its tales. But basically, nasty things should not happen, ever, and so there is usually little difficulty in having the shop or manufacturer put matters right. They do not want their pride and joy Wonder Flash out there with a sign: 'It broke.' As ever, your best protection here is in dealing with reputable people—bike shop, manufacturer, or framebuilder—who are serious about their business. But play fair. Just about any bike can be broken if you try hard enough. Bouncing a lightweight racing bike up and down kerbs or thrashing it through a rocky streambed is abuse, pure and simple, and if the machine breaks you are not entitled to a refund or free repair.

Aluminium has much less resistance to fatigue than steel. The do's and don'ts of building in aluminium were learned before the computer age, through pragmatic trial and error, and there were some rude, tragic surprises. Around 1981, for example, Lambert bikes with aluminium forks were recalled because the fork blades were snapping apart, with thoroughly nasty consequences for their luckless riders. There were no hidden metallurgical flaws or untoward celestial aspects. The designers simply hadn't made the forks strong enough. Lambert are no longer with us, and I think that modern aluminium bikes are no more prone to break than steel bikes—i.e. very rarely. The relevant factor here is again not the materials, but the care and skill of manufacture. With reputable companies and builders you should be on safe ground.

A more realistic concern with aluminium bikes is involuntary disassembly, or failure of tube joins. Aluminium is difficult to weld. Many builders glue rather than weld their frames, and every once in a while a frame does come unstuck. However, there is usually ample warning through the joint loosening rather than parting all at once. It is then very simple to clean the parts up and glue them back together. In any case, glues are improving rapidly, and are frequently stronger than the materials they join.

Welding is an entirely satisfactory method of joining large diameter aluminium tubing, although true skill is essential. It's not a job for the village blacksmith, or even someone who can work well with steels. Mass-produced aluminium bikes are a comparatively recent phenomenon, and there may be more information forthcoming on the long term, in-service durability of welded aluminium joints. My personal preference is for glued joints, as they are simple to work with.

Carbon fibre frames are glued together, usually via lugs made from aluminium. They are light and strong and have performance levels that make questions about wear and tear seem banal. If you want (and can afford) the best, then carbon fibre is an option you must consider. Titanium frames are too new on the market for feedback on in-service durability, but titanium is renowned for resistance to fatigue, and welding has little appreciable effect on its strength. A problem with a titanium frame would almost certainly be because of design or builder error, a difficulty that could arise with any material.

Design

The design or geometry of a bicycle frame varies according to its intended purpose and the type and weight of rider. The two fundamental types of bikes are road and off-road, and within each category there is a similar basic choice: going quickly and energetically, or more slowly and comfortably. Sport or utility. Generally, performance bikes have a taut ride and quick handling, while bikes made to carry baggage have an easy ride and slow, predictable handling. The difference between road and off-road bikes is one of degree: hot, quick off-road bikes are usually relatively tame on properly surfaced roads and, conversely, docile road bikes used off-road may classify as competition machines.

Dimensions	Racing	Fast Road	Touring	Mountain bike
Angles	73-75°	72-74°	72-73°	68-72°
Wheelbase	38.5-39″	39-41″	40-42″	42-45″
Fork rake	1.4-1.75″	1.75-2.2″	2.2-2.5″	2-2.75″
C'stay Length	16-16.5″	16.2-17.5″	16.5-17.7″	17-18.5″
B/B Height	10.5-11″	10.5-10.75″	10-10.75″	11.5-13″

The first crude indication of a bike's character is the wheelbase, the distance between the two wheel axles. On road bikes this ranges from 38.5 inches for racing models to around 42 inches for touring models. On mountain bikes the range is from around 41 inches to 45 inches. Wheelbase is an additive function of the relative angles at which the tubes are joined, and their length. Tightly built, short-wheelbase frames with steep angles and short tubes are 'stiff', while long-wheelbase frames

with more relaxed angles and longer tubes are 'soft'. These terms lend credibility
to the simplistic, widespread tenet that stiff frames have a harsh ride and soft frames
a comfortable ride. More relevant to ride comfort are the type of wheels and tyres.
Variations in frame design are for performance, degree of stability, and room for
carrying things. Racing bikes need to be quick and nimble, and there usually isn't
enough room to mount mudguards, carrier racks, and the like. Touring bikes want
stable, predictable handling—so you can relax and enjoy the view—and of course
need enough room to carry equipment without discomfort to the rider. But fast bikes
can be comfortable as well as efficient, and one popular model is the sport, or fast,
touring bike, with a wheelbase of 40-41 inches.

Going into all this business a little more deeply, the kick or speed of a bike is
largely determined by the tightness of the rear triangle formed by the seat tube,
seatstays, and chainstays—more
simply, the length of the chainstays. On a hot road-racing
bike this could be as little as
15.75 inches, leaving no room
between tyre and seat tube for
a mudguard (or on a showroom
floor, your finger). On sport
touring bikes the interval is
16.25-17 inches, and on
machines for fully loaded touring it is 16.5-17.75 inches.
Mountain bikes run hot at
around 17.5 inches and more
sedately at around 18.5 inches.
Simply, short chainstays make

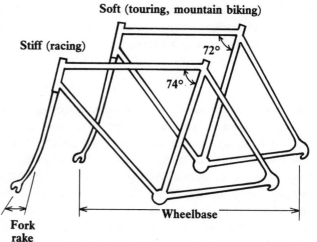

for quick acceleration and climbing, and nimble handling; long chainstays reduce
snappiness but increase stability and room for carrying things.

The speed with which a bike handles, and the degree of directional stability, is
largely determined by the tightness of the front end. This is a function of the head
tube angle, and of the fork rake. The tighter the head tube angle, the faster the
bike reacts to steering input. Bikes with fork rakes of 2 inches or longer tend to
be stable, especially at low speeds; fork rakes under 2 inches give nimble handling
and better stability at high speeds.

Design elements are often mixed in different ways. The classic road racing bike
is tight both front and rear, for maximum performance. Many triathlon bikes,
however, mix a tight rear with a more relaxed front. This is because in competition, a triathlete is likely to be tired, and to welcome a bit of help in staying on
course.

Bottom bracket height relates to the centre of gravity and stability of a bike, and
ease of touching the ground with a foot when seated on the saddle. Touring bikes
have low bottom brackets to aid stability when loaded with baggage, and to make

frequent stops easier. Racing bikes have higher bottom brackets for pedal clearance when cornering, and mountain bike bottom brackets are highest of all, for clearance over rough ground. With a low bottom bracket it is usually possible to start and stop the bike without leaving the saddle. However, the pedals are more prone to ground when cornering—an unpleasant, scary experience that can make you nervous about 'laying the bike over'. A high bottom bracket may require that you leave the saddle when stopping and starting, but adequate pedal clearance when the bike is up and going is a great aid to confident bike handling.

One quick way to annotate bike design and function is via the frame angles formed to the top tube by the seat and head tubes. On a classic touring bike these are likely to be 72° parallel. As the frame tightens and becomes a sport touring bike with more emphasis on performance, the frame angles steepen to, say, 73° parallel. For road racing they are likely to be 74° parallel. As a progression these figures are broadly accurate, but individual bikes vary a fair bit. Thus, some aluminium racing frames are steeply pitched at 75° seat and 74° head, and yet are comfortable because the material has good shock-absorbing qualities. The frame built by Jack Taylor of England for his Superlight Tourist model uses a 73° seat and 71° head. The bike is particularly designed for stability and comfort with heavy touring loads.

The first and most fundamental requirement of a frame is that it fits the rider. If frame angles have to differ from the 'norm', then so be it. For example, women generally have less reach than men, and short women in particular have limited reach. On bikes that are correctly sized for their legs they are stretched out too far for their torsos. It's uncomfortable and can be very painful. The solution is to shorten the top tube, and since you cannot just whack a chunk out of it without messing up the rest of the bike, the solution is effected by steepening the seat tube angle to 75° or 76°—a 'stiff', 'harsh riding' racing geometry. Try telling that to those lucky women who have travelled thousands of comfortable miles on properly fitting bikes!

Frame angles depend on the length of the frame tubes, not the other way round. They do run to pattern, with steeper frame angles for faster, more lively bikes. Most people will find a good fit on standard frames, with the aid of correct saddle positioning and stem length to adjust for minor variations (see Fitting). But go for fit and comfort first, and let the design follow suit.

Diamond-pattern frames are with us in no small part because they conform to the narrow definition of a bicycle established by the Union Cyclist Internationale (UCI), the governing body of cycle sport. The UCI says that a bicycle is not a bicycle unless it has a frame formed from three tubes. Flight of the dodo—the death knell has sounded for frames made from sticks. Composites are the new materials, and one enormous asset of these is the ease with which they can be worked and shaped into various forms. Some firms are producing traditional stick-design frames in composite materials, but the most exciting configuration is monocoque—single piece, with nary a frame angle in sight. The means to hold the wheels, cranks, forks, saddle, handlebars, and everything else are contained in one cohesive unit. Monocoque designs

Monocoque frame bike—a new and exciting configuration. Note single fork blade! Designed and built by Mike Burrows.

are aerodynamic, light, and strong, but the most significant advantage is that strength and flex are almost infinitely variable; in theory at least, it is now possible to build the absolutely perfect bicycle, with every performance characteristic precisely as desired.

At this writing monocoque designs are banned from sanctioned bicycle racing by the UCI, and exist in prototype or custom-built form only. But I've got a funny itch that feels like the first mountain bikes. Monocoque designs are efficient, sleek, and appealing, and I think people will want them, UCI or no. One of the manufacturers of 'outlaw' bikes might well introduce a monocoque model soon, and if so, be sure to look it over. It's the way to go.

Summary

The frame is the most important element in the quality and vitality of a bike. Within reason and the purpose of the bike, you want the best frame you can afford. Alloy steels are the traditional materials for frames, and the parameters for quality, performance, and value are well understood; you'll get what you pay for, from refugee gas pipe through to the finest in ultra-light, ultra-tech tubing. Aluminium frames are a more recent introduction and have advantages in lightness, comfort, and (in large diameter tubing) stiffness. Some models are remarkably economical, and others are quite expensive. Titanium, and composite frames in carbon fibre, Kevlar, and other exotics are the top of the performance and cost tree, are wildly exciting, and too recent for information on durability.

Wheels

After the frame, the wheels—tyres, rims, spokes, and hubs—are the most important components of a bike. The frame is the vitality, the wheels the point of translation into motion. Their effect on performance and comfort is enormous. A bike frame is fairly immutable. Once completed and painted, it is very unlikely to go back to the torch or glue-pot for changes and modifications. The range of options offered by wheels, however, are under your direct control. This makes them worth knowing about in some detail.

A bicycle wheel is one of the strongest engineering structures in existence. This is because weight has a greater effect on a wheel than anywhere else on a bike. The best way to appreciate the old saw 'an ounce off the wheels is worth a pound off the frame' is to hold a wheel by the axle ends and move it around in the air, and then do so again while spinning the wheel. The faster the rotation, the greater the 'weight', or inertia, and the harder it is to move the wheel into a new plane of rotation.

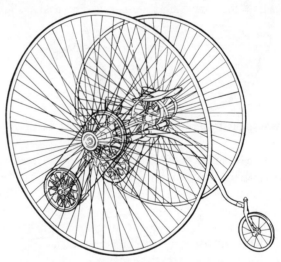

Otto Dicycle, 1881

Bicycle wheels are built with spokes and rims to keep weight to the minimum and reduce the force of gyroscopic inertia. If weight did not matter they could be a solid one-piece design, like automobile wheels. The other important considerations in wheel design are comfort and durability, and basically it is a straight trade-off: lighter is quicker, stiffer riding, and more fragile; heavier is slower, softer riding, and more durable. The type of bike, rider, and conditions of use determine the balance of priorities. Wheels for racing on smoothly surfaced roads for example, are lighter and slimmer than wheels for touring with heavy loads on gravel tracks.

A wheel is a package where the components—tyre, rim, spokes, and hub—tend to follow suit in weight and quality. Stout tyres, wide rims, and thick spokes go with touring bikes and mountain bikes. Light tyres, narrow rims, and slender spokes go with sport and racing bikes. Generally, heavier wheels are better able to cope with bumps, potholes, and rough surfaces, and lighter wheels are faster but harsher riding. Much depends on the rider. 'Comfortable' for a beginner usually means a wheel that does not skitter at the sight of a pebble. The fact that it is heavy and slow is inconsequential. For an advanced rider, however, a slow wheel is usually uncomfortable because it is hard to move. Comfort in such a case is a taut wheel that responds quickly and rolls easily.

Tyres

There are two types of wheels: high-pressure (HP) wheels have wire-on tyres on HP rims, and sprints have tubular tyres on sprint rims. Wire-on tyres are the familiar type with an open casing, where the two edges of the casing nestle within the lips of a U-shaped rim. The casing edges are reinforced with beads of wire or Kevlar, so that they retain shape and stay inside the rim when the inner tube is inflated. It's a straightforward design that is easy to manage when changing a tyre or extracting the inner tube to mend a puncture.

With tubular or sew-up tyres the casing edges are sewn together, completely surrounding the inner tube. A sprint rim has a slightly concave, smooth top with no lips and the tyre is held in place with glue or shellac. In the event of a puncture, a complete tubular tyre is much quicker to replace than a wire-on tyre, an advantage when racing. However, mending a puncture in a tubular is a time-consuming, fiddly business.

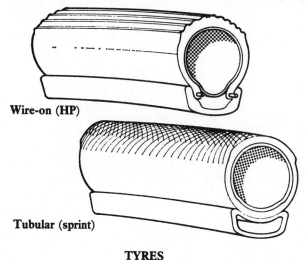

Wire-on (HP)

Tubular (sprint)

TYRES

Where sprints score is in reduced weight. Sprints are inherently lighter than HP's, and the difference in performance is very noticeable. The same bike when fitted with sprints handles and responds more quickly than when fitted with HPs. As a result, sprints—laboriously sewn together casings, sticky glued rims, and all—are the preferred choice for racing.

Sprints are top of the performance tree, but not by much. Wire-on tyre technology has seen enormous development in recent years. Models range from 2.125-inch wide, heavy-duty knobblies for off-road use, down to 0.875-inch wide, ultra-light treadless road screamers that in terms of rolling resistance (not weight) are just as fast as tubulars. Between the two extremes is a vast spectrum of tyres catering to just about every need.

There are two traditional systems for sizing tyres and—curses—they are not interchangeable. American and British sizes are in inches: 27 × 1.25 (or 27 × 1¼) means a tyre diameter of 27 inches and a cross-section or width of 1.25 inches. Continental sizes are metric: 700 × 28C means a tyre diameter of 700 mm and a width of 28 mm. Neither system is accurate: for example, mountain bike 26-inch tyres need smaller rims than road 26-inch tyres. A more precise metric system of annotating tyre sizes is now coming into international use, and consists of a two-figure number, a dash and a three-figure number, as in 32-620. The first figure gives the tyre width, the second the diameter of the rim it fits. Both are in millimetres.

Commonly Known as	Standard Designation
Road	
26 × 1.25	32-597
26 × 1.375 (650 × 35A)	35-590
26 × 1.5 (650 × 35B)	35-584
27 × 0.875	23-630
27 × 1	25-630
27 × 1.125	28-630
27 × 1.25	32-630
27 × 1.375	35-630
28 × 1.5 (650 × 35B)	35-584
650 × 35A (26 × 1.375)	35-590
650 × 35B (26 × 1.5)	35-584
700 × 19C	19-622
700 × 20C	20-622
700 × 23C	23-622
700 × 25C	25-622
700 × 28C	28-622
700 × 35C	35-622
700 × 35B (28 × 1.5)	35-635
Mountain bike	
26 × 1.5	37-559
26 × 1.75	44-559
26 × 2.125	54-559

The 700C is the same diameter as the sprint rim used for tubular tyres, and makes it possible to interchange HP and sprint wheels on the same bike. This is a handy feature for weekend racers who use their bikes for commuting and training during the week. The 700C is also the common Continental size, a point to note if you plan to tour in Europe. You cannot mount a 700C on a rim for a 27-inch tyre, or vice versa, and in most cases you cannot interchange 700C and 27-inch wheels on the same bike. It's got to be one or the other. If you plan to tour abroad, or to run a racing bike, now or perhaps later, or simply have a choice, then standardize on 700C.

Until recently, the common tyre size in Britain was 27 inches and the usual advice was to use it because replacement tyres were easier to find. This idea dates from a time when 27-inch wheels were the mainstream size, tyres failed regularly, and the various models were slow and little different from each other, so that the main concern was how easily and cheaply a replacement tyre could be bought. Nowadays 700C tyres are readily available, and modern tyres are a dynamic component that you select for the balance of speed, grip, comfort, and durability that suits you. Replacement time is a moment for contemplating delicious possibilities from the comprehensive ranges in bike shops, not settling for whatever el cheapos are available in the local chain store.

If you run good rubber and replace tyres before they are completely worn, then you should very rarely suffer worse than a mendable puncture. In any case, for a replacement tyre in an emergency you should carry your own spare! It's not much good being out in the middle of Dartmoor (or anywhere on a Sunday morning) and needing a spare of whatever size. If complete self-sufficiency is important, then carry a spare. Happily, there are lightweight wire-on tyres that fold to a very compact size, and are easily carried on a bike.

Mountain bikes and roadsters generally use 26- or 24-inch wheels, which are stronger because of their smaller diameter and generally more robust construction. Tyres in these sizes usually favour strength over speed, but high-performance models are rapidly increasing in number. Tyres for 20-inch wheels are soft and slow, to help cushion the inherent stiffness of the wheel.

In general, wide tyres have a more comfortable ride, better traction on loose surfaces such as gravel and in wet conditions, and are the most durable. Narrow tyres have a stiffer ride, less traction, and are more vulnerable to punctures and bruising— but they go. The mainstream tyre width for most 27-inch/700C wheel road bikes is 1.25-inches/32 mm, a category that embraces everything from rugged, heavyweight expedition models to lightweight, Kevlar-bead, high-performance models. Next step up the speed ladder are narrow-section, 1.125-inch/28 mm and 1-inch/25 mm wide tyres. These are very much for performance, have a stiff ride, and are fragile: one bad hit on a monster pothole can be terminal. But they are great fun, particularly for skilled riders who enjoy zest and sparkle in a bike. At the slow end of the ladder, 1.375-inch/35 mm wide tyres are the job for outback touring with very heavy loads, commuting on really mean streets, slippery conditions, and deep gravel.

The 1.25-inch/32 mm category is very flexible. The tough models are very tough, and the high-performance models are very fast, but still practical for durability and traction. For sport riding and race training, narrow-section tyres give maximum performance—and a few grey hairs if the road is wet and slippery.

Tyres for mountain bikes follow similar basic principles except that the width range is from 1.375 to 2.125 inches. The narrow models are usually for properly surfaced roads or competition, and the wide models are for hard off-road bashing, and for traction in sand and mud. There are also dual-purpose tyres with a uniform tread pattern or continuous ridge at the centre for speed on the road, and knobs on the sides for traction in dirt.

How a tyre is built also affects performance. The tread material can be soft, for better grip, or harder, for greater durability. It can be thin, for minimum rolling resistance, or thick, for greater strength. The casing is made of layers of fabric, with the number of threads per square inch (tpi) ranging from around 35 to 106. A high tpi number indicates a light, supple tyre with low rolling resistance and good cornering adhesion, but one that is vulnerable to cuts and bruises. A low tpi number indicates a stout, rigid tyre with higher rolling resistance and less adhesion, but better able to resist misfortune.

All these various characteristics can be mixed and matched to meet particular requirements. There are tyres made for superior traction in wet conditions, tyres with belts of bullet-proof Kevlar in the casings to help prevent punctures, and a host of other variations. The point to bear in mind is that tyres are a dynamic part of a bike, and greatly increase the range of options under your control.

If the bike you buy is a good one, and designed for an express purpose (such as heavily loaded touring), then it may be fitted with high-quality tyres. The majority of production bikes, however, must compete vigorously on price, and so in most cases the tyres will be merely average—good enough, but easily improved on.

Good tyres can cost a fair bit, it is worth checking around before you buy. Articles in periodicals are rarely based on hard information, but the advice of bike shops is usually straight. Specialized is a leading brand, some would say the best, with a wide range of models to suit every purpose and pocket. Michelin is another top name. Nutrak, Avocet, and Panaracer have good models, and Continental, Clement, Wolber, and Vittoria are all in there pitching hard.

Rims

Rims are made in steel or alloy. Alloy is what you want. Steel is just too heavy. A bike with steel rims handles like a barrel of nails, takes an age to get into motion, and can take the rest of your life to stop. Most bicycle brakes are the calliper type that work by pressing two blocks against the sides of the rim. In dry conditions this works well with alloy rims, and only just with steel rims. In wet conditions alloy rims have less braking power, but are still functional. In the case of steel rims, however, braking power piffles to almost zero, and it is often more effective—true—to stop by dragging your feet.

In times past steel rims were sometimes recommended for steamroller strength. But like tyres, modern alloy rims are available in a range of weights and strengths,

Tubular   HP straight-side   HP box-section

RIM PROFILES

and you can pick what you need for the job. Mountain bikes are made to withstand dreadful hammerings—like 30 mph across rocky streambeds—and without exception use alloy rims. For ultimate performance and strength, top-line rims are made from specially hardened alloys.

Approximate Alloy Rim Weight	Application
Sprints	
290-325 g	Time trials
325-350 g	Time trials/road racing
350-400 g	Road racing
Wire-ons	
380-400 g	Racing/high performance
400-450 g	High performance
450-550 g	Touring

A good match between tyre and rim widths is important. For example, most rims made to mount 1.25-inch wide tyres will accept a slightly narrower 1.125-inch tyre, but not a 1-inch model. Conversely, very narrow rims for 0.875- and 1-inch tyres will sometimes stretch to 1.125-inch tyres, but rarely to 1.25-inch. It's more than a simple yes or no fit. A rim and tyre work together and have an optimum performance profile. When a tyre is too narrow for the rim it tends to take the shape of a wedge, and impact resistance and grip are greatly reduced. The wheel is more easily damaged by bumps, the ride is hard, and handling is skittish and uncertain. There's less of a problem if the tyre is too wide for the rim, but sometimes the rim swims about within the tyre, so that the bike feels indeterminate and queasy when cornering. When tyre and rim are correctly matched, the profile is similar to a button mushroom, with the tyre (cap of mushroom) wider than the rim (stem). Ride is firm and handling is certain; the bike is 'willing' to take a corner.

Rim Width	Normal Tyre Width Range/ Maximum Stretch
Road	
19-20 mm	19-25/28 mm
22 mm	25-28/35 mm
26 mm	28-35 mm
Mountain bike	
22 mm	35-50 mm
28 mm	37-54 mm
32 mm	44-54 mm

Good quality rims are eyeletted: the holes for the spoke nipples are reinforced with metal eyelets, just like shoes. Generally, box- or modular-section construction gives the most strength for the least weight. Part of the rim is hollow—in cross-section, a shallow rectangle or 'box'. Rims that are sturdier all around can use a simpler channel-section design shaped like a U.

Top brands with excellent quality in all models are Super Champion, Mavic, and Saturae. Other good names are Ambrosio, Araya, Wolber, and Weinmann. Bike manufacturers understand the performance and durability advantages of good rims and, for the most part, fit models suitable for the type and price range of bike.

Spokes

The most highly stressed parts of a wheel are the spokes. In materials there are three types: galvanized rustless, chrome- or nickel-plated, and stainless steel. Galvanized spokes have a dull finish but are strong. Plated spokes are glittery and pretty but need polishing to prevent rust, and are slightly weaker than galvanized. Stainless steel is generally reckoned the best, but is more demanding of wheelbuilding technique. In design, there is plain-gauge, the same diameter throughout, and double-butted, with the stressed areas at the ends of the spoke thicker and the mid-section thinner. Plain-gauge spokes are easier to work with, and give a stiff wheel that can carry on for a while even if a spoke breaks. Double-butted spokes are more elastic and supple, and if correctly tensioned will in theory give an even stronger wheel.

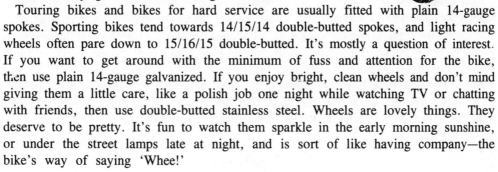

Touring bikes and bikes for hard service are usually fitted with plain 14-gauge spokes. Sporting bikes tend towards 14/15/14 double-butted spokes, and light racing wheels often pare down to 15/16/15 double-butted. It's mostly a question of interest. If you want to get around with the minimum of fuss and attention for the bike, then use plain 14-gauge galvanized. If you enjoy bright, clean wheels and don't mind giving them a little care, like a polish job one night while watching TV or chatting with friends, then use double-butted stainless steel. Wheels are lovely things. They deserve to be pretty. It's fun to watch them sparkle in the early morning sunshine, or under the street lamps late at night, and is sort of like having company—the bike's way of saying 'Whee!'

Hubs

There are two types of hubs: steel three-piece and alloy single-piece. Steel hubs malfunction as a matter of course, and should be studiously avoided. You'll only find them on very cheap bikes not worth having.

Alloy hubs are universal on decent lightweight bikes. They attach to the bike with conventional axle nuts, or via quick-release (QR) levers which work instantly. Quick-release hubs are standard for lightweight road bikes, and are a welcome convenience when servicing the bike, travelling with it by car, train, or aeroplane, and when locking up on the street (the front wheel is removed and locked together with the frame and back wheel to a rigorously immobile object).

The hub illustrated is a high-flange design used for racing and sport riding. The flange is the part with all the holes where the spokes are attached. According to theory, the stiffness of a wheel is proportional to the flange diameter squared. Hence, commuting and touring bikes often use low-flange hubs for a softer, less stiff ride, while performance bikes usually have high-flange hubs for greater responsiveness. (In adverts and manufacturers' catalogues, the terms high-flange and low-flange are usually abbreviated as H/F and L/F. In America, hubs are large-flange and small-flange, so if you see a U.S. advert or catalogue with the term L/F hub, it means a high-flange and not a low-flange model.) Opinion is divided as to which type is stronger. A high flange reduces the torque load on the spokes, but increases the angle at which the spokes join the rim, trading one problem for another. Tandems require high-flange hubs to allow room for additional spokes. For solo bikes, flange size is less important than the overall quality of wheel building.

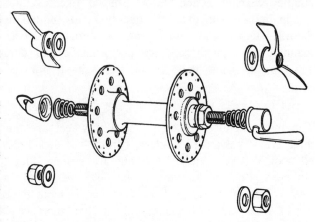

Low-class alloy hubs such as Atom and Normandy, and anonymous cheap models from the East, can deform at the spoke holes, thereby promoting spoke breakage. The top-class brands are Campagnolo, Shimano, SunTour, Mavic, and Specialized, followed at an interval by Suzue, Zeus, Ofmega, Maillard, and Miche. Most of these manufacturers offer models in several different price ranges.

Many hubs have seals to help protect the bearings from dirt and water. This can be a useful feature, but make sure that the hub is user-serviceable. Some hubs can only be serviced at the factory, an unnecessary inconvenience.

Ye Total Wheel

Wheel quality depends partly on the quality of the parts used, and partly on the design, but the thing that makes a good wheel is—a human being. There are all kinds of automatic wheelbuilding machines, and some of them can make a good head start at putting together a wheel, but the final, crucial touch is human. One important function of a bike shop is to check and true the wheels before a new bike is given to a customer. A craft, an art—call it what you will—truing a wheel is something like playing a banjo or guitar. You learn the strings and the notes, you practise, and then your fingers have the music.

A pair of top-class, fully handmade wheels can cost as much as a complete basic bike. Yup. But this buys superior performance and strength, and value for money reliability exceeding tnat of half a dozen sets of cheap wheels. Now very obviously, basic bikes cannot afford handmade wheels with jewel-like parts. In fact, cheap wheels will not stand much more than 6 months of regular urban commuting, and just one long tour with a heavy load can be finis. One important reason why many people upgrade from cheap bikes after a year or so is that they get fed up with dodgy wheels and broken spokes.

It may be discouraging to hear that wheels can be a source of grief. The other side of the coin is that wheels can be really good. In fact, wheels can transform a bike—and you are not just limited to one set of wheels. It's increasingly common to run two pairs of wheels, one for heavy going, the other for sport and fun. So, you might buy a very quick road bike with light, fancy wheels, and plan to run heavier, no-nonsense wheels when using the bike for commuting or loaded touring. Or, for economic reasons you might buy a bike with a fairly good frame and so-so wheels, and upgrade the spinners when you can afford to do so.

One basic governing factor for options in wheels is the quality of the frame. Good wheels will not make a dull frame go whiz. This is why first and foremost you go for a good frame, and then next—good wheels!

Transmission

The transmission turns power at the pedals into work at the rear wheel—motion. There are three main types: single-gear, hub multi-gear and derailleur multi-gear.

Single-Gear

A single-gear transmission consists of the basics: pedals, cranks and chainwheel, chain, rear sprocket, and freewheel. It's simple, strong and reliable, and fine for flat terrain when you've plenty of time for accelerating the bike to speed. But for hills and stop-and-go traffic a single gear ratio (number of times the rear wheel turns for each complete rotation of the cranks) is limiting. The human body does not churn out slathers of energy. In a low gear ratio (fewer turns of the wheel for each rotation of the cranks) good for climbing hills, you'll run out of breath trying to spin the cranks fast enough for speed on the level. In a high gear ratio (more turns of the wheel for each rotation of the cranks) good for speed on the level, climbing will agonize your muscles and eventually bust your knees. The way to flexibility is a hub or derailleur gear system with multiple gears.

Hub Gears

Hub gears are internal; the mechanism nests safely within the hub shell where nothing can get at it. The basic design is nearly 100 years old and is used on utility bikes all over the world. It's as tried and true as they come. Most makes have 3 speeds, with adequate range for ordinary utility use over moderate terrain. Sturmey-Archer also offer a 5-speed model with a slightly greater range.

Hub gears are easy to shift. Most are controlled by an external shift lever that can be operated at any time, whether the bike is moving or not. The relatively rare semi-automatic 2-speed is pedal-operated. When pedalling is momentarily stopped, the unit shifts, up or down as the case may be. Hub gears are simple and reliable, but have performance drawbacks. One is that the intervals, or jumps, between gears are large, which makes it difficult to maintain a steady, efficient pedalling rate. Another is fundamental: the mechanism itself consumes a lot of the rider's output. The amount of power lost through internal friction is a matter of some debate, but 18 per cent is an oft-cited figure.

Derailleur Gears

Derailleur gears live out in the open air, exposed to wet, dirt, and knocks. They appear crude: to change gear ratio, pieces of metal poke at the chain, knocking it from one sprocket or chainring to another. And yet, derailleur gears in good condition can be up to 99 per cent efficient in delivering power to the rear wheel. This is why they are the universal choice for performance bikes.

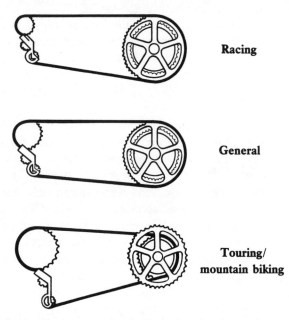

Racing

General

Touring/
mountain biking

The range of gear ratios in a derailleur system depends on the size of the chainrings on the crankset (the business with the pedals), and the size of the sprockets, or cogs, on the freewheel (the spiky business on the rear wheel). Large on the front to small on the rear makes the wheel go around more times for each rotation of the cranks—speed. Small on the front to large on the rear makes the wheel go around fewer times for each rotation of the cranks—torque. Chainrings and sprockets go up and down in size a tooth at a time, and so derailleur systems are very flexible in size and pattern of gear ratios.

Derailleur systems divide into two general design categories: competition and touring. In racing the need is to keep the human power plant churning away at peak efficiency. There's one thing to do—go. The gear ratios are tightly clustered in a narrow range: close-ratio gears. In touring and general riding the need is to extend the work range as widely as possible. There are many things to do, from lazing along boosted by a tail wind to climbing stiff gradients while laden with baggage. The gear ratios are broadly spaced: wide-ratio gears.

Derailleurs

A derailleur (or mech, in bikie parlance) moves the chain from sprocket to sprocket (rear), or chainring to chainring (front). The rear mech also keeps the chain taut by wrapping it through a spring-loaded arm. With close-ratio gears the sprockets on the freewheel are near to each other in size, and there is less chain to gather in. A typical competition mech is therefore lightweight and compact, with a short arm, and shifts quickly and precisely. With wide-ratio gears the sprockets are further apart in size and there is more chain to gather in. A touring or mountain bike mech is therefore usually larger and mechanically more elaborate, with a long arm, and shifting is not as whiz as with a competition unit.

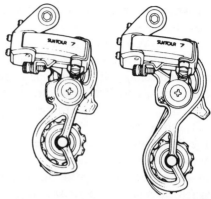

Short arm mech   **Long arm mech**

Derailleurs come in good, better, and best quality grades. Just about all of them work. The differences relate to weight, mechanical sophistication, speed of shifting, strength, finish, and range or capacity. Competition and mountain bike designs are usually strong, touring designs range from simple and strong to complex and vulnerable. For example, the Huret Duopar is a touring mech justly renowned for smooth shifting over widely spaced sprockets even when under load. It is almost as famous for breaking. The complex mechanical articulation that allows it to zoom from a small sprocket up onto a mega-sprocket is also the means for the unit to destroy itself if something gets out of turn. A mech like the Duopar is fine for a rider who loves precise shifting and knows how to handle the unit. Unless handled carefully, however, a Duopar can turn cannibal and tear itself to bits. Such traumas are reasonably rare. Most bike manufacturers prefer to fit reliable equipment, and use simple and strong touring mechs. You're likely to consider a very sophisticated model only as a replacement or to upgrade. If you enjoy lightness and precision, then by all means try a high-tech whizzer. If you want the thing to work

RIDING FIXED

The most sophisticated and fastest transmission is none at all—a single-ratio fixed gear with no freewheel. When the back wheel turns, so do the cranks. The only way to stop pedalling is to stop the bike.

Riding fixed is a traditional European method for winter training. At the end of the road racing season the multi-gear bike is put away, and replaced with a fixed-gear machine. Sometimes the bike is a track model made for the job, but often it is just an old, stripped-down road bike that can en-

dure the grunge and grime of winter. The classic gear ratio is 63 inches, which is low and easy to spin.

The bike is used for everything. With only one gear ratio the rider is forced to learn how to spin the cranks at blinding speeds. There's no other way to make the bike move, or to stay with it on the downhills. The rider becomes progressively more supple, fluid—and fast. On return to the multi-gear bike there's no holding him or her. It is said, with justice, that you do not know how to ride a bike until you have ridden fixed for at least a season.

even when you make a mistake, then stick with the more robust models made for mountain bikes.

For some years now the cycle components market has been dominated by two major Japanese firms, Shimano and SunTour. They maintain a running, ding-dong battle, competing vigorously throughout comprehensive ranges from basic budget models through to state-of-the-art models at the forefront of technology. In the short term, one or the other firm may momentarily forge into the lead, but the other usually soon catches up.

The derailleur was invented in 1933 by Tullio Campagnolo, a name that has stood ever since for the pinnacle of elegance and efficiency in cycle components. Many road racing cyclists regard the Campagnolo Record series derailleurs as the best available. Certainly, the finish and assembly of Campagolo components is particularly fine, and while some of their designs are conservative, Campagnolo is race-proven for strength and durability. When the chips are down the most important quality is that the equipment works. At times, SunTour and Shimano have the technological edge, but Campagnolo has the pedigree of victory.

Where the Japanese firms score decisive points is in the important areas of low- and mid-price components—the kind most often seen on production bikes, and that most people use. Savouring top-line equipment is fun, but the impressive thing is that you can buy a decent derailleur for the price of a meal—in a fairly cheap restaurant!

Gearing—the size and pattern of gear ratios in a transmission—is a major factor when selecting a derailleur, and this subject is covered in the chapter Fitting and Gearing. Read it before buying a bike.

Shift Levers

The shift lever is the means for moving the derailleur from sprocket to sprocket (or chainring to chainring) and then holding it in place. Mechanically, there are two kinds: open and indexed.

An open shift lever depends on simple friction or a ratchet to keep the lever in position. When shifting from one gear to another, aligning the derailleur so that

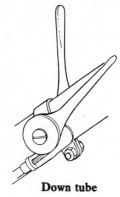

the chain meshes smoothly with the sprocket is done by feel and ear—a knack that comes more easily to some people than others. An indexed shift lever has stops for each correct position; alignment of derailleur and sprocket is completely automatic—a marvellous facility at any level of riding ability.

Down tube

Stem

With the exception of the Campagnolo Syncro 2 lever, indexed shifting requires that shift lever and derailleur must both be designed for indexed operation. Derailleur and shift lever are supplied as a system, and combining units from different manufacturers usually won't work. Another point is that tolerances in an indexed system are stringent. All parts must be firmly mounted, the sprockets must be precisely equidistant from each other, and the control cable without slack, or the system will malfunction. Which could be very daunting but for the saving grace: a selector switch for indexed or normal operation. An indexed system can be changed to normal, non-indexed mode anytime you want—and the performance is still wizard. Eat your cake and have it, too! This versatility is one reason why indexed shifting systems are gaining so rapidly in popularity. Indeed, these days it is hard to find a bike without indexed gears.

One problem with indexed gears is of their own making. Their performance is so good that they set a new standard—and then have trouble living up to it. The things are fiddly. A little slack in the cable, a chance knock of the derailleur against a pole, a bit of muck in the works, and the system goes out of whack. Although you could just switch to non-indexed mode, the appeal of indexed operation is usually strong enough to make you fiddle until the thing works again.

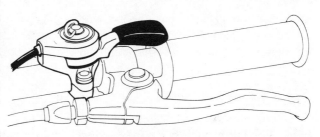

Thumb-shifter

Generally, shift levers are paired with derailleurs, SunTour for SunTour, Shimano for Shimano, and so on, and generally, quality is commensurate. A basic mech will have a simple friction lever that moves easily when releasing derailleur spring tension and needs more pressure when tightening the spring. A better mech will have a lever with ratchet or clutch mechanism that moves easily in either direction.

Shift levers are mounted in various places: on the down tube, on the handlebars, at the handlebar ends, and on the stem. Down tube mounting is the classic method for bikes with drop handlebars. It allows short control cables, giving maximum feel and quick response when shifting. One's hand falls naturally to the down tube position, which is on the centre line of the bike and thus has the minimum adverse effect on bike stability.

Handlebar-end shifters use long cables, and because these increase the amount of slack in the system, shifting

Bar-end

is sloppier and less precise. Mounting on drop handlebars often requires the drilling of holes in the handlebar, and there have been instances where this has led to corrosion and a complete snapping apart of the handlebar while the rider was under way. Handlebar-end shifters are a matter of individual preference, as they are fairly rare on production bikes.

Thumb-shifters are a blessing from the evolution of mountain bikes. They are designed for flat handlebars and mount just inboard of the brake levers, so that both gears and brakes can be operated without removing hands from the bars. They're lovely.

Stem-mounted shifters are a bad idea. They were developed because they look easy to use. But in a crash they can puncture your gut or tear off the family jewels. Thumb-shifters are infinitely better, and much friendlier.

Cranksets

Cranks and chainwheels are made of aluminium alloy or steel. Designs vary in the method used to attach the cranks to the bottom bracket axle. The Ashtabula is a one-piece crank, chainwheel, and bottom bracket in steel, and is most often seen on

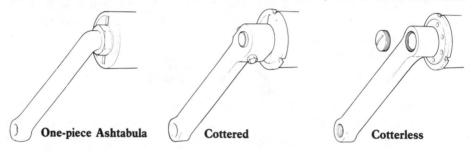

One-piece Ashtabula   **Cottered**   **Cotterless**

BMX and cruiser bikes. Cottered cranks are fastened to the bottom bracket axle with a wedge-shaped cotter pin, and are usual on cheap roadster bikes. Alloy cotterless cranks use a recessed bolt to fix the cranks to the bottom bracket axle, and are used for low-price bikes through to superbikes.

Cotterless cranksets vary considerably in type and quality. Low end of the scale are one-piece cranksets with a fixed chainring, found on basic-grade roadsters, commuting bikes, and cheap sports bikes. When the chainring wears out, the whole unit has to be replaced, at modest cost. Although a fixed chainring limits the possibilities in gear ratios, this is often of little consequence for a utility bike.

Cotterless cranksets with detachable chainrings divide into two categories, racing and touring. Racing cranksets are highly stressed, and for maximum strength, long arms are used to mount the chainrings. This limits the minimum size of chainring that can be fitted. Touring bikes need low-ratio gears, and on touring cranksets the arms are short, so that smaller chainrings can be used. Competition cranksets usually have two, fairly closely spaced chainrings. This gives adequate range

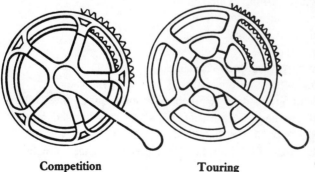

Competition   **Touring**

CHANGING THE RINGS

One sin committed by all too many bike manufacturers is the fitting of competition cranksets to basic, heavy bikes that will be used primarily for general riding and touring. It is then impossible to fit small chainrings in order to obtain the lower gear ratios that these bikes so desperately need. Another lingering trap for the unwary are cranksets for which replacement chainrings are unobtainable. Chainring patterns vary from manufacturer to manufacturer and model to model. They divide into a number of compatibility groups of which four or five are mainstream. Parts availability on these is usually very easy. With some of the more obscure models it can be non-existent. A final point is minimum chainring size. If you're buying a bike for touring and/or off-road riding, then the ability to fit a small 24T inner ring is usually an asset.

Names: Campagnolo, Shimano, SunTour, Stronglight, and TA are all excellent. SR and Sugino have many good value models. There are also lesser known brands, such as Specialized, Mavic, Avocet, Miche, Ofmega, Galli, and Gipiemme, that include both high-class and good value equipment. The difficulty with specific recommendations is that crankset names and model designations shift and change like night clouds scudding before the moon. Manufacturers and distributors come and go. When buying a bike, ensure that it has the right type of crankset for your needs, and if it accepts spares, that they exist in the here and now.

for close-ratio gears and fast, reliable shifting—the shift lever needs only to banged one way or the other. Doubles can also be used for touring by simply reducing the size of the chainrings so that all the ratios are in a low range.

The best policy with gear ratios is to concentrate them where you need them most, but a lot of people want it both ways: wide-range gearing with low ratios for easy climbing, and big ratios for speed. The range of a double can be extended by using chainrings and/or freewheel sprockets well apart in size, but then there are large jumps between gear ratios and shifting is ragged. A better method for creating wide-range gearing is to use triple chainrings. These are virtually standard on mountain

Shimano Biopace rings

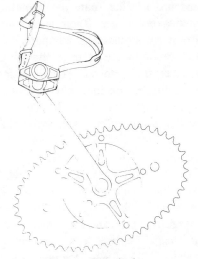

Durham Elliptical

bikes and very common on touring bikes. Triple chainrings allow a wide spread of gear ratios to be spaced evenly, and make the transmission mechanically more coherent. A triple needs a bit of technique and time for shifting, but is usually smoother than a double stretched to maximum capacity. In times past triples were in some disfavour because they were often sensitive and fiddly. The advent of mountain bikes requiring very wide-range gearing spurred improvements in this area, and triples now work very well. They are fine for beginners, and for whenever wide-range gears are required. See the chapter Bike Set-up for more information.

Cranksets with oval chainrings have become quite popular for touring bikes and mountain bikes. These vary the gear ratio during each revolution of the cranks, and there are two schools of thought regarding the best way to match ratio with the strong and weak parts of the rider's power stroke. Method one positions the crank so that the ratio is largest when the crank is moving from 1 o'clock to 6 o'clock. Method two, as used by the Shimano Biopace, is just the opposite: crank movement from 1 o'clock to 6 o'clock is the easy (smallest ratio) segment of crank rotation. Method one is a straightforward attempt to take maximum advantage of the most powerful portion of crank rotation, the downstroke. Method two is more complex. The gear ratio is eased during the downstroke, thereby increasing pedal momentum and power, and the greater speed of the cranks is then met by a larger gear ratio as the cranks move through the dead or weak positions at 12 and 6 o'clock. The change of pace also makes it easier for the leg muscles to synchronize the transition from downward movement to upward movement.

Oval chainrings, whether used by method one or two, have their merits—principally, an increase in torque that is most useful at slower pedalling cadences. Put another way, oval chainrings work, but not for cyclists! Behind that cryptic comment is the quintessential lore of cycling: all through the years aspiring cyclists have diligently applied themselves to mastering the art of spinning the cranks at speeds of 85 rpm and up. It's the route to optimum performance. Oval chainrings are rarely used by professional racers. Their fast/slow/fast/slow rhythm is not conducive to rapid cadences. However, tourists and mountain bikers have different needs than racers, and the better low-speed torque of oval chainrings is often useful when climbing, or moving slowly over tricky terrain. Oval chainrings are good for people who pedal slowly, and to a limited extent, may also be beneficial for beginning racers. They do work, some people like them hugely, and it's pretty much a matter of try and see—but so far at least, not for professional racing.

Chains

Chains used to be simple, cheap, and black. Nowadays chains come in a variety of colours and designs, and are made with better quality steels using sophisticated hardening and plating processes. They are stronger, lighter, and much faster at changing gear. There are two main types: standard-width, and narrow-width. Narrow chains are made for use with compact freewheels (opposite), and usually also work with standard freewheels. Standard chains are too wide to work smoothly with compact freewheels.

Chains from manufacturers such as SunTour, Shimano, and Regina are designed to be used with their own transmission systems. The important area of design variation is in link sideplate shape, which is important to speed and ease of shifting. Mixing chains and freewheels from different manufacturers sometimes gives ragged performance, particularly with indexed gears. Sedis is a popular independent brand with a comprehensive range of chains that always seem to work well.

Freewheels

The freewheel is attached to the rear hub and holds the sprockets, or cogs. These may be five, six, or seven in number. Five-speed freewheels have standard spacing between sprockets, 6-speed freewheels have standard or compact spacing, and 7-speed freewheels have compact spacing. A compact 6-speed is the same width as a 5-speed, and a 7-speed is the same width, or nearly so, as a standard 6-speed. Compact freewheels require a narrower chain than standard freewheels.

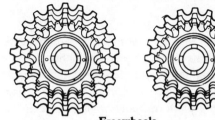

Freewheels

In general, 7-speed freewheels are best suited to fast road and racing bikes. The extra width of the freewheel requires more wheel dish—insetting the hub by using shorter spokes on the freewheelside of the hub—which weakens the wheel. This is one reason why sturdy touring and mountain bikes favour 5- and 6-speed freewheels. freewheels.

HOW MANY SPEEDS?

In Ye Olden days, derailleur gear bikes were called 10-speeds, because the common gearing pattern was a pair of chainrings running to five sprockets on the freewheel. These days, you'll find anything from 5 to 21 speeds, with one to three chainrings running to from five to seven sprockets. The availability of many speeds has dazzle appeal, but as a rough rule of thumb, more is not always better.

You probably already know that a 10-speed only has eight usable ratios, because it is mechanically harmful to run the chain from the large front chainring to the large rear sprocket, or from the small front chainring to the small rear sprocket. Freewheels with six and seven sprockets magnify this restriction by their greater tendency to produce gear ratios that duplicate each other. Thus, a 2F/7R rig that is supposed to have 14 speeds may still have only eight different usable ratios!

In a close-ratio racing set-up, however, a 7-speed freewheel is useful, because it allows quick shifting within the range defined by the size of the front chainring in use. The fact that some ratios may be duplicated is less important than speed and precision of shifting sequence. A 7-speed freewheel also permits the fitting of a 12T sprocket (13T is the minimum with a 6-speed freewheel) for a big, fast final drive ratio—achieving the same effect by using a larger chainring will also raise the ratios obtained with all the other sprockets, and this general rise in range may not be what the rider wants. In sum, 7-speed freewheels are best confined to racing bikes with close-ratio gears, or to bikes with triple chainrings. If you want maximum reliability, in wear and in performance, stick with 5-speed freewheels.

Standard freewheels thread onto the rear wheel hub. Pedalling winds the freewheel on tight, and it is rarely easy to get it back off. A cassette freewheel slides onto a spline and is much easier to assemble and disassemble. However, each type of cassette system is unique in hub design, which precludes using standard freewheels. You're limited to the one system.

Freewheels are highly stressed, and reliability is the paramount factor. Sitting by the roadside and trying to sort out a freewheel—assuming you have the tools to get that far—is an odious pastime, even for a bike mechanic. The current favourite for reliability and strength is Maillard. SunTour and Shimano are fine. If you are offered a Regina CX, turn it down: I've a large collection of fractured, split, and just plain busted CX freewheel bodies. The problem may have been limited to a particular production batch, but at £24 apiece, I'm not having any more.

Pedals

Pedals are like shoes: intimate, and considerably varied in function, fit, and comfort. The pedals on most production bikes are basic and will need replacement within a year. If you have preferences it is probably worth making a substitution at the time of bike purchase. There are three basic types of pedals: cage, platform, and system (special design).

Parallel cage pedals have the same shape on each side and can be used either way up. Most models for road bikes can be fitted with toe clips. The pedal is then dual mode: toe clip or open. This arrangement is attractive for people new to toe clips. Parallel cage models for mountain bikes are beefier and the cage side edges are more deeply serrated to give shoes a firmer grip. Only some models accept toe clips.

Quill cage pedals are a racing design made for use with toe clips and cleats. Only one side is right way up.

'Bear Trap'

The quill is a small protrusion on the end of the pedal that helps keep the foot in place. The under-side of the pedal is rounded, for extra clearance when corner-

ing. Cleats are a small plastic or metal plate attached to the sole of the shoe. A thin slot in the cleat engages with the rear cage side of the pedal. Tightening the toe clip strap snugs the cleat firmly over the cage side and ensures that the shoe stays attached to the pedal. This improves both performance and safety.

Metal platform

Quill cage

Cage pedals are designed for minimal weight and are intended to be used with cycling shoes that have a stiff sole for supporting the foot. Using them with ordinary shoes may lead to foot cramps on long rides.

Platform pedals have a larger surface area for supporting the foot. Most of the metal and nylon road models are made for use with toe clips and cleats, and have a raised ridge to engage the cleat. Off-road models also usually accept toe clips, but not cleats. They often have raised studs on the platform area to help grip the shoe. Rubber platform pedals can be used either way up and do not accept toe clips. They are primarily for simple utility and cruiser bikes.

Toe clips and cleats are a classic method for attaching to pedals, but for a secure grip the strap must be tight and this can lead to numbness or discomfort in the foot. Loosening the strap brings relief, but then there is a risk of pulling out of the pedal and possibly losing control of the bike.

The solution to this problem is a system pedal and cleat designed to work as a unit. There's no toe clip or strap. The pedal includes a mechanism that automatically grips the cleat when the rider steps into the pedal. The process is just like a step-in ski binding, and in fact the leading range of designs come from Look, a ski equipment manufacturer. So long as the pedalling forces are vertical, the cleat stays firmly attached to the pedal. The method for disengagement is particular to each make and model, but is usually a simple rolling motion of the foot to the side.

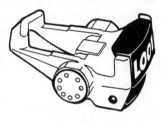

Look system pedal

System pedals are lovely. They have a better grip than toe clips and cleats, and yet are usually easier to disengage. There's no toe clip strap cutting painfully into the foot. Weight and bulk are reduced. A really minimalist model like the AeroLite weighs 74 g in steel and but 48 g in titanium, as against a minimum of around 200 g for a standard pedal with a toe clip and strap. A system pedal can only be used with a specific design of cleat. This restriction does not matter when the bike is a personal machine used only by you.

Pedals range in cost from a few pounds to over £100. Inexpensive pedals wear out after about 5,000 miles. With regular maintenance good quality pedals will turn in 100,000 miles—literally cheaper in the long run. However, if early retirement is forced on a pedal by damage from a fall or grounding on a corner, the economic advantage goes to the cheap pedal.

Names: The SR rubber platform pedal with an alloy body is the best of its type. At peanut prices the parallel cage Lyotard 136 is a favourite standby, and the steel platform Lyotard 23 is known for smooth, reliable performance. The slightly dearer alloy SR platform pedal is popular for touring bikes. The Campagnolo range of quill pedals is excellent in quality and value throughout. Shimano and SunTour both make fine pedals. I've always had a soft spot for MKS pedals. They work fine and don't cost the earth. In system pedals the Look models have established a convincing record of performance and reliability—they're a common sight at race meetings.

Selecting an appropriate pedal depends on riding style, the kind of shoes used, and a host of other variables. Many of these are discussed elsewhere in this book. After reading the mountain bike chapter, for example, you should know if you need massive son-of-Jaws pedals with jagged cage sides, or slimmer pedals with toe clips. Pedals are personal. Think through your needs, examine and fondle the hardware— and choose whatever you fancy best.

Brakes

Bicycle brake designs differ in their balance of braking power, weight, mechanical precision, and expense. They are a dynamic part of bike performance, and it is important to know how different kinds of brakes mix and match with different kinds of bikes. You can't possibly enjoy yourself on a bike unless you understand the brakes, and know what you can do with them. For example, side-pull brakes are fine for racing bikes, because they have all the stopping power that lightweight machines with thin tyres can safely use. Fitting the same type of brake on a cheap, fake mountain bike is tantamount to suicide, because it does not have the power to cope with the greater forces generated by heavy bike weight and strong grip of wide tyres. Moreover, brake performance on a fine, sunny day is one thing; performance in wet or muddy conditions, or with heavy loads, is quite another. There are three basic kinds of brakes: hub, disc, and calliper.

Hub Brakes

Coaster brakes are for the rear wheel and are usually pedal-operated. They are easy to apply but hard to control and can cause a skid by locking up the wheel. They do not have real stopping power. It's a skid or next to nothing. Skidding to a stop is excessively exciting at high speeds, wears out tyres very quickly, and takes too long. Coaster brakes have poor heat-dissipating qualities and can burn out on a long downhill descent. In short, they are very Mickey Mouse, and usually found only on beach cruiser bikes and specialized BMX freestyle machines. As a means of stopping they are like tossing out a rock held to the bike with rope—not serious.

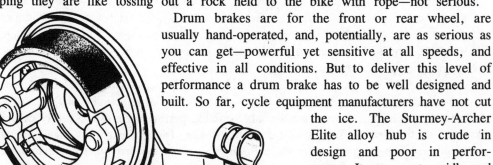

Drum brakes are for the front or rear wheel, are usually hand-operated, and, potentially, are as serious as you can get—powerful yet sensitive at all speeds, and effective in all conditions. But to deliver this level of performance a drum brake has to be well designed and built. So far, cycle equipment manufacturers have not cut the ice. The Sturmey-Archer Elite alloy hub is crude in design and poor in performance. It wears out rapidly and does not work when wet. The French MaxiCar drum brake sometimes found on European

Section: Sachs drum brake

tandems gives a general retarding effect, but stopping power is not electric. The same applies to models from Huret-Sachs. Good drum brakes are wonderful, and perhaps we will eventually see viable models from major manufacturers. At this writing they are obtainable only from custom builders, at custom prices.

Disc Brakes

Disc brakes are about the same story as drum brakes. They are powerful and are used on tandems and tricycles. The commercial models are too heavy for solo bikes. Good lightweight models are custom equipment. Disc brakes work well but tend to be finicky; they need to be kept in close adjustment, and a few drops of oil or other lubricant on the disc can greatly reduce braking power. For the requisite investment of time, energy, and money, drum brakes give better results.

Calliper Brakes

Braking for most bikes is through the use of a calliper mechanism to press a pair of blocks (or shoes) against the wheel rim. There are five design types: side-pull, centre-pull, cantilever, U-type cantilever, and roller-cam cantilever.

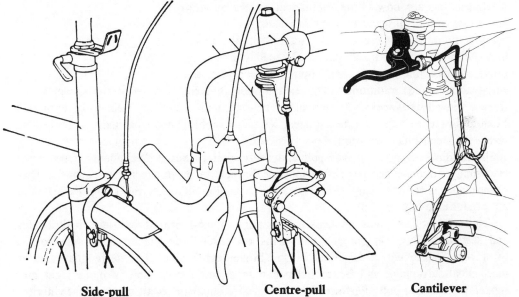

| Side-pull | Centre-pull | Cantilever |

Side-pull brakes pivot two calliper arms on a single bolt and are made in two versions: inexpensive, for cheap bikes, and expensive, for use on quality bikes. Cheap side-pull brakes have long, widely-spaced arms in order to reach around mudguards and thick tyres. They are stamped out of steel and chromed to prevent rust. The design, and crude method of manufacture, result in a sloppy mechanism with erratic, weak performance. Perversely, cheap side-pulls are common on bikes that have the greatest need for decent brakes: heavy utility machines, and small-wheel bikes with steel wheels. Quality side-pull brakes are a totally different affair. They are cast in alloy and milled to precise tolerances. Better models are cold forged for greater strength and rigidity. The mechanism itself is tidy and compact, with short arms. A direct cable connection between the brake lever and the calliper arms gives positive feel and control. Lightness and precision make the quality side-pull the usual choice for racing bikes.

Centre-pull brakes use two pivot bolts, one for each calliper arm, and operate by pulling on a yoke cable connecting the two arms. This gives a mechanical advantage which reduces the amount of force required at the brake lever. The two arms balance each other, and need adjustment less frequently than a side-pull design.

Side- and centre-pull brakes stop equally well. The more rigid side-pull is better for speed control (as opposed to coming to a halt). At speed, the greater mechanical slack in a centre-pull mechanism makes it inclined to snatch and exert more deceleration than necessary or safe. (Mind, this is starting to split hairs. The Tour de France has been won using bikes with centre-pull brakes. Much depends on quality of manufacture.) In times past, ease of operation and maintenance made centre-pull brakes the common choice for sports and touring bikes. They are still better than a side-pull for such machines, but are now being supplanted by the superior and more powerful cantilever brake design.

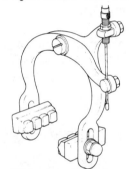

Wide-arm side-pull

For a racing bike, a good side-pull has all the power that can be safely used with the small road contact area provided by thin tyres. A side-pull is compact and aerodynamic—and traditional. The better models stand more as jewel-like works of art than simple mechanical devices. One very upmarket Modolo brake features washers plated with 24k gold. This is actually a legitimate means of retarding corrosion.

The dominant marque in side-pull and centre-pull brakes is Weinmann. They make everything from inexpensive basic stoppers through to professional grade jewels. Dia-Compe also cover the range. For class, Campagnolo, Shimano, SunTour, and Modolo all produce lovely models.

Cantilever brakes pivot on bosses (mounting points) brazed onto the fork blades and seatstays. Two separate calliper arms on either side of the wheel are joined by a yoke cable, which is pulled by the brake lever cable. The design has greater mechanical advantage and better balance than a centre-pull, and is more rigid and lighter than a side-pull. Performance is naturally superior in all respects: sensitivity, ease of application, and sheer raw power. Cantilever brakes are SOP for mountain bikes and heavy-duty touring bikes.

Some manufacturers produce 'solo' model cantilever brakes with shorter arms and blocks than the conventional 'tandem' models. These stinge on performance, which is not the idea. If you go for cantilevers, do not settle for less than full-size arms and blocks.

Top of the performance tree in calliper brakes is the roller-cam design, originated by Charles Cunningham, a mountain bike designer and builder. As with a cantilever, the arms are separate and pivot on bosses alongside the wheels, on the fork blades and chainstays. There is no yoke cable. The ends of the calliper arms have rollers which ride on a wedge-shaped plate; when the plate is pulled via the brake lever and cable, the arms are pushed apart and press the blocks against the wheel rim. The design has a high mechanical advantage, and performance is so hot that many mountain bike builders install a roller-cam brake on the back

Compact Shimano 7400

wheel only, and a regular cantilever on the front. Some people have found that a roller-cam on the front runs too much risk of locking the wheel and pitching the rider over the handlebars.

Roller-cam brakes are fairly well limited to expensive mountain bikes and custom touring bikes. The design is intricate and the mounting point for the rear brake, on

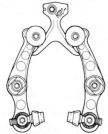

the chainstays just behind the bottom bracket, gives maximum exposure to fouling from mud and stones. It is said with some fairness that the roller-cam is a 'California' brake; fine for use in a dry climate, but not suitable for the muddy conditions frequently encountered by British mountain bikers. It's best to enclose the brake in a special protective pouch, and to make cleaning and lubrication a frequent task. This kind of fiddling about

Roller-cam design

is all right if you want and can use top-notch brake performance. If you just want to fit brakes and have them work when required, then a plain cantilever design is a better bet.

The U-type cantilever brake is a recent introduction. Like a centre-pull brake, it uses a yoke cable to actuate two arms, each mounted on separate pivot bosses brazed onto the frame. In performance, U-brakes are more tractable than roller-cam brakes, but not as powerful; they are prone to mush out on steep descents. U-brakes are fairly easy to adjust, but some bike mechanics say that servicing is difficult. Perhaps U-brake designs will improve, but at this writing, cantilever and roller-cam brakes are better.

Cantilever, roller-cam, and U-type brakes require brazed mounting bosses on the frame. A bike without the required mounting bosses for cantilevers can have them added at a later point in time, but this involves stripping down the bike to the bare frame, and then repainting it after the brazing work is done. This is OK for a conversion of an old bike, but not very economic for a new bike. Roller-cam and U-brakes can use the same bosses, cantilevers have bosses in a different location. You can't change from one type to the other, and within the roller-cam/U-brake category, different models have different mounting positions. It's a bit of a mess, and when considering a bike with cantilever brakes you need to find out what other brakes can or cannot be fitted to the existing bosses. Bike manufacturers are starting to standardize in this area and the problem is therefore receding, but watch your step with bike models that have been discontinued, used bikes, and 'on sale' brakes that may be obsolete designs.

At this writing the best cantilever brakes are the Shimano models, followed at an interval by Dia-Compe. Oddly, the Weinmann cantilever is crude and not very good. For an economic roller-cam brake look to SunTour. More pricy, but best, is the Wilderness Trail Bikes Speedmaster roller-cam. A few small builders make their own roller-cam or other special design brakes; you have to assess these individually, and consider availability of parts.

Just entering the market are hydraulic brakes for bikes. The brake lever drives a piston which compresses fluid in a cyclinder connected to the brake mechanism by a flexible tube. This type of mechanism is standard for car brakes, and is extremely powerful. One interesting model, the Mathauser hydraulic brake, is a calliper type attached with a single pivot bolt, as with centre- and side-pull designs, but the units mount behind the forks and stays and transfer blocks transmit the very strong braking forces to the frame. Another prospective gem comes from Magura, the motorcycle brake manufacturer whose products were used by early mountain bike inventors. The Magura hydraulic brake is also calliper in general shape, but the brake block travel is straight-line and therefore should need little if any adjustment. The Magura unit is new and needs a design tweak or two, but expect to find it on high-class mountain bikes in the near future. Hydraulic systems are the norm for serious power, and down the years many people have chased the goal of a fluid-operated cycle brake. As with internal hub gears, hydraulic brakes use quite sophisticated design and engineering to produce a mechanism that, externally, is simple and easy to use. It looks as if Mathauser and Magura have turned the trick.

Brake Levers

Brake levers come in two types: flat handlebar and drop handlebar. Flat handlebar brake levers as found on roadsters and commuting bikes are simply a basic means to make the brakes work. Brake levers for mountain bikes are more sophisticated. They are shaped for comfort under steady use, and top models have features like adjustable reach to accommodate different hand sizes.

Brake levers for drop handlebars all have the same general shape, but subtle variations from manufacturer to manufacturer can be important. This is because a lot of riding is done with the hands on the hoods, and the fingers resting on the levers. Make sure that the levers fit your grip, as some makes are only suitable for large hands.

On some bikes the brake levers include a second 'safety' or 'dual' lever underneath the straight section of the handlebars. These were originally developed for use on touring bikes, to increase the number of positions from which the brakes can be operated and help rider comfort when making long descents. Marketing flacks quickly took to promoting them as 'safety' levers, implying that they could help avoid or mitigate an accident. The truth is precisely the opposite.

Dual levers have to travel a long distance before the brakes engage. If the system is not closely adjusted, it is possible for the 'safety' lever to bang uselessly against the handlebar while you carry on to destruction. Even when adjusted properly, dual levers need 20-30 per cent more distance for a stop than standard levers. If you're riding top of the bars and an emergency arises, there is no time to change your mind and dive for the standard levers. All you can do is clutch the inferior alternative and hope for the best. What's more, in the top of the bars riding position, bike control and handling is reduced. This is safety? Finally, hands on the brake hoods is one of the most popular riding positions. The hardware on most dual levers makes impossible the fitting of rubber hoods which are essential for comfort in this position. Bah. You don't find dual levers on good bikes. It's as simple as that.

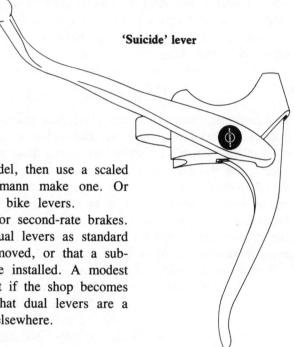

'Suicide' lever

Dual levers are sometimes touted as good for people with small hands. More bah. If you have small hands and can't find a suitable lever in a standard model, then use a scaled down junior racing lever. Weinmann make one. Or switch to flat bars and mountain bike levers.

Whatever you do, don't settle for second-rate brakes. If the bike of your choice has dual levers as standard equipment, insist that they be removed, or that a substitute unit without dual levers be installed. A modest charge for this service is fair, but if the shop becomes tacky, or tries to convince you that dual levers are a good idea, then buy your bike elsewhere.

Brake Blocks

With calliper brakes it is essential that the brake block and rim materials are properly matched. Rims are steel or alloy, blocks are rubber, leather, or synthetic. Rubber works well on steel or alloy in dry weather, but in wet conditions, poorly on alloy, and sometimes not at all on steel. You haven't lived until you've careened for a few miles down a long hill on a dark, wet night, wondering if each moment will be your last. Rubber blocks are acceptable only for lightweight racing bikes with alloy rims and a minimum of mass to retard. Leather blocks are designed for steel rims only and will chew an alloy rim to bits. They work well in the wet, but badly in the dry, and aren't acceptable for anything. Synthetic blocks outperform all others on alloy or steel rims in the dry, and are in the top performance class in the wet.

The only liability of synthetic blocks is that they can be too effective. A panic-stricken novice rider could clamp down on the front brake too hard and cartwheel the bike. However, synthetic blocks are expensive and the vast majority of new bikes are therefore fitted with rubber blocks. These are more even-tempered in performance and will suffice for a novice rider until he or she becomes adept at braking. But graduation to synthetic blocks, which are stronger in wet conditions, should be an early priority. Aztec, Mathauser, and Kool Stop are good brands. Of these, Mathauser is initially the most expensive, but it's also the most durable and therefore economic in the long term.

Summary

When I was a kid most of the neighbourhood bikes had sneaker brakes—a foot jammed against the back tyre. It worked pretty good. Proper brakes are a lot better, and currently, the best of the readily available and affordable types are the cantilever and roller cam designs. I don't see the point of anything less, except on a road racing bike, or a used bike that is not going to be pressed hard.

Handlebars, Stem, and Saddle

It would make very good sense for bike manufacturers to supply their machines without handlebars, stem, or saddle, and leave selection of these items to the individual bike buyer. It's more than a matter of personal taste or style. These components are the interface between rider and machine and are the means for making the bike comfortable and efficient. People are like blades of grass: similar, but never exactly alike. A small variation in stem length, for example, can be the difference between a bike that gives you an aching back after a few miles, or one that you can ride forever. The vital subject of fitting is detailed in the chapter Bike Set-up; here, there's just a quick skim through the hardware.

Handlebars are, with the exception of one-piece handlebar and stem designs, held in place with the stem, the height and length of which determine handlebar position. On very cheap bikes stems and handlebars are made of steel, but otherwise, alloy is the norm. There are two basic shapes for handlebars: flat and downswept, or dropped. The Maes pattern is the most

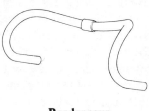

Bucket

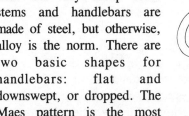

Maes

common downswept version and is suitable for racing, touring, and general use. The Randonneur pattern is for touring; the upswept portions give firm bracing points for the hands when riding in an upright position. The Pista is a pure racing pattern, with little purchase for riding upright.

Flat handlebars come in three general applications: racing, general, and moun-

Randonneur

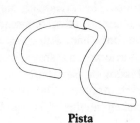

Pista

tain bike. The flat bars used on low-profile racing bikes have the ends pointing forward and up, rather like horns. Until recently, profile bars were rarely used outside of time trial and track events, but they are now increasingly popular for general use. The configuration provides good support for the rider, a strong grip point for the hands, and immediate access to brake and gear controls. With traditional dropped bars people do most of their riding in a semi-crouched position with their hands on the brake lever hoods, rather than in a full crouch with their hands on the lowest part of the bars, the hooks. Profile bars are more comfortable to ride than brake lever hoods, and yet still have a top bar section that allows the rider to change to a more upright position for a change of pace. Lost is the ability to ride on the hooks, but on the other hand, profile bars can be lowered until the position is as fierce as the rider wants—they were made for racing in the first place. Bear in mind, however, that profile bars are fully effective only when used on frames with short head tubes, either because the frame is small in size, or has a top tube that slopes down to the head tube. On a standard diamond-frame with a level top tube, profile bars will give a high riding position

Flat bars for general use as found on roadsters and commuting bikes are sort of like bucket handles: a means to get a grip and steer. Mountain bike handlebars are a totally different story. They are a dynamic part of bike performance and an essential aspect of comfort.

Profile

There are two basic types: one-piece, with bars and stem as a single unit, and two-piece, with separate bars held in a stem that can be a two-prong Slingshot design, a single-prong, four-bolt design, or a single-prong, one-bolt design. One-piece bars are extremely strong. They come in various nuances of shape: low, high, short, long, narrow, wide, and the choice has to right first time out, because it can't be changed. On the other hand, once the shape is right, one-piece bars are great; the design is strong, simple, and gives a convenient platform for carrying things.

Two-piece bars give greater flexibility in positioning. Different reach stems can be used, and the bars themselves can be rotated for subtle changes in configuration. The whole approach is more minimalist and flexible, and is the current trend for most mountain bikes. Two-piece bars flex more than one-piece bars, however, and are not as strong.

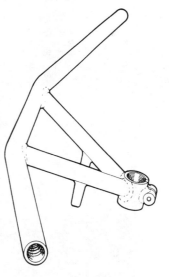

Bullmoose

Mountain bike bars are made in steel or alloy. For once, steel does not indicate cheap. Mountain bikes are made for thrashing and hammering. Steel bars can take repeated abuse more readily than alloy bars, which fatigue much more easily. An alloy bar (of any kind, road or mountain bike) which has had a severe bend should

be discarded, because it could fail without warning. Steel can be manipulated with a much greater margin for safety. This said, the weight/performance advantages of alloy bars make them popular.

I'm not big on fancy bars. The best accolade for bars is that they work so comfortably and well that you don't notice them. Once you find a set of bars you like, keep them, even if you change bikes.

There are two basic types of saddles. One is the mattress design, wide and comfy and often fitted with coil springs or other shock-absorbing mechanism. It's made to go with flat handlebars and a riding position that puts most of the rider's weight on the saddle. The other type is the racing design, narrow and hard and made for use with drop handlebars. These distribute the rider's weight more evenly and allow a saddle shaped to reduce friction between the legs.

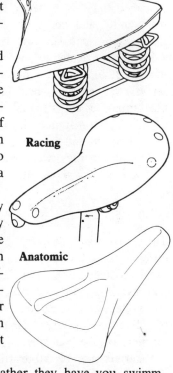

Mattress

Racing

Anatomic

Saddles are about as personal as you can get. Fit and comfort are very individual. What is bliss for one person can be a torture rack for another. This leaves bike manufacturers in a fix. Even if they supply a good saddle, not everyone is going to like it. Partly because of this, and partly because of economics, most production bikes are fitted with indifferent saddles. Some people do not notice; others will be well advised to substitute a better saddle at the time of bike purchase.

Leather saddles are the traditional type and can be very comfortable after 500 miles of riding. (Some people try to shorten the break-in interval by treating their saddle to oil baths, incantations, hot ovens, and beatings with rolling pins. These drastic measures are sometimes effective, but are regarded with horror by saddle manufacturers.) If you get on with a leather saddle you'll never find better, but it takes time and a hard behind. Rain will damage an unprotected leather saddle. If you opt for leather, buy the best—Brooks.

Plastic saddles are cheap, and feel like it. In hot weather they have you swimming about in your own sweat. They have the advantage of lightness, which is good for short distance races where weight is important. They are also impervious to weather, and can be a good choice for utility bikes that will often be left out in the rain.

Saddles with a base of plastic, a layer of foam or polymer, and a top cover of leather are the most common type, and with good reason. They need no break-in and rate very highly for comfort. They are engineered to meet specific requirements: racing models are thin and spartan, touring models are wider and softer. Some have what is known as an anatomic design, with the base shaped to allow extra room and padding where the pelvic bones make contact. These are popular for mountain bikes, as they allow freedom of movement and yet provide some insulation against shock.

Women have wider pelvic bones than men. This fact has now been recognized by most saddle manufacturers, but only for mixte-frame bikes; diamond-frame bikes are fitted with 'male' model saddles. If you are a woman, be sure to have a saddle made for your physique. The difference in pelvic bone width is easily catered for, but I have yet to find a manufacturer producing saddles that take into account the shallower female pubic arch. One drastic but apparently effective means of dealing with the problem is to simply cut away those portions of the saddle which cause discomfort.

Man or woman, if you buy a bike and the saddle is not to your liking, exchange it immediately for a better one and pay the price difference. You will spend many, many miles and hours on your saddle, and if you pinch pennies on this item you will be so reminded, for truth, by a sore behind and inflamed crotch.

My recommendation for a starter saddle is a fairly soft, foam or polymer filled model. But look out. Only you can say what is a good saddle. Two of my friends set off for India on their bikes, and after two days both were bitterly swearing a blue streak at the discomfort of their saddles—one a leather Brooks Pro, the other a Sella Italia anatomic filled with foam. When raging pain brought them to a halt, they switched saddles as a last resort. Suddenly all was bliss, and the rest of the 6,000-mile journey went without a hitch. The only way to know about saddles is to try them for yourself.

General Summary

There are many different brands of bicycles, and each manufacturer usually produces a range of models in different price grades. In the upward progression from basic all-steel bikes, you find an increasing use of aluminium alloy for the components, and for the frames, alloy steels, aluminium, and then finally, titanium, and composites such as carbon fibre and Kevlar. At any point in the progression a 'good' bicycle is one where design and materials work in harmony to fulfill the intended function of the machine.

Materials can be arbitrarily sorted into four grades:

1. Cheap—Frame of low-carbon steel; steel components.

2. Basic—Frame of high-carbon steel with small alloy content; alloy components except for steel wheels.

3. Medium—Frame of chrome-moly steel, or seamed double-butted steel, or aluminium; alloy components throughout.

4. High—Frame of seamless double-butted steel, or aluminium, or composite carbon fibre or Kevlar, or titanium; alloy or carbon fibre components throughout.

This is how it all stacks up:

Design	Materials
1. Beach cruiser—Extra soft frame, 2-inch wide tyres, hub brake, 50 lb.	Cheap to basic. Anything better might as well be a mountain bike.
2. Heavy roadster—Soft frame, 1.5-inch wide tyres, hub gears, calliper brakes, 50 lb.	Cheap but robust.
3. Light roadster (English Racer)—Soft frame, 1.375-inch wide tyres, hub gears, calliper brakes, 35 lb.	Cheap to basic. Anything better starts to become a commuter bike.
4. Commuter (town)—Soft to medium frame, HP wheels with 1.25-inch wide tyres, derailleur gears with medium-range ratios, calliper brakes, flat bars, 25-30 lb.	Basic to medium. Anything less is a light roadster, anything more is over the top.
5. Sports (10-speed)—As commuter, but medium- to high-range ratios, drop bars, 30 lb. Knock-around general transport.	Cheap to basic. Anything better will be more specific in design and function.
6. Touring—Soft frame, HP wheels with 1.25-inch wide tyres, derailleur gears with low- to medium-high ratios, cantilever brakes, drop bars, carrier racks, 26-30 lb. Steady, relaxed loping, with full baggage if required.	Basic to high. Quality determines range and baggage capacity: basic is OK for weekend jaunts but not a run to Alaska.
7. Fast (sport) touring—Medium to stiff frame, HP wheels with 1- or 1.125-inch wide tyres, derailleur gears with medium- to high-range ratios, side-pull or centre-pull brakes, drop bars, 24-28 lb. Lively, performance-minded riding with light loads.	Medium to high. Anything less will shy on performance.
8. Fast road (training)—Stiff frame, HP wheels with 1- or 1.124-inch wide tyres or sprint wheels and tubular tyres, derailleur gears with closely-spaced, high-range ratios, side-pull brakes, drop bars, 21-26 lb. Full on for the fast lane and entry level racing. Baggage: credit card.	Medium to high. Anything less is a joke that manufacturers call a 'look-alike'.
9. Racing—Stiff frame, sprint wheels and tubular tyres, derailleur gears with closely-spaced, high-range ratios, side-pull brakes, drop bars, 18-22 lb. For joy and racing.	High. Anything less isn't so.
10. Mountain bike (ATB)—Soft to medium frame, 24- or 26-inch wheels with 1.4- to 2.125-inch wide tyres, derailleur gears with low- to medium-high-range ratios, cantilever, roller-cam, or U-brakes, flat bars, 24-30 lb. All-terrain—in country or city.	Low (look-alike) to medium (a taste) to high (real thing).

Selection
Part II

You want a bike suitable for your needs and budget. But in both areas it is usually wise to push a little, so that your bike has some open potential. Suppose, for example, that fitness is a priority, and that you would like to get in some vigorous exercise over a regular 5-mile commute to and from work, and on occasional day rides. A commuting bike would be fine for the commute, but once you were seasoned you would find edge-of-capacity riding out of character for the bike. A good fast tourer would better encourage 'going for it'. But suppose the roads for that 5-mile journey are mined with jagged craters, and there are byways—dirt tracks, abandoned railways, open fields, who knows what—that look worth exploring. A lively mountain bike is the odds-on choice. You won't go quite as fast on properly surfaced roads, but you'll have lots of fun and all the room for improving fitness that you can take.

The classic error for novices is to under- or over-buy. They are interested in cycling but shy of 'all the fancy stuff', and opt for an all-steel machine good enough for local use, but that only gives a taste of what is possible when adventuring or going for a turn of speed. A year or so later they are back at the shop, laying down the money for a better machine.

The opposite extreme is to want the best money can buy. The prospective cyclist acquires a lightweight racing bike for commuting and quickly tires of a sore behind, endless punctures, and buckled wheels. The bike spends its life in a shed.

Evaluate and understand your own needs carefully, and then go for a bike that has some fun in reserve. Some bit, some thing, some aspect, that tickles your fancy and scratches a dream. This is the main trick for success with a bike. At root, fun is the reason for cycling. Commuting, racing, touring, hauling the groceries and laundry, off-road bashing—all are experiences. Sure racing is fun. You can also really get off on hauling a heavy load with a nifty trailer. Pick what appeals to you.

One little word of caution. Anti-establishment machines are fun. It's very relaxing to drift down the road on an Old Faithful held together with rust—sort of like joining hands with the stream. The bike is greater than you are. But if you're looking at a bike as a pragmatic tool, then you want a good one that works cleanly and well. That's why I'm big on a bike that is just that little bit better and more satisfying—a machine that you can move and grow with.

The converse is not to buy more bike than is comfortable. Own the bike and use it, not have it tell you what to do. Hot, fine-tuned machines require a commensurate level of mechanical attention and riding ability. You can't leave them around loose. If your primary requirement is a thrasho utility bike to get you from here to there, and that can stand time spent outside, then buy that sort of machine.

Confounded for choice? You're not limited to just one bike. Start with what you like best. Then later, treat yourself again!

The Exact Machine

The problem with recommending specific bikes is that brand names, bike models, and prices can change rapidly. Like people, bicycle manufacturers have good times and bad times. A well-established company can merge with another, and until the two groups harmonize, quality may suffer. Or, a firm that has been in the doldrums may decide to capture a larger slice of the market, and offer a range of bikes at exceptionally good prices—for a while. Once business picks up, so do the prices.

Select a bike by first working out a solid idea of the design, quality level, and features you want. Then look around and see what's going. Without being tiresome, seek as many opinions as possible. The best sources of advice and counsel are bike shops. They want you as a customer. Most shops have particular lines of bikes to sell, but this cuts both ways. There are many reasons why a shop will stock certain bikes and not others. If the shop looks half-way decent then the fact that it sells a given machine can be a recommendation in itself. If you can't find that Wheelie Wonder that is supposed to undercut any rival by at least £150, it may because the thing is a mangled pile of garbage that no dealer wants to touch with a barge-pole. Listen to what the shops say. Yes, they will try to sell you what they have. But like food in a restaurant, what's on for the day may be the best thing.

The design, quality level, and features you want in a bike may cost more than you can afford. This is where matters can get really sticky. The temptation is to get as much as you can, but it is not a good idea to buy on price alone. In the end you pay, one way or the other. Better a good-quality, basic bike than a poor-quality, medium-grade bike. If your budget is limited, then look to a used machine (see Buying a Bike).

Don't let price chasing lead you into a department or discount store. These places do not sell worthwhile bikes. In the chapter Buying a Bike I explain some of the vital role of a bike shop in making a bike work. This applies double to cheap bikes. Even if all you want is a basic, all-steel runabout, buy it from a bike shop! The one you get from a discount store is likely to break, and when you take it along to a bike shop for fixing, odds are they will say no. The reason is that the bike is wrong from the ground up and not worth trying to fix. It's a waste of your money. If you cannot afford a new bike from a bike shop, buy a used machine.

Women

Unless you have a very particular need for an open frame without a top tube, go for a diamond frame. An open-pattern frame is structurally weaker and less responsive than a diamond-pattern frame. There are fewer models and sizes, and all too

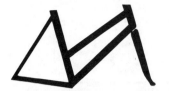
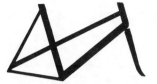

Conventional woman's frame   **Mixte frame**   **Triangulated (diamond) frame**

often the 'woman's' version of a production bike has an inferior specification compared with the 'man's' version. Worse, the lack of a top tube does not change the length of the bike for a better fit. All the way around it is not much of a deal, and my advice is to go for the better value and performance of a diamond frame. If you are on the short side you may have a problem finding a diamond-frame production bike in your size. They are made; locating one is a matter of persistence.

One builder specializing in bikes for women is Georgena Terry (140 Despatch Drive, East Rochester, NY 14445, USA). She has a neat solution for the smaller frame sizes: a 24-inch front wheel. This allows the bike to be proportioned correctly for length without fouling up the handling qualities, and to have a head tube of reasonable size. If you are among the some 75 per cent of women who are 5′7″ or less, then a Terry bike or similar custom-built frame is really worth considering.

Custom Bikes

One grand bit of fun is to build up your own bike, starting either with a frame off the shelf, or a frame custom-built to order. Strictly speaking, off-the-shelf frames will serve the needs of most people, but the satisfaction of having a unique, made-to-measure frame, finished and decorated exactly as you wish, can be tremendous.

The old-time master framebuilders are a dying breed and their work is in great demand, but there are also many young, new framebuilders who turn out excellent products at very competitive rates. Many of them are to be found in smaller communities and rural areas where overheads are low, and many are into participation and dialogue. They'll talk with you, analyse your needs, and let you see the frame actually being built. It's wonderful fun all around, but

The Terry bicycle

bear in mind that time is money and be prepared to pay a fair price for custom service. In regard to details of a prospective frame, make all the suggestions you like, but never ask a framebuilder to do something he or she does not want to do. The responsibility for ultimate success rests with the builder, and it is not fair to press for a scheme that could turn out wrong.

A custom bike is one of life's great pleasures. But in view of the cost you may want to leave this one until you have run a bike or two and have a sound idea of what you want.

QUADRANTS!!!

TRICYCLE No. 8.
World-famed Gent's Roadster.

TRICYCLE No. 14.
For Lady.

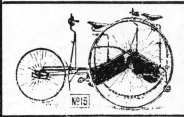

TANDEM No. 15.
Suits all Riders.

SAFETY No. 13.
Ball Steering.   Band Brake.

SAFETY No. 17 (Regd.).
Extremely Popular.

Send for our Catalogue, which is supplied free on application, and see what Riders say about these Machines.

Makers: THE QUADRANT TRICYCLE CO.,
SHEEPCOTE STREET, BIRMINGHAM.

Special Bikes and Trikes

Small-wheel Bicycles

Small-wheel bikes with open, step-through frames and 16- or 20-inch wheels are heavy and slow, unstable, and have lousy brakes. On paper, a small-wheel bike looks appealing: a one-size-fits-all machine that can haul groceries or serve as a general runabout. Many models are shopper versions with baskets that come off quickly so

they can be taken into the shop. Neat. But small wheels are stiff, and are usually shod with wide, soft tyres for an acceptable ride. This makes the wheels slow. A bike weight of 35-45 lb adds to the drag. But the real wash-out is the first time the brakes are applied in wet weather. Nada. Zilch. The ride is perhaps forever. Small steel rims and crude calliper brakes are marginal in performance when dry, and utterly worthless when wet.

Small-wheel shopper

If you need a general runabout suitable for all the family, look for a small-frame mountain bike with alloy wheels. If some people in the family are short, models with 24-inch wheels are available. Fit a long seat post with a quick-release clamp for instant size adjustment. For hauling things, equip the bike with big, wire mesh baskets.

Folding Bikes

A folding bike can be a viable means of dealing with specific situations and conditions. In fact, it can be a real treat. But a folding bike is not a means to eat your cake and have it, too. The key to success is that the ability of a folding bike to reduce in size serves a useful purpose. If not, you are better off with a regular bike.

One oft seen 'folder' is a standard small-wheel bike, hinged at the middle of the frame. It's one of the great tortures. The thing is a disaster as a bike, and folded, it is an awkward, unmanageable mangle of sharp protrusions and filthy greasy bits. There's no good way to lay hands on the thing, and when you finally do, it's too heavy to move more than a few feet at time.

If you want a bike that folds compactly so that you can store it easily, or put it in a car boot, consider the Dahon. It reduces to 8 × 18 × 28 inches, or about the size of a small suitcase. When folded, a third castor wheel comes into service, and this allows the whole package to be trundled along the ground. Good, because the Dahon is too heavy to carry for any distance. It's a useful machine where the problem is storage: in your home, at work, or in a car, boat, or aeroplane. In comparison with other folding bikes the performance and ride of the Dahon is very good. One weak point is the rear brake, which is not fierce.

If portability is the prime requirement, one very good bike to consider is the Bickerton, an aluminium folder with 3- or 5-speed hub gears that weighs in at around 23 lb, and reduces to a compact 9 × 20 × 30 inches. A stout fabric bag on the front handlebars will hold up to 40 lb of groceries or whatever, and doubles as a carrier for the bike when it is folded.

At 23 lb the Bickerton is easy to manage. It's no trouble at all to take along in a taxi-cab, train, bus, or aeroplane. It can be checked into cloakrooms and other places that would never touch a regular bike. Storage in a home with limited space is a snap.

As a bike, the Bickerton is good, but unusual. It has the fundamental asset of light weight, which gives responsiveness and good hill climbing. Design and materials give the frame surprising flexibility, so that despite the use of small wheels, the ride is very comfortable. You can go all day on it. One 55-year-old grandmother rode her Bickerton across the entire United States.

The chief disadvantage of a Bickerton is that when under way it feels loopy, like it was made out of rubber bands. If you pour power into the pedals and heave

mightily on the bars, the bike indeed does go twang, sometimes in several directions at once. You can't have everything. The Bickerton is a great folder and all right as a bike so long as you work with it, slipping in the power steadily and smoothly. On descents it is best to keep the speed down; the small wheels make for fast, tender handling. But they are alloy, and the braking is adequate if not fantastic. Bicker-

Original all-alloy Bickerton

ton have also just launched a new model with 20-inch wheels front and rear that should have slightly better handling.

Another folding bike to examine is the Brompton, available in two models (25.4 lb and 28.4 lb), with 16-inch wheels and 3- or 5-speed hub gears. It folds to 22.2 × 21.5 × 9.6 inches and is cleverly designed with a set of castor wheels so that the bike can trundled along when folded (like a suitcase with wheels).

If full-size bike performance is paramount, an interesting model to consider is the Montague Folding ATB. This is a 26-inch wheel mountain bike that reduces to approximately 12 × 28 × 32 inches—a neat trick accomplished by using two seat tubes, one inside the other. Folding is literally three snaps: the quick-release levers for two seat clamp bolts and the front wheel. It's new, and I've not had a ride on one, but reviews in the cycle press are good. For information, contact Impex Southern Ltd., Ketts Hourse, Winchester Road, Chandlers Ford, Eastleigh, Hants SO5 2FZ.

Another option to consider if you like a full-size bike is—a full-size bike! I travel a fair bit, and rarely without a bike. The usual first choice machine is Midnight Express, a lightweight mountain bike that strips down very quickly using just two hex keys. The lot pops into a bike bag padded with a sheet of air-bubble plastic and some extra clothes, zip zip, and I'm gone. If they nick me at the airport check-in, the excess charge is for an item of sporting equipment, and costs only a few pounds—a bargain. The bike has no racks or mudguards and so the package, while substantial, is manageable on a train or bus, and will easily slip into a car boot. At journey's end the dividend is a versatile, full-on bike that can go wherever, on- or off-road.

Montague folding bike

Folding bikes raise all kinds of possibilities. Londoner Paul Fagin did a 20-city tour of China by aeroplane—with a Bickerton. What a combination! He covered a lot of ground and a wide range of cultures and environments, was able to explore each area in close-up detail, and yet was fully mobile, with the ability to use any type of transport.

There are many reasons for using a folding bike: ease of storage, mobility when travelling, commuting mixed-mode together with a car, aeroplane, boat, or train, ease of storage, etc. Priorities are up to you. But if you go for a folding bike, make sure that it will do what you want. If you've a deep pocket, another possibility for a portable bike is the Moulton AM, discussed below.

The Moulton AM

The Moulton AM is a unique design justly described as an engineered bike. The most obvious innovative feature is full independent suspension for both front and rear wheels. Unlike other small-wheel bikes which use squishy tyres for a comfortable ride, the Moulton design small-diameter wheels are narrow, hard, and very fast. Moultons are both extremely comfortable and efficient.

Many advantages accrue from the combination of suspension and small wheels. There is room for wide, platform carrier racks that can manage bulky, heavy loads.

Dursley Pederson

Perhaps most exciting of all, there is room for a generously sized Zzipper fairing. This means greatly improved aerodynamics and a new dimension in speed. The Moulton AM-14/S has a gear range of 30-117 inches, and can use it. Other things being equal, catching one needs another AM-14/S, or a full-bore HPV. A standard racing bike hasn't a hope. The fairing is also excellent protection from rain and dirt.

A disadvantage of the suspension is that the bike bobbles like a trampoline if you hammer it hard. The suspension is adjustable, and can be tuned to suit a strong rider, but the AM is still a bike that wants a smooth riding technique. Over a distance, the reduction in fatigue awarded by the suspension is worth a lot more to performance than the ability to snap off in a sprint.

The Moulton AM does not fold, but only a single hex key is needed to disassemble the bike into two halves. There's an optional bag to carry it, and while the package cannot be classified as slim and neat, it is manageable enough for travelling.

There are three models. The AM-2 has a two-speed, pedal-operated hub gear. It is a simple town bike, and you'd have to be wealthy indeed to buy one just as a light runabout. Most people want something more flash: either the AM-7 with 7-speed derailleur gears, or the full house AM-14/S with 14-speed derailleur gears. I agree. At this level, you should go all the way.

The Moulton AM is a class machine. It's beautifully made and handsomely finished and is an assured classic. And it costs a bomb. No more than any other really top-flight superbike perhaps, but a hefty sum. The real issue is not so much the cost, which in raw mechanical terms is fair enough, but what you want. For many people, owning an AM is a passionate affair filled with satisfaction, delight, and adventure. Other people agree that the bike is very gee whiz, fun, and useful, but have other things they'd rather spend their money on. It is a question of temperament and interest, not right and wrong. If you enjoy innovative engineering and superb building, and can write four-digit cheques without flinching, then look over a Moulton.

Tandems

Tandems offer a number of advantages and disadvantages over solo machines. Two strong riders can move a tandem along very briskly, as overall weight is less and wind resistance is cut in half. A tandem will outrun a solo on a downhill run. Uphill, a tandem is slow. But over gently undulating terrain the greater mass of the tandem increases momentum and helps to iron out small hills. The long wheelbase gives excellent stability, and a smooth ride.

Two riders of unequal strength can have rest periods for the weaker rider on the easy parts of a ride, and put in the muscle together when climbing hills. Togetherness is a definite plus feature of tandem cycling; it is easy to talk, and there is something very pleasant about the shared physical effort. There's a whole new collection of skills to learn before the pilot (front) and stoker (rear) work together smoothly. It's a process that is the making of some people, and the undoing of others.

Tandem disadvantages stem chiefly from sheer size. A tandem handles awkwardly in traffic, needs a roof rack for transport by car, and takes up a lot of storage space.

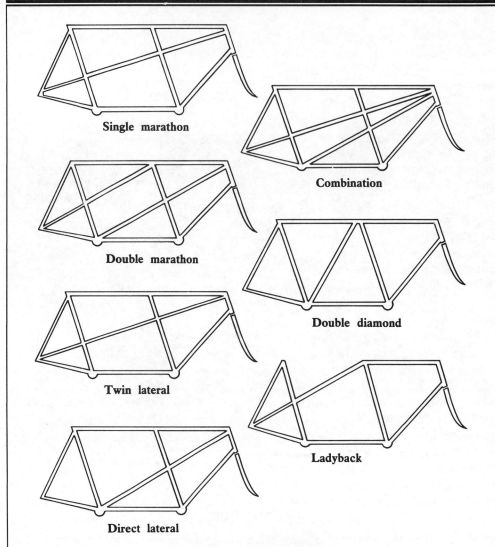

Single marathon

Combination

Double marathon

Double diamond

Twin lateral

Ladyback

Direct lateral

TANDEM FRAMES

Tandem frames are designed to reduce side-to-side flex while still retaining a reasonably comfortable ride. Two popular compromises are the marathon and twin lateral designs. Both use long diagonal tubes running from the head tube all the way back to the rear drop-outs. These provide lateral bracing against the flex caused by powerful pedalling and sharp changes of course. With the marathon, a single tube splits at the seat tube to run on either side of the rear wheel; with the twin lateral, two thin tubes are used for the entire length.

The double marathon has two diagonal bracing tubes for a very stiff and strong geometry. The direct lateral, which is popular with American builders, uses a single diagonal tube from the head tube to the rear bottom bracket, and beefy chainstays. The stiffest and heaviest is the combination, which uses both marathon and direct lateral tubes. Double diamond frames are common, because they are easy to build, but tend to flex at the front bottom bracket. Ladyback tandems look all right on a TV show, but are much too flexible for serious riding.

Only a lightweight (35-45 lb) derailleur-gear tandem is worth owning. The heavyweight (90 lb) models are just too much work to pedal. With the weight of two riders a tandem has to have first-class brakes. At the minimum, cantilevers with oversize blocks. This would be for a lightweight racing tandem for use by experienced riders. Touring tandems should have cantilevers, and a drum or disc brake. The latter is primarily for speed control on long descents, so that the calliper brakes do not overheat the rims and cause a tyre to burst.

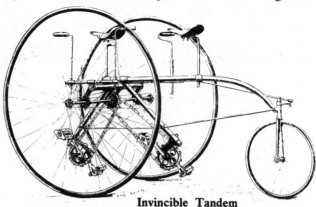
Invincible Tandem

Wheel quality is critical. The hubs should be made for tandem use, with 11 or 15 mm axles; standard 9.5 mm axles are not strong enough. There should be at least 40 spokes, better yet 48, in 13 or 14 gauge. The rims should be known for their strength, for example the Super Champion Module 58.

It's well worth figuring out just what you'd like to do with a tandem. For sport and speed you've got to go a quality and fineness route similar to that for a solo racing bike. It's not a machine for lumping around. For casual fun and games a more robust model with 26-inch or 650B tyres is a better bet; the ride is more comfortable, and handling is good enough even for unproperly surfaced roads. The ultimate in worry-free tandems are the mountain bike versions; excellent builders of these are:

● Tom Ritchey, 1326 Hancock Avenue, Redwood City, CA 94061, USA.

● Santana, P.O. Box 1205, Claremont, CA 91711, USA.

Look carefully into the whole business of tandems before you buy. A good tandem is expensive and any compromise on quality will cost dearly. A tandem must be soundly engineered and constructed in order to stand the stress of two riders. Historically, large manufacturers have not done well with tandems; the good ones come from smaller, specialized firms and builders. It's best if the people who make and sell the equipment use it as well. Then you get straight information. See if there is a bike shop within reachable distance that specializes in tandems, and check adverts in cycling magazines. Some builders to try are:

● Tom Avon Cycles, 7 Chessells Street, Bedminster, Bristol.

● Bob Jackson, 148 Harehills Lane, Leeds, West Yorkshire LS8 5BD.

● George Longstaff, Albert Street, Chesterton, Newcastle-under-Lyme, Staffs ST5 7JF.

● Mercian Cycles, 28 Stenson Road, Cavendish, Derby DE3 7JB.

● Tony Oliver, Maes Meredydd Uchaf, Rhosybool, Amlwch, Anglesey, Gwynedd, Wales.

● Harry Quinn, Ivy Tower Farm, St. Florence, Tenby SA70 8LP.

● Ken Rogers, 37 Berkeley Avenue, Cranford, Hounslow, Middlesex.

●Swallow Frames & Cycles, 2 Stannetts, Laindon North Trade Centre, Essex SS15 6DJ.

●Jack Taylor Cycles, Church Road, Stockton-on-Tees, Teeside TS18 2LY.

Two tandem clubs that can give practical advice based on experience are:

●In Tandem, Crowfoot, Herts Ferry, Portsmouth Road, Surbiton.

●The Tandem Club, Box TC, The Cyclists' Touring Club 69, Meadrow, Godalming, Surrey GU7 3HS.

Side-by-side

A tandem in a class of its own is the companion, or sociable bicycle, with the saddles set side-by-side rather than in-line as with an ordinary tandem. It looks weird but works a treat and is easy to ride. Anyone who can ride an ordinary bike can just get aboard and go.

A large frontal area gives poor aerodynamics and precludes using a side-by-side for long or quick journeys. However, at speeds up to 15 mph on local excursions and on tours where speed and distance are not the object, it is a complete stone gas. You can talk, hold hands, and even kiss.

Some very lovely side-by-side bikes were made by Barrett Cycles, Angola, NY 14006, USA. They might still be going. A recent introduction comes from Buddy Bike, 77 Mowat Avenue, Toronto, Ontario, Canada M6K 3E3 1T4. The models I've seen are a touch basic, but seem to work perfectly well.

Tricycles

There are trikes and there are trikes! The type popular in retirement areas usually have 20-inch wheels to keep the weight down low and are quite stable as long as they are not pushed hard. A large rear basket handy for carrying groceries, golf clubs, gold bricks, or whatever is a popular accessory. People with poor balance or co-ordination, brittle bones, or other problems, should seriously consider a tricycle. Bear in mind, though, that many old folks do just fine with conventional two-wheelers, and there are a number of bicycle clubs whose members are all over 70.

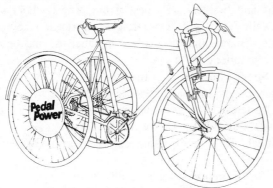

One type of tricycle has a fixed gear, so that the pedals and wheels always move together. People with limited motion in their legs have sometimes found that the exercise provided by this arrangement improves leg mobility.

People with a taste for the unusual might consider a lightweight racing or touring tricycle with 26- or 27-inch wheels.

Higgins differential-drive tricycle, c. 1950

In no way is this an old-age toy. Many an experienced bicyclist has come a cropper first time out on a trike. It must be steered around a corner, a sensation completely at odds with the handling of a bicycle, and rider weight must be counterbalanced to the inside on even a moderate bend. It is quite easy to lift a wheel, and down-hill bends must be approached with caution. Changes in the camber of the road also easily upset balance.

Part of the appeal of trikes is that they are challenging to ride. Many adherents are crack bicyclists out for still more thrills. But trikes also have practical advantages: they're good for carrying things, can stop and park without difficulty, and stay upright under slippery conditions. We ran a big tandem trike as the family cycle for some years, and the different combinations of adults, kids, and babies that could be hung on the thing was quite dazzling.

Beeston Humber Tandem

Kits for converting solo and tandem bicycles into trikes are available from Rogers, Swallow, and Longstaff (addresses below). These work, but you need to be mechanically proficient, or have the services of an able shop. The process involves fiddly details that are essential, such as new arrangements for braking.

In Britain, a trike is called a 'barrow', and dedicated adherents have banded together as: The Tricycle Association, 92 Graham Gardens, Luton, Herts. Builders include:
● Bob Jackson, 148 Harehills Lane, Leeds, West Yorkshire LS8 5BD.
● George Longstaff, Albert Street, Chesterton, Newcastle-under-Lyme, Staffs ST5 7JF.
● Ken Rogers, 37 Berkeley Avenue, Cranford, Hounslow, Middlesex.
● Swallow Frames and Cycles, 2 Stannetts, Laindon North Trade Centre, Essex SS15 6DJ.
● Jack Taylor Cycles, Church Road, Stockton-on-Tees, Teeside TS18 2LY.

At the opposite end of the scale from the racing and touring trikes are the utility machines. These are workhorses that often weigh 100 lb unladen, but that can manage loads of up to 500 lb. One increasingly favoured application for utility trikes is as mobile vending stands for sandwiches, ice cream, vegetables, or whatever is going. Many are lovingly decorated and maintained by their owners and are really pretty. I'm prejudiced, of course, but feel that pedal power and street trading are a balanced combination that go together well. The people who go in for motorized premises always seem pressed, and a bit wan. Pedal power has low overheads.

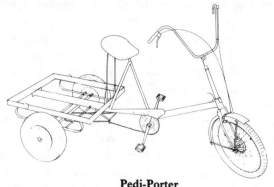

Pedi-Porter

Load-carrying trikes have a great variety of industrial and commercial uses. A few examples would be: moving gardening equipment around estates and parks; moving anything that a human being can pick up around a warehouse or shipping depot; delivering groceries and take-out meals; and collecting rubbish from small bins. There are a zillion other applications—just look at countries like America, the Netherlands, and China. The great point in favour of utility trikes are that they are highly economical, and use only the amount of power needed for the job at hand. They are also noise- and pollution-free. If you can think of and suggest an application for a utility trike where you live or work, you will be doing yourself and everybody else a big favour. A good range of carrier bicycles and tricycles is manufactured by W. R. Pashley Ltd., Stratford-upon-Avon, Warwickshire CV37 9NL.

Sailing Tricycle

The Rans Company, 408 Milner, Hays, Kansas 67601, USA, manufactures sailing tricycles. These have a sail (about 30 square feet) just like on a boat, and will see 50 mph—be sure you have enough room!

Reproduction Antiques

From time to time small firms or builders produce reproductions (faithful copies) or replicas (rideable modern equivalents) of antique cycles. If you are interested in something really different, this may be for you.

Rans

If you opt for an early design like an Ordinary, or a Star, obtain a book such as *Collecting and Restoring Antique Bicycles* by G. Donald Adams (Tab Books Inc., Blue Ridge Summit, PA 17214, USA), with directions for riding. It is just as easy to 'come a cropper' with a modern Ordinary as an old one. A variety of bikes and trikes based on nineteenth century designs are made by Rideable Bicycles Replicas, 2447 Telegraph Avenue, Oakland, CA, USA. In 1981, one of their machines completed a 1000-mile tour down the length of England without a single mechanical problem.

In America, the revival of interest in classic 'paper-boy' bikes led Columbia to re-issue their 1952 Five Star model in a limited edition. Fitted with mock petrol tank and coil spring shock absorbers, a streamlined chrome bullet headlamp, and white-wall tyres, and richly finished

Replica Ordinary

in two-tone green and cream paint, the Five Star looked stunning in adverts and on magazine covers, but has proved tacky and disappointing in real life. If you'd like a bike of this kind an original model is a better investment.

In *The Evolution of the Bicycle 1867-1939* Tom Norton describes the Dursley Pedersen as: '. . . perhaps the most comfortable and novel cycle ever designed.' Launched at the 1897 Stanley Show in London, the bike had two utterly unique features: a hammock saddle woven from 45 yards of silk cord, and a frame made entirely from very thin, lightweight tubing, in a sophisticated design based on principles used in bridge construction. Comfortable, elegant, and extremely light (a folding model produced for the British Army c. 1900 weighed a scant 15 lb), the distinctive Dursley Pedersen was one of the first of the de luxe type of cycles to become popular with the middle and upper classes, and was produced until 1914.

The availability of replica Pedersens is episodic. The design was revived a number of years ago by a blacksmith in Denmark (the Copenhagen Pedersen), and more recently, by Chris Margenout and friends in England (the Cheltenham Pedersen). The Cheltenham model, finely built in Reynolds 531 tubing, came closest to the quality and light weight of the original but is no longer produced. The Copenhagen Pedersen, made of heavier tubing and more plainly built, is nonetheless still an elegant machine and a great deal of fun to ride. Models with specification to customer's requirements are available from Swallow Cycles, 2 Stannetts, Laindon North Trade Centre, Laindon, Essex SS15 6DJ.

Children's Bicycles

Children need and deserve good bikes. For children, bikes are motion and growth incarnate. Freedom, and a means to learn all kinds of new skills and accomplishments.

Bikes are important tools for children, but are often treated as toys to be bought as cheaply as possible. The market is littered with worthless junk—tin can assemblies with sleeves of plastic for bearings—that is sold entirely on the basis of price. Even King Kong would have trouble making one of these things go. Try turning the cranks or one with your hand and see. Your little nipper with tiny legs no longer than your forearm hasn't got a chance. Of course he or she will leave the stupid thing to rot. It isn't even worth giving away. Cheap kid's bikes are a complete waste of money.

A better child's bike costs a reasonable piece of change, because it is just as complex to make as a full-size bike. But it works! The return value in terms of play and work is incredible. I've watched many young children (under age 4) play with bikes for oh, one or two hours at a stretch, every day, for months on end. They just keep on whizzing and whizzing. If you're looking for something to get the kids out of your hair, a bike is one of the best things going.

A good bike gives genuine play value, and it lasts. You can pass it down in the family, or sell it for a recovery of a lot of the purchase price. If you are on a tight budget or have a swarm of offspring to mount, then buy used. Basic quality is more important than newness, and anyhow, joint participation with dad or mum in sprucing up an old bike is far more interesting for most children than spending money at the store. Local classified adverts, 3 x 5 WANTED cards at laundrettes, school meetings, etc., will do the trick.

A child can enjoy a bike at age 2 or even sooner, but not necessarily as a means of transport. The initial use may be as a house or as a study in mechanical engineering. Let the child move at his or her own pace and they will eventually figure out what the thing can do. Keep a careful eye on matters. A toddler can easily catch a finger in moving bits. For a very young child, a proper tricycle is far more stable and safe than a bicycle with training wheels, which upsets easily. An excellent, sure-to-please chain-drive tricycle is the Pashley Pickle.

A child is ready for a bicycle at about age 4 or 5, depending on individual development, co-ordination, and interest. Don't use training wheels. They are dangerous, and retard learning. The best way to teach anyone, young or old, to ride a bike is to let them do it themselves. Remove the pedals, and lower the saddle so that the rider can touch the ground with their feet when mounted. Show him or her how the bike steers. Let them push with their feet, as with a scooter. After a little progress, put them on a bit of ground with a gentle downgrade. Each individual scoot will progressively become longer and longer. When they can go for a good stretch without touching the ground, replace the pedals and watch them go. Keep them on level ground until they also learn how the brakes work.

The ideal first bike for a youngster should have:
●Pneumatic tyres for a comfortable ride, easier pedalling, and effective braking. Solid rubber tyres are three times harder to pedal, provide a harsh, jolting ride, and give bad braking.
●Ball bearings for the headset, bottom bracket, and wheels. Plastic sleeve bearings give bad handling and steering, poor efficiency, and wear out quickly.
●A large seat range adjustment so the bike can grow with the child.
●Brakes that work. It's surprising how many do not. The type is a matter of the individual child. I prefer calliper rim brakes, because they are easy to tune and service, but many young children do not have hands large and strong enough to work the levers. If this is the case, go for a pedal-operated coaster brake.

Once a child is about age 7, a whole new world opens up—BMX. This started as small fry, dirt track racing. It has now blossomed into incredible developments like freestyle, with levels of bike handling that have to be seen to be believed. A group of freestylers look like fish underwater, spinning and darting, diving and swooping—except they are doing it on terra firma and in the air!

The whole thing about BMX is that it is real time. A lot of the development and spread of adult mountain bikes was directly due to BMX technology. Mechanically, most BMX bikes are far superior to most adult bikes. They have to be. In the broadest sense, BMX is like truth. You can't fake a bunny hop or placing in a race heat. Junk iron doesn't cut the ice.

All you have to do is pick up a good BMX bike to appreciate why any kid would want it. It's light. It'll go. And it's unbelievably tough. It is made to leap into the air, zoom off things, crash—and come back for more. Does your little nipper have a chance of being hurt doing this kind of thing? You bet. But not mortally. In fact, not even seriously, if he or she uses the right equipment—a helmet, full-length trousers, elbow-pads, and gloves. BMX is a microcosm of the big world.

You can only show off if you've got the stuff—and that takes dedication and hard work. In BMX, jerks are not well regarded, because they are not working with the reality.

BMX is wired up short, just like kids are. It's on a scale that they can manage, and safely. All they need is a bit of ground someplace and they're off, messing around and learning new tricks. I've never really believed in the business of aping adult activities by putting kids on junior road bikes and dragging them on 50-mile tours. Yes, kids like riding, sometimes for long distances, but I don't think roads are the place for it until they are age 13. Until then, they simply haven't got the attention span to cope with the many dangers. Too many get wiped out; per mile cycled, the highest accident rate by far is for under-16s.

One reason I'm an off-road fan is that the whole family can do it, dogs and all. Whether it's the park next door, the seacoast, or a run in the mountains, we can all be together, and yet each of us can ride as hard or as softly as we want. But I'm getting ahead of myself.

The main point is that children deserve good bikes. Adults have cars, they have money in their pockets for public transportation—kids generally just have a bike. It should be a good one. There are lots of options. BMX of course. There are also junior mountain bikes with 20-inch wheels that are really a treat. Tough, lots of gears, mega-brakes, and easy to handle. My kids like cycling—small coincidence— but their interest quadrupled when they acquired junior mountain bikes.

How do you pick out a good kid's bike? The same way you pick out a good adult bike. You're looking for quality tubings, alloy components, and good building. And it can cost. Junior mountain bikes and road bikes aren't so bad. Some of the BMX machines can break your back. If little junior becomes serious about racing or freestyle stunts then you may be in for some real dramas about finance. I think that here, you start to get into what family is all about. How much or how little money is less important than how you both handle it. Working out what the resources really are, and how they can be distributed, is part of learning how things happen.

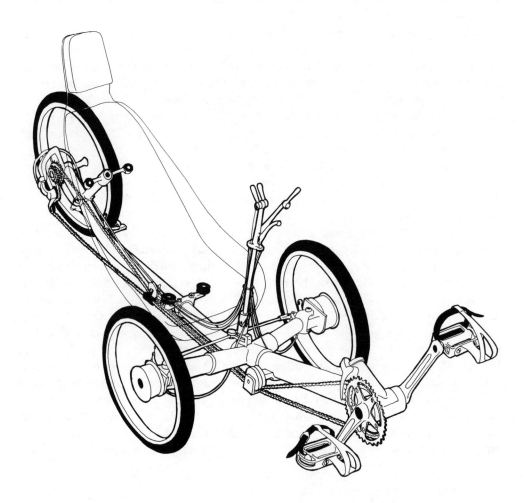

Windcheetah SL.
Fast, exceptional agile tricycle designed and built by Mike Burrows of Norwich. The SL
stands for street legal. An optional fibre glass body shell can be fitted, either with a hard top,
or a fabric convertible top. Popularly known as the Speedy, the machine has been a
consistent winner of Practical Vehicle Competitions in America, Canada, and Europe. It is
also a wicked contender on tight, twisting racecourses—and in traffic.

Buying a Bike

The best place to buy a new bicycle is a bike shop. You can sometimes save money at a department or discount store in the short term, but you are virtually guaranteed headaches and problems that will prove more costly in the long term. In the first place, the quality of merchandise from non-specialist sources is almost always inferior. Secondly, manufacturers assemble bikes only up to a point; final assembly, adjustment, and tuning is left to the mechanic who sets the bike up for use. Department and discount stores do not employ trained bicycle mechanics, and so the bikes they sell are often in bits and pieces, or have been put together by some cretin who has literally done more harm than good. Even the finest machines can have a defect or other problem requiring expert attention. It takes a good bicycle mechanic to assemble a new bike without damaging anything, check all the parts, and iron out the inevitable defects. Even then, problems are not likely to be over. If a department or discount store gives a guarantee—few do—they have no mechanics to take care of in-service problems. And if there is some totally basic defect in a machine you buy, it takes weeks for a refund or replacement.

A bike shop will assemble the machine. Although you must check their work, chances are they'll do the job right. If some problem comes up later they are available right away to fix it, and so are replacement parts. You get a guarantee on parts and labour good for a year or more.

The more local a shop you can deal with, the better. Any bike shop must meet certain basic requirements in quality of bikes and in service, but convenience means a lot. A guarantee on a shop 50 miles away is useless for anything except a major disaster. Most of the repair problems with new bikes are fairly minor and can be dealt with in a few minutes. Bike shops often have a backlog of repair jobs, however, and typically give first priority to customers whose bikes were purchased from the shop. So if there is a local shop and they don't have what you want, see what they can do. Perhaps they can order a bike for you. If their brand of bike is not the one you had in mind take a good look at what they offer. All other things being equal, as they may well be since many manufacturers use the same components, the convenience of a local shop is an excellent reason to switch brands. Just make sure you get a fair value. Ask about servicing and parts. If their guarantee isn't good enough, ask for better terms. Don't expect, however, that a small shop will be able to offer as good a deal as a high-volume, super-powered emporium. What you pay a little extra for is the fact that they are around the corner. Also, perhaps the general feeling and vibes are better.

At any rate, stay away from discount and department stores. I have not regaled you with horror stories about machines purchased from such places, but they are legion, and cover everything from kids' tricycles to ultra-fancy racers. The tiny bit extra you spend in a bike shop buys an awful lot.

Check the Yellow Pages, ads in cycling magazines, and any local oracles for the locations of bike shops near your home. Visit them. Bike shops vary a good bit in character. Some are dedicated strictly to high-class racing bikes, others to plain utility machines. Some shops are small and cramped and are useful only when you know exactly what you are looking for, while other shops are large and have comprehensive displays of bikes for direct examination. Either type can do the job: the important thing is that you are made to feel welcome, and are offered service. These are the things you want to know:

● Does the shop have the sort of bikes you are interested in? Ask for leaflets that you can take home and study.

● Is the shop interested in your needs? Correctly matching the kind of bike and customer is the fundamental requirement for success, and good advice in this area is one of the things you are paying for.

● Will you be able to take a test ride? (Nice days only, so bike does not get wet and dirty—mountain bikes excepted!)

● What sort of servicing does the shop offer? What are the guarantee terms? A free post-sale service should be standard.

The Buy

Once you've boiled your options down to two or three bikes and one or two shops, you're ready for the main event: the buy. To ensure the best attention of the shop, avoid doing this on Saturday, Friday evening, or Monday morning, when they are likely to be busy. Wear suitable clothes and shoes and have a bit of tissue or rag handy in your back pocket.

Before whizzing off on a test ride (or on any strange bike, for that matter) check that the handlebars and saddle are tight, the brakes firm, the gears function, and the wheels run free and true. Simple stuff, yes, but many an experienced rider has had an unhappy surprise from a loose or poorly adjusted component on a strange bike.

Vary the pace of your test ride: try out low- and high-speed handling, riding over rough surfaces, cornering, and braking, but don't press the bike too hard, or expect too much. Any new bike feels strange for a while. If you are actually uncomfortable, and the feeling persists, ask the advice of the shop. Sometimes an adjustment of saddle height or stem length will cure the difficulty. If not, try another bike. When you've found the bike you like the most, buy it.

If you are interested in substitutions, this is the time to specify what you want. You might need a shorter stem, drop instead of flat bars, or a better saddle, to

name a few common swaps. Although you are trading one item for another, the shop is entitled to charge for labour, and any difference in value. Then there are accessories such as racks and lights. Sort it all out and get the money down to the bottom line. The shop may ask you to return for the bike, later that day if there is time, the next day if not, and are entitled to a deposit. Ensure that the sales receipt has the frame number of the bike, and your name and address.

Taking Delivery

Anticipate that any new bike will have something wrong with it. Dealing with a good bike shop minimizes this possibility but by no means eliminates it. When I picked up a new dream machine from one of NYC's finest shops I was too bedazzled to give it anything but the most cursory inspection. As I accelerated away from the shop the rear hub and freewheel exploded in a blizzard of metal flakes and chips. Most problems you are likely to encounter are not apt to be so spectacular, but the point cannot be emphasized too strongly that a thorough inspection of any new bike is necessary.

Collect the bike at least two hours before shop closing, so you have plenty of time to sort out fine points and make adjustments. Look the bike over carefully, checking that all the bits are tight and tidy, and of course that the brakes and gears work. Take it out for a good spin, and check the following:

● Frame for straightness. Stand behind or in front of the bicycle and see that the wheels are in line. Next, hold the bicycle by the saddle only and wheel it around. If the frame or forks are bent, it will tend to veer to one side. Finally, at some point when you are clear of traffic hold the handlebars as lightly as possible, even riding hands-off if you have this skill. The bicycle should go straight, in control, without pulling to one side. Reject any bicycle which fails these tests. A bicycle which will not track accurately is tiring and unsafe to ride.

● Wheels should spin easily. When the bike is held clear of the ground the weight of the valve stem should push the wheel around until the valve positions at six o'clock. (Because tubes and tyres are not always uniform in consistency, sometimes the valve will settle in a different position.) Wheels should be centred in fork arms or chainstays. If a wheel can be moved from side to side and there is a clicking sound, the hub bearings are out of adjustment. Check that the rim is true by holding a pencil next to it and spinning the wheel. Brace the pencil on a fork arm of chainstay to keep it steady. Side-to-side movement of wheel rim should not exceed one-eighth of an inch.

● Pluck spokes. All should be evenly tight and give the same 'twang'.

● Brake blocks should hit rims squarely and not drag when released.

● Gears should work smoothly and with no slippage. Test first with wheels off ground and then on a ride.

● Pedals and chainwheel should spin easily but without side-to-side play.

You may think that all this is a lot of trouble to go through. I have bought a fair number of new bikes for myself, family, or friends. There was something wrong with every one of them, and a few I rejected outright. You will save yourself a lot of grief if you invest some time at the outset on careful inspection.

A bike inspection is something that a good bike shop will regard with tolerant amusement, because they do not expect to be caught out. A bad shop will register irritation and this is immediate grounds for concern. Your interest and participation should be welcomed, not discouraged. But be fair. You can't expect some basic machine to sing with quality, or for the shop to spend all day fiddling with it. What you do have the right to expect of any bike, whatever it costs, is that it is roadworthy.

After you purchase a bike, check that all nuts, bolts, and screws are secure. Every last one. After riding 50 miles or so, repeat this operation. New bicycles 'bed in', there is microscopic wear where parts meet or are joined together, and it is very common, for example, for the brake bolts to work loose. Cranks, particularly the cotterless type, are bound to need tightening. See the appropriate section under Maintenance for details.

Used Bikes

Used bikes are a good way to save money. Expect to pay about 75 per cent of list price for a machine in excellent, as-new condition, and about 50 per cent of list for one in average condition.

Sources of used bikes depend on where you live and your own initiative. Some bike shops sell used machines, but turnover is quick and you will need some luck to catch the machine you want. The cycling magazines often have a sprinkling of good machines in their classified adverts; again, move quickly if you want to score.

If you are really trying to go on the cheap, look around locally. There are a lot of forgotten bikes mouldering away in garages, attics, and sheds. They often have some minor fault like a broken brake or gear-shift cable, and are no problem to make roadworthy. If you just start asking around in your neighbourhood, put up WANTED notices in laundrettes and on bulletin boards, you may well turn up a prize bike for a song.

Most cities and communities have local classified publications listing all kinds of stuff—including bikes—for sale. Check also the classified ads in the regular papers. Often a sale of household effects includes a bicycle. Auctions are sometimes good. A good bet in the spring are local bulletin boards at universities and colleges. Put up some cards yourself or take an ad in the student newspaper. Naturally, the more prosaic a bike you seek, the faster you will be likely to find it. But if you just put the word out wherever you go, something will eventually turn up.

Understand exactly what sort of bike you are looking for. Converting a racing bike into a touring bike can be expensive—new freewheel, chain, chainwheel sprockets, and possibly new derailleurs and wheels. Be particularly careful of winding up with a lemon. Try to find out the history of the machine. It's best if you can talk to the owner. Was he or she interested in the bike and in taking care of it? Or did they just leave it out in the rain? Where did they ride? And not least of all, what questions does the owner ask of you? Do they care that the bike is suitable for your needs? I would much rather pay a little extra for a well-loved bike than save a few pounds on a machine with a dubious or unknown past.

In inspecting the bike, cover all the points listed for a new bike. Pay particular attention to the frame. Wrinkled paint on the forks or where the top and down tubes meet the head tube can indicate that the bike was crashed. So can a coat of nice new paint. I know of instances where badly repaired crash-damaged bikes have fallen apart, killing their unfortunate new owners. What you want to see are a certain number of inevitable nicks and scrapes, but no major dents, rust spots, or welds.

Count into the cost of a used bike a complete overhaul and lubrication, including possible replacement of cables, chain, and sprockets. Read the sections on Maintenance and Repair in this book to learn how to assess components for wear and useful life.

A final word about used bikes relates to the next problem, keeping your bike. There are plenty of stolen bicycles for sale. Many street markets are venues for stolen machines, and in some areas you can even order the type of bike you want—

theft to specification. Price is usually about 25 per cent of list, often less. With such a flourishing industry it hardly seems a crime to get a bike this way. It is. Legally and morally. Simply put, you are helping to steal. Additionally, it is not some giant money-greedy corporation's candy bar or rip-off piece of junk which you are stealing, but a possession somebody quite probably loves and cherishes.

Keeping Your Bike

This is a serious problem. Something like 100,000 bikes are stolen every year. If you do not take suitable precautions, then the loss of your bike is virtually certain. Unless the bike is post-coded (see below), recovery is extremely unlikely. Stolen bikes are very small beer for the police, and few forces have the time or inclination to check serial numbers against lists of stolen bikes.

Security is your responsibility. It's up to you to outfox the opposition, and the best method is to minimize the opportunities for theft. At home and at work the bike should be kept indoors. This is usually simple enough at home, but can require ingenuity at a place of work. In America, many employers provide bike parking facilities and other welcome perks such as changing rooms and showers. The employers know that cycling is good for health, and that healthy employees produce more work. In Japan, which is famous for productivity, exercise periods during working hours are often compulsory. In Britain, all too many places of business regard bikes with decided disfavour, and offer no help with parking. How you meet the problem depends of course on the particular circumstances. As a general rule of thumb there will be some nook suitable for a bike; a little-used storage room or closet, space down in the basement or utility room, etc. If this fails, look afield: a nearby garage or other facility might be more accommodating.

Sometimes you will just have to park on the street and here, the vital element is the strength of your locking system. There's only one effective answer: a lock with a performance guarantee that pays you back the value of your bike if it is stolen as a result of the failure of the lock to prevent the theft. Ordinary cable and chain locks are no good, because they can be cut in seconds with common tools.

I once arranged a bike theft for a magazine article. We locked a bike to a fence railing on a busy London street, positioned a photographer on the first floor of a building directly opposite the bike, and sent in our very own professional 'thief'. The dirty deed was accomplished within seconds. A voluminous raincoat concealed the actual snipping of a cable lock, which the thief tidily tucked away in a pocket before absconding with the bike. People only yards away did not notice a thing. We could hardly believe how easy it was. We repeated the experiment six times, progressively making the theft more and more obvious. On the final go, the thief marched directly up to the bike, hauled out the snips and cut the cable lock in full open view of nearby pedestrians, and still got away with the bike. One person took notice of what was happening, but did nothing about it.

Locks with performance guarantees are made of specially hardened and treated metals, have intricate key mechanisms, and various other features designed to make them as bomb-proof as possible. One unfortunate individual in Newcastle locked up his bike with a Citadel lock, and lost the keys. It took the combined resources of the police, the fire brigade, and the engineering department of the local technical school a day and a night to open the lock.

Until recently, guaranteed locks really were just about invulnerable, but thieves have learned new tricks. In the mecca of bike theft, New York City, it is common to see 'invulnerable' locks beefed up with extra parts improvised from lead pipes and other plumbing hardware. It's a necessary defence against techniques that will break certain kinds of locks. One manufacturer has amended the guarantee on their lock with the sticker: 'Guarantee not valid in New York City'. That misbegotten thieves have succeeded where fire and police departments have failed is perhaps a twisted testimonial to the human spirit—but in any case, sooner or later we can expect the same level of expertise here. The best lock you can find is your baseline for security, but is only a start. When locking up on the street you should:

● ALWAYS lock your bike. It takes but a moment to snatch a bike. Thefts where the owner left the machine for 'just a few seconds' are legion. If you don't physically have your hands on the bike, it should be locked up.

● Lock your bike to seriously immovable objects such as heavy fences, lamp-posts, or parking signs.

● Lock the frame, and both front and back wheels.

● Be selective about when and where you lock the bike. Slum neighbourhoods are a bad bet at any time. Even if the bike is not stolen, bits and pieces may get stripped off it. In any neighbourhood, look for a busy, well-travelled spot, not a dark alley.

● Try to enlist help. The cashier for a cinema will usually keep an eye on your bike. Newsagents and other merchants will often help, particularly if you are a regular customer. The local cafe may give you indigestion, but if the chef waves a cleaver at anybody who bothers your bike, the place is worth cultivating.

A stout lock is a substantial piece of hardware. The majority of high-security locks are the U-shaped type, with a bar that bridges the ends of the U. Most standard models are large enough to fit around a parking sign pole, the bike frame, and both wheels (front wheel removed from forks). There are also smaller, lighter models just big enough to lock the frame to a pole. These can be useful when a lock is only a contingency measure (an unexpected stop on your way to work, for example). Large models designed for motorcycles are also available, but they are decidedly bulky and heavy. The two leading brands of U-locks are Citadel and Kryptonite.

Chain-type locks are not as secure as U-locks, but will fit around lamp-posts, trees, and other street furniture too bulky for a U-lock. At this writing the only chain lock with a performance guarantee is the No-Crak, a massive piece of equipment that will discourage most thieves on looks alone.

Have your bike post-coded. This involves the stamping of your house number and postcode on the bottom bracket and enables the police to return your bike if they recover it after a theft. Various police departments, bike shops, and cycle campaign groups will perform the service for a modest charge or even for free. Do it. The other day I was in a bike shop when a police officer came in to look over a bike.

He casually mentioned that down at the station they had five very expensive recovered mountain bikes, and no way of locating the owners.

Insure your bike. One gang of filth foiled in their attempt at theft by a good lock vented their frustration by wrapping the bike around a lamp-post. A not uncommon evil is cutting the bike frame itself, just to get the components. These things happen, and the only resource is insurance. The cheapest way to obtain this is as an extension of a household policy. Insurance services are also available through cycle campaign groups, racing and touring organizations, and some bike shops. Effective policies that give new for old on the bike and also cover accessories are expensive, but are more worthwhile than cheap policies with limited cover.

If you do get a bike you must accept the possibility that it will be stolen. I succeeded in keeping my first good bike for years and years. It went when my flat was ripped off. More recently, my beloved first Speedy was stolen while in the care of a friend. The problem never ends. It hurts a lot when a cherished bike that you have shared all kinds of experiences with suddenly vanishes to feed some junkie's habit. Try not to forget that it can happen to you, accept it, and the elaborate security precautions you must take will have a slightly less paranoid tone.

Basically, thieves steal because they can get away with it. It isn't a matter of poverty, social inequality, or diminished opportunities. Mercy and consideration are the qualities the thief lacks, and there is no simple answer for this problem. Theft is simply something that is around, like rain. In face of the problem the main thing you can do is keep your own head together and to this end, prevention is a lot better than cure. Make awareness of security a constant part and parcel of how you use your bike.

Successfully locking your bike is only one aspect of bike security. Depending on your age and sex, and the value of your bike, you are also subject to direct assault while riding. Usually this crime occurs in parks and other semi-isolated places, and to a lesser extent on slum streets. In form it can vary from seemingly friendly and casual interest on the part of strangers who would like to 'try your bike out', to someone leaping out from behind a parked car, knocking you flat with a club, and riding away on your bike. This once happened to an entire pack of racers in New York's Central Park. The attacking gang got away with 10 bikes.

Once assaulted, there is little you can—or should—do unless you are an action freak or have experience in physical combat. No bike is worth a cracked skull or a knife in the gut. You would not have been jumped in the first place if your opponent(s) did not have an advantage.

On the other hand, it is sickening and degrading to be ripped off. If you're up against three guys armed with knives and clubs, then quit. If you are simply up against an aggressor who is forcing you into the role of victim, then fight. On principle. It's OK to lose a bike, the crown jewels, or a million pounds. You are worth more. What's not OK is to lose your own self-respect. Most bullies are both motivated and stimulated by cowardice. Deep inside, they are scared themselves, and bullying is a way of denying this. If they sense rabbit in someone else, they go for them. If they sense fighting spirit, they may back off. There are lots of circumstances where you can and should fight, win or lose. Where you draw the line is up to you. Fighting takes experience. Bullies may be cowards, but of needs, many of them are experienced, quick, and vicious. Know what you are doing; foolish bravery can get you killed. In any case, do not let a violent encounter take you by surprise. Think about and prepare for it now.

For example, one kind of attack consists of a group of people fanning out across a street with the obvious intention of stopping you. What do you do? Stop and negotiate? You might as well just hand your bike over. Is that what you want to do? There may be room enough for a quick U-turn and fast sprint away. Suppose there isn't? William 'Sundown Slim' Sanders (a fun bike journalist) has a succinct answer: CHARGE! Shake off the victim mentality, pour on the power, yell like a maniac, and head directly for one of the people blocking you. Don't aim at a gap between people, pick someone out and genuinely try to hit them. In the end, most anybody will make a scrambling effort to get out of the way. This is the kind of thing you can do only if you are prepared. Otherwise you will just roll to a dumb stop, wondering what if anything you can do, and one of the crowd will 'try your bike out'.

Of course if you can avoid confrontations in the first place, so much the better. Stay out of isolated areas in parks at any time, and out of parks altogether at night. If you travel through rough neighbourhoods move along at a smart pace, and try to stick to well-lit streets. Above all else, be alert. Look for likely ambushes and for people who seem unduly interested in you. If a few people suddenly cross the street and intersect your intended path, you've genuine cause for alarm. Vanish if you can. It's not just the bike. One friend of mine who ignored the portent of a gang of four men moving into his path was knocked off his bike by a simple touch on the handlebar, and then for fun, was propped up against a fence and methodically beaten to a pulp. He was kicked on the head over 30 times. My friend is happy—and lucky—to still be alive.

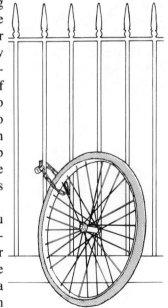

In weighing the pros and cons of owning a bike you have to make a realistic evaluation of your own situation. If you work in a crummy neighbourhood and your employer won't let you bring your bike inside, you're screwed (and should get another job). If you are a woman in an urban area you are a more likely victim of direct assault. If . . . if . . . I think that the advantages of owning a bike outweigh the disadvantages. But riding a bike exposes you to the world in new ways, and it would be unfair not to tell you about the problems you could encounter. Be prepared!

. . . **gone!**

Fitting
and Gearing

Getting the most out of a bike requires a good fit; the right frame size, with correct placement of the handlebars, seat, and controls. The various formulas and methods listed here have historic precedent. At first, a riding position that is 'according to the book' may feel odd. Give yourself at least 50 miles to get used to the new arrangement before making alterations. You may find the 'odd' position considerably more efficient and less fatiguing than a supposedly comfortable position. On the other side, everyone is a little different, and some variation from the norm may be in order. Just give the orthodox position a fair trial, and make changes gradually.

For how to make alterations in seat, handlebar, stem, and brake lever positions, look up Adjustment under the relevant heading in the Maintenance and Repair sections.

Fitting
Frame

Frame size is measured from the seat lug to the centre of the bottom bracket axle. There is no single infallible method for calculating correct individual frame size. For example, three popular rules of thumb are:
1. Inside length of leg from crotch bone to floor, measured in stocking feet, less 9" for heights to 5'10", 10" for heights 5'10" to 6'1", and 11" for heights over 6'1".
2. Height divided by 3.
3. Two-thirds inside length of leg.
Thus, a person 6'8" tall with a 32-inch inseam would have a frame size of (1) 23 inches, (2) 22.6 inches, and (3) 21.3 inches! In fact, correct frame size is a matter of trial and error, and experience in what is right. The start has to be with a live human being. A man and a woman of the same height, for example, have different leg lengths (hers are longer). A man and a woman with the same leg lengths have different arm lengths (hers are shorter). Consequently each has different needs.

A few bike shops have fitting machines—static gadgets that you climb aboard, and that are then adjusted until fit is ideal. You know the correct frame size, saddle height, stem length, handlebar rake, and so on. Great stuff, but I'd like to walk you through how it is done by eyeball.

Firstly, find a diamond-frame bike that you can comfortably straddle with your feet flat on the ground. If the top tube digs into your crotch, you can be sure sooner or later of a nasty slam where it hurts the most. There should be an inch to spare, more if you are 5'10" or taller.

Next, set the saddle height so that when you sit on the bike with your heel on the pedal, your leg is almost straight. Between 2 and 4 inches of seat post should be exposed; if less, try a smaller frame, if more, a larger frame. In general, women will be happier with a smaller frame and an extra-long seat post, because their (comparatively) shorter torsos and arms will be more comfortable on a smaller bike.

Novices are prone to select a frame which is too large. An oversize frame feels a bit more secure and steady, and may have a slightly easier ride, as small frames tend to be stiffer than large frames. A novice may have had only a few rides, and 'feel right' on a frame that in fact is a little too big. Only with time and miles does the rider come to appreciate the deftness and responsiveness of a correctly sized frame.

It pays to carry out the sizing exercise first thing, before looking at bikes or frames. You might be one of those lucky people who fits a common size without a hitch. Or you might be someone who really needs a frame at say, 19.5 inches maximum. This requirement eliminates a lot of bikes that would be a waste of time for you to consider.

There is little harm and possibly even merit in a slightly undersize frame. A longer seat post and stem will put matters right. But do not oversize by more than one-half inch. An excess of 1 inch or more will adversely affect handling, speed, and most importantly, comfort.

A mountain bike is harder to size than a road bike, because the bottom bracket height tends to vary more. The rough rule is 3-4 inches smaller than a road frame. A lot depends on what you are going to do with the bike. For town and road riding a larger frame is fine. For serious off-road work a smaller frame is essential. There should be at least 4 inches of daylight between your crotch and the top tube. This may dictate a sloping top tube. Again, the usual tendency is to go for too big.

Saddle

The position of the saddle determines the fitting of the rest of the bike. For most riders the correct fore-to-aft position is with the nose of the saddle 1.75 to 2.5 inches behind a vertical line through the crank hanger.

When comfortably seated on the saddle with feet on the pedals and with cranks parallel to the ground (3 o'clock/9 o'clock), a plumb line (weight and string) from the centre of the forward knee should pass right through the pedal spindle.

The taller the person, the further back the saddle. However, there are many variations. Touring riders often use a slightly rearward saddle position together with handlebars set on the high side. They are interested in comfort and steady power over long distances. Sprint riders and traffic jammers who use brief bursts of sharp energy use a more forward saddle position. This is one reason why sprint frames come with a steeper seat tube angle. For around-town use, if you are a vigorous rider, you may like a more forward saddle position. For extended going and best overall efficiency, however, stick to the normal position.

The horizontal tilt of the saddle, i.e., height of the front relative to the rear, is crucial. There is, in your crotch, a nerve. Pinching it even slightly over a long ride can disable you with numb crotch for weeks. Start with the saddle dead level, and if you experience any discomfort, immediately lower the nose a degree or two. It can make all the difference. This adjustment is much easier if you have a good-quality seat post with micro-adjusting bolts.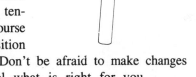

You may find yourself trying out different kinds of saddles. Each type may need a slightly different horizontal tilt. For example, padded anatomic saddles have a tendency to bounce the rider forward, and the usual recourse is to tilt the nose up a degree or two. This position could be very uncomfortable with a harder saddle. Don't be afraid to make changes and experiment. With time you will know by feel what is right for you.

Most saddles are set too low. A rough rule of thumb is that while sitting on the bike with your heel on the pedal at its lowest point, your leg should be almost straight. This means that when riding with the ball of your foot on the pedal, your leg is almost but not quite fully extended at the bottom of the stroke.

A precise formula for the best saddle height has been worked out in a series of tests. Measure inside leg length from crotch bone to floor without shoes. Multiply this length (in inches) by 1.09. Example: $32'' \times 1.09 = 34.88$, or $34\frac{7}{8}''$. Set saddle so that distance A from top of saddle to centre of pedal spindle in down position with crank parallel to seat tube is $34\frac{7}{8}''$.

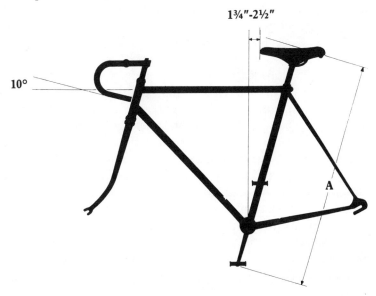

The 1.09 formula was put together by experts. They found that an alteration in saddle height of 4 per cent of inside leg measurement from the 1.09 setting affected power output by approximately 5 per cent. Once you've set the saddle height by this formula, leave it alone for a while before making changes.

Handlebars

By and large, dropped bars and profile bars are more efficient and comfortable than conventional flat bars.

1. A much greater variety of positions is possible. Not only can you select the best

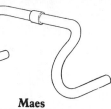

Maes

position for conditions, such as low down when headed into the wind, but being able to shift about and bring different muscle groups into play greatly increases comfort, to say nothing of power.

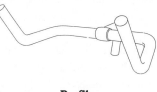

Profile

2. Because weight is supported by both the hands and posterior, road shocks and bumps rock the body rather than jar it. With flat bars, most if not all of the body weight rests on the saddle. With dropped bars and profile bars, a portion of body weight supported by the arms, and because the torso is inclined forward, when the bike goes over bumps the body tends to absorb shock by pivoting at the hips. Leaning

Fitting

forward stretches the spine, and this also helps in absorbing shock. Flat bars force the rider into an upright position where the individual vertebrae of the spine are pinched together, and because there is no pivoting at the hips, each and every jolt and bump is transmitted directly up the spine, greatly increasing fatigue.

3. The better distribution of weight allowed by dropped or profile bars makes the bike more stable, and improves handling and steering.

A choice between dropped bars or profile bars is really a matter of individual preference. Because profile bars have one basic riding position, it is logical to place thumb-shift or bar-end gear levers on the ends of the bars, so that both brake and gear controls are immediately to hand. It's a good arrangement for maximizing control, and is favoured by many dispatch riders for hard riding in urban traffic. Profile bars still have a flat top section that allows the rider to sit up and relax. Do note, however, that profile bars are designed to be used with frames that have short, low head tubes; used on a diamond-pattern frame that is correctly sized for the rider, they will give a high riding position.

Mountain bike handlebars are a very different kettle of fish from traditional flat bars. Some competition riders use dropped bars on mountain bikes, but flat bars are customary. Unlike the flat bars on a 'sit up and beg' roadster, mountain bike handlebars support part of the rider's weight and are very much an active feature of the bike. They are usually wider than dropped bars, for greater leverage, and the single riding position keeps the brake and gear levers literally at the rider's fingertips. The configuration is expressly designed for maximum bike handling and control, and is excellent for use in traffic provided the bars are not too wide. In the big, open spaces, wide bars are great; in traffic they tend to snag car rear-view mirrors, lorries, pedestrians, and what-else. Bars that are too wide are easily trimmed with a hack-saw, but first move the controls inboard and try the new position out before taking irrevocable action.

Drop bars range from 38 to 42 mm in width, with 44 mm sometimes available. If you have wide shoulders, bars with a narrow span will compress the chest and impair breathing. If you have narrow shoulders, wide bars won't do any harm.

Handlebar height is very important. For conventional use handlebars should be set so that the uppermost section is just level with the saddle. Sprint bikes have the bars a whole lot lower, and if you do a lot of traffic riding you may want to set yours down a bit. Be careful of an overly 'fierce' position, however; the gain for short-term speed will be at some cost to overall efficiency.

The stem should position the bars so that the distance between the nose of the saddle and the rear edge of the centre of the handlebars equals the distance from your elbow to your outstretched fingertips. Take the trouble to get this one right, particularly if you are female. There are two ways to check:

1. Sit on the bike in your normal riding position while a friend holds the bike steady. Without moving your torso, remove one hand from the handlebars and let the arm dangle fully relaxed. Then rotate your arm in a large arc without stretching. If, as your hand comes back to the bar, it is ahead of or behind the other hand, the bars need to be moved.

2. When comfortably seated on the saddle with both feet on the pedals and with cranks parallel to the ground (3 o'clock/9 o'clock), a plumb line (weight and string) from the centre of the forward knee should pass through the pedal spindle.

Brakes

Brake levers on flat bars should be set between 30° and 45° below horizontal to prevent damaged fingers in the event of a fall. On dropped bars set up for racing the

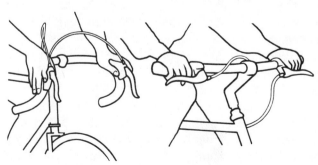

hands are often primarily on the hooks, inside the curved section of the bars, and the brake levers are usually set at approximately 3 o'clock so as to be within ready reach of the fingers. Tourists and urban riders, however, tend to use a more upright position and to place their hands on the tops of the bars, or in traffic, on the brake lever hoods. In such instances, for comfort, and a secure grip when braking hard, the levers should be set at around the 2 o'clock mark. With this arrangement I like to have the ends of the bars raked 10° from the horizontal. This allows the 3 o'clock racing position to be created by simply rotating the bars until the ends are horizontal.

Toe Clips

Use them! Toe clips are what cycling is all about. They are essential for full pedalling and riding skills. You might be worried about being trapped to the pedal. This is extremely rare. In fact, for safety reasons it is far, far more important to have your feet firmly attached to the pedals. Toe clips may look awkward, but with a little practice you'll soon slip in and out of them without a thought (see Riding). Be sure to have them correspond to your shoe size: small for small, medium to size 8-9, and large for size 9-10 and up. Go for larger if you wear bulky shoes. To avoid scratching up fancy shoes, either fit toe clip pads or mask the clips with cloth tape.

Cleats

Cleats are metal or plastic strips fastened to the soles of cycling shoes. Used together with toe clips they hold your foot to the pedal with a vengeance, and are unsafe for traffic riding unless you use very loosely set straps. But they are essential for racing and great for touring and mountain biking.

When using cleats be careful not to force your feet out of natural alignment. A little twist one way or the other can really wreck your knees. If you experience discomfort with cleats then seek professional advice from a qualified bike shop or sports coach. Don't use cleats if they hurt.

Modern cycling shoes have adjustable cleats. A good fitting method is to set the adjusting screws semi-tight, so that when the cleat is on the pedal, you are able to adjust its position by twisting your foot. Ride the bike for a while, experimenting with different positions until you are comfortable, and then properly tighten the adjusting screws. To fit traditional nail-on cleats, first ride your bike for a few miles so that the soles of your shoes take an impression from the pedals. Then simply place the cleats so that the cleat gap is aligned with the rear cage edge.

Crank Length

The cranks on Ashtabula and cottered cranksets are usually 165 mm long. Cranks for cotterless cranksets range in length from 160 mm to 180 mm. The usual size on road bikes is 170 mm. Some bike manufacturers supply 165 mm cranks on small frames, and 175 mm cranks on large frames. Many mountain bikes are fitted with 175 mm cranks for extra torque.

Correct crank length is a function of rider size, riding style, and skill. A person 6'4″ tall is not going to be too happy twiddling short 160 mm cranks, and a person 5' tall is going to have a long stretch to spin 175 mm cranks. Broadly, long cranks are for slow pedalling and delivery of torque through leverage, and short cranks are for fast pedalling and delivery of torque through momentum. Another element is clearance when cornering or going over rough ground. It's surprising how much difference a few millimetres can make. Long cranks on a touring bike with a low bottom bracket, for example, will usually make the machine prone to ground a pedal when cornering. If you are an old codger with no intention of hurrying anything, then longer cranks will provide a bit of welcome advantage. If you like to dive in and out of corners, stay off long cranks unless the bike is a criterium racer or mountain bike, with a high bottom bracket.

Unequal Legs

Some people have legs that are different in length. The result when riding a bike can be inexplicable back, hip, and leg pains. If a qualified orthopaedist or sports physician confirms that this is the problem, the method for compensation is to use pedals of different heights. TA have an Piste Orthopaedic pedal with interchangeable cage plates of different heights, obtainable by a bike shop on special order from Ron Kitching. Alternatively, any good engineering workshop should be able to make up new cage plates for a pedal with removable plates.

Gearing

Fitting also includes the selection of gearing. Understanding this subject requires some knowledge of basic riding technique. Some of the information I am going to give you now is rather technical. Just use it as required.

When I bought my first derailleur-gear bike I was surprised to find that the gear ratios, instead of each having a separate range like on a car, overlapped considerably. One gear wasn't much different from the other. The reason is that in pedalling there is a cadence rate (number of crank revolutions per minute) which is the most efficient—quick enough to avoid fatigue from pressing too strongly on the pedals (pain in the legs), but not so quick that the rider becomes starved for oxygen (panting). For most people the optimum cadence rate is 65-85 rpm, racers run 120-130 rpm and up. The idea behind a multitude of gears is to allow the rider to maintain the same cadence regardless of terrain.

In consequence, racing bikes usually have close-ratio gears, with each ratio near in size to the next, while touring and mountain bikes usually have wide-ratio gears, with much greater differences between each ratio. The reason for this is that touring and mountain bikes encounter more varied conditions, frequently pack heavy loads up steep grades, and are more likely to be used by novice riders. You need to be fairly proficient and fit in order to comfortably use close-ratio gears.

What determines ratio? The number of teeth (T) on the front chainring divided by the number of teeth on the back sprocket (or cog). Thus, 60T front to 15T rear is a ratio of 4:1. For competition a typical set-up might be a rear cluster of 23-21-19-17-15T, matched to front chainrings of 49/52T. For touring it might be 28-24-20-17-14T rear and 40/50T front.

To make notation easier, gear ratios are calculated into a single number. The formula is:

$$\frac{\text{Number of teeth on front sprocket}}{\text{Number of teeth on back sprocket}} \times \text{wheel diameter} = \text{gear ratio}$$

Gear ratio numbers are expressed in inches, as in '80-inch' gear. This is an arbitrary reference, as gear-inch number is not a measurement of how far a wheel will travel for each rotation of the cranks. In fact, the system is derived from the high bicycle, where a gear of 60 meant that the driving wheel had a diameter of 60 inches. Thus, for one rotation of the cranks, a modern bicycle with a 60-inch gear will go the same distance as a high bicycle with a 60-inch diameter driving wheel. If you want to know how far a wheel will travel per crank rotation, add *pi* to the gear-inch formula:

$$\frac{\text{Number of teeth on front sprocket}}{\text{Number of teeth on back sprocket}} \times 3.14 \times \text{wheel diameter} = \text{distance}$$

In general, 100 inches is the top range and is hard to push, 90 inches is more common, 80 inches is the usual speed gear, 70 and 60 inches are the most often used, 50 and 40 inches are for hills, and 30 and 20 inches are for extremely steep terrain and/or heavy loads. A lot depends on the kind of bike involved. For example, my mountain bike has a gear range of 28 to 80 inches, my racing safety bike is ranged from 47 to 108 inches, and my HPV goes all the way from 30 to 144 inches. Same rider, but very different machines and riding conditions.

There are other factors besides range to consider in setting up gears. Ease of transition from one gear to another is important. If you have to shift both front and back sprockets every time, it is laborious. For example:

Rear		14	17	21	26	31
Front	52	100.2	82.3	66.9	54	45
Front	47	90.4	74.5	60.2	48.6	40.8

means that to run up through the gears consecutively requires continuous double shifts. On the other hand, a set-up like:

Rear		14	15	17	19	21
Front	54	104	97.2	85.6	76.7	69.4
Front	38	73.2	68	60	54	49

means that you can run up through the gears using only one shift of the front derailleur. (Never use the small front to small rear or big front to big rear. I will explain why later.)

If you use wide gaps front and rear there is almost bound to be some duplication of gears:

Rear		14	17	21	26	31
Front	52	100.2	82.3	66.9	54	45
Front	42	81	66.7	54	43.5	36.4

and yet, curiously enough, many good bikes are set up this way. It really depends on what you want the bike for, because in balancing the various factors of range, ease of shifting, and number of different gears, you are just going to have to make compromises.

Stock gearing on many production bikes is definitely a compromise:

Rear		14	17	20	24	28
Front	52	100	83	70	58.5	50
Front	42	81	67	57	47	40.5

This selection of ratios is adequate for town riding, but the bottom 40.5-inch gear is not low enough for touring in hilly terrain or carrying heavy loads.

Tourists want lower gears spaced closely together, and the classic method for doing this is to use smaller front chainrings and a modest spread of cogs:

Rear		15	17	19	21	23
Front	46	83	73	65	59	54
Front	28	50	44	40	36	33

By dropping sprocket sizes a little more and widening their range, we come to a little whizzer known as the Montague:

Rear		14	16	18	20	22	28/30
Front	42	81	71	63	57	51.5	
Front	26		44	39	35	32	25/23

These patterns have a lot going for them: four closely spaced ratios at the low end of the range for climbing hills, a simple shifting sequence, and four good ratios for level ground. The drawbacks are a big jump between the small and large chainrings, and a limit on top speed.

One way of obtaining low ratios while still keeping speed gears is to use a big 34T rear sprocket:

Rear		14	18	23	30	34
Front	52	100	78	61	47	41
Front	42	81	63	49	38	33

This gives a wide range, but the large jumps between ratios make it difficult to maintain an even pedalling cadence, and many of the ratios are duplicates. Another method is to reduce the size of the small chainring as:

Rear		14	17	20	24	28
Front	52	100	83	70	58.5	50
Front	36	69	57	48.5	40.5	34.7

The advent of 6-speed blocks and narrow chains makes it possible to have both fairly closely-spaced gears, and a 'stump-puller' for hills:

Rear		13	15	18	21	26	32
Front	52	108	93.6	78	67	54	44
Front	42	87	75.6	63	54	43	35

This arrangement gives a reasonable hill-climbing gear, a good spread of middle and high gears, and an 'overdrive' for zooming down hills.

Racing and fast road bikes want narrow jumps between gears, as in this 14-speed arrangement.

Rear		12	13	14	15	17	19	21
Front	52	117	108	100	93	82	73	66
Front	42	94	87	81	75	66	59	54

The main points to bear in mind when working out a selection of gear ratios are:
1. Emphasis—for touring and mountain biking, a good range of low gears; for competition, a good range of high gears; and for town riding, a good range of middle gears.
2. Bottom low—for touring in hilly terrain this should be around the 20-inch mark. A gear this low is thought by some to be for weaklings and called a 'granny' gear. With it, however, you will be able to pedal when others have to walk. Do not confuse touring and racing, the appropriate ratios for each are different. The strongest rider I know is Tim Gartside, a long-distance tourist who when tested on a bicycle dynamometer, broke it by blatting out more than 1.9 horsepower. Tim subsequently set a world record bicycle speed in the HPV Bluebell, pushing a 256-inch gear. For touring, Tim uses a bottom gear of 19-inches. So do many other very strong riders.

Town bikes want a bottom gear close to 30-inches, and competition bikes can start with a 45- or 50-inch gear.
3. Top high—there are many world champion riders who like to use big gears. In general, however, most racers gain speed by pedalling faster, not harder. The great Eddy Merckx, for example, used a 77-inch gear when he broke the 1 hour time trial record. For practical purposes anything over 100 inches is an overdrive giving more speed on downhills. Fine if you like excitement or are racing, but otherwise, consider that the hard work—and main need for gears—is going UP the hill. Let gravity do the work down the other side, while you relax and enjoy the view.

Consider also the long term. In Europe, juvenile (under 16) racers are limited to a maximum gear of about 76 inches. This is to prevent injury to their legs and force the development of correct riding techniques. I wish this had happened to me. I would have stronger knees, and be a much better bike rider.
4. Shift sequence—make it as simple as possible. You want it all to happen easily. Double (front and rear together) shifts are fun when you want to be artistic, but not when you are panting for breath and fighting for a tight edge of momentum.
5. Derailleur capacity—this is a function of the difference in size between the large and small sprockets, and large and small chainrings. (A 14-28T block has a 14T difference, and 42/52T chainrings have a 10T difference, for a total of 24T. The arm of a rear derailleur for use with this system must able to wrap 24T worth of chain.) Competition derailleurs with short arms usually range from 22T to 28T capacity. Touring derailleurs run up to 32T or 34T, and the big 'uns hit 38T.

Another aspect of rear derailleur capacity is maximum front chainring difference.

This can be from around 12T to 18T and is generally linked to overall chain length capacity; a derailleur that wraps a lot of chain will usually also cope with large differences in chainring sizes.

Front derailleur capacity is a straightforward function of the difference in chainring sizes. Competition units are as low as 14T, and hefty units for use with wide-range triple chainrings are 26T or more. Note: some of the mega-capacity front changers do not work properly unless there is a minimum difference of 6T between each chainring.

American product liability laws require that derailleur gears on production bikes must be idiot-proofed by being capable of shifting to any possible combination of front chainring and sprocket. This means that many gear systems on American bikes are needlessly bulky and awkward in terms of chain length, and size of derailleur needed to manage same. In real life it is silly (and harmful, see below) to pair the big chainring with the largest rear sprocket, or the small chainring with the smallest rear sprocket. If you eliminate these combinations which you should never use, the system can be set up with less chain, and a lighter, more responsive derailleur.

6. Derailleur sprocket size—the largest size rear sprocket that a derailleur can handle. If a derailleur is marked for a 30T sprocket, it is usually unable to mount a larger sprocket such as 34T. This is a function of the mechanical range of the derailleur itself, and not the amount of chain to wrap. Broadly, competition derailleurs work best on close-ratio freewheels kept well within capacity. Touring derailleurs work well on wide-ratio freewheels and indifferently on close-ratio freewheels.

7. Number of gear ratios—6- and 7-speed freewheels (which give 12 and 14 speeds with double chainrings, 18 and 21 speeds with triple rings) are common on production bikes. Set up with close-ratio sprockets they are great for competition, but are more trouble than gain when set up with a wide range of sprockets for a town or touring bike. For one thing, gear ratios have a greater tendency to duplicate, negating the point of the exercise. For another, a narrow chain is required, which makes shifting more fiddly. To make room for the 7-speed model freewheel, and certain of the 6-speed model freewheels, the wheel must have more dish (off-set of the hub) and is therefore weaker—not the thing for bumpy urban streets or heavyweight touring. Finally, a 7-speed block matched to double chainrings in actual practice gives 10 speeds at most and not 14.

Why? Because even with a 5-speed block and double chainrings you should never run the big front chainring to the big rear sprocket, or small front chainring to small rear sprocket. It causes the chain to cut across at too severe an angle, creating excessive wear, a tendency to rub the derailleur cages, and reduced efficiency. With a 7-speed block the problems are even worse. At most you can use only 5 of the 7 rear sprockets on each front chainring, and it is better to limit the number to 4—a rather anaemic total of 8 speeds out of a possible 14. Throw in a couple of duplicated gears and you are down to 6 usable ratios—the minimum that even a poorly designed 5-speed block/double chainring combination will produce!

One good reason, however, for using a 7-speed block, is that a 12T final drive sprocket can be fitted. This is the easiest way to obtain a big gear ratio for maximum speed on descents. Otherwise, if a 13T or 14T final drive sprocket is used, the only way to obtain an overdrive ratio is to increase the size of the front chainring, and this will throw a spanner into the size and balance of all the other gear ratios.

Triple Chainrings

For really effective wide-range gearing, the route to take is triple front chainrings. You will not gain all that many more ratios, but they will be exactly where required and certain types of difficult shifts will be easier. With a triple the inner chainring should be the smallest available, say 28T, 26T, or even 24T. This allows the use of a moderately sized largest rear sprocket, saving weight and improving shifting. It is always much easier to drop the chain from a large to a small front chainring than to lift the chain up from a small to a large rear sprocket. With a triple, shifting into low range is a simple matter of banging home the shift lever for the front derailleur.

The next advantage of a triple is that the middle chainring can be ideally sized for level cruising, and can be used on all of the rear sprockets without chain deflection problems. Most of the time you just run on the middle ring, and have only one shift lever to worry about.

When there is a tail wind or downgrade it's up onto the big chainring and go. Since the middle range of ratios are nicely taken care of by the centre chainring, you can afford to have a selection of final drive ratios plus an overdrive ratio off the big chainring.

A triple is a bit tricky when shifting to the middle chainring. At first, you will have to look at and centre the derailleur with each shift. But with practice you'll be able to do it by feel. Another factor is that a long chain, and long-arm derailleur to keep it under control, makes for slower shifting. It takes a while for all that hardware to settle into place.

If you want a triple chainset, sort matters out at the time of bike purchase. Triple rings require a longer bottom bracket axle to adjust the chainline and keep the inner chainring clear of the bike frame. Some double chainsets can be converted to triples, but getting everything to work properly can take a lot of fiddling about. Better if the bike is set up as a triple in the first place.

Gears for You

Gearing is a peculiar subject. Some people dote on gear ratios and spend long hours calculating the permutations of various different gearing systems. Others go into a catatonic trance at the first mention of the subject. Both reactions ignore what is perhaps the most important element: you.

The function of different gear ratios is to keep you churning away smoothly and efficiently over a range of conditions and terrain. Finding your best gear ratios and gear-shifting system is a matter of getting out on a bike and seeing what works.

You should soon enough be able to identify four or five recurring types of circumstances, each best met with a particular gear ratio. Thus, on my mountain bike Midnight Express the gear ratios each have names: Winch; Uphill Start; Downhill Start; My Most Marvellous Climbing Gear; Cruising; and Bombing. Each has been selected by a pragmatic process of trial and error. My Most Marvellous Climbing Gear is the exact ratio that I can comfortably spin for long periods while climbing shallow gradients. It's also the gear best suited for bucking a stiff headwind, pulling

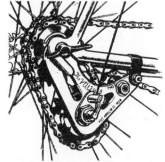

strongly out of a tight corner, or on the flat, lightly spinning along to loosen up my legs. Winch is a stump-puller that will lift me up any hill I'm likely to encounter in my area. Cruising is my normal riding gear, and Bombing is for sprints and shallow descents.

The way to create a gear system of this type is to first work out a broad estimate of the range you think would be good: say, from 30 to 75 inches, and a combination of chainrings and sprockets to match, say, 30/40T front and 14-24T rear. Basically, the chainrings govern the gear ratio ranges as a whole, and the rear sprockets the exact gear ratios within those ranges. Now, suppose you find that when riding the 40T front to a 14T rear, you are frequently stymied. The gear is OK on flat, smooth ground, but any slight upgrade forces you to move to the next sprocket up, say a 16T, and that one isn't quite right either, because it is too easy. Right, you swap the 14T for a 13T—that gives you a nice bombing gear—and the 16T for a 15T—your main riding gear—and bingo! you are smooth and have power on tap. What are the ratios involved? You can work them out, but they don't really matter; if you walked into a bike shop and asked for a 70-inch gear, you'd get a blank stare. You have to ask for a specific component such as a 15T sprocket, and you might as well think

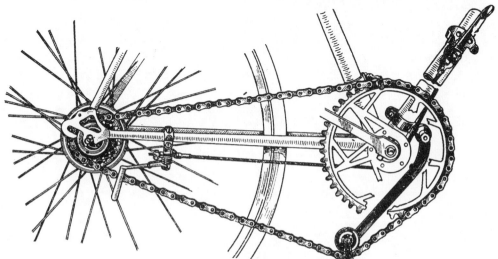

The Osgear (Constrictor Tyre Co.)

that way to start with. Thus, most riders talk in terms of 'I like 52/15', and 'What a descent, 54/13 all the way!'

The pragmatic approach can be continued almost indefinitely. Once you find the ratios you like best you can turn to matters such as shifting patterns. For example, suppose you want to be able to make the shift from your Cruising ratio to your slightly smaller 'Dig Out' ratio with lightning speed. One way to do this is to have a half-step difference between the front chainrings, so that a shift at the front has half the value of a shift at the rear. You use a rear sprocket that gives you the appropriate Cruising ratio when the chain is on the large chainring, and when you Dig Out you simply snick the chain onto the smaller chainring. It's about the fastest shift there is, which is why a half-step front is a common racing set-up.

Gear ratios are a fairly complex subject, and it helps a lot to know the whys and hows of shift patterns, half- and full-steps, derailleur capacities, and all the rest. But the starting point is you and your needs. Once you start riding, the areas in the gearing set-up that need improvement will be clear enough.

Summary

A bike is an extension of your body. It is all right for cycling to hurt because you are riding vigorously, or hardening yourself and extending your range. But the bike itself should be comfortable. If there are aches and pains that do not go away with a bit of riding and conditioning, then carefully review the fit of the bike.

In performance terms, a bike should work for you, not force you to try and keep up with the bike. In general, the key concept is moderation, and particularly in the vital area of gear ratios, you'll gain skill and strength more rapidly if you start out using modestly sized ratios and simple shifting patterns, and then upgrade in pace with your own development.

GEAR RATIO CHART FOR 27 INCH WHEELS

Number of teeth on sprocket

Number of teeth on chainring

Sprocket	24	25	26	27	28	29	30	31	32	33	34	35	36	37	38	39	40	41	42	43	44	45	46	47	48	49	50	51	52	53	54	55	56	57	58	Sprocket
12	54.0	56.3	58.5	60.8	63.0	65.3	67.5	69.8	72.0	74.3	76.5	78.8	81.0	83.3	85.5	87.8	90.0	92.3	94.5	96.8	99.0	101.3	103.5	105.8	108.0	110.3	112.5	114.8	117.0	119.3	121.5	123.8	126.0	128.3	130.5	12
13	49.8	51.9	54.0	56.1	58.2	60.2	62.3	64.4	66.5	68.5	70.6	72.7	74.8	76.8	78.9	81.0	83.1	85.2	87.2	89.3	91.4	93.5	95.5	97.6	99.7	101.8	103.8	105.9	108.0	110.1	112.2	114.2	116.3	118.4	120.5	13
14	46.3	48.2	50.1	52.1	54.0	55.9	57.9	59.8	61.7	63.6	65.6	67.5	69.4	71.4	73.3	75.2	77.1	79.1	81.0	82.9	84.9	86.8	88.7	90.6	92.6	94.5	96.4	98.4	100.3	102.2	104.1	106.1	108.0	109.9	111.9	14
15	43.2	45.0	46.8	48.6	50.4	52.2	54.0	55.8	57.6	59.4	61.2	63.0	64.8	66.6	68.4	70.2	72.0	73.8	75.6	77.4	79.2	81.0	82.8	84.6	86.4	88.2	90.0	91.8	93.6	95.4	97.2	99.0	100.8	102.6	104.4	15
16	40.5	42.2	43.9	45.6	47.3	48.9	50.6	52.3	54.0	55.7	57.4	59.1	60.8	62.4	64.1	65.8	67.5	69.2	70.9	72.6	74.3	75.9	77.6	79.3	81.0	82.7	84.4	86.1	87.8	89.4	91.1	92.8	94.5	96.2	97.9	16
17	38.1	39.7	41.3	42.9	44.5	46.1	47.6	49.2	50.8	52.4	54.0	55.6	57.2	58.8	60.4	61.9	63.5	65.1	66.7	68.3	69.9	71.5	73.1	74.6	76.2	77.8	79.4	81.0	82.6	84.2	85.8	87.4	88.9	90.5	92.1	17
18	36.0	37.5	39.0	40.5	42.0	43.5	45.0	46.5	48.0	49.5	51.0	52.5	54.0	55.5	57.0	58.5	60.0	61.5	63.0	64.5	66.0	67.5	69.0	70.5	72.0	73.5	75.0	76.5	78.0	79.5	81.0	82.5	84.0	85.5	87.0	18
19	34.1	35.5	36.9	38.4	39.8	41.2	42.6	44.1	45.5	46.9	48.3	49.7	51.2	52.6	54.0	55.4	56.8	58.3	59.7	61.1	62.5	63.9	65.4	66.8	68.2	69.6	71.1	72.5	73.9	75.3	76.7	78.2	79.6	81.0	82.4	19
20	32.4	33.8	35.1	36.5	37.8	39.2	40.5	41.9	43.2	44.6	45.9	47.3	48.6	50.0	51.3	52.7	54.0	55.4	56.7	58.1	59.4	60.8	62.1	63.5	64.8	66.2	67.5	68.9	70.2	71.6	72.9	74.3	75.6	77.0	78.3	20
21	30.9	32.1	33.4	34.7	36.0	37.3	38.6	39.9	41.1	42.4	43.7	45.0	46.3	47.6	48.9	50.1	51.4	52.7	54.0	55.3	56.6	57.9	59.1	60.4	61.7	63.0	64.3	65.6	66.9	68.1	69.4	70.7	72.0	73.3	74.6	21
22	29.5	30.7	31.9	33.1	34.4	35.6	36.8	38.0	39.3	40.5	41.7	43.0	44.2	45.4	46.6	47.9	49.1	50.3	51.5	52.8	54.0	55.2	56.5	57.7	58.9	60.1	61.4	62.6	63.8	65.0	66.3	67.5	68.7	70.0	71.2	22
23	28.2	29.3	30.5	31.7	32.9	34.0	35.2	36.4	37.6	38.7	39.9	41.1	42.3	43.4	44.6	45.8	47.0	48.1	49.3	50.5	51.7	52.8	54.0	55.2	56.3	57.5	58.7	59.9	61.0	62.2	63.4	64.6	65.7	66.9	68.1	23
24	27.0	28.1	29.3	30.4	31.5	32.6	33.8	34.9	36.0	37.1	38.3	39.4	40.5	41.6	42.8	43.9	45.0	46.1	47.3	48.4	49.5	50.6	51.8	52.9	54.0	55.1	56.3	57.4	58.5	59.6	60.8	61.9	63.0	64.1	65.3	24
25	25.9	27.0	28.1	29.2	30.2	31.3	32.4	33.5	34.6	35.6	36.7	37.8	38.9	40.0	41.0	42.1	43.2	44.3	45.4	46.4	47.5	48.6	49.7	50.8	51.8	52.9	54.0	55.1	56.2	57.2	58.3	59.4	60.5	61.6	62.6	25
26	24.9	26.0	27.0	28.0	29.1	30.1	31.2	32.2	33.2	34.3	35.3	36.3	37.4	38.4	39.5	40.5	41.5	42.6	43.6	44.7	45.7	46.7	47.8	48.8	49.8	50.9	51.9	52.9	54.0	55.0	56.1	57.1	58.2	59.2	60.2	26
27	24.0	25.0	26.0	27.0	28.0	29.0	30.0	31.0	32.0	33.0	34.0	35.0	36.0	37.0	38.0	39.0	40.0	41.0	42.0	43.0	44.0	45.0	46.0	47.0	48.0	49.0	50.0	51.0	52.0	53.0	54.0	55.0	56.0	57.0	58.0	27
28	23.1	24.1	25.1	26.0	27.0	28.0	28.9	29.9	30.9	31.8	32.8	33.8	34.7	35.7	36.6	37.6	38.6	39.5	40.5	41.5	42.4	43.4	44.4	45.3	46.3	47.3	48.2	49.2	50.1	51.1	52.1	53.0	54.0	55.0	55.9	28
29	22.3	23.3	24.2	25.1	26.1	27.0	27.9	28.9	29.8	30.7	31.7	32.6	33.5	34.5	35.4	36.3	37.2	38.2	39.1	40.0	41.0	41.9	42.8	43.8	44.7	45.6	46.6	47.5	48.4	49.3	50.3	51.2	52.1	53.1	54.0	29
30	21.6	22.5	23.4	24.3	25.2	26.1	27.0	27.9	28.8	29.7	30.6	31.5	32.4	33.3	34.2	35.1	36.0	36.9	37.8	38.7	39.6	40.5	41.4	42.3	43.2	44.1	45.0	45.9	46.8	47.7	48.6	49.5	50.4	51.3	52.2	30
31	20.9	21.8	22.6	23.5	24.4	25.3	26.1	27.0	27.9	28.7	29.6	30.5	31.4	32.2	33.1	34.0	34.8	35.7	36.6	37.5	38.3	39.2	40.1	40.9	41.8	42.7	43.5	44.4	45.3	46.2	47.0	47.9	48.8	49.6	50.5	31
32	20.3	21.1	21.9	22.8	23.6	24.5	25.3	26.2	27.0	27.8	28.7	29.5	30.4	31.2	32.1	32.9	33.8	34.6	35.4	36.3	37.1	38.0	38.8	39.7	40.5	41.3	42.2	43.0	43.9	44.7	45.6	46.4	47.3	48.1	48.9	32
33	19.6	20.5	21.3	22.1	22.9	23.7	24.5	25.4	26.2	27.0	27.8	28.6	29.5	30.3	31.1	31.9	32.7	33.5	34.4	35.2	36.0	36.8	37.6	38.5	39.3	40.1	40.9	41.7	42.5	43.4	44.2	45.0	45.8	46.6	47.5	33
34	19.1	19.9	20.6	21.4	22.2	23.0	23.8	24.6	25.4	26.2	27.0	27.8	28.6	29.4	30.2	31.0	31.8	32.6	33.4	34.1	34.9	35.7	36.5	37.3	38.1	38.9	39.7	40.5	41.3	42.1	42.9	43.7	44.5	45.3	46.1	34
35	18.5	19.3	20.1	20.8	21.6	22.4	23.1	23.9	24.7	25.5	26.2	27.0	27.8	28.5	29.3	30.1	30.9	31.6	32.4	33.2	33.9	34.7	35.5	36.3	37.0	37.8	38.6	39.3	40.1	40.9	41.7	42.4	43.2	44.0	44.7	35
36	18.0	18.8	19.5	20.3	21.0	21.8	22.5	23.3	24.0	24.8	25.5	26.3	27.0	27.8	28.5	29.3	30.0	30.8	31.5	32.3	33.0	33.8	34.5	35.3	36.0	36.8	37.5	38.3	39.0	39.8	40.5	41.3	42.0	42.8	43.5	36
37	17.5	18.2	19.0	19.7	20.4	21.2	21.9	22.6	23.4	24.1	24.8	25.5	26.3	27.0	27.7	28.5	29.2	29.9	30.6	31.4	32.1	32.8	33.6	34.3	35.0	35.8	36.5	37.2	37.9	38.7	39.4	40.1	40.9	41.6	42.3	37
38	17.1	17.8	18.5	19.2	19.9	20.6	21.3	22.0	22.7	23.4	24.2	24.9	25.6	26.3	27.0	27.7	28.4	29.1	29.8	30.6	31.3	32.0	32.7	33.4	34.1	34.8	35.5	36.2	36.9	37.7	38.4	39.1	39.8	40.5	41.2	38

Number of teeth on chainring

GEAR RATIO CHART FOR 26 INCH WHEELS

Number of teeth on chainring

Number of teeth on sprocket

Sprocket	24	25	26	27	28	29	30	31	32	33	34	35	36	37	38	39	40	41	42	43	44	45	46	47	48	49	50	51	52	53	54	55	56	57	58
12	52.0	54.2	56.3	58.5	60.7	62.8	65.0	67.2	69.3	71.5	73.7	75.8	78.0	80.2	82.3	84.5	86.7	88.8	91.0	93.2	95.3	97.5	99.7	101.8	104.0	106.2	108.3	110.5	112.7	114.8	117.0	119.2	121.3	123.5	125.7
13	48.0	50.0	52.0	54.0	56.0	58.0	60.0	62.0	64.0	66.0	68.0	70.0	72.0	74.0	76.0	78.0	80.0	82.0	84.0	86.0	88.0	90.0	92.0	94.0	96.0	98.0	100.0	102.0	104.0	106.0	108.0	110.0	112.0	114.0	116.0
14	44.6	46.4	48.3	50.1	52.0	53.9	55.7	57.6	59.4	61.3	63.1	65.0	66.9	68.7	70.6	72.4	74.3	76.1	78.0	79.9	81.7	83.6	85.4	87.3	89.1	91.0	92.9	94.7	96.6	98.4	100.3	102.1	104.0	105.9	107.7
15	41.6	43.3	45.1	46.8	48.5	50.3	52.0	53.7	55.5	57.2	58.9	60.7	62.4	64.1	65.9	67.6	69.3	71.1	72.8	74.6	76.3	78.0	79.7	81.5	83.2	84.9	86.7	88.4	90.1	91.9	93.6	95.3	97.1	98.8	100.5
16	39.0	40.6	42.3	43.9	45.5	47.1	48.8	50.4	52.0	53.6	55.3	56.9	58.5	60.1	61.8	63.4	65.0	66.6	68.3	69.9	71.5	73.1	74.8	76.4	78	79.6	81.3	82.9	84.5	86.1	87.8	89.4	91	92.6	94.3
17	36.7	38.2	39.8	41.3	42.8	44.4	45.9	47.4	48.9	50.5	52	53.5	55.1	56.6	58.1	59.6	61.2	62.7	64.2	65.8	67.3	68.8	70.4	71.9	73.4	74.9	76.5	78	79.5	81.1	82.6	84.1	85.6	87.2	88.7
18	34.7	36.1	37.6	39	40.4	41.9	43.3	44.8	46.2	47.7	49.1	50.6	52.0	53.4	54.9	56.3	57.8	59.2	60.7	62.1	63.6	65.0	66.4	67.9	69.3	70.8	72.2	73.7	75.1	76.6	78.0	79.4	80.9	82.3	83.8
19	32.8	34.2	35.6	36.9	38.3	39.7	41.1	42.4	43.8	45.2	46.5	47.9	49.3	50.6	52.0	53.4	54.7	56.1	57.5	58.8	60.2	61.6	62.9	64.3	65.7	67.1	68.4	69.8	71.2	72.6	73.9	75.3	76.6	78.0	79.4
20	31.2	32.5	33.8	35.1	36.4	37.7	39.0	40.3	41.6	42.9	44.2	45.5	46.8	48.1	49.4	50.7	52.0	53.3	54.6	55.9	57.2	58.5	59.8	61.1	62.4	63.7	65.0	66.3	67.6	68.9	70.2	71.5	72.8	74.1	75.4
21	29.7	31.0	32.2	33.4	34.7	35.9	37.1	38.4	39.6	40.9	42.1	43.3	44.6	45.8	47.0	48.3	49.5	50.8	52.0	53.2	54.5	55.7	57.0	58.2	59.4	60.7	61.9	63.1	64.4	65.6	66.9	68.1	69.3	70.6	71.8
22	28.4	29.5	30.7	31.9	33.1	34.3	35.5	36.6	37.8	39.0	40.2	41.4	42.5	43.7	44.9	46.1	47.3	48.5	49.6	50.8	52.0	53.2	54.4	55.5	56.7	57.9	59.1	60.3	61.5	62.6	63.8	65.0	66.2	67.4	68.5
23	27.1	28.3	29.4	30.5	31.7	32.8	33.9	35.0	36.2	37.3	38.4	39.6	40.7	41.8	43.0	44.1	45.2	46.3	47.5	48.6	49.7	50.9	52.0	53.1	54.3	55.4	56.5	57.7	58.8	59.9	61.0	62.2	63.3	64.4	65.6
24	26.0	27.1	28.2	29.3	30.3	31.4	32.5	33.6	34.7	35.8	36.8	37.9	39.0	40.1	41.2	42.3	43.3	44.4	45.5	46.6	47.7	48.8	49.8	50.9	52.0	53.1	54.2	55.3	56.3	57.4	58.5	59.6	60.7	61.8	62.8
25	25.0	26.0	27.0	28.1	29.1	30.2	31.2	32.2	33.3	34.3	35.4	36.4	37.4	38.5	39.5	40.6	41.6	42.6	43.7	44.7	45.8	46.8	47.8	48.9	49.9	51.0	52.0	53.0	54.1	55.1	56.2	57.2	58.2	59.3	60.3
26	24.0	25.0	26.0	27.0	28.0	29.0	30.0	31.0	32.0	33.0	34.0	35.0	36.0	37.0	38.0	39.0	40.0	41.0	42.0	43.0	44.0	45.0	46.0	47.0	48.0	49.0	50.0	51.0	52.0	53.0	54.0	55.0	56.0	57.0	58.0
27	23.1	24.1	25.1	26.0	27.0	27.9	28.9	29.9	30.8	31.8	32.7	33.7	34.7	35.6	36.6	37.6	38.5	39.5	40.4	41.4	42.4	43.3	44.3	45.3	46.2	47.2	48.1	49.1	50.1	51.0	52.0	53.0	53.9	54.9	55.9
28	22.3	23.2	24.1	25.1	26.0	26.9	27.9	28.8	29.7	30.6	31.6	32.5	33.4	34.3	35.3	36.2	37.1	38.1	39.0	39.9	40.9	41.8	42.7	43.6	44.6	45.5	46.4	47.4	48.3	49.2	50.1	51.1	52.0	52.9	53.9
29	21.5	22.4	23.3	24.2	25.1	26.0	26.9	27.8	28.7	29.6	30.5	31.4	32.3	33.2	34.1	35.0	35.9	36.8	37.7	38.6	39.4	40.3	41.2	42.1	43.0	43.9	44.8	45.7	46.6	47.5	48.4	49.3	50.2	51.1	52.0
30	20.8	21.7	22.6	23.4	24.3	25.1	26.0	26.9	27.7	28.6	29.5	30.3	31.2	32.1	32.9	33.8	34.7	35.5	36.4	37.3	38.1	39.0	39.9	40.7	41.6	42.5	43.3	44.2	45.1	45.9	46.8	47.7	48.5	49.4	50.3
31	20.1	21.0	21.8	22.6	23.5	24.3	25.2	26.0	26.9	27.7	28.6	29.4	30.2	31.0	31.9	32.7	33.5	34.4	35.2	36.1	36.9	37.7	38.6	39.4	40.3	41.1	41.9	42.8	43.6	44.5	45.3	46.1	47.0	47.8	48.6
32	19.5	20.3	21.1	21.9	22.8	23.6	24.4	25.2	26.0	26.8	27.6	28.4	29.3	30.1	30.9	31.7	32.5	33.3	34.1	34.9	35.8	36.6	37.4	38.2	39.0	39.8	40.6	41.4	42.3	43.1	43.9	44.7	45.5	46.3	47.1
33	18.9	19.7	20.5	21.3	22.1	22.8	23.6	24.4	25.2	26.0	26.8	27.6	28.4	29.2	29.9	30.7	31.5	32.3	33.1	33.9	34.7	35.5	36.2	37.0	37.8	38.6	39.4	40.2	41.0	41.8	42.5	43.3	44.1	44.9	45.7
34	18.4	19.1	19.9	20.6	21.4	22.2	22.9	23.7	24.5	25.2	26.0	26.8	27.6	28.3	29.1	29.8	30.6	31.4	32.1	32.9	33.6	34.4	35.2	35.9	36.7	37.5	38.2	39.0	39.8	40.5	41.3	42.1	42.8	43.6	44.4
35	17.8	18.6	19.3	20.1	20.8	21.5	22.3	23.0	23.8	24.5	25.3	26.0	26.7	27.5	28.2	29.0	29.7	30.5	31.2	31.9	32.7	33.4	34.2	34.9	35.7	36.4	37.1	37.9	38.6	39.4	40.1	40.9	41.6	42.3	43.1
36	17.3	18.1	18.8	19.5	20.2	20.9	21.7	22.4	23.1	23.8	24.6	25.3	26.0	26.7	27.4	28.2	28.9	29.6	30.3	31.1	31.8	32.5	33.2	33.9	34.7	35.4	36.1	36.8	37.6	38.3	39.0	39.7	40.4	41.2	41.9
37	16.9	17.6	18.3	19.0	19.7	20.4	21.1	21.8	22.5	23.2	23.9	24.6	25.3	26.0	26.7	27.4	28.1	28.8	29.5	30.2	30.9	31.6	32.3	33.0	33.7	34.4	35.1	35.8	36.5	37.2	37.9	38.6	39.4	40.1	40.8
38	16.4	17.1	17.8	18.5	19.2	19.8	20.5	21.2	21.9	22.6	23.3	23.9	24.6	25.3	26.0	26.7	27.4	28.1	28.7	29.4	30.1	30.8	31.5	32.2	32.8	33.5	34.2	34.9	35.6	36.3	36.9	37.6	38.3	39.0	39.7

Number of teeth on chainring

Number of teeth on sprocket

Riding

Anybody can ride a bicycle. Proper cycling is another story, and here, technique counts more than anything else. Physical condition of course plays a part, but skilled 50-year-old grandmothers can and do run rings around fit young adults. Attention to the basics of technique will make riding easier and more enjoyable, and help you realize your capacities and abilities. Riding well is part of the fun—and there is always room for improvement!

Shifting

Broadly, shifting is a matter of synchronizing pedal pressure and crank rotation with movement of the shift lever. Let your skill develop gradually. Back off if you start to get damaging 'clunk' sounding shifts. These are caused by incorrect timing. The way to do things fast is to do them right. Once you get the knack, smooth, split-second gear changes will be second nature.

Hub Gears

To shift up to a higher gear, ease pressure on pedals while continuing to rotate cranks, move shift lever to next gear, and resume pedal pressure. Extra-fast shifts may be made by maintaining pedal pressure, moving the selector, and then pausing pedalling momentarily when the shift is desired. If done too hard, this may damage gears. Going down to 1st from 2nd or 3rd, and when coming to a stop, back-pedal slightly. If not stopping use same procedure as for up-shifts.

Derailleur Gears

Shift derailleur gears only while pedalling. To see why, hang your bike up so that the rear wheel is off the ground, rotate the cranks, and manipulate the gear-shift levers so you can see how the derailleurs work. Shifting a derailleur without pedalling may result in a bent or broken chain or gear teeth. If you park your bike in the street, always give the gears a visual check to make sure passers-by have not fiddled with them. It happens often.

Ease pedal pressure when shifting. The exact amount depends on the kind of shift and equipment involved. For example, in a front changer down-shift the chain is knocked off a larger chainring down onto a smaller chainring. This is mechanically easy and is usually quick. In an up-shift from a small to a large chainring, however, the chain must climb up while overcoming the spring tension provided by the rear derailleur. If the difference in chainring sizes is large, up-shifts will take a bit of time.

There are three types of shift lever mechanisms: simple friction, friction with a clutch or ratchet device, and indexed. Indexed levers automatically stop in the right place for each gear. Friction shift levers do not have stops for the different gears, and you have to learn where they are by feel and ear. Do not let the front derailleur cage rub the chain. Sometimes a front changer will shift only if it is overset; once the shift is completed the lever must be reversed slightly to position the changer so that the chain does not rub against the derailleur cage. It's easy to do, because you can look right down and see what is happening.

Aligning a rear changer so that the chain meshes smoothly with the selected sprocket is not as easy. It's a matter of ear and feel; no untoward grinding or chattering noises, and a smooth sensation at the pedals. Some old-fashioned rear derailleurs need back-and-forth shift lever movement; a generous motion to initiate the shift, and then a slight reverse direction adjustment to bring everything into alignment. Many modern designs, on the other hand, are very responsive and shift with just a touch of the lever. Experiment with your own system to see what works best.

Indexed systems are automatic, but sometimes work best with a bit of the old-fashioned 'over-shift' technique. If up-shifts are slow, try pushing the gear-shift lever slightly beyond the stop for the gear ratio you want. It's a slightly delicate operation, because you need to stop just short of actually snicking the lever into the stop beyond the one you want. Time and practice will give you the knack.

Do not run the big front chainring to the big rear sprocket, or the small front to the small rear. It causes the chain to cut across at too severe an angle, greatly increasing wear and reducing efficiency. Proper shifting should also take into account the demands of cadence (see below).

Pedalling

Ride with the ball of your foot on the pedal, not the heel or arch. The fundamental technique for easy cycling is called ankling. This is where the foot pivots at the

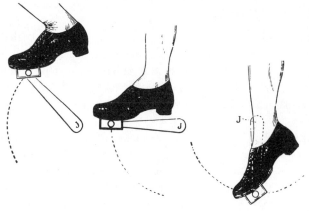

ankle with each revolution of the crank. Start at the top of the stroke (12 o'clock) with the heel slightly lower than the toes. Push with the ball of the foot and simultaneously pivot at the ankle on the downstroke so that the foot levels out between 2 and 3 o'clock, and continue this motion so that at the bottom of the stroke the toes are lower than the heel. The main thing to strive for is smoothness and steady, even pressure. Practise this slowly, in a high gear, and away from traffic so you can concentrate on watching your feet.

Toe clips are a great boon. They allow you to have a feather-light touch on the pedals with no fear of losing grip. In fact, you cannot spin properly without them. They are completely safe. Smooth-soled conventional shoes can always be slipped out of the pedal even if the straps are tight. If using cycling shoes with cleats or ridges, keep the straps loose when riding in traffic.

The technique for getting under way is simple: start with loose straps. Straddle the bike, slip a foot into a pedal at the 1 o'clock position, and tighten the strap. Push off, using the downstroke of this crank to get you under way, and simultaneously reach down with the free foot, give the pedal a light tap to spin the toe clip around to the proper position, slip in foot, and tighten strap. It sounds more complicated than it is. The key is the deft, light tap to the pedal to bring the toe clip around so you can slip your foot in. Practice will soon make it second nature. When coming to a stop, reach down and loosen one strap so you can get your foot back in easily when under way again. Do not worry about being trapped by toe clips. I have made zillions of emergency stops and have always been able to get my feet free. On the other hand, do not tempt fate by riding in heavy traffic with ultra-tight straps. And if you use sneakers or other soft-soled shoes (bad—not enough support), or cleated bicycling shoes, keep the straps loose when conditions warrant.

Cadence

This subject was mentioned in connection with gearing. Briefly, human beings pedal most efficiently at a certain number of crank rotations per minute. The optimum cadence varies with the physical condition and technique of the individual rider. Generally, novices run 60-85 rpm, experienced tourists approach 100 rpm, and racers run 120-130 rpm and up.

Most people gear too high and pedal too slowly. They don't think they are going anywhere or getting any exercise unless they are pushing against resistance. It is precisely this pushing which creates fatigue. It is much better to pedal rapidly against relatively little resistance. Especially when first starting with a bike, always try to pedal as rapidly as you can without going into orbit. As a rough rule of thumb, if your legs are on fire, you are pushing too hard; if you are gasping for breath,

you are spinning too fast. Maintaining a comfortable balance between these two extremes is the primary reason for having lots of gears; always shift up or down as necessary to maintain an even cadence. Learn to shift just before you need the new gear. Do not let a hill slow down your cadence, for example, but shift just before you hit it, and as needed going up. The way you will be able to churn along will be edifying.

Bumps

When you come to bumps, potholes, cables, etc., put most of your weight on the pedals and handlebars. This allows the bike to pivot underneath you, reducing shock for both you and the bike. You know how motorcycle scramble riders stand up on the pegs? Like that. Over washboard surfaces with lots of little bumps, use a higher gear ratio than normal; pushing against the pedals will increase the amount of weight supported by your legs.

Braking

Try to use your brakes as little as possible. This will help you to anticipate traffic conditions in advance. Be careful of braking too hard and skidding, or pitching

yourself over the handlebars. It is the front brake which does most of the work, and the more rapidly you decelerate, the more work it can do. This is because weight is transferred forward, increasing the coefficient of friction between the front tyre and the road surface. Simultaneously, weight on the back tyre is lessened slightly, decreasing the coefficient of friction and making it more liable to skid. The technique for a rapid or panic stop is thus one of moving body weight to the rear while progressively increasing pressure on the front brake and simultaneously holding pressure on the back brake just below the point where the wheel will lock and skid. It is a co-ordinated sequence of events that can only be learned by practice. Start with quick stops from low speeds and gradually increase velocity. Really throw your butt back as you hit the brakes, transferring most of your weight onto the pedals. This helps lower the centre of gravity. Get to the point where you are stopping the bike just as fast as you can. Simulate emergency stops by having a friend cue you at unexpected moments.

Once you master hard braking, keep your technique fresh and sharp with regular practice. Knowing is not enough. The reflexes have to be kept in shape so that in a real emergency, you make the right moves without cognition. Some people feel foolish doing this sort of thing—cowboy. Fah. Better to burn some rubber and have an idea of what you can do with your bike. It's also a dynamic check on the condition of your brakes.

In slippery conditions, or when banked hard over in a turn, favour the rear brake. The rear wheel does have a greater tendency to skid, but if it slips you may still be able to keep yourself upright, and at worst will land on your hip. If the front wheel washes away you've a good chance of landing on your face.

In wet conditions frequently apply the brakes lightly to wipe water off the rims. Don't get caught napping, otherwise you may need four or five times the distance for stopping with dry brakes.

Going down long hills avoid overheating the wheel rims by pumping (on-off-on-off-on etc.) the brakes. Always be able to stop. If you find yourself wondering if the brakes will work—say on a very steep pitch—find out at once. Ride within your experience. If the descent is longer or steeper than you've made before, periodically stop and check the rims for overheating.

On the other side of the coin, if you've got a clear road don't be afraid to let the bike move out and breathe. Past 20 mph you've got a free speed control—air resistance. For speed, a racer will tuck into a full crouch, tighten in the elbows, and hold the pedals at 3 and 6 o'clock. If you sit bolt upright with arms and legs splayed apart, you'll find that air drag is often all you need to keep speed at a comfortable level. An important advantage in using this technique is that the mechanical brakes are kept fresh and ready.

Turning

If you ride a bicycle, then by definition you can turn it. But there are different methods and styles of turning.

Under way, a bicycle is in a constant state of imbalance. A tendency to lean one way will be corrected by the rider, the bike will move through centre of balance to lean the opposite way, and the rider will correct again. Most turning consists simply of taking advantage of a lean in the desired direction. Instead of correcting, the rider allows the lean to continue and thus effects a turn. The feeling is that the rider has changed balance and the bike has followed suit, and in that bicycle geometry is designed for a certain amount of self-steering, the feeling is accurate enough. The rider does in fact change balance. This type of turn has two faults: it is slow, and it puts rider and bicycle weight in one single line down to the point of tyre contact with the road.

In racing, and in traffic riding, it is often necessary to turn—FAST! This can be done by hauling back on the handlebar end opposite to the direction in which you wish to go. The bike will move out from under you, you will start to fall, and then you will TURN. Can you see it? In the 'normal' turn you topple to one side gradually; in the 'haul handlebar' turn you snatch the bike out from underneath you, and immediately fall into a turn. It is very handy for avoiding unexpected obstacles such as broken glass. In effect, you go one way, the bike goes the other, and afterwards you catch up with each other. Like panic braking, this type of turn must be learned slowly, and with lots of room for manoeuvring.

Another type of turn consists in laying down the bike, while you remain relatively upright, i.e., the bike 'leans' more than you do. This is useful when the road surface is rough, because then part of the rider's weight pivots as the bike moves up and down, lessening the load on the wheels. Better for the bike, better for you. It is also a quick turn, although not as fast as hauling handlebar.

Yet another type of turn consists of leaning the body more than the bike. This is a very standard technique for fast riding on shale and gravel, and is thought to lessen the chances of skidding. When I unexpectedly encounter a wet manhole cover or oil slick while turning I throw the bike up while keeping my own weight down. This, and the lay down turn, can be done by moving the whole bike underneath you while you pivot sideways at the hips, and can be accelerated by hauling on the handlebars as well.

Haul, lay down, and set up turns are esoteric in description but relatively simple in practice. You can learn them in a backyard or empty parking lot. For your own safety you should be able to execute a haul turn instantly, whenever circumstances require.

Climbing

Climbing technique depends on the length and pitch of climb, the kind of bike, and the condition and nature of the rider. A racer is more likely to 'honk'—stand up out of the saddle and use body weight to help drive the cranks around. A heavily laden tourist is more likely to drop into bottom gear and twiddle up—stay in the saddle while spinning the cranks lightly and rapidly.

Unless you know that you can attack a hill and win, it is generally better to start calmly and moderately and keep some strength in reserve. On very long climbs do not look at the top; concentrate on the immediate moment and surroundings, and on maintaining a steady rhythm. If there is a long downgrade after the crest, keep your legs moving as you coast down, to prevent them from stiffening up.

Fast is Safe

Every cyclist must know how to ride in traffic, just as pedestrians have to know how to cross the street. Simply, cycling in traffic is dangerous. Fear of an accident with a car is the principal deterrent to cycling, and is an amply justified concern—nervousness when first venturing into traffic indicates a sound mind. However, with time and experience you can learn to ride with a level of knowledge and skill that greatly reduces the risk of accidents. The outcome of riding in traffic depends less on the situation than on what you do. But the element of risk is constant. Something can happen out of the blue, through no fault of your own, that wipes you off the face of the earth in a twinkling.

Taking a bath is also a risky affair. And people die unexpectedly in bed. The amount of traffic riding that suits you is entirely your decision. Although the basic principles are the same, there is a considerable difference between mixing it up with heavy weekday commuter traffic and cycling to the park on Sunday. I'll help you as best as I can, but the go/no go decision is yours.

The most important thing to understand about riding in traffic is the need for attentiveness. You must be alert at all times and know everything that is going on, from the size of the pebbles on the road to the debris which might fall on you from a construction project to the number and type of vehicles before and behind you—absolutely everything. Traffic riding requires total concentration. There is no time for day-dreaming or idyllic pastoral pleasures.

Some people are just born inattentive. If you are one of these and a survivor, you've probably learned to steer clear of risky places and situations. Perhaps you prefer walking to cycling or driving a car, because it leaves your mind free to wander. Great, but if you ride a bike then it should be off-road, or on cycle paths. If you let your mind wander while you are cycling in traffic, you may only survive as a statistic.

It's not all bad. Attentiveness has benefits. Total engagement is refreshing. For example, I like physical challenges but spend a lot of time pushing a keyboard. For me the change of pace that jamming through traffic provides is often exhilarating. As they say, it takes your mind off your troubles. More to the point, once you gain experience you are still alert, but relaxed. Moving easy. Is crossing the street a C. B. DeMille production for you? In a more relaxed state attentiveness is fun; you see more, notice more, feel more. Every once in a long while I give a ride a miss. I might be unhappy, and perhaps not attentive enough. Or out of sorts, and inclined to be too aggressive. But if I'm feeling good it is hard to keep me off a bike. And if I'm marginal, I know from experience that a bike ride will probably chase the blues away and cheer me up.

There are at least two drawbacks to riding in traffic that have no redeeming features: air pollution and harassment.

Air Pollution

Inhaling car exhaust fumes and other pollutants is a serious health hazard for cyclists. The physical activity of cycling increases the effectiveness of the body's own natural defence mechanisms against airborne pollutants; in comparison with motorists in the same locations, cyclists have lower blood levels of lead and carbon monoxide. Still, in traffic you are at nose level with the source, and it cannot possibly be good for you.

What are you in for? It's difficult to say exactly. One statistic that has been around for years is that the average urbanite inhales the equivalent in particles and poisons of two packs of cigarettes a day. I've got a much more personal index. I used to do training rides in the local park early in the morning, before it opened at 7 a.m. and cars entered the road. On each outing I tried to shave a few seconds off my best lap time. It was edge-of-performance riding, and if I was late and the park opened and just one lousy car got on the road, I felt the difference. Even after the car disappeared out of sight, the fumes hanging in the air made me dizzy, cut down on the amount of oxygen I was getting, and slowed my time.

Motor vehicles are pretty well the beginning and the end of the air pollution problem, contributing up to 85 per cent of all air pollution in urban areas. They emit lead, unburned petrol, nitrogen oxides, sulphur oxides, carbon monoxide, hydrocarbons, and grit. The worst for the cyclist are lead and carbon monoxide.

Up to 99 per cent of the lead in the air comes from petrol combustion. Across Britain, the weight amounts to some 7,500 tons annually. In London alone, nearly 4 tons of lead pollute the air each day. For the urbanite, this means breathing air containing up to 10,000 times as much lead as would occur naturally, and carrying a body weight of lead 500 times greater than when his or her ancestors relied on biomechanical and renewable energy sources. Fruit and vegetables grown within the London area contain so much lead that health authorities have declared them unfit for human consumption.

How dangerous is lead? Very. The list of possible damages is amazing, and ranges from headache, a string of severe disabilities including arthritis, gout, and heart disease, through to simply shortening your lifespan. Lead damages the brain, liver, kidney, and central nervous system. But perhaps the worst is that lead makes you stupid. Researchers the world over have shown that children exposed to high lead levels are associated with low intelligence and verbal skill, bad hearing, and slow reaction times. In Europe it is now estimated that one in three children is suffering damage from lead pollution.

Most countries saw the light ages ago. The Russians eliminated lead from petrol in all their major cities as early as 1959. In America the 1970 Clean Air Act established requirements for vehicle emissions, and now half the cars there run on unleaded petrol. Just about all the cars in Japan run on unleaded petrol, and ditto all new cars in Australia from 1985 onwards. West Germany, Sweden, and Switzerland all have greatly reduced levels of lead in petrol, and the Germans plan to eliminate it completely. In Britain, however, the government and the motor vehicle industry have consistently resisted lowering the level of lead in petrol.

Lead is added to petrol in order to raise the octane rating and reduce combustion instability, or engine 'knock'. Lead also promotes mechanical wear and tear, however, and so to get it back out of the motor, scavenging agents are also added to the petrol, along with carcinogenic anti-wear agents. It's a real witch's brew, and completely unnecessary. There is now a cheap octane improver of very low toxicity, MTBE (methyl tertiary butyl ether), which burns better and does less damage to the engine. MTBE is not used because the major oil companies have a good thing going in lead additives. The firm Associated Octel controls the majority of the markets for lead additives outside North America, and is owned jointly by BP, Chevron, Mobil, and Texaco. In 1979 net profit before tax was £6.8 million. Associated Octel got government subsidies as well, and two Queen's Awards for exports.

In terms of immediate risk, carbon monoxide is the greatest hazard for the cyclist. Cars push nearly 4 million tons of the stuff into the air every year. Carbon monoxide is a classic poison which interferes with the oxygen-carrying capacity of the blood. Long before it kills, this action results in decreased alertness, headaches, vague dizziness, and nausea. Just the thing for riding in traffic. For bonuses, heart problems, memory loss, emphysema, and cancer. Whee.

On a broader canvas, emissions such as nitrogen oxides and hydrocarbons contribute to forms of photochemical pollution. One such is ozone, which in high levels can cause eye, nose, and throat irritation, and affect the respiratory system. Another is acid rain, a chemical pollution that is destroying forests and lakes across Europe— and so also livestock, wildlife, and fish.

There are two ways of reducing the levels of carbon dioxide, nitrogen oxides, and hydrocarbons emitted by cars. One is the so-called 'lean-burn' engine which is reasonably effective at coping with carbon monoxide and nitrogen oxides, but does little to remove hydrocarbons. The other is the catalytic converter which is in effect a filter, and only works with lead-free petrol. Converters are effective against carbon monoxide, nitrogen oxides, and hydrocarbons, and have been widespread in America since 1975. They are also used in Japan, Canada, and Australia.

The world's leading catalyst manufacturer is—British! At last count they have sold 55 million converters, every last one of them overseas. Why doesn't the British motor industry and its trade association, the Society of Motor Vehicle Manufacturers and Traders, want to know about converters? Because they have opted for the lean-burn engine in an attempt to reduce cost and thereby obtain a commercial advantage over Japanese, European, and American car manufacturers. The bill for this goes to you— by air.

Will the government help? No. There is already an existing EEC Directive on controlling vehicle emissions, but the government have stated that they will not necessarily enforce this. They are instead lining up with the motor industry and supporting the lean-burn engine. No wonder Britain has the unhappy distinction of being the dirtiest country in Europe.

As a cyclist you are better off with regard to pollution than a motorist or pedestrian, but minimize your exposure when you can. Try to avoid congested routes by travelling back streets and through parks, and when possible, avoid riding during the peak traffic rush hours, and on heavily used steep hills, which is where cars really pour out the junk. Your chances are a lot better if you take in an adequate amount of vitamin C. It reduces the toxicity of all sorts of things, including lead, carbon monoxide, and nitrogen dioxide. Some people feel that the alleged benefits of vitamin C are a lot of hogwash. Others—some of them pretty smart—think the stuff is useful. A well-balanced diet with as much real, fresh food as possible, will help in equipping you to deal with pollutants. One nice thing about cycling is that your fuel is important, and this creates a predisposition for foods that are actually nutritious. So to some extent, matters take care of themselves.

Cycling is a biological activity that naturally makes you aware of the terrible problem of air pollution. If you want to help in the fight for clean air, give tangible support to the group at the forefront of battle: Friends of the Earth, 26-28 Underwood Street, London N1 7JQ.

Harassment

Motorists routinely harass cyclists. Sometimes it is unintentional, and sometimes it is deliberate.

Traffic involves many points of conflict where resolution is up to the road users themselves. Driving a car in traffic requires controlled aggression; an indication to other road users of what is to happen next, followed by action. In light traffic this give and take usually goes smoothly enough, but in heavy traffic it can easily get out of hand. Just as when the mouse population in a cage is intensified and the mice become progressively more and more frenetic, motorists in heavy traffic tend to be more aggressive. The more retarded the journey and the more futile their efforts at advancement, the more angry they become.

Matters are made worse by the fact that only a few people treat motor vehicles strictly as a means of transport. Ego, status, and territory are all closely intertwined with motor vehicles. It is these psycho-

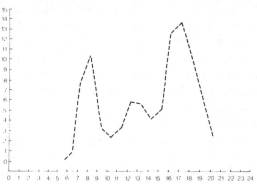

Percentage of casualties per hour of the day

logical factors, rather than mechanical aspects such as braking capacity, which are the main cause of 'accidents'. Driving a car is a sexually based expression of power and potency. That this leads to risk-taking is clearly reflected in insurance premium rates: higher if you are young, male and/or operate a powerful car, lower if you are experienced, female and/or operate a vehicle of modest power. The common denominator is greater or lesser aggressiveness.

Traffic is an environment of regularized confrontation involving fundamental instincts and emotions—a sanctioned madhouse. It doesn't have to be that way, but it often is. In such circumstances the physical vulnerability of a cyclist is a serious disadvantage. Motorists have strong metal cocoons; cyclists have nothing. In any direct confrontation, they lose. And as the insurance premiums show, some motorists are much more aggressive than others. Many will not hesitate to cut up a cyclist.

For beginning cyclists the confrontative and competitive aspects of riding in traffic appear stupid and daunting. What's the sense of stacking up a bike against a car? Novices tend to ride very timidly, and to make matters even worse by failing to take right of way when appropriate.

Intermediate cyclists know enough moves to feel victimized when a motorist is too aggressive. At this stage, frustration with the unfairness of it all can be acute, and the reaction to abuse from a motorist one of extreme and unsettling anger. If the first instinctive reaction to danger is to cower, the second is to strike back. Often this is a great idea. For many motorists who endanger cyclists, the fact that their protective shells are not all-embracing is a shocking revelation. But this method of operating has serious drawbacks.

In most bike-car confrontations the cyclist is helpless to do anything but preserve life and limb while the motorist escapes. When the cyclist finally does catch up with an errant motorist, the accumulated frustration can erupt in violent anger that is all out of proportion to the circumstances. Sometimes it is rough justice, and sometimes it is wrong. Either way, in the long run rage is debilitating and at odds with having a good time. And while venting your spleen may make you feel better, an altercation

FEMALES—WARNING

Female cyclists are subject to harassment from motorists and passers-by. In form, this ranges from insulting lewd comments to outright assault, where a motorist will reach out and knock a moving female cyclist to the ground. I do not have statistics on this sort of thing, but it most definitely happens, and female cyclists must take warning.

In a fantasy world, an endangered cyclist would be a reincarnated Bruce Lee, and beat the attacker senseless. In real life it is hard to get up after being knocked off your bike because someone goosed you, or clouted you with a baseball bat. This kind of thing happens, to both men and women.

Please be scared now, it might help you to be careful.

is likely to push the motorist into behaving even more wrongly in an effort to be right—the usual defence for stupidity is anger.

Part of becoming a skilled cyclist is learning to stay out of trouble in the first place. You'll ride careful but comfortable. Most of the potential bad incidents can be spotted in advance and avoided, including the unconscious or deliberate evils of motorists. Your own skill is what determines if your journeys are smooth and easy, or jerky and hard.

But there is one category of motorist for which there is no good answer: killers who deliberately mow down cyclists. It happens more often than most people imagine.

Homicidal intent with a car is difficult to establish. Typically, when a cyclist dies at hands of a motorist, the worst charge is negligence, and the penalty a fine and perhaps a period of time for which the motorist's licence is suspended. Often there is no penalty at all. Killers know that if they off someone with a gun, they are in trouble. If the instrument is a car, it is called an accident.

It is one thing to dice with a motorist for space and territory, and quite another to find that someone in a car is trying to kill you. There are no good answers for this problem. An immediate counter-attack is usually impractical; you are too busy trying to stay alive. If matters do get to the state where you can fight back on a physical level, you may well wind up facing criminal charges. Proving that a motorist has made a deliberate attack is difficult, but if you pull a motorist out of a car and beat him or her senseless, and/or use weapons, then an attack is clearly evident, and you may be the one who goes to the dock. Do not confuse life and justice. There are times when you should retaliate, and later on I explain some of the methods for doing so. But in general, responding to the threat of danger with anger is non-productive, serving only to destroy your peace of mind and, possibly, get you into trouble.

Why am I telling you all these wonderful, cheerful things? How would you like it if I said to go swimming in a stretch of ocean, and neglected to mention that the waters were infested with sharks? The analogy is interesting, because the patterns are very similar. Cars and sharks alike have their ways of moving and doing things. Sharks are feared out of proportion to the actual danger they present. People with the right temperament who know what is going on can handle sharks comfortably. There are right moves and wrong moves—but sometimes sharks just up and bite. Cars are the same. There are right moves and wrong moves for riding in traffic, but sometimes cars just attack. If you ride in traffic there is always a chance that you won't come back. In Britain, hundreds of cyclists are killed every year. No matter how good you are, you might be one of them. If you cannot accept and deal with that possibility, then do not ride in traffic.

Riding

There are innumerable physical hazards to look out for when riding in traffic, but motor vehicles are your main concern. Theory says that bikes have the same rights and privileges as other types of vehicles. The facts are otherwise.

A motor vehicle is an inherently rapid piece of equipment. For motorists, anything which obstructs forward progress—such as a slow-moving bicycle—should not be there. They may be wrong, but it is essential to understand how they think. As a cyclist you are a relative nonentity. As often as not, motorists will cut you off, make turns right in front of you, or sit on your tail when there is no room to pass. It never occurs to them to put on the brakes and give you room to manoeuvre, as they would for another car or lorry.

Many motorists are incompetent, under the influence of alcohol or drugs, or all of these things. Any cross-section of drivers will find elderly, obese, and otherwise infirm people with the motion capacity of a frozen sloth. They may think they are all right when in charge of a motor vehicle, or even hot stuff (drunks especially), but the truth is that their control of a vehicle is marginal. If something untoward happens they are unlikely to react in time, or correctly. Such people are also unlikely to be cyclists themselves, and therefore unfamiliar with how cyclists behave.

Riding successfully in traffic requires a blend of determination and knowing when to give in. For example, try never to block overtaking cars. But if it is unsafe for you to let them pass, then do not hesitate to take full possession of your lane so that they *can't* pass. Both you and the other person have exactly the same right to use the street or highway. Possession of a motor vehicle confers no additional rights or privileges. It is very important that you understand and believe this. You have nothing to apologize for. You are not blocking or in the way. If anything, you are owed a vote of thanks for using a minimum amount of energy, not polluting the environment, and not endangering lives. At the same time you have to be practical. A lot of motorists are outright maniacs. No matter how right you are, any confrontation with a motor vehicle will see you the loser.

As a cyclist you may not always be accredited a rightful place in the scheme of things, but you should nevertheless be capable of riding according to the Highway Code. In general, you are supposed to ride as well to the left as is consistent with safety; obey traffic signs and signals; give way to pedestrians at zebra crossings; and signal turns and stops. Left turn is left arm held straight out to the side, right turn ditto with the right arm, and stop a downward patting motion of the extended right arm. If the Highway Code is unfamiliar to you, then get a copy of the Code from a post office and study it. You can also enrol in the National Cycling Proficiency Scheme which trains and tests in the fundamentals of cycling and the code. It takes only a few hours and is free. Inquire at your local police station or school. Perhaps best of all is the 'Bike-Mate' scheme run by various cycling campaign groups. This pairs you with an experienced cyclist in your area who keeps you company on your first few rides, showing you the ins and outs of handling traffic, the local short cuts, and other useful lore. For information, contact The Cycle Campaign Network, Tress House, 2 Stamford Street, London SE1.

This may all seem a bit much to you. The popular image of cycling is that it should be happy-go-lucky and carefree. Not in traffic. Getting about on roads is a serious business which, if it is to be done safely and with consideration for the rights of others, requires that you know what is going on. I bad-mouth motorists

KNOW YOUR ENEMY

There are sharks, and there are sharks. Some are harmless, or attack only in specific circumstances, but certain kinds are dangerous as a matter of course. Motorists are the same. The key differential that shapes the danger potential of a motorist is personality. It's the basis for car sales, and is the critical element in road safety and crashes. The story is clearly reflected in car insurance premium rates, where drivers are risk-graded by age, gender, and driving record. Young males are the most crash-prone, middle-aged females the least. Why? Simply, males and the young are more aggressive. Another element is driving record. A history of offences or crashes predicates more of the same, and again, personal attitude is an important factor: in one study, motorists convicted of drunken or reckless driving were asked to rate their own driving abilities; the majority described themselves as being as good as, or better than, most drivers.

Cars are risk-graded in insurance groups (IG) from 1 to 9 by power to weight ratio, general performance, and cost. IG 1 is safest, IG 7 and up is the red danger zone—IG 8 costs 400 per cent more than IG 1, and IG 9 for high-performance cars is available only by individual quote. Basically, the faster and more expensive the car, the more likely it is to have a crash.

Drivers and cars combine in different ways to increase or decrease the degree of potential danger. A 5-year old, modestly powerful IG 5 car is quite dangerous with a young buck at the wheel, and safer when piloted by a kind grandmother. Note cost as an important factor; the young can rarely afford advanced instruments of warfare such as very expensive IG 9 BMWs and Porches, and make do instead with older models of large-engine IG 7 and 8 Rovers and Fords, or, if money is short, with ancient, small-engine family saloons pepped up with go-faster stripes, chromed wheels, and faulty silencers—IG 20, if there were such a category. Note also that the cost factor cuts both ways; it is money and not skill that enables the operation of a dangerous IG 8 or 9 car, and so while some drivers of such vehicles are well-meaning enough, very few are competent. Recent studies suggest that there could be a link between expenditure of over £20,000 on a car, and low intelligence.

As a cyclist you need to be able to rate the danger index of drivers and cars at a glance. You'll find out about this sort of thing soon enough, but meanwhile, here is an essential shortlist:

● Rover 3500. IG 8. The worst. Muscle car driven almost exclusively by aggressive males, as compensation (according to marketing studies) for stunted penes. Equivalent to Great White Shark (JAWS), violent and dangerous in the extreme. Really—stay away from them.

● Ford Capri. IG 8. Classic muscle car, older models favoured by young drivers who regard motoring as a form of combat.

● Ford Granada. IG 8. Mixed-mode muscle/status car, older models are hand-me-downs for people who haven't made it up the ladder, or who are slipping back down, and Granada drivers therefore tend to be bitter, vicious, and sometimes totally demented.

● BMW. IG 7-9. In new models, *nouveau riche* drivers who think they are high-performance pilots because of the cost of the car, but real ability is very thin, and blunders are frequent—ask any auto body repair shop. Drivers of older models are usually desperate for an upward shift in class, and are quick to challenge cyclists and pedestrians for road space.

● Volvo. IG 6-8. Middle of the middle class. Loaded with safety features—for the driver, who is often oblivious of cyclists. Not malevolent, but through sheer elephantine ignorance, a considerable danger nonetheless.

● Ford Sierra. Company car favoured by people in a constant hurry, and more than willing to cut up cyclists.

● Vauxhall Astra. IG 5-7. Amother popular company car, noted for hard-nosed, abrupt behaviour and frequent insurance claims.

● Morris Marina. Famous for a body design that severely restricts the driver's ability to see.

● Renault 25. IG 8. Yuppie performance car given to shooting ahead at every oppor-

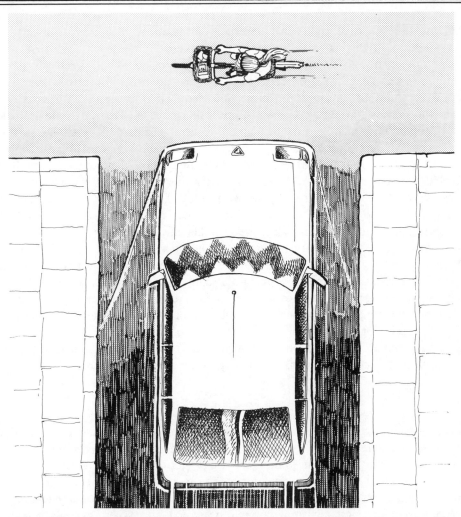

tunity. Like the infamous Jaguar E-type sports cars, few Renault 25s—or their drivers—ripen to an old age.

● Citroen 2CV. Small, sewing-machine engine and quaint but practical body design. Drivers are normally considerate of other life forms, but are governed by a constant need to preserve momentum, and often charge hills no matter what.

● Mini-cabs. Usual identifying characteristic is an add-on aerial held with a suction cup or magnet, trailing a wire into the interior of a 4-door saloon or estate. Mini-cab drivers do not have the training of licensed taxi-cab drivers, and combine less skill and forbearance with greater aggressiveness.

● Skip lorries. Big, wide, and very un-friendly. Drivers are paid per delivery, and push hard to make as many as possible. Known killer of cyclists.

● Postal vans. Big, pushy, and aggressive, especially at close quarters.

The list goes on, and the basic pattern remains the same: aggressiveness, power, and speed are coefficients of high crash rates; the less of these qualities, the fewer crashes. I say crashes, because accidents are events without apparent cause, a term that cannot be applied to the outcome of mixing powerful cars with drivers in every physical and emotional condition, from depression and apathy through to hysteria and in-coherent fury. What happens on the roads is not at all down to chance, and if you pay careful attention to the other players, you can vastly better your odds.

a lot, but they do have rights that deserve consideration. Moreover, claiming your own status and rights is possible only if you know the rules in the first place.

Rules are relative to time and place. In America many motorists charge through red lights as a matter of course. There, you are not long for this world if you rely on the rules of the road for protection. You have to assume that if there is a way for someone to get you, the attempt will be made. The only rule is to survive. The result is anarchy. In Britain the general standard of road behaviour is more advanced, and most road users abide by the rules. You can usually count on motorists to stop for red lights, and they rightfully expect the same of you. If you can abide by the rules, do so. We'll all be better off. But there are times and places when it is safer to make your own rules. For example, it is often better to jump a light so that you have time to get out of the way of faster vehicles. In countries like Holland, early start green lights for cyclists are the norm. I think that personal safety takes priority over regulations, but be sensible and discreet when breaking or bending the rules. Running a light and scattering pedestrians right, left, and centre is rank selfishness; slipping through when no-one will be bothered is rarely offensive. Do note, however, that in law, cyclists are dangerous characters subject to prosecution for endangerment of self or others, recklessness, dangerous riding, speeding, and riding under the influence of drugs or alcohol. You can be charged for traffic violations on a bicycle, and if you supply a motoring licence as identification, any convictions become part of your driving record.

Rolling

●Hands near or on brake levers at all times. With modern synthetic brake blocks you should be able to exert the maximum braking force the tyres will stand. If you are on a bike with poor brakes and must stop or die, try twisting the front wheel as you apply the brakes. So long as you're not going too fast, the bike will melt into the ground in a controlled crash as the wheel and forks buckle.

●Keep your eyes constantly moving both fore and aft. When looking behind do not twist your head; duck it down. Easier to do, quicker, and smoother. Do this constantly. At any moment you might have to swerve to avoid an obstacle, and must know if you have the room to do so. A rear view mirror will contribute greatly to safety, comfort, and speed.

●Be definite. Save meandering for country lanes where you can see for a long way in both directions. Ride in a straight line. Signal all turns clearly. Make right turns from the right lane and left turns from the left lane, if on a wide street. If you are going to do something, do it. Being definite takes the form of a certain amount of aggressiveness. Don't get bulldozed into immobility—nobody is going to give you a break. Make and take your own breaks. As far as most motorists are concerned, you either don't exist or are some alien foreign object which they want behind them. Draw attention to yourself and be super-clear about your intentions. Colourful clothing is a good idea.

●Always assume the worst. You can't see around the stopped bus? *Assume* a pregnant woman who is the sole support of 21 children is going to come prancing out. There is a car waiting to cross your lane? *Assume* it will, because *it will*. In four out of five accidents involving bicycles and motor vehicles, the motor vehicle committed a traffic violation. Always ride within a margin of control which allows you to stop or escape should absolutely everything go wrong.

●Look for openings in traffic, driveways, streets, petrol stations, etc., that you can duck into should the need arise. Try to plan where you would go should you and the bike part company. The natural tendency in a collision situation is to try desperately to stop. Many times your interest will be better served by launching yourself over an obstacle. Far better to hit the road at an angle than a car head-on.

●While not exceeding a speed which gives you control, try to keep moving. Within reason, avoid using your brakes. This will have the effect of making you figure out well in advance what traffic situations are going to occur. There is a car double-parked in the next block. Are you going to be able to swing out to pass it? Also, a lot of the danger from other vehicles in traffic comes from differences in velocity. If you are going slow, cars bunch up behind, crowd, become impatient, etc. A bike can easily keep up with and pass a lot of traffic. You may find it a bit unnerving to run neck and neck with taxi-cabs and lorries at first, but it is safer than offering a stationary target. Try to integrate yourself with the traffic.

●To this end, always be in a gear low enough to give you power and acceleration. In heavy traffic an even cadence is difficult to maintain, but try to keep your feet churning away and avoid getting stuck in a 'dead' high gear. As a cyclist, you have only a fraction of the power available to the motorist. To stay integrated with traffic requires that you be prepared to accelerate hard and quickly.

●On the other hand, do not tailgate. Car brakes are better than bike brakes. Most bike accidents consist of the bicycle running into something. Leave plenty of room up front. This is where motorists accustomed to running bumper to bumper will try to pressure you from behind, even though you are moving at the same speed as the car you are following. Maintain position and if they give you the horn, mix them up by giving them a friendly, cheerful wave. (I used to give them the finger, but too often this irks them into tailgating even more closely, the opposite of what I want.)

●Be extra-cautious at intersections where you already have right of way. Cars coming from the opposite direction and turning right will frequently cut straight across your path. Even if the vehicle is seemingly waiting for you to pass, don't trust it, for at the last moment it will leap forward. Letting a motor vehicle precede you to clear the way through an intersection or dodgy situation is often a good tactic. Motorists who will not hesitate to cut up a cyclist become lambs if the cyclist is shadowed in the lee of a big bus or lorry.

Another danger at intersections are cars coming up alongside from behind and then making sudden left turns. One way to stop this is for you to be in the centre of the lane. However, if the intersection you are entering has a light which is going to change soon, then traffic from behind may be storming up at a breakneck pace. You'd better be out of the way.

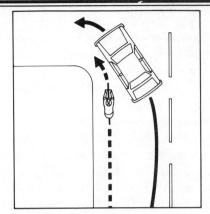 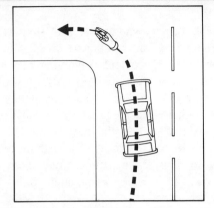

LOW SIDE. Car overtakes and pushes cyclist into the kerb.   **HIGH SIDE. Car is forced to follow cyclist.**

●In any city anywhere in the world, taxi-cab drivers are a hazard. All things are relative and in London, for example, most cabbies are decent. In America cabbies have the highest ulcer rate of any occupational group, as well they might, considering their working conditions and driving skills. Abilities vary, but most are just no good. New York City cabbies are the bottom of the barrel.

The reason taxi-cab drivers are often a problem is that they are professionals. Driving in traffic every day, they soon learn exactly what is going on and become accustomed to moving ahead at every opportunity. It is second nature, and does not even require hostile intent on their part. It is just something that they do. Every day. As long as you ride clearly and decisively, most cabbies will treat you with respect. If you start fumbling about, however, then they will quickly become impatient, and shunt you in behind a bus, or cut you off, or submit you to some other unpleasantness about which you can do nothing.

One particular hazard from taxi-cabs is their predilection for passing cyclists with too little room to spare. Again, it is a natural consequence of the cabbie's skill—most of them know where they are to the inch—and constant desire to forge ahead. A cyclist needs spare room to either side to allow for hazards such as potholes and other obstructions. If a taxi-cab is pressing you from behind and space is limited, either take and hold enough room for your own safety, or pull over and wave the taxi-cab on by.

Bear in mind that cabbies drive for a living. I don't enjoy it when a taxi-cab suddenly swerves in front of me in order to pick up a fare, but I do recognize that the driver needs to bring home the bacon. Make extra allowances for working drivers. If a cabbie or driver of a delivery vehicle does something truly untoward and dangerous, slang them; otherwise, live and let live.

●Very often you will be riding next to parked cars. Be especially careful of motorists opening doors in your path. Exhaust smoke and faces in rear view mirrors are tips. Even if a motorist looks right at you and is seemingly waiting for you to pass, give her/him a wide berth. Believe it or not, you may not register on her/his consciousness, and she/he may open the door in your face.

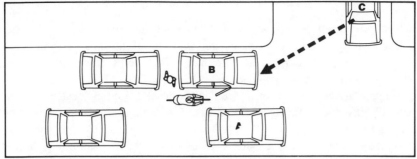

LOW SIDE. Cyclist is vulnerable to opening door of car B, and invisible to driver of car C at junction.

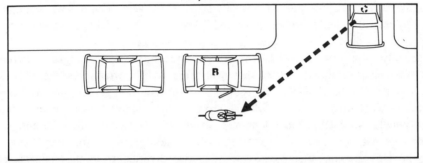

HIGH SIDE. Cyclist is clear of opening car door, and visible to driver of car at junction.

● The law requires you to ride as far to the left side of the left lane as is consistent with safety. This is a very elastic and sometimes abused definition. Cyclists have been ticketed for causing an obstruction by riding too far to the right, and there have also been instances of opening car door/cyclist accidents where the cyclist was held to be at fault. Always allow enough manoeuvring room to avoid road litter and potholes. Pass parked cars with room to spare should a door open. If somebody objects to your 'obstructing', ignore them. You are not obliged to risk your life for their convenience.

If the road or street is too narrow for overtaking vehicles to pass you with enough room, then ride bang out in the centre of the lane. Do not let them pass, or if it is a two-way road or street, make them pass in the opposite lane. You want room. Vehicle drivers may hoot and fume, but this is far safer for you than letting them pass with only inches to spare. You are equally entitled to road space and safe passage.

A common problem is a double-parked car or other obstacle that narrows the road space, bunching traffic into a single line. If you are to one side with the vehicles passing by in a steady stream, joining the line takes good timing. Blocking a motorist is all right if you obviously have no alternative, but not for long. The trick is to pick a gap that gives you reasonable clearance for the obstacle, signal your move, and go. If the stream of traffic is irregular, you can leave joining the queue until fairly late; if the stream is dense, make your move earlier, to avoid the risk of being boxed-in by an unkind motorist.

●On multi-lane roads or streets where there is a left-turn-only lane at an intersection, and you intend to go straight through, get into the right through-lane well before the intersection. Ditto if there is a bike lane. This helps minimize the chance of a left-turning vehicle cutting you off.

Lane changing in fast, thick traffic can take muscle. John Forester, author of the comprehensive *Effective Cycling* (MIT Press, Cambridge, Massachusetts, USA) and a noted authority on riding in all conditions, does a lane change by establishing eyeball-to-eyeball contact with a particular motorist while positioning himself with the clear intention of moving right (or left). If the motorist makes room, Forester then changes lane. The method has a distinct advantage in that both hands stay on the brakes, where they belong in heavy traffic. However, if you have enough room in front to take one hand off the bars and stick it out in a jabbing, emphatic signal, the situation is then much clearer to other road users.

One curiosity is that motorists sometimes understand body language better than signals. Glancing in the direction that you want to go often gets the idea across.
●The important general factor in relations with motorists is communication: here is what you want to do, here is what I want to do. Awareness is the key. Intensely mistrust people who natter on telephones while driving. They are inherently stupid. Ditto drivers eating ice-cream, guzzling soft drinks or beer, fondling their mates, lighting up fags, picking their noses, or otherwise diverted from the principal activity at hand. If a car is poised to enter the stream of traffic in which you are riding, and the driver is looking the other way, every alarm bell in your head should go off. You want eyeball contact. Hi there is no guarantee that a motor vehicle driver will do the right thing, but it does improve your chances.

It helps a lot if you know what is going on. You've got to be able to read other drivers and vehicles. For example, an astounding number of people expect big lorries and buses to contravene basic laws of physics. If you understand the problems of large vehicles there are many little courtesies you can extend that will be repaid in kind. Professional drivers appreciate craft. By the same token, don't expect someone grinding along in a wreck loaded with screaming kids to have much of a grip on what's happening. It is not that they mean harm, the problem is that they are not there in the moment. Keep track of neighbours. A young kid in an old heap with go-faster stripes who keeps alternately flooring the throttle and brakes is someone to stay away from. If something goes wrong—little old lady or doggie in the road or other surprise—young charger is likely to foul up. A big moving van may be awesome in size, but is better close company because the driver is a professional who is more likely to have his or her mind on the job.

Be aware of general conditions. Motorists are more aggressive in heavy traffic at peak travel periods, and also when driving under the influence of alcohol. Alcohol diminishes physical skill, mental judgement, and inhibition threshold. Drunks who cannot steer in a straight line imagine that they are racing trim, and are much more inclined to try and prove it. A motorist does not have to be over the legal limit to become more unskilled and belligerent. There is no amount of alcohol which is 'safe'. In Finland, motorists may not have any alcohol at all, not even from medicine, and the penalties for infringement are severe. The proof is in the pudding; Finland has fewer accidents, particularly of the drink-related type. In Britain, drinking and driving is a tacitly approved game that is a contributing factor in 25 per cent of accidents and over 1,100 deaths a year. Be particularly wary if you are out on the road at pub closing time. Friday and Saturday nights are the worst.

●Keep an eye on the road surface. Watch out for broken glass, stones, potholes, etc. Plenty of bumps and potholes are big enough to destroy a bike—and you. Going over bumps, cables, etc., get off the saddle and keep your weight on the pedals and handlebars. This is when toe clips and straps are reassuring.

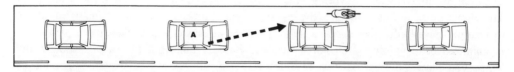

LOW SIDE. Cyclist has no room for avoiding potholes or litter, and is invisible to driver of car A.

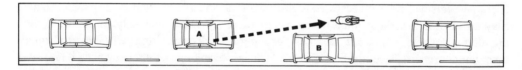

HIGH SIDE. Cyclist has room to maneuver, and can be seen by driver of car A. The fact that car B has moved out slightly also helps signal the presence of the cyclist to the driver of car A.

●Quite a few things can dump a bike:

Oil slicks in the centre of traffic lanes at busy intersections and on sharp curves. Whenever cars stop or turn hard, a little oil drops off. The resulting slick can send you off the road or sliding out into the middle of a busy intersection.

Newly wet streets. There is a light film of oil which until it is washed away mixes with the water to make a very slippery surface.

Wet manhole covers and steel plates can dump you in a hurry. So can wet cobblestones, wet autumn leaves, loose gravel, and sand. Wet paint stripes (such as at zebra crossings) are a particular hazard.

Many storm sewers are just the right size to swallow up a bicycle wheel.

●Ride with the traffic. Sometimes when there is no traffic coming the other way, it is better to ride in the opposite lane.

●The velocity of traffic on motorway-style roads which have no parking is usually too high to permit safe cycling. If you run in the centre of the lane, you block traffic. If you go to the side, cars whizz by you at high speeds with only inches to spare. Stick to streets with parked cars and look out for opening doors.

●Cars and lorries have a habit of pulling out unexpectedly and without signalling.

Look out for driveways, building entrances, construction projects, taxi-cab ranks, and any other possible source of a vehicle. Remember, you don't exist for many drivers. They look right at you, the image is flashed on their brain, but they don't comprehend. They don't *see* you.

And perhaps some do. One time in New York City I had the lights in my favour at an intersection with a police car waiting on the cross street. The eyes of the driver fixed steadily on me and he waited until I was just going through the intersection before pulling through a red light and right in front of me. Expect the unexpected.

● Pedestrians are awful. They don't think 200 lb of bike and rider coming towards them at 30 mph means anything, and will frequently jaywalk right in your path. The other side of this coin are the cyclists who hurtle past pedestrians with inches to spare. They don't always make it. Any collision between a cyclist and a pedestrian is going to be a painful affair for everyone. Respect the right of way of pedestrians. When you have the right of way, use a whistle or yell—and give way if you have to.

● Kids. As much of a hazard to the cyclist as to the motorist. Any child has the potential to race out suddenly into the street.

● Other cyclists. The fact that someone is riding a bike does not mean that they are on your side. Like other categories of road users, many cyclists do stupid things. Stay clear of other riders unless you know them, or they obviously know what they are doing. When you come up to a group of cyclists waiting at a traffic signal, take your proper place in the queue. When overtaking another cyclist it is your responsibility to keep clear, and make sure you do; if your front wheel touches the other bike, you will probably go down like a shot. By the same token, if a cyclist presses you hard from behind, let them by if you can, but otherwise, hold your line.

● Lights. Although lights at night are a legal requirement, many cyclists ride without them. This is insane. Lights help make you visible to motorists. Rear reflectors and pedal reflectors are useful. Wheel reflectors and front reflectors are useless and can be heaved into the rubbish. Lights are what might help you to be seen. The various kinds are discussed in Accessories. CAUTION: using lights does not mean you are safe. Some motorists will take no notice of you even if you are lit up like a starship. I know a lot of people who had to be convinced of this the hard way.

● Footpaths. It is illegal to ride on a footpath. However, a cyclist is closer to a pedestrian than a car is to a cyclist. Mixing cyclists and pedestrians together on footpaths is not only much safer than mixing cycles and cars on roads, it is not even dangerous. The accident statistics from Stevenage, where pedestrians and cyclists have shared common paths for years, bear this out. A number of factors make this so, but the most fundamental is that the cyclist, like the pedestrian, is vulnerable and exposed and has every interest in avoiding conflicts.

Riding on footpaths must be done with discretion—dashes through Sunday parks filled with strollers and wandering dogs are apt to end badly—and you must give priority to pedestrians, dismounting if necessary. But many footpaths are little used and offer a more sensible transit than running with the road traffic. Just remember, however rational your case, to ride on a footpath makes you liable to infringement of the law, an alternative you may prefer to risking your life.

Fast Is Safe

Cycling in traffic seemingly involves girding yourself for battle and inducing a constant state of morbid apprehension for your life. At one level this is true. The idea of mixing cars and bicycles together is crazy. Cars are an atavistic idiocy responsible for millions of deaths and injuries. It is entirely logical to want nothing whatsoever to do with them.

However, once you have a working appreciation of the hazards to be encountered in traffic, you will find that the situation can be made to work to your advantage. Riding fast promotes your own safety. This is because moving quickly demands that you anticipate and avoid the dangerous situations that would otherwise retard your journey. The best way to do this is to ride on what I call the high side—out in the mainstream of traffic.

So long as you shift along quickly enough to keep pace with the other road users, riding the high side is safer than trying to stay out of the way by keeping to the low side, near the gutter. Riding the high side largely eliminates hazards such as road litter, opening car doors, cars overtaking and turning left across your path, and stray pedestrians stepping off the pavement. All of these are a greater danger than the risk of being struck from behind by a motorist. Furthermore, on the high side you are more visible to motorists than when on the low side.

Emotionally, riding on the high side is more satisfactory than hiding in the gutter and waiting to be hit. Clear assertiveness diminishes rather than increases tension for the cyclist. The aim is to pass along smoothly, neither accelerating nor decelerating excessively. The mark of a good traffic rider is that she or he is in the right place at the right time. This skill is a function of awareness and a positive orientation, whereas tension is the negative outcome of worrying about finding yourself in the wrong place at the wrong time. Just reducing the need to slow down or stop will itself make for a more relaxed journey.

This is not an endorsement of a wholesale speed trial or kamikaze style of riding. Initially, the approach to learning about cycling hazards must be defensive. First save your neck. Once you have learned the ropes, however, treat riding in traffic as a game, and play it hard: the faster you can go, the safer you will be.

Having it back

An accident is a surprise. It is not the same thing as losing control of a bike because you pressed too hard. An accident is something you didn't expect. You need to know what to do when an accident starts to happen. The problem is not so much knowing what to do, however, as being able to do it.

Most people react to an imminent crash with panic. They may freeze into immobility and do nothing, or blindly clamp down on the brakes and lose directional stability. This can make a bad situation fatal. For example, if a car is about to hit you from the side and you death grip the brakes, the rear wheel is likely to lock up and send you down in a slide, to be rolled up underneath the car. If at the moment of impact you instead try to get clear of the bike and make a dive for the bonnet of the car, you may slide along to the windscreen and perhaps even over the roof. Not fun, but the survival chances are much better than if you are underneath the car.

Panic-induced muscular tension increases physical damage in a crash. The person who falls or is thrown and is able to stay loose and relaxed will suffer less injury than a person who tenses and tries to save him or herself. The ability to exercise the best of a series of bad options, and stay physically relaxed in a situation offering damage, can only be learned through experience. If you do not know how to fall, try to have someone with training—fighting experts, skydivers, skiers—give you some pointers. Fast off-road riding with a mountain bike is useful. A few spills are inevitable, and as long as they are in loose dirt, usually little damage results. This kind of play is even better on snow and ice.

Practise the braking and turning techniques discussed in the Riding chapter. Think of how to use them in various circumstances. If a car pulls up alongside you and then unexpectedly turns left, cutting you off, a sudden application of the brakes will simply pile you into the car. A rapid haul turn, however, just might avoid an accident, and if you do hit, you will both be going more or less in the same direction. Suppose a car pulls out in front of you from a side road or driveway. There may be enough room for a haul turn so that you hit the car a glancing blow. If there is not enough room to turn, then brake as hard as possible without skidding, and just before hitting the car launch yourself clear of the bike. You may be able to sail right over the car. Stay loose and roll when you hit the road.

If you are hit from behind. DO NOT BRAKE. Try to get away by steering to the side.

Having It Back

When a motorist does you dirt, one acceptable response is an explosive yell. It's the cycling equivalent of blowing a horn to signify potential or immediate danger.

A good yell can help you to release some of the adrenalin energy that danger generates. It can make a motorist just a touch uncomfortable, and is more effective if there are passengers in the vehicle. A lot of ruckus and commotion means that the motorist is doing something wrong, and the more passengers as audience, the greater the awareness of discord.

One of the most frequent sins of the motorist is to overtake a cyclist and then suddenly brake and turn left. The motorist knowingly creates trouble for the cyclist, and expects to get away with it through sheer greater size. This is a moment of opportunity. The cyclist is usually in the blind rear quarter of the vehicle and invisible to the motorist, who will be under some tension about the outcome of his or her misdeed. In such circumstances, a well-timed yell can startle the motorist into a momentary loss of vehicle control. If there is a nearby obstruction, the motorist may hit it.

Another unsettling tactic in a situation where a motor vehicle is actively risking an accident is to hit it hard with the flat of your hand. This makes a tremendous bang (especially if done on the roof). The best time for a direct attack is when a vehicle entering the roadway from the left and turning right cuts across your path. By swerving behind the vehicle, you create the welcome safety of diverging trajectories and with good timing you can give it a noisy bash on the flank. Do not use this ploy without a clear escape route. If you bang on a vehicle which is running alongside and crowding, you are just asking for the motorist to panic and do something wrong, or for a hot-head to give that little twitch of the wheel that will smear you forever.

One defence is attack. At close quarters you have the advantage of knowing where you are to the inch. Few motorists are that good. If someone starts to crowd you, one tactic is to call their hand by moving in close. You can run very tight if need be. Most motorists can't handle it and will give way. In heavy traffic this technique can also be used to brush motorists into giving you enough room. A completely different but effective ploy is to wobble unsteadily, which suggests that you are barely in control and might do anything next. The motorists' instinct is to shy away.

The cyclist is a guerrilla; maintaining a clear escape route is always paramount. Some club riders have been known to spray concentrated Ribena on a maleficent motorist's windscreen; the stuff takes an age to clear away, allowing ample opportunity for the cyclist to vanish. I cannot personally recommend this sort of thing. It might cause an accident in which totally innocent people were hurt. Moreover, enraging motorists only makes them nastier, and more willing to victimize cyclists. If you are tempted to tweak the tail of a motorist, think of the other cyclists who will also cross that motorist's path.

Think also of the basic odds. Some cyclists actively harass motorists. Sooner or

later they get more than they bargained for. David and Goliath routines are fun as games, or if you just don't want to back down, but if you get hurt doing this kind of thing, don't complain.

Remember, some motorists are certifiably insane. They will endanger you for fun, or to satisfy competitive emotions that are incomprehensibly stunted and malformed. If you start razzing them, they may literally try to kill you. It's happened to me more than once, with and without preliminaries. I don't mind a slanging match and a few choice insults, but mortal combat against a nutter armed with a 5000-lb car is too much. Experience—not just my own—records that the most frequent trigger for outright homicidal fury in a motorist is giving them the finger. I don't know why this particular gesture is so provocative, but don't use it unless you are ready for real trouble.

It is sometimes tempting to deliberately have an accident. The most appealing moment is when a motorist noses out in front of you from a side road, forcing you to slam on the brakes to avoid a collision. Sooner or later it will cross your mind to slack the brakes and hit the side of the vehicle, rolling on your shoulder and back over the bonnet or boot to a safe landing, but thereafter continuously complaining of a pain in your back requiring hospital examination, full involvement of the police, and a claim against the motorist's insurance company.

There are yet more tactics and actions for dealing with motorists, and some of them are pretty extreme. But wars never do anyone much good. At the end of the day, I've found that the ultimate put-down for motorists is simply to pass them.

Commuting

Commuting to and from work is a great way to enjoy cycling. If you live in the country then conditions for commuting will usually be excellent, and most kinds of bikes can be used for the job. If you live or work in an urban area, as most people do, then consideration should be given to the type of bike, selection of equipment, and general method used for the journey.

Bike

Road racing, cyclo-cross, and track bicycles each have distinctive characteristics appropriate to their intended use. So does the urban commuting bicycle. Many city streets are obstacle courses filled with bumps, potholes, uneven surfaces, steel plates which are slippery when wet, broken glass, bits of sharp metal, and other rubbish. In heavy traffic there is often not enough room for a cyclist to avoid an obstacle. A machine for these conditions must be tough. Theft is a constant problem in cities. An obviously expensive bicycle is more likely to be stolen, or stripped for parts. Finally, most regular commuters prefer a bike that requires a minimum of maintenance.

Several different types of bicycle are capable of coping with urban conditions. Each has advantages and disadvantages according to your particular situation and needs.

The classic heavy roadster offers a soft ride which helps to iron out the worst of the bumps, robust tyres which have a fighting chance of surviving glass and other road litter, and an upright riding position which allows a good view of traffic conditions. However, at 50 lb, heavy roadsters are hard work to pedal, and are not suitable for long journeys or steep terrain.

The 3-speed hub-gear roadster is lighter in weight and uses narrower, faster tyres, but is still not much of a speed machine or hill-climber. One performance improvement is to fit alloy rims and high-pressure tyres. An inexpensive way of improving hill-climbing ability is to fit a larger rear sprocket of 22 or 24 teeth. This limits top speed to around 20 mph, but this is adequate for most traffic conditions. Roadsters are not the most valuable of bicycles, but are easy to resell. Security is a problem.

Derailleur-gear road bikes are the obvious choice for long journeys and/or steep terrain. Models made expressly for commuting usually have alloy components, flat bars, mudguards, and a comfy saddle. Another good choice is a touring bike. A generous wheelbase and fork rake, strong rims with thick spokes, and stout tyres, will maximize comfort and stability over rough surfaces. Sealed bearings for the bottom bracket, headset, hubs, and pedals will help minimize maintenance.

Security is a problem. The best answer is someplace inside at work. If not there, see if you can promote something in another building. For locking up on the street, the only answer is a lock with a performance guarantee (see the chapter Buying a Bike for details). Some people keep a collection of locks at their work parking place, and carry a small lock in case of need. Others disguise a high-quality frame with a coat of dull-looking, sloppy paint, and substitute low-grade components (saddle, derailleurs, chainset). The resulting bike looks like an old banger but still goes fairly well. When locking up on the street some people take the additional precaution of disabling their bikes by slacking off the brakes or wheels, or removing the saddle.

The ultimate machine for urban cycling is the mountain bike. On an ordinary lightweight road bike, the sight of a jagged, yawning pothole will set your senses screaming with alarm. On a mountain bike you can laugh and attack the thing. Wide tyres and handlebars give a sure grip and utterly superior low speed handling. The

A PRACTICAL DEMONSTRATION—I.

County Councillor (to distinguished foreign guest): "You will get an admirable idea of how we sand the roads on an extensive scale. With this huge van we can cover the ground in one-third the time, and distribute ten times the quantity of —

A PRACTICAL DEMONSTRATION—II.

Councillor: "Great Sahara !!! —!!!"
Visitor: "Ah! Malheur!! —— a mort!!! —— sacre-e-e-e-e-e-e-e!!!!"

only thing that will stop quicker than a mountain bike is a long wheelbase recumbent, and I wouldn't want to live on the difference. When it comes time to snap away from a traffic light, a good surge through the extra-long cranks can leave even a pure road racing bike in the dust. You can go where you like—blazing down the fast lane, up and down kerbs, along canal tow-paths, straight through parks—the mountain bike will do it all and more.

Many mountain bike tyres designed for off-road use run well enough on properly surfaced roads. The trick is to inflate the tyre to a high pressure. Tyres rated at 35-45 psi will often take up to 80 psi without flinching. There are also models (such as the Panaracer Ibex or Ritchey Quad) that are dual-rated: around 40 psi off-road, 65-80 psi on-road. If you want to be more precise, run two sets of wheels, one with road tyres, the other with big gnarly knobbies for off-road bashing. This also allows you to have different ranges of gear ratios for each type of riding. For minimum fuss when making a switch, use the same size rims and model of freewheel. I prefer 22 mm rims, as they are very good with the 1.4-inch wide Specialized Nimbus tyre, and will also mount 2.125-inch wide knobbies. The more usual 28 mm rims do not match happily with tyres less than 1.75 inches wide. A 1.75-inch road tyre goes well enough, but the 1.4- and 1.5-inch models are lighter and more sprightly. The Specialized Nimbus is a wet weather tyre that grips the road like a leech. It's pretty good off-road, too, so long as conditions are not muddy. Completely bald, high-performance tyres go like silk and corner like a dream, but are very vulnerable to cuts from glass.

One way to bypass the security problem is to use a lightweight folding bike. These machines go where you go and can be tidily tucked away under a desk or in a restaurant cloakroom. If it suddenly starts to pour cats and dogs and you do not feel like getting wet, a folding bike is little trouble to take on a bus, train, or taxi-cab. This makes such a machine the favoured contender for mixed-mode transport. In performance, lightweight folding bikes are reasonable, but small wheels do not have the stability of large wheels over bumps and through potholes, and braking capacity is not of the first water. If you can, ride large wheels.

Routing

Bikes move in different ways than other vehicles. They can cut down back alleys, whiz through parking lots, and what have you. Even if you know the territory over which you plan to commute, it is worth obtaining a map and giving it a good study. Local cycle campaign groups and bike shops may have information on routes best suited for cycling. Very often, things are not what you thought they were. Working out good commuting routes is a matter of trial and error. What you are looking for are streets and roads that allow you to keep moving, but that do not embroil you in the worst of the traffic. A good ride is more important than the fastest possible journey. Start by drawing a straight line on the map between home and work. Pick out a trial route, bearing in mind whatever you know about the area. A direct route, for example, might crest three hills that you could avoid entirely with a slightly longer route. Or, perhaps there is a way to have one short, sharp climb, and then gentle downgrades for the rest of the journey.

Hard rules are difficult to suggest, because it all depends on where you are. London is not the same as Edinburgh, and neither is anything remotely like Stevenage. Explore. For the first few journeys allow at least twice the time you think you need. This gives a comfortable margin for problems, rest stops, sorting out parking, and so on. Relate what you discover to the map. You'll usually find that there are one or two obvious options to check out. After a week or two you'll probably have the optimum route down pat, but keep on exploring. You never know what you might find and anyway, it is fun to have different routes to run.

In some areas you are required to use cyclepaths if they are available. This can be a real problem, because many cyclepaths are badly designed and dangerous. They are littered with broken glass, cross-traffic, pedestrians, and parked cars. All too often they were built to get bikes out of the way of cars, not for bikes to run on. Some cyclepaths pass through desolate, ill-kept areas and are all right in daylight, but risk muggings during night-time. Other cyclepaths route alongside well-travelled streets or roads, but are then beset with dangerous cross-traffic for driveways, petrol stations, shopping centres, and such-like. You're safer out on the road. On the other hand, you might be lucky and be able to use a cyclepath built by people who knew what they were doing. Lots of them are really lovely, and in some places you can cover most of a journey without ever seeing a car. There's no way I can predict the exact conditions in your area; you'll have to look yourself.

An option that not many people know about are canal towpaths. Despite the abundance of 'No cycling' signs, you can cycle on towpaths administered by the Waterways Board if you need to do so in order to reach work or school, and have a permit (£1, from the British Waterways Board, 7th Floor, Gresham House, 53 Clarendon Road, Watford WD1 1LA). Canal towpaths are car-free and can be an idyllic part of your route, but be sure to ride with special care and consideration for other towpath users.

Joy

Commuting by bike is a wonderful way to get to know an area. It is easy to divert and explore—a new road, a hidden courtyard, a quiet mews, or whatever. I've lived and worked in and around various parts of London for years now, and each change of location has been accompanied by a galaxy of new things to see. I've found new restaurants, shops, neighbourhoods, farms, paths paved with the same stones trod by men in armour—the list is endless.

On the other side, you get to know some routes better than the back of your hand. You know every pothole and every bump, how the lights go, and a thousand and one other comprehensive details. If you want, you can elevate running a commuting route to an art form, timing the lights and junctions so that you flow through the entire journey like silk. You can go hot, really crowding the pace and chopping a little off your best time. Or go easy and see the sights. One of the best things about commuting by bike is that the route and kind of ride is your decision—every time!

Pointers

Keep the weight down. It's tempting to take along every tool you think you might need, a full set of waterproof garments, maps, and something for luck. But once the load gets up to a certain point you become a baggage-laden tourist rather than a rider—and no small part of the fun is riding. It's also a drag to have to cope with an assortment of gear when off the bike. I've boiled the essentials down to a few things—patch kit, spare tube, short pump, Mafac tool kit, and rain cap. In winter, lights. It all fits in a small saddle pouch or handlebar bag. Anything else I need I find or improvise. If I'm shopping or carrying along papers and books, I use a backpack or large shoulder bag. If you must regularly cart a lot of heavy gear, use a single pannier, and stow your important goodies in an ordinary plastic shopping bag to keep them dry in case of rain (no pannier is 100 per cent waterproof).

Cycling is warm work and, in cities, can expose you to a fair bit of dirt and grime. Wear cycling clothes and shoes if you can. They're much more efficient and comfortable. Invest in a high-quality cycling jacket that is waterproof but that breathes—see Accessories for more information. I keep an assortment of conventional glad rags at the office, and change to fresh clothes on arrival. If you're unlucky and not easily able to do this at your place of work, find a nearby public convenience or cafe with a loo and do a transformation—Shazzam!

You may want to limit your cycle commuting journeys to fine weather at first, but once the bug takes hold, you'll find that you want to use the bike if you can. When in doubt, ride. Rain and other miseries are a pain, but it's worse to miss a ride and then discover that, after all, it only drizzled. If the heavens cascade and you get soaked, it's not the end of the world—particularly if you have dry clothes available at the end of the journey.

The present deplorable state of Kingston Bridge

Country Roads

Touring is one of the real joys in biking. The only better way to see the countryside in close-up detail is by walking. Touring by bike has the advantage of mobility and luggage-carrying ability, however, and you can still always pause to explore an area or have a good look at something.

Touring can be done in a tremendous variety of ways. You can go for an afternoon's jaunt or spend a summer or more travelling thousands of miles. You can go as a self-contained unit with your own camping gear, or ultra-light with only a credit card as baggage and stay in inns, guest houses, and hotels. You can count the miles travelled, or concentrate on the scenery (yeah!). Your journey can include transit by auto, bus, train, boat, and plane, so that you can hop from one interesting place to another. You can have a plan, or absolutely none at all. Touring is a call to adventure, beauty, and new sights and experiences.

There's a lot to touring, and plenty for you to think about. At the same time it can be quite simple. Any bike headed for the sticks should have a tool kit, unless you don't mind pushing your bike a few miles to a bike shop and/or the possibility of an overnight stay until it opens. Equipment makes a difference, but the main thing is to get out there. My greatest, happiest tour was on a battered 1935 BSA whose vital parts shed like water.

Part of the fun of touring is figuring it out and planning or not planning for yourself. Some people insist that the only way to tour is with a meticulous

'A merry heart goes all the way,
　Your sad tires in a mile, a.'—*Shakespeare*

and detailed plan; others heave map and compass into the bushes and go wherever fancy takes them. For some the fun and relaxation comes as a result of planned and concentrated effort; for others it is through not thinking about anything. There is no 'right' way to tour. Each to his or her own. Accordingly, this chapter simply tries to give basic information about touring. It is not a step-by-step guide. It's up to you to decide where and when you want to go, and what sort of equipment you expect to need.

Resources

Books

There are plenty of books on cycle touring. One of the best is *Bike Touring*, by Raymond Bridge (Sierra Club Books, San Francisco, California, USA). It's enlightening, and full of detailed advice on bikes, equipment, planning—and enjoyment. *The CTC Route Guide to Cycling in Britain and Ireland*, by Nick Crane and Christa Gausden (Penguin Books, London, and Oxford Illustrated Press, Sparkford) is a classic that contains much useful lore, and 365 routes that reach the furthest corners of Britain. Good reading and a ride on the funny side is *Bike Tripping*, by Tom Cuthbertson (Ten Speed Press, Berkeley, California, USA). A tome full of basic information is *The Bicycle Touring Book*, by Tim and Glenda Wilhelm (Rodale Press, Emmaus, Pennsylvania, USA). *Cycling in Europe*, by Nicholas Crane (Pan Books, London, and Oxford Illustrated Press, Sparkford) is enticing and amusing, and has many useful pointers on designing and planning tours. *Cycle Touring in Britain and the Rest of Europe*, by Peter Knottley (Constable, London) has detailed chapters on tour preparation. *Weekend Cycling*, by Christa Gausden (Oxford Illustrated Press, Sparkford) is meticulous, clear, and colourful. The no-holds-barred mega-expedition is well covered by Nicholas Crane in *Richard's Mountain bike Book* (Oxford Illustrated Press, Sparkford). There are many other books, often written to cover areas outside Britain, but replete with general touring information. Pop along to a bookshop or well-stocked bike shop and see what strikes your fancy. Touring is a very individual affair, and for books in this area, the author's general attitude and tone can be more important than the absolute amount of information supplied.

Touring Clubs and Groups

A good way to get into heavy touring is to join a club or group. You get a planned tour, the benefit of a group leader who will set a pace within your capacity, and lots of free friendly help and advice. Tours can vary a good bit in character. Some are spartan and fast, others are gently paced and followed by a sag wagon to carry baggage and spare parts for the bikes.

First and foremost of the touring clubs is the Cyclists' Touring Club, Cotterell House, 69 Meadrow, Godalming, Surrey GU7 3HS. Membership (write for cost) includes the *Cycle Touring Club Handbook*, a thick list of 3,000 recommended accommodation addresses, places to eat, people who can fix bikes, and CTC local information officers for Great Britain; a list of overseas touring correspondents; information about touring areas, equipment, and travel by air, rail, and sea, including ferries, tunnels, and bridges; a catalogue of books and maps for Great Britain, the

Continent, and Morocco available through the bookstore; and a complete exposition of club services. For the tourist, the most important of these is the touring department, which has available a large library of comprehensive, personally researched tours complete with maps. The touring department will also plan and suggest tours for routes and areas you request, and will advise on cycle and personal equipment, gears, maps, and travel books. Other CTC services are too numerous to mention.

The CTC has 55 District Associations. Each has a programme of rides throughout the year, mainly on Sundays but also during the week. There are also local, national, and foreign tours led by experienced members, numerous national competitions and rides, and an annual grand celebration and get-together, the York Rally.

An essential organization for the economy minded is The Youth Hostels Association, Trevelyan House, 8 St Stephen's Hill, St Albans, Herts AL1 2DY. They have over 5,000 hostels in 64 countries, many in beautiful and historic areas. The hostels are sometimes spartan, but always serviceable. You provide your own sleeping bag, and help a bit with the chores. Inexpensive, and you can cook your own food. The association stores sell camping and touring equipment, have a tourist service, and run guided tours.

Organized Rides and Holiday Tours

A type of tour especially popular with newcomers is the organized ride complete with cook, bike mechanic, and van for carrying luggage, spare parts, and flaked-out riders. Tours can range in scope from simple day outings to the three-week, 900-mile John O'Groats to Land's End Great British Bike Ride. The best known organizer of these is Bike Events, P.O. Box 75, Bath, Avon BA1. Many others are listed in the spring issues of cycling periodicals.

You can also get your feet wet on a mass day ride such as the annual London to Brighton. Mass rides are popular throughout the country, and are in effect 'cyclists' days' where the organizers plan and map the routes, obtain permissions and co-operation from the police and other authorities, and arrange for food and drink, bike mechanics, sag wagons, and transport home. A big ride like the London to Brighton will see over 25,000 cyclists swarming along the roads and are an awful lot of fun. The focus of the event is enjoyment, and every effort is made to ensure that people have a good time. The spirit of camaraderie is tremendous and there's always a helping hand if you need it. If you've never done a 50- or 60-mile run, a mass ride is an excellent way to do it. Check with any bike shop for the rides going in your area.

A number of holiday resorts offer bike tours either based from the resort itself, or stopping over at selected inns and hotels. Tours are graded for different levels of rider ability and strength, and rental machines and equipment are often available.

Check the cycling periodicals and also the holiday issues of daily newspapers for holiday tours. As with any other type of package holiday, there are good outfits and bad, and a colourful brochure does not necessarily indicate that you will have a good time. A simple test for any prospective resort is to ask for the names of two or three people in your area who have been there. A quick telephone call or visit will then produce all the information you need.

Solo

Where you go depends on your own temperament, interests, physical condition, and available equipment. If you favour back roads off the beaten track and camping, you are going to have to deal with equipment for both you and the bike; touring on better roads and sleeping in inns means less and lighter equipment. Limit your initial rides to 20-30 miles, and work up to longer hours and overnight stays as you become stronger and more experienced. A novice can do 60 miles in a day, but only on a one-time basis. Over-long daily distances will make a tour into a relentless grind. You're out there to have fun, not to set endurance records. Balance hard runs with days of relaxation and shorter jaunts. One good trick is to ride within an area rather than from point to point. If you become tired, home base is not far away, and if you feel like riding until the morning star rises, you can do that too.

General information on touring, brochures, accommodation lists and so on can be obtained from tourist authorities:
- British Tourist Authority, 64 St. James Street, London SW1 1NF.
- Scottish Tourist Board, 23 Ravelston Terrace, Edinburgh EH4 3EU.

Riding

I recommend taking the smallest, least travelled roads practically possible. These are B-class roads and smaller. They are usually more interesting in terms of scenery, and less travelled by cars. Motor vehicles in the country are a serious hazard, because the speed differences between cycles and cars are much greater. On dual-lane roads the vehicles run at 70 mph, often bunched so tightly together that the drivers' vision

is limited to the vehicle they are following. When they come up on a cyclist there is no time to swing out and give room. This danger is acute at night-time. A sensible alternative for the cyclist are the little-used footpaths that often parallel dual-lane roads, but keep a keen eye out for broken glass and other litter.

On the two-way A- and B-class roads many cars move smartly, particularly if the driver is a regular who 'knows the road'. In a bend where a car moving at 50-60 mph suddenly encounters a cycle moving at 10 mph, and with limited space for manoeuvring, a bad situation can develop a lot faster than the many drivers who over-rate themselves think is possible. There are fewer car/bike accidents in the countryside, but for cyclists, a far greater proportion of them are fatal.

The best bet for the cyclist are small roads which keep vehicle speeds down to about 30 mph, at which rate there is almost always enough time and room to prevent serious crashes. Small roads meander and increase point-to-point travel time, but are usually more interesting. The idea of cycling in the first place is to savour and enjoy; if you need to get someplace fast, take a train!

An alternative to roads are bridlepaths (which cyclists are legally entitled to use) and footpaths (which they are not). These honeycomb Britain and I have taken many long tours touching roads for only a mile or so. The scenery is usually fantastic, and the riding is often challenging and demanding. A mountain bike is the natural choice for this sort of thing, but I've done it many, many times on perfectly ordinary bikes.

Look to the mountain bike chapter for pointers on how to behave in the off-road countryside. So far as the legality of footpaths is concerned, be guided by the immediate situation. A popular walking area filled with Sunday strollers is a poor choice and you should dismount and walk. Most times, however, no-one else will be around and you will have the outdoors to yourself.

Another off-road option are canal towpaths. Most of these have 'No cycling' signs, but in fact, you may cycle on towpaths administered by the British Waterways Board if you have a permit. The necessary piece of paper costs £1 (British Waterways Board, 7th Floor, Gresham House, 53 Clarendon Road, Watford WD1 1LA), and your letter of application should give a specific reason for needing a permit, such as commuting to work or school. The canals and other inland waterways were Britain's first transport network and thread through many scenic and interesting areas. Quiet and calm, they are popular with strollers, fisherfolk, and others who enjoy a bit of peace. In this world, a bike is a high-speed vehicle that can cause alarm; keep in tune with the environment by riding with studied, obvious consideration for others.

Safe country riding is largely a matter of common sense. Most of the rules for traffic riding apply here also.

● Always carry identification, written information on your particular medical or health requirements, and enough bail-out money to get you home should you or the bike pack it in.

● The cardinal rule is 'what if'? Look and think ahead. Don't, for example, time your riding so that you and an overtaking car reach a curve at the same time. If a car—or worse yet a lorry—comes the other way there just isn't going to be enough room.

● Bear in mind the tremendous relative velocity of cars. In traffic you can pretty much keep up, but in the country cars will have up to 70 mph over your 5-15 mph. If you crest a hill and there is no oncoming traffic, move over into the opposite lane for a while. This avoids the hazard of drivers coming from behind who cannot see you over the brow of the hill.

● Try to have a place to duck into should everything go wrong. Where will you go if that tractor pulls out? If a car comes around the corner on your side of the road are you going to try for the ditch or a tree? You may wreck a bike going off into a field, but this is a lot better than colliding with a car. Think about this as much as you can and try to make it an automatic process. If an emergency does arise, instead of freezing in panic you may be able to save your life.

● Be particularly wary, when you have speed up, of people doing odd things. Cannon-balling down a hill you may be doing 40 mph, a fact that many motorists and ped-

estrians do not comprehend. They see a bicycle, and automatically class it as slow and unimportant, dismissing it from mind (as you can be sure they would not do for a large lorry), and step or drive out onto the road, or pass, or whatever. This capacity for visual recognition with no subsequent cognitive comprehension may seem bizarre, but I assure you it is so. Never trust other road users.

● After running through puddles or wet grass, dry your brakes off by applying them slightly as you ride. Running down steep hills do not hold the brakes steadily, which can cause overheating, but pump on and off. This tells you if you have stopping power in reserve—which you always should.

● Run to the left, but leave room to manoeuvre in case you encounter road litter, potholes, or whatever.

● On two-lane roads watch out for overtaking motorists coming towards you in your lane. They often do not see or just plain ignore a bicycle coming towards them. When this happens, claim your space by moving out to the centre of your lane; most on-coming motorists will return to their side of the road. Some will not and you must be prepared to make an emergency stop on the shoulder of the road. A rotten tomato or bit of leftover lunch is handy for such moments.

● Beware the Hun in the Sun. At sunrise and sunset motorists with the sun in their eyes may not see you.

● Rural farm traffic is a law unto itself. Many farmers operate machinery on local public roads as if they were in the middle of a field. Make allowances. Like cabbies, farmers are working drivers.

● Watch for loose gravel, dirt, or sand, especially at driveway and side road entrances.

● Bridge gratings, cattle grids, railway tracks, etc., can all swallow up a bicycle wheel and send you flying.

● Give horses plenty of room. A bike is a strange phenomenon for many horses and, moreover, often it is the horse and not the rider who is in charge.

Dogs

Dogs and other creatures of the field and air are a menace to the cyclist. I was once attacked by a determined and large goose. Dogs are the main problem, though, and you need to keep a constant lookout for old Towser. It is no fun to spend a month picking bits of gravel out of your legs and face because a dog knocked you off your bike. If you are bitten outside of Britain and the dog gets away, you will have to undergo a long and extremely painful series of rabies shots.

There are many theories about why dogs attack two-wheeled vehicles. I think that the spokes make a noise which drives them nuts. There are also a number of dog owners who take a not-so-secret pleasure in having vicious, attack-prone animals, and others who should not try to take responsibility even for a cockroach. One couple expressed puzzlement to me after their dog bit my riding companion. Every time the dog misbehaved, they said, they beat it until their arms hurt: why wouldn't it obey? With treatment like that, any dog will become vicious and irrational.

Understanding that old Poochie may not be directly at fault does not make being bitten or knocked off your bike more fun. Dogs are livestock, fully the responsibility of the owner, and excepting dogs crazed by disease, can be trained to leave cyclists alone. I like dogs very much and accept that some adjustment to their particular natures and quirks is necessary if they are to be around. I do not accept being knocked off my bike by some giant hound. If the owner will not control the dog, I will.

Most dogs attack according to a pattern. They circle to the rear of the cyclist and come up from behind. Sometimes, if you already have speed up and are on level ground or a downgrade with a clear road ahead, you may be able to sprint and outrun a dog. More often this is not possible—you've been taken completely by surprise, there is an upgrade, or other traffic about—but in most cases there is still no serious problem. Nine times out of ten, dogs are normally friendly. All you have to do is stop, dismount, and face the dog directly. That's all. Simply stop. Often he will come up wagging his tail and wanting to make friends. Dogs enjoy excitement and action, but very few dogs relish a serious fight.

It is important to get the reflex of stopping if you are not going to outrun the dog. People do get bitten, but the majority of injuries happen because the cyclist panics, loses control of the bike, and crashes. Unless you are extraordinarily accomplished, it is very difficult to ride a bike and deal with a dog at the same time. By stopping, you immediately increase your ability to control the situation. This said, the next priority is to clear off; dogs are territorial animals and are usually less interested in hurting you than in defending their patch of ground. Leave by walking away like all 'normal' (to the dog) people do, and the dog will consider the job done.

The tenth time, when a dog won't let you move away and still threatens attack: the main thing when dealing with a vicious dog is to have *confidence*. As a human being you are one of the largest mammals on earth and a formidable contender in a fight. Suppress your fears and radiate the notion that any dog that messes with you will regret it for the rest of his days, if he lives that long. Point your arm at the dog and in firm, commanding tones say 'Go Home', 'Depart Ye Henceforth', or whatever articulation you can muster. Only the rarest of dogs will attack a human being who appears confident and obviously prepared to deal with matters. Continue to speak firmly, keep your bike between you and the dog, and slowly walk away.

If the dog attacks: one defence is aerosol pepper sprays made for exactly this purpose. They have a range of about 10 feet and are light enough to clip to the handlebars or your belt. The drawback is that they don't always work. You have to be accurate and get the stuff into the dog's eyes, not always an easy trick when there is a lot of excitement and fast movement. Even when the spray is accurately directed, there have been plenty of instances where dogs (and people, too) have come back for more.

There isn't a dog alive that will come back for another faceful of water mixed with hot pepper sauce or powder. The solution can be sprayed from a water bottle or ex-container for detergent, shampoo, etc., all of which are easily carried on a bike. An advantage of this method is that you can practise spraying until you are proficient. Also, although a pepper solution will make a lasting impression on a dog, and probably cure him forever of bothering cyclists, it won't do any permanent damage.

If you have no weapon and can't or won't climb a tree, get a stick or large rock. No? The bicycle pump. Ram it down the dog's throat. In any event, don't run, cower, or cover up, because the dog will only chew you to ribbons. *Attack*. A small dog can be scooped up by the rear legs and heaved away. A hard landing will almost certainly put other thoughts in the dog's mind. With a big dog you are fighting for your life. If you are weaponless try to tangle the dog up in your bike. Use your legs to kick at the dog's stomach and genitals. If you have got a pump or stick and the dog is moving too fast for you to ram it down his throat, hold the pump by both ends and offer it up to the dog horizontally. Often the dog will bite the stick/pump and hang on hard. Immediately lift the dog up and deliver a very solid kick to the genitals. If you have no pump or stick, throw rocks, or use a heavy rock as a club. If worst comes to worst, and you are forced down to the ground by the dog, ram your entire arm down his throat. He will choke and die. Better your arm than your throat.

Not nice. Neither is the dog problem. There are 6 million dogs in Britain, and according to a recent report by Dr David Baxter and Professor Ian Leck of the Department of Community Medicine at Manchester University, 210,000 people a year are bitten severely enough to require hospital treatment. The further number of people with lesser injuries or simply given terrible frights is unknown. Baxter and Leck estimate that the cost of road accidents caused by dogs is £40 million a year. In America, dogs cause 8 per cent of all bicycle accidents. I don't have a comparable figure for Britain, but it is a rare cyclist who does not have a dog story to tell.

It is rightly said that there are no bad dogs, only bad dog owners. Trained attack and guard dogs rarely go out of control. It's the darling Poochies and Lassies with careless or incompetent owners who are the problem. If you are attacked or even just threatened by a dog, make every effort to identify the dog and its owner. Ask in local homes, shops, petrol stations, and so on. Report any attack to the police, whether you find the owner or not. This is a real responsibility, because the next cyclist or little child to come along might not as lucky as you. Be as clear as possible about the appearance of the dog and any particular markings it has. If the dog has a previous history of trouble, the police will probably know about it. Any dog is allowed one bite, and a charge is then issued to the owner to keep the animal under control. A second bite is a very serious matter and the third bite is terminal: the dog is put down. I've lived with and loved dogs all of my life and find this possibility extremely distressing, but I like even less the prospect of serious personal injury or even death because a pet is out of control. The law gives fair warning and opportunity for owners of attack-prone dogs to mend their ways. Anyone who truly loves a dog will take the trouble to see that it is able to get on in the world without coming to harm, and if they do not know how to train a dog, professional help is available.

If you are bitten by a dog, however lightly, obtain immediate medical treatment. Any damage sustained as a result of a dog attack, hitting a dog, or seeking to avoid hitting a dog, while cycling in accord with legal requirements, is the full responsibility of the dog owner. If the owner is unco-operative, just find a solicitor. Unless you have done something completely hare-brained (no lights at night, whizzing through a public park, etc.) the law is completely and absolutely on your side.

Technique

Cadence plays an extremely significant part in the technique of long-distance touring. In short sprints you can drain your body's resources and strength, but on a long tour, energy output must not exceed your body's ability to replenish fuel and oxygen continuously. Which makes it sound simple: just take it easy and have something in reserve. Not quite.

If you are interested in covering a lot of ground (not everybody is) and in feeling comfortable, then you must strive for an exact balance between energy output and the body's ability to synthesize and store energy. There is a *pace* which works best. Go too fast and the result will be fatigue and possibly strained muscles that will dog you throughout the tour. But go too slow, and you will become sluggish and lethargic, and mistake this for genuine tiredness.

A rough indicator of pace is respiration and heartbeat. You simply cannot sustain for long periods a level of effort which makes you pant hard, or causes your heart to hammer. The pace you can maintain depends on your physical condition, not on your strength. A simple test is to talk or whistle; hard climbs and exciting moments aside, when touring you should be able to converse, or carry a tune.

I particularly recommend that you take it easy at first, sticking to the lower gears and not pushing hard against the pedals. This will help you to find your own cadence and pace, and perhaps avoid excessive initial effort. Most people tend to lean into it hard the first day. The result is strained and sore muscles, and the next day they can hardly move. You'll go farther and faster if you take it easy at the start.

Riding position can make a tremendous difference. Going into the wind try to get low down. With a strong tail wind straighten up and get a free push. On the Continent many riders use homemade 'sails' resembling kites strapped to their backs. These are effective even with a quartering wind. Position determines the muscle groups in use: hands high on the bars eases the back, stomach, arms, and hands; down positions do exactly the opposite and are the best for hill-climbing.

Equipment

Bike

Choice of bike depends on the kind of touring you do. A hub-gear roadster is durable, but heavy weight and an inefficient gear train make it a poor choice for distance work. For all-round use, a derailleur-gear bike is best by far. It can be set up to favour durability and carrying heavy loads, or to favour performance and speed. Proper touring bikes have wide-range gears, mounting points for pannier racks and mudguards, and are usually equipped with cantilever brakes. (See the Bike Anatomy chapter for details.) Many sports bikes can be modified for touring, and the discussions of luggage, lights, etc., below will suggest what bits and pieces are necessary for your needs. You can also just slip a credit card into your pocket and head out on a lightweight, no-frills racing bike. The most important thing is for your bike to be geared correctly for the terrain you will encounter, and the kind of riding you want to do. (See the chapter Bike Set-up).

My favourite all-round touring machine is a lightweight mountain bike. It's not quite as fast as a road bike, but it is tough and will stay together through thick and thin. Tyres can be mounted that are reasonably swift and fleet on properly surfaced roads, but that can cope with dirt tracks and cross-country bashing. To me, touring is about freedom, and that's what a mountain bike delivers. If I want to really scream down the road (or enjoy armchair comfort), I ride an HPV! (See the chapter Zzzwwaaaammo!)

If you want to mix transportation modes frequently, going by bus, train, plane, or car from one place to the next, you might find a portable folding bike the most convenient. Personally, for this sort of thing I prefer a lightweight mountain bike with quick-release wheels. It can be popped into a bike bag, and while the package is something of a lump, this method bypasses the anti-bike contingent when you use public transport.

Tyres

On a 27-inch wheels use 1.375-inch expedition-grade tyres for poor roads and/or very heavy loads. For more performance, use lighter 1.25-inch high-pressure gumwalls, and if you really want to blast along, then use narrow-profile, 1- or 1.125-inch high-pressure (100 psi) tyres. Many shadings and variations are possible within each of the basic size categories—for example, narrow-profile tyres with Kevlar belts in the casings to help prevent punctures. But the general rule is: the narrower, harder, and lighter, the faster, and the more punctures.

With mountain bike 26-inch wheels, durability is rarely a problem. You can select tyres for the kind of performance you need. For road tours I use a lightweight 1.4-inch road tyre, and take it easy when going off-road over sharp rocks and rough ground. If my intention is to blast along rubble-strewn paths and tracks, or to clamber around on high ridges, then I mount big, stout 2.125-inch gnarlies and take a little longer on the climbs.

Tool Kit

What you need depends on how far you go and how well you maintain your bike. I keep a basic tool kit and expand it with extra tools and parts when necessary. At the minimum, have:

Tyre repair kit and levers.
Adjustable spanner, 4- or 6-inch.
Screwdriver with blade- and cross-tips.
Chain tool and spare links.
Brake and gear cables, long (cut to proper size later).
Any special hex keys required for your bike.
A few assorted nuts and bolts, and a bit of tape.

For longer journeys add:

Spoke key.
A few spokes (tape them to one of the stays) and nipples.
Brake pad.
A special multi-spanner to fit hub cones and lock rings (make sure it works), or hub cone spanner and assorted spanners as required.
Freewheel remover.
Cotterless crank extractor.
Lubricants, including grease.
Any special gizmo you might need.

Sounds like a lot, but it can all be packed into a compact bundle. On group rides cut down on the number of spare parts per rider, and share one set of tools. Your lighting system as a matter of course should carry spare bulbs. Include a bit of wire and tape for longer runs.

There are any number of special multi-spanner tools that are supposed to handle any problem a cyclist might encounter. A few of these work and are all right as an emergency tool, but most them are awkward and a few are downright worthless. For mechanical work you want good tools expressly designed and made for the job. This said, if you keep your bike in good condition then it is unlikely to malfunction or break, and the tool kit can be purely a contingency measure. It's on this basis that I'm quite fond of the Mafac tool kit. The tools are tinny and cheap, but very lightweight and compact; the kit will slip into a shirt pocket or tuck away out of sight underneath the saddle. I keep the good tools at home, and a Mafac kit (plus hex keys if required) on each bike.

For mending yourself, a basic first-aid kit. I generally also carry: a multi-purpose pocket knife, compass, waterproofed matches, button thread for clothing repairs, game snares, or fishing line, and, when appropriate, a snake-bite kit. If you are fond of following sudden fanciful notions and exploring odd byways when riding a bike, then a lightweight survival blanket is worthwhile insurance. Again, all this stuff can be reduced to a compact bundle.

Lights

A requirement at night. Many tourists like dynamo lights as they are consistently bright and less expensive than battery lights. However, some people do not care to pedal against the resistance of a dynamo, and the wiring tends to snag and break at inconvenient moments. Unless fitted with a storage battery adding up to 1 lb weight, dynamo lights go out when the bike stops.

Battery lights are simple, can be used off the bike for map reading or roadside repairs, and left off the bike altogether on a fast day run. They are the best for off-road riding, as they do not dim if you go slowly, and there are no wires to snag.

Dynamo lights are brighter than ordinary battery lights. Specialized rechargeable battery systems, however, are bright and can also be dynamo powered if necessary. They are the route to go if you want to be definitive. See the lights entry in Accessories for details.

For road riding I strongly suggest using a flashing light such as the Starlight or Belt Beacon (see Accessories). A useful item is the Matex torch, which straps on the arm or leg and shows a white light to the front, red light to the rear. It will also do as a camp torch or for roadside repairs. You should have an extra light of some kind as a back-up in case one of the main lights goes kaput.

Mudguards

A great pleasure in wet going and on rough back roads. Plastic models are light and easily removed when not needed, but eventually warp. Alloy and stainless steel models are sturdier, and offer mounting points for lights and other knick-knacks. They tend to transmit sound, but this can be cured with a coat of undercovering paint from an auto shop.

Bicycle Shoes and Cleats

There are two basic choices: shoes made to be used without cleats and suitable for walking when off the bike, and shoes made for use with cleats and suitable only for cycling. In theory, if you are really rolling on the miles and want the strongest possible shoe, then cleats give the maximum get up and go. In reality, many ultralong distance tourists are perfectly happy with dual-purpose cycling/walking shoes, and they have the advantage of not having to carry an additional pair of shoes for use when off the bike.

Start off with a pair of dual-purpose shoes. They'll be useful for general riding. If you find them suitable for touring, fine. If not, buy a pair of proper cycling shoes with cleats. In my experience nothing beats these for comfort and efficiency.

Baggage

Loading a touring bike is an art. There are two cardinal principles: load low and load evenly. Piling gear up in a high stack, or all in one place, creates tremendous instability. Bicycle carriers are designed to distribute loads properly. There are three basic kinds: handlebar bags, saddlebags, and panniers. People travelling light can get by with a saddlebag. These fasten to the seat and seat post and are available in various sizes, from little larger than a wallet to bags that can hold a lot of gear.

An alternative or supplement to the saddlebag is the handlebar bag. These give ready access for maps, food, cameras and other things you need often. On drop handlebars the weight has an adverse effect on steering, but this is not a problem with flat handlebar mountain bikes. If you want to carry a camera in a handlebar bag, it should be the type which is held by a wire frame slung from the handlebars, and secured by elastic tension cords to the front forks. This will help minimize the tiny sharp vibrations which are particularly harmful to cameras.

A revolution in cycle baggage occurred with the introduction of the Blackburn Low Rider front pannier rack. Instead of holding the panniers up high, this rack centres the panniers on the front hub. The improvement to bike handling over standard front pannier racks has to be experienced to be believed. On a drop handlebar bike, front panniers will carry more than a handlebar bag and access is fairly easy. On a mountain bike, front panniers tend to get in the way when riding off-road through tricky bits.

Campers will want rear panniers and, for the best load distribution, front panniers as well. Panniers come in one of two basic designs: single-bag, which allows maximum cramming in of gear, and multi-bag, which separates gear into compartments for easy access. Most panniers made today are quick on or off the bike, and some can be converted into backpacks.

Good brand names are Freedom, Karrimor, Carradice, Pakit, Cannondale, and Eclipse. I have used Freedom, Karrimor, and Eclipse with good results, but different models suit different uses. You really need to go to a bike shop and inspect the merchandise personally.

Panniers want the support of a stout carrier rack. Those supplied on production bikes are usually flimsy. There are two types: aluminium alloy and steel. Aluminium alloy racks are light and strong, and while breaks are very rare, they have been known to happen. In such an instance special equipment is needed for a repair. The original Blackburn racks have many copies, and with these you get what you pay for. So far as I am concerned, there is no substitute for the real McCoy.

Although the manufacturer would never recommend this, heavy-duty Blackburn racks are strong enough to carry a passenger.

Steel racks are less expensive and of course heavier than aluminium alloy racks, but have the advantage of being easy to repair with ordinary welding equipment—handy if you are far afield. The Karrimor rack has been around for donkey's years and is a proven performer.

When you load your bike, put heavy gear at the bottom of the bags, and light, bulky stuff like sleeping bags at the top. Give yourself a few shakedown trial runs. Nothing is quite so irritating as rebuilding a luggage rack in the middle of a tour. After the rack bolts and screws have bedded in, use a sealing material such as Loctite to hold them firmly in place.

Maps

A compass is not only useful in conjunction with a map, but can itself guide you in the general direction you want to go without strict routing. Sometimes it is fun to dispose of maps altogether. Just go where fancy takes you, and ask directions along the way. You get to meet people, and often they can suggest really interesting routes, scenic attractions, swimming holes, and the like. But have a map in reserve.

As well as keeping you on a desired route, maps have the vital function of keeping you off main roads and out of industrial areas. Motorist's maps are not detailed enough. Excellent are the Ordnance Survey (OS) maps, a catalogue of which is available from Ordnance Survey, Romsey Road, Maybush, Southampton SO9 4DH, and also at many bookshops.

Working out a selection of maps that will be useful without enshrouding you in a blizzard of paper takes a bit of planning. The best method is to start at home, with OS 1:250,000 (about 4 miles to 1 inch) maps. Once you've established the main route, then for local navigation nothing can beat the OS 1:50,000 maps, which show individual buildings, private roads, churches, ancient ruins, telephone call boxes, and the like. If you are riding bridlepaths and cross-country, then you will find 1:50,000 maps essential. The difficulty is that some 200 of these maps are required to cover Britain, and a selection for a tour can be extraordinarily bulky (and expensive!). If you are loping along on roads, a practical compromise are the ½-inch scale Bartholomew's maps, obtainable in book shops or direct from John Bartholomew & Son Ltd., 12 Duncan Street, Edinburgh EH9 1TA.

Clothing

This is rather obviously a function of climate. There is a quite real danger of hypothermia if you are ill-clad while topping a high alpine pass in conditions of freezing rain; and equally, you can be fried cherry red if you ride unprotected under a blazing sun. The best guide for this sort of thing is simple experience gained on short excursions.

Shorts are pretty much universal garb except in winter. Proper cycling shorts have no seams through the crotch, and should be lined with terry-cloth or other soft material for additional comfort. Some liners are removable for washing, and it then makes sense to have two liners, one for using, and one for the wash. Traditional racing shorts are lined with chamois, which is very comfortable, but after washing the chamois must be rubbed with softening cream to prevent hardening. Since you're not supposed to use underpants with chamois liners, you wind up doing a lot of rubbing. Terry-cloth liners are much more convenient. Sort out your shorts before you go; comfort is important.

For an upper garment the common T-shirt is fine by itself in good weather, and a good undergarment when the temperature dips. Cycling jerseys are cut long to cover the kidneys when the rider is crouched over the bars, and usually have large pockets at the rear that will hold maps, food, gloves, and even a compact spare tyre. Wash and wear synthetic garments provide a high convenience factor. However, they are often uncomfortable to wear during sustained physical activity, and my own preference is for clothing made of cotton, wool, or silk. For jackets and waterproof gear, see the discussion in Accessories.

Camping Gear

Membership of the Camping Club of Great Britain and Ireland Ltd., 11 Lower Grosvenor Place, London SW1 0EY, includes an International Camping Carnet, insurance services, a handbook on camping, and a guide to 1,500 sites in Great Britain and Ireland. Site lists are also available from the British Tourist Authority, Thames Tower, Black's Road, London W6 9EL.

Personal experience and preference are the main basis for scope and choice of camping equipment. Some people need a prepared camp site with loos, showers, and even a TV set. Others get by with a bivvy sack and a candle. If you are unfamiliar with living outdoors, do some research before investing heavily in a lot of paraphernalia. One excellent and definitive tome is *Backcountry Bikepacking*, by

W. Sanders. If you plan to go far afield, *The Survival Handbook*, by Anthony Green-bank (Bell & Hyman, London) is full of nitty-gritty information on how to start a fire without a match, manufacture a compass, ward off frost-bite, and other Out There essentials. *Bike Touring*, by Raymond Bridge (Sierra Club Books, San Francisco, California, USA) has a good section on low-impact camping.

I grew up in the forests of the Catskill Mountains in New York State, and in those Good Old Days 'camping' was not a singular or equipment-orientated activity. It was taken for granted that people could get along in the outdoors. Most of what was needed was already there: boughs for making shelters and beds, water to drink, fish and game to eat, and firewood without end. To this day I find the idea of a portable stove ridiculously synthetic; camping should be the evening-caught trout grilling on a glowing open fire. But even in the still reasonably remote Catskill Mountains the water is no longer fit to drink, the rabbits are diseased, and the fish are few and far between. If you cut boughs or build an open fire, a vexed Forest Ranger is likely to turn up and serve you with a summons.

When we lived and played in the woods we did not disturb things very much. No seasoned outdoors person uses anything but old, dead wood for fires, and none of us ever burned down a forest through carelessness. We certainly didn't pollute the entire water table, or kill all the fish. We burned or buried our rubbish—which was precious little anyhow—and as much as possible left things as we found them.

Modern times are odd. In some places there is more game (but not fish) than before. But the old ways won't work. There are just too many people. If all forage off the land, the cumulative effect is devastating to the environment. In many places you can no longer forage, hunt, fish, build fires, go swimming, or do anything to anything. Look, don't touch, keep your dog on a lead, and keep your nose clean, too. That's how it is, from the American Rocky Mountains to the European Alps, and of course especially in a well-populated country like Britain, and so if you intend to go camping, you must be self-sufficient in every respect.

Camping is a popular activity, and there are camping equipment stores in most cities and towns, but be selective. A lot of the gear is designed to be carted around in an motor vehicle; cyclists require light weight and quintessential function.

Herewith the main items to think about:

1. Sleeping bag. Some sort of shelter and a fire for warmth and cooking can always be improvised with a fair degree of success, but only the most skilled can keep warm in a bad bag. (If you are truly stuck and in genuine danger of freezing, build a fire and let it burn for a while. Then shift the fire and sleep on the ground it has warmed. You can do this two or three times in a night, and be tolerably comfy.) A poor bag weighs more, and if you freeze and can't sleep, this will give you ample time to brood on the economic and practical merits of having invested in something that would do the job in the first place. Get the best bag you can afford. Also, although your bike has carrying capacity and most of your touring is apt to be in warm weather, I suggest you keep other possibilities such as back-packing or tours in the autumn (fantastic!) in mind.

The best bags, pound-for-pound, are filled with down. Down has the greatest range (temperatures at which the bag will work), resiliency (bag packs small), recovery (gets loft back when unpacked), wicking properties (carries moisture away from body), and moral character. The less expensive, lighter (filled with 1½-2½ lb of down) models are OK for warm weather. I suggest a multi-layered and/or openable bag that will also take a flannel insert. This gives optimum range and comfort.

When down becomes wet it turns into a useless soggy mess. One way to avoid this is to enclose the sleeping bag in a waterproof Goretex bivvy sack. This increases the range of the bag, and should you lose or not want the tent, the bivvy sack will get you through. There is also a new product, Nikwax TX·10, that the manufacturers claim will waterproof fabric, and fillings such as down, wool, or polyester, so that wet no longer causes loss of loft. It could be worth a try (Nikwax, Durgates Industrial Estate, Wadhurst, E. Sussex TN5 6DF).

One particular bag that has been around for a while and that has a lot of testimonials is the Buffalo. This is a system of two outer bags and four inner bags that can be mixed together in various ways, allowing you to tailor the bag for specific conditions. (Buffalo, Meersbrook Works, Valley Road, Sheffield S8 9FT.)

The least expensive bags contain synthetic fillers such as 'Dacron 88' and 'Astrofill'. These weigh about 6 lb—a lot of weight for a cyclist—and are OK for warm weather and low altitudes. They are awful when wet.

2. A ground sheet such as a triple-purpose (rain cape, tent) poncho. A sheet of thin plastic or even a large rubbish bag will do.

3. Sleeping mattress or pad. Air mattresses (avoid plastic ones) are comfortable but

TO CYCLISTS
THIS HILL IS
DANGEROUS

S.T DADD

bulky. Ensolite pads are thin, but warm and comfortable. Karrimor's Karrimat is a proven performer.

4. Tents come in all shapes, sizes, and grades. Conditions and personal preference dictate choice. Tents are good for protection against bugs, rain, and to ensure privacy. Bivvy bags are minimalist and give a good view of the stars. Polythene sheets can be rigged into a decent shelter with only a little effort and are extremely cheap and light. A poncho is just as good.

5. Cooking stove. Cheapest are the solid fuel jobs such as the Esbit, which will fold and actually fit into a pocket. The flame on these cannot be controlled, which means no cooking inside a tent, and in windy conditions matters can get impossibly out of hand.

More tractable are gas stoves with throw-away cartridges. These burn clean and pack tidily, but the cartridges have an annoying habit of running out when least expected; for regular use you will need to carry a refill.

Liquid fuel stoves variously use paraffin, meths, white gas (in America), diesel, or petrol. Some will run on only one type of fuel, others will digest the lot.

Operating a paraffin stove is something of an art. First the burner must be pre-heated with meths. Then you prick the jet with a wire to clear any possible obstruction, open a tap and, if all is well, the emerging paraffin vaporizes and ignites. If something is amiss, then the stove goes out and enshrouds you in a cloud of oily black smoke. Paraffin stoves are one of the few mechanical devices known to possess intelligence. They always wait for the key moment when your back is turned before malfunctioning and erupting in a ball of flame (although there is no particular danger, so long as you are within quick striking distance of the controls).

Meths stoves are simple and reliable. An excellent make is the Swedish Trangia, which comes complete with its own frying pan, two saucepans, handle, and kettle. The Trangia is clean and will cope with high winds. The snag is the cost and availability of meths. In fact, with paraffin, white gas, and meths you will always have to plan ahead, and ensure that you have an adequate supply. This can make your life miserable with, for example, a compulsory Saturday morning ride in a torrential downpour to make town before the shops close.

Petrol is more easily available and is relatively cheap, but can blow you to kingdom come. So long as you are careful there should not be a problem, and many experienced tourists swear by the excellent performance and economy of stoves such as the Optimus 99. I think a petrol stove is fine if you are using it all the time and well in the habit of following the necessary precautions. For sometime use, white gas, meths, or paraffin stoves are better, as their quirks are merely inconvenient and amusing rather than fatal. As for gas stoves, I abhor a world filled with empty gas cylinders.

If you plan to camp a lot and want a good stove that performs when required, even under adverse conditions, you'll have to pay for it. Most of the models in bike and general camping shops are built down to a price, not up to a standard of performance. Check out shops devoted to quality mountaineering equipment. If you don't mind venturing afield, the stoves put out by MSR, Box 3978 Terminal

Station, Seattle, Washington, 98124 USA are luscious. Their X-GK is an expedition-grade corker that will burn anything, anytime, anywhere. The WhisperLite model runs on white gas and is popular because it is inexpensive (but not cheap), lightweight, and compact.

For utensils I prefer a steel pot, a steel frying pan that will serve as a lid for the pot (and simultaneously keep its own contents warm), and a steel cup that can also go on the fire. Avoid aluminium utensils, they are toxic. Skewers can be used on their own, or to form a grill, and are very compact.

6. Food. Dried lightweight foods are extremely convenient and palatable enough, but not to everyone—try one at home before buying enough for a journey. I suggest carrying enough for emergencies only, however, and trying for fresh food along the route. Stock up on supper and breakfast at about 4 o'clock. Mixtures of dried fruit, grains, dried milk, protein powders, yeast, etc., are nourishing, tasty, and easy to carry. Many health food shops have a dried fruit and nut mixture called trail food. Always have something more advanced than a candy bar in reserve, just in case you get stuck.

Mail Order

The U.K. catalogue mail order firm I know about is Field and Trek, 3 Wates Way, Brenchwood, Essex CM15 9TB. They've plenty of good gear. Slightly flakier but entertaining is Survival Aids, Morland, Penrith, Cumbria CA10 3AZ. If you like to peruse juicy camping equipment catalogues, try some of the U.S. firms. The goods are appealing, and there is no problem ordering them from Britain, but Her Majesty's Government will charge import duty on the purchase price and carriage cost, and VAT on top of that.

● L. L. Bean, Freeport, ME 04033, USA. Not deadly cheap, but quality equipment which works.

● Early Winters, 110 Prefontaine Place South, Seattle, WA 98104, USA. Wide selection of high-quality equipment.

● Herter's, Route 1, Waseca, MN 56093, USA. My favourite. Chest-thumpers, and slanted towards hunting and fishing, but sound equipment at very low cost.

● Recreational Equipment, P.O. Box C-88125, Seattle, WA 98188, USA. Excellent equipment at good prices.

Please . . .

If you camp or otherwise hang out in the countryside, please be tidy. Litter is not only aesthetically vastly unpleasing to other people, but is also very dangerous for animals. Livestock and wild creatures can cut themselves on tins and glass, and choke to death on plastic bags. Take away all your rubbish and if you find extra, do yourself a favour and take away as much as you can of that as well. In a very real sense the countryside belongs to everybody. But the people who live and work there are getting increasingly fed up with the sloppy ways of tourists and 'outsiders'.

In popular holiday areas there are farmers and other locals who really hate tourists, and with good cause. As a result, more and more real estate is being closed off. Do your bit to reverse this trend.

Getting There

Other forms of locomotion complement bicycles very well. Most people live in cities, and unless you know the back routes and byways that go out of town, reaching a nice bit of countryside by bike can be an exhausting journey. Some people enjoy doing everything by bike; others like to mix transportation modes. It's a great way to travel. You have the benefit of mobility and covering a lot of ground, and yet are able to explore interesting areas in detail.

Cars

A bike with wheels off will fit in the boot of many economy cars and certainly on the back seat. For carrying several bikes you can buy or make a car carrier. There are two types, rear-end and top. Rear-end versions usually hold two bikes and are easy to load. The bikes tend to scratch each other, however, and collect a lot of road grit. It's also hard to get into the boot. Top-mounted carriers hold four to five bikes. Each bike must be firmly strapped down, which can be a laborious process, but the machines are kept clean, separate, and out of harm's way.

Car carrier racks are available from any good bike shop. I particularly like the LP range. This includes a Universal rack which will mount on a conventional car rack.

When loading, alternate direction for three or more bikes. Seat on one cross-bar, handlebars on the other. Careful of brake and shift cables. Lash down with toe straps or elastic luggage straps at contact points, and especially the handlebars, since these hold the bike upright. Guying, running straps from the side of the car to high points on the bike (like with a sailboat mast), is a *good idea*. A belt-and-braces approach is important; at 60-70 mph the wind force on a roof-mounted bike is terrific. At fuel and rest stops, check that the lashings are secure, and that the rack itself is firmly attached to the car.

Aeroplanes

Airlines routinely handle bikes, and some will provide a special box for a bike. Some airlines carry bikes for free, others levy a charge. This is often a flat fee (around £10 or so) for an item of sporting equipment—the same rationale applies to golf clubs, skis, and similar gear. Prepare the bike by removing the pedals and the rear derailleur if you have one, and loosen the stem so that the handlebars can be twisted parallel with front wheel. Protect the frame and chainwheel with a broken-up cardboard box or a sheet of air-bubble plastic. Deflate the tyres to half-pressure.

There are two schools of thought regarding the best method for shipping a bike: roll-on, and boxed. A bare bike is in fact much easier for a baggage-handler to manage. It can just be rolled along, and is light and easy to pick up. The difficulty is that if something goes wrong—a shift in cargo or whatever—the bike is easily hurt. Most airlines make you sign a release of indemnity absolving them of any responsibility for damage to the bike, and you must therefore carefully weigh convenience against the prospect of a mangled bike. If you want to maximize protection for the bike, use a box or purpose-made bike bag.

A large cardboard box can be obtained from any bike shop. It's far from proof positive against injury, and a common tactic is to line the sides of the box with thin sheets of hardboard. All in all, it is a fair production, and when you arrive at your destination, there is then the problem of what to do with the box. If you are returning home from a different airport you cannot take the box along. If you are returning from the same airport then you can check the box into storage, but this can prove expensive over a long holiday and in any case, in these security-conscious days airport baggage-check stations are unenthusiastic about large boxes.

A more convenient solution is a purpose-made bike bag. These come in two types: hard-shell case, and fabric bag. Hard-shell cases are usually made of fibreglass and are exceedingly strong. They cost a bomb, and are heavy enough to require castor wheels in order to be moved around. A hard-shell case is sensible only if you frequently travel by air, and have a place at your destination point to store the case. Fabric bags are lightweight and fairly easy to manage, and at destination point, can be folded up and carried on the back of the bike. They are not great shakes as protection for the bike, and it is wise to line the bag with stiff cardboard or hardboard, and wrap the bike in bubble-plastic or extra clothes. But for me at least, so far so good. I've travelled often using a stoutly made Carradice Pro Bag, always with success.

Buses

Here your bike lies flat on its side in a luggage compartment with a lot of other junk that can bang into it. Use a stout box or reinforced bag. If you know the bus and driver, and the vehicle is not crowded, then it may be feasible to simply slip the bike in as is.

Railways

Trains are perfect for speeding you to a particular area, or for skipping over uninteresting sections on a long tour. No special preparation of the bike is necessary, other than labelling it with your name and destination station. Load the bike into the baggage van yourself, checking with the van guard for the best out-of-the-way location. Use elastic straps to hold the bike firmly in place, lock it, and take away your panniers and other gear. British Rail has an impossibly complex method for allowing or disallowing the carriage of bikes on its various trains. They have a guide leaflet, *The British Rail Guide to Better Biking*, that you should be able obtain from any station. It's best, however, to ask directly and be guided accordingly. Whatever the rules, final say rests with the van guard. Being nice to these people will pay dividends. You can always fox everybody by using a box or bike bag; the bike then goes as personal luggage, for free.

Warning: do not ever ship an unaccompanied bike by British Rail unless it is over-insured to the point of windfall. One bike shipped to me via British Rail was mangled into a worthless pile of junk—frame, forks, and even the cranks bent beyond repair—and the question of compensation did not even arise. Insure, and be prepared for the very worst.

Touring Abroad

'Going foreign' with a bike is a particularly satisfying way of travelling, as it allows you to explore and savour a country to a degree not otherwise possible. In most places people admire and respect cyclists, and are exceptionally helpful and friendly. For uninteresting or arduous sections of the journey you simply use public transport.

The Continent

The book to have is *Cycling in Europe*, by Nicholas Crane (Pan Books, London, and Oxford Illustrated Press, Sparkford). It covers the best touring areas in 16 European countries, is full of all the information you need, and is fun to read. *Adventure Cycling in Europe*, by John Rakowski (Rodale Press, Emmaus, Pennsylvania, USA) is by a 250,000-mile veteran and is a gold-mine of useful tips as well as a country-by-country information guide. Twenty-seven countries are covered in *Cycle Touring in Britain and the Rest of Europe*, by P. Knottley (Constable, London), a handy guide with chapters on preparation and planning, and also a country-by-country information guide.

The best single source of current information is the Cyclists' Touring Club. They have information sheets, pre-planned tours, maps, and insurance and travel services which make them unbeatable value for the tourist. They also conduct tours. So does the Youth Hostel Association, and membership includes a number of useful guides and handbooks. (A full list of European cycletouring organizations is given on page 363 of this book.)

And then there are always the traditional aids to travel—the Michelin Guides and various sightseeing tomes. These can be very useful. One of the nicest things about cycle touring is that you are not obliged to make a plan and stick to a schedule. Even in crowded holiday areas you should not have much difficulty in finding accommodation if you just veer off the beaten track—which a bike makes easy.

Riding

You ride on the right (starboard!) side of the road, of course. You won't find this difficult, but watch out for moments when your body reflexes scream for a wrong move—the first time you face dazzling car headlamps at night, or when sprinting away from danger. Anytime there is a bit of a panic your body automatically seeks safety— possibly on the wrong side of the road. Therefore, for the first couple of days ride cautiously and allow ample time to think things through before making moves.

Most of the rules are the same as in Britain. You are not allowed to use footpaths (but take cues from local riders), and must use a cyclepath when there is a round blue sign with a white bicycle in the centre. At junctions, traffic from the right has priority unless a sign advises otherwise. In roundabouts, existing traffic must give way to traffic entering the roundabout—the opposite of the British rule. In general, don't rely heavily on right-of-way. European driving standards vary enormously; particularly in small villages and on back roads, locals tend to do as they please. Most European motorists respect cyclists and you should not have any untoward problems, but they have their crazies, too. Watch out for European motorcyclists; they ride like the very devil.

Africa

Bicycles are a common form of transport for Africans, but their machines are of course extremely stout and sturdy, as often there is simply no road at all. In Morocco, for example, south of the Atlas Mountains and into the Sahara Desert, the roads are dirt tracks resembling streambeds. Most of the locals simply cycle over the desert itself. In contrast, the roads in Northern Morocco are quite negotiable, and there are not many cars. Similar varied conditions prevail throughout Africa.

Unless you run a local bike, parts are a problem, and in many areas so is thievery. Cyclists in Africa have been trapped in disease quarantine areas. There is always an ongoing selection of wars, revolutions, famines, and other excitements to interest the tourist. In many places life is less than cheap. Still, I would say the prospects for cycle touring are good. Beyond odd articles in the cycle press there is not much annotated information, but I know a fair number of people who have toured in Africa.

They all seem to be self-reliant, energetic, and able to get on well with people.

A highly entertaining read with useful snippets of information is *Bicycles Up Kilimanjaro*, by Richard and Nicholas Crane (Oxford Illustrated Press, Sparkford). It's primarily about the Crane cousins' mountain bike ascent of Kilimanjaro, Africa's highest mountain, but the wry comments about reaching the place give a good picture of the kind of problems you might encounter. Nicholas Crane is also one of the authors of *Richard's Mountain bike Book* (Oxford Illustrated Press, Sparkford), and his chapters are essential reading if you fancy a mega-expedition to some remote corner of the world. Betina Selby has taken and chronicled a number of interesting journeys in India, Israel, Egypt, and other countries, and her books *Riding the Mountains Down, Riding to Jerusalem,* and *Riding the Desert Trail* (Chatto & Windus, London) all provide useful practical information.

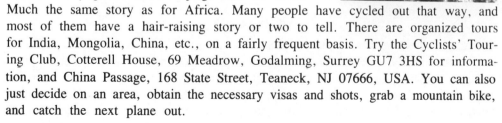

Asia and the Pacific

China—Cycling Association of People's Republic of China, 9 Tiyuguan Road, Beijing, Tel: 75 1313.
Much the same story as for Africa. Many people have cycled out that way, and most of them have a hair-raising story or two to tell. There are organized tours for India, Mongolia, China, etc., on a fairly frequent basis. Try the Cyclists' Touring Club, Cotterell House, 69 Meadrow, Godalming, Surrey GU7 3HS for information, and China Passage, 168 State Street, Teaneck, NJ 07666, USA. You can also just decide on an area, obtain the necessary visas and shots, grab a mountain bike, and catch the next plane out.

The Americas

Canada—Canadian Cycling Association, 333 River Road, Vanier, Ottowa KIL 8B9 Ontario.
Mexico—Todo en Bicicleta, c/o Morales, Pirineos 239, Col Porteles, Mexico 13 DF.

United States

Bicycle touring is a fine way to see the United States. If you are interested in major cities you must exercise care with regard to personal safety. The level of violence in some urban districts makes them 'no-go' areas unless you have a local guide.

American motorists tend to be slip-shod and—bad combination—aggressive. The idea that cars take precedence over any other vehicles is more prevalent than in Britain, and the problem of motorists not noticing or thinking about cyclists is worse. Many American cars are large, softly sprung, and do not handle well. Roads are wider and straighter, and accordingly, American drivers do not have the same level of skill as their European counterparts, who have to cope with narrow, twisting roads. On the plus side, American roads frequently have a three- or four-foot wide hard shoulder marked off with a white line, and a bike can often tuck into this space.

Cycle touring is popular in America, and especially in the countryside, you will be quite safe so long as you take the trouble to seek out local advice and lore. In certain parts of the country, for example, you have to take care when riding at night; snakes sometimes come onto the road to enjoy the radiant heat created by the daytime sun. It's easy enough to learn about these things; most Americans are warm, open, friendly people.

Books

Some of the books mentioned at the start of this chapter cover the United States. A lot of basic information is in *The Bicycle Touring Book*, by Tim and Glenda Wilhelm (Rodale Press, Emmaus, Pennsylvania, USA). The Bicycle USA *Almanac* (address below) is an absolutely essential 'where to go' with state-by-state information on climate, terrain, maps, contacts, etc. Also vital is the Bikecentennial *The Cyclists' Yellow Pages* (address below). There are lots of other books and booklets in American bookstores and bike shops, many are regional publications with exact particulars on local resources and conditions.

Organizations

●Bikecentennial, P.O. Box 8308, Missoula, MT 59807.
Born with the Bicentennial in 1976, this organization has gone from strength to strength in helping and serving cyclists of all types. Membership includes discounts on equipment, maps, and accommodation, and a raft of literature including the reference book, *The Cyclists' Yellow Pages*. Bikecentennial are particularly big on touring, and have organized tours, route services, insurances, and just about anything else you might need or want. Get in touch with them if you want to tour the states.
●Bicycle USA, Suite 209, 6707 Whitestone Road, Baltimore, MD 21207.
Run by the League of American Wheelmen, a touring and general cycling activity organization that is over 100 years old. They've got publications, all manner of tours and events, cycling instruction, and most everything else. Well worth contacting.
●American Youth Hostels, Room 828, P.O. Box 37613, Washington, D.C. 20013-6161.
Good equipment and books. About 250 hostels, sometimes spartan but always serviceable. Tours in the United States and abroad. Inexpensive.
●International Bicycle Touring Society, 2115 Pasco Dorado, La Jolla, CA 92037.
An easy-going outfit for adults only. Tours are followed by a sag wagon, overnight stays in motels and inns at moderate rates.

There are many other touring organizations, both private and public. The Bikecentennial *Yellow Pages* and Bicycle USA *Almanac* both list local touring clubs.

Holiday Tours

Commercial holiday tours abound in America, and can be a great way to enjoy the country. Most of your problems are solved at a single stroke; all you have to do is get there. Here are a few established firms:

● Country Cycling Tours, 380 Lexington Avenue, New York, NY 10168.
● Country Roads, P.O. Box 10279, State College, PA 16805.
● Sierra Club, 530 Bush Street, San Francisco, CA 94108.
● Vermont Bicycle Touring, Box 711, Bristol, VT 05443.

There are many, many others. Try to obtain copies of the spring issues of American cycling magazines; they are loaded with adverts for holiday tours.

Maps

The best source is the U.S. Geological Service, who publish contour maps for each state. If you know the exact area you'll be in, they also have local maps down to 1:24,000, a scale which shows walls, footpaths, tiny streams, etc. These are too detailed for any but the most local use, but are extremely interesting. Many map stores carry the USGS maps, or you can order them direct (for local maps ask first for free state index map):

East of the Mississippi	West of the Mississippi
US Geologic Survey	US Geologic Survey
Washington District Section	District Section
1200 South Eads Street	Federal Center
Arlington, Virginia 22202	Denver, Colorado 80225

Odd bits

If you plan a tour which includes travel by rail, be chary of baggage handlers. The make-work contingent has rigged it so that a baggage-handler must load the bike aboard the train—badly. Stories of bikes mangled into oblivion by these clods are legion. Insist on personally supervising loading, or don't go. However, train journeys arranged by people who know the ropes, such as Bikecentennial and Bicycle USA, are apt to work out well.

If you take your own bike with you, you'll have the assurance of a machine that has already been sorted out, and can concentrate on your holiday. There are a lot of nifty American bikes, however, and it is understandably tempting to buy one there. Fine, but if you do this, allow at least a couple of days to check out and fine-tune the bike before setting off into the wild blue yonder.

Take along or purchase the best lock you can find; bike theft in America is very common.

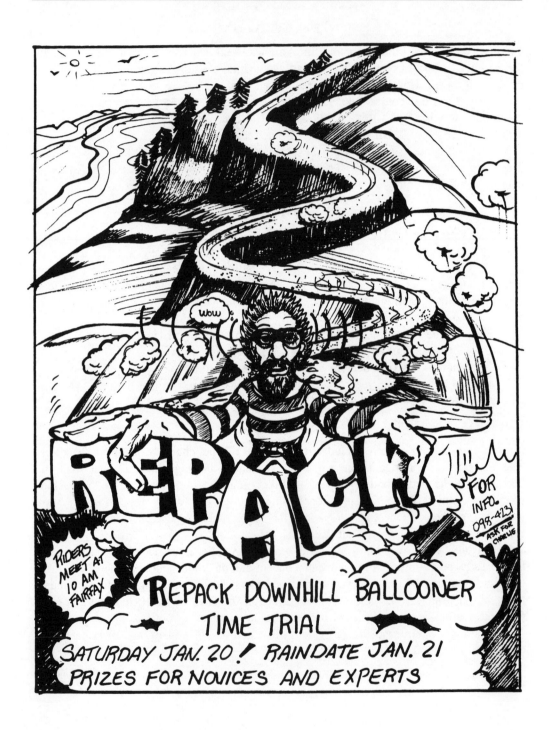

Mountain Bike!

The mountain bike is an invention which is changing the world. It's the cycling equivalent of a Land Rover, with strong wheels and tyres, very wide-range gear ratios, and mega-powerful brakes. There have always been bikes for hard work and rough roads. Bikes were important in the development of wilderness areas such as the Australian Outback and Alaska, and most of the Third World relies heavily on bikes for transport. But the bikes were, and are, very heavy.

The vital difference with mountain bikes is that they are made with the lightweight alloys and components generated by BMX technology and the boom in adult sports bikes. The result is a machine that is both lightweight and incredibly tough. It's everything a bike should be. Other than for road racing, if you are to have only one bike then a mountain bike has to be the main contender. Nothing else on two wheels is so useful, so versatile, and so much fun.

Fun is how it all started. Mountain bikes are an American invention, born in Marin County, California, in the mid-1970s. It's a great story, and is well told by Charles Kelly, father of the mountain bike, in *Richard's Mountain Bike Book* (Oxford Illustrated Press, Sparkford). Here's Kelly on the beginnings:

1976

It has been an unseasonably dry winter in northern California, and the three young men are sweating profusely as they push strangely modified bikes up the steep dirt road in the cool air. The subject of their breathless conversation is a detailed analysis of the condition of the road surface, which resembles an excavation site more than it does a road. On occasion one or another will stop and look searchingly back down the hill, perhaps kicking dirt into a small depression or rolling a rock to the side of the road.

These young men belong to the same adrenalin-driven breed that will always be found exploring the limits of human performance; in other circumstances they might be skiing off cliffs, jumping out of aeroplanes, or discovering America. In this instance they have developed their own unique athletic challenge, a race whose participation is limited to a few dozen local residents who know about it and have the unusual cycling equipment necessary to take part. The road they are on is the racecourse.

After more than half an hour of hard work, scrambling and pushing but hardly ever riding their bikes, the trio reaches the crest of the hill, where the road they are on intersects another equally rough dirt road. A small crowd of about fifteen other cyclists, similarly equipped and including a couple of high-energy women is gathered at the intersection. These people have come up by a slightly easier route that follows a properly surfaced road up part of the hill, but they have also had to ride a couple of miles of steep and rough road to arrive here. The three recent arrivals casually drop their bikes on the road, which has become a jumble of modified machinery.

Most of the crowd is in their twenties, but there are a few teenagers and one grizzled individual who claims to be fifty. All are wearing heavy shirts and jeans, and most are also wearing leather gloves and heavy boots. None is wearing a helmet.

Although the scene seems to be chaos, order begins to appear. One of the group takes out of his backpack a well-thumbed notebook and a pair of electronic stop-watches. Moving slowly through the crowd, he begins compiling a list of names. The notebook is the combined scoring system, archives, and publicity for the race, since it contains in addition to today's scoring all the previous race results and the telephone numbers of all the participants. Apparently races are not scheduled, they are spontaneously called together when the sun and moon have assumed appropriate aspects.

As names are taken the note-taker assigns a starting order based on the rider's previous performance and experience. Those racing for the first time are first on the list, followed by those with the slowest previous times. The current course record-holder is accorded the honour of starting last. Now starting times are assigned to the names on the list and a copy of the list is made. The watches are started simultaneously and the note-taker hands one copy of the list and one of the watches to an 'official timer' whose appearance is undistinguished from the rest of the crowd. The timer takes a moment to tape a bottle cap over the reset switch on his watch, then he jumps on his bike and disappears down the hill.

For the next ten minutes the adrenalin content of the air builds while riders attend to their pre-race rituals. Some sit quietly eating oranges, some joke nervously or talk excitedly. Others make minute adjustments to their bikes, adjusting brakes, perhaps letting a little air out of the tyres, or repeatedly shifting the gears, still undecided about which ratio to use for the start.

After an interval that is too short for some and too long for others the first name on the list is called. Up to the line steps a nervous young man who has by now tried every one of his gears without making a decision. He tries a few more last-second shifts as he rolls his bike to the line, which is a rough scratch inscribed in the road surface by the heel of the starter's boot. This is his first race, and he spends his last few seconds at the top of the hill asking questions about the course faster than anyone can answer, although answers are immaterial because he isn't listening anyway.

The starter props the young man up by holding his rear wheel, and as the rider stands on his pedals his legs are quivering. The starter intones, 'Ten seconds . . . five . . .' Anticipating the start, the rider tries to explode off the line a second before the starter says, 'Go!' But the starter is used to this and he has a firm grip on the wheel, which he releases as he gives the signal. Thrown completely off-balance and draped over the handlebars by his premature jump, the novice wobbles off the line for a few yards before finding the throttle and accelerating to the top of a small rise 100 yards off and then disappearing from sight.

The sport going on here is so unusual and possibly even dangerous that it is unlikely to catch on with the public as a Sunday recreation, but the participants couldn't care less. They are here to thrill themselves, not a distant crowd, and in that respect this is a pure form of athletic endeavour untainted by any commercial connection.

The bicycles in use are as unique as the sport. They are all old balloon-tyre frames dating from the thirties to the fifties; most of them were built by the Schwinn Company but a few other rugged and otherwise extinct species are represented. The standard set of modifications includes the addition of derailleur gearing systems (either 5-speed or 10-speed), front and rear drum brakes, motorcycle brake levers, wide motocross handlebars, handlebar-mounted shift levers, and the biggest knobby bicycle tyres available mounted on heavy Schwinn S-2 steel rims. A few reactionaries cling to their 1- or 2-speed coaster brake models, but the majority have drum brakes and gears, and this looks to be the wave of the future.

The riders affectionately refer to their machines as 'Clunkers', 'Bombers', or 'Cruisers', depending on the owner's local affiliation, and there are not more than 200 of the advanced models in northern California.

Certainly people have been riding old bikes on dirt roads in all parts of the world as long as there have been old bikes. These northern California riders have successfully crossed old news-boy-type bikes with the modern '10-speed', and the result is a hybrid that is perfectly adapted to the fire roads and trails of the Northern California hills. In the process of field testing their modifications the researchers have shattered every part to be found on a bicycle. Rims, hubs, handlebars, cranksets, seatposts, saddles, gears, chains, derailleurs, stems, pedals, and frames have all been ground to fragments along with some exterior portions of a number of clunking enthusiasts, who apparently will make any sacrifice in the name of science.

During the early experimental stage some riders recognized the steep dirt road now known as Repack as an ultimate field test for both bike and rider. This rarely used fire road loses 1,300 feet of elevation in less than 2 miles. In addition to its steepness, it features off-camber blind corners, deep erosion ruts, and a liberal sprinkling of fist-sized rocks. The name 'Repack' stems from the coaster-brake era; after a fast trip down the hill the rider would heat the brakes to the point where all the grease in the hub turned to smoke, and it was time to repack the hub. . . .

In its history from 1976 to 1984, Repack saw no more than 200 individuals take part. In spite of this, the name has assumed legendary status among mountain bikers. This status may or may not be deserved, but it is certain that this unlikely event was the meeting place and testing site for the people who brought mountain biking to the world. Among the participants were course record-holder Gary Fisher, who helped put gears on Marin's 'clunkers', and who is also responsible for some of the standard refinements by adding 'thumb-shifters' and the quick-release seat clamp. Joe Breeze holds the second-fastest time, and his designs and framebuilding were the breakthrough that created the modern mountain bike. Tom Ritchey raced at Repack on a borrowed Schwinn Excelsior before he ever built a mountain bike; Tom's influence can still be seen in the designs of most mass-produced mountain bikes. Another early builder, Erik Koski, raced his designs there. For my part, I was the race organizer, scorer, and Keeper of the Records; in 1976 I had a frame built specifically for the purpose of racing there, the first custom mountain bike I know of. (This frame did not live up to my expectations, so I persuaded Joe Breeze to build me another one. Two (his and mine) turned into ten, the prototypes of the modern machine.) . . .

By 1979 several northern California builders were making major strides in off-road design, inspired by the feedback from each other's efforts. In addition to Joe Breeze, these included Erik Koski, Jeffrey Richman, Jeff Lindsay, and of course Tom Ritchey.

In 1979 Ritchey's frames became the first offered on the market commercially.

Even at the staggering price of about $1,300 a copy, he could not keep up with the orders. About the same time Marin County brothers Don and Erik Koski designed the 'Trailmaster', and shortly afterward Jeff Lindsay introduced his 'Mountain Goat'. In 1980 Specialized Bicycle Imports of San Jose, California, bought four of Ritchey's bikes and used them as the starting point for the design of the first mass-produced mountain bike, the Japanese-made Stumpjumper, which appeared in 1981. With the appearance of this and other mass-market bikes shortly afterward, the movement took off.

What the early Californian inventors only dimly foresaw was that their creations are the perfect transport for a much nearer wilderness: the urban jungle. Bikes that can zoom along rock-strewn trails and ford streams have no trouble with bumpy, potholed streets. With modern tyres some of these machines are as at home on the road as on the dirt. In fact, these practical and extremely hardy vehicles have become the first choice for urban cycling: today, one in three bikes sold is a mountain bike.

Kinds of Mountain Bikes

Mountain bikes are a people's invention and are not fettered by UCI regulations or other silly ideas about how things should be. Mountain bikes incubate innovation and development, and in this area, new things will continue to appear for a long time to come. At this writing, I see four general kinds of mountain bikes:

1. Touring/Downhill. The early Californian riders were famous for 75-foot sideways slides into corners, and speeds of 35-40 mph on rocky trails. Bikes developed for this kind of riding are generous on wheelbase and fork rake, and tend to go for strength with, for example, wide 32 mm (1.25-inch) rims and full-size 2.125-inch wide tyres. The most recent models introduced by builders like Ritchey, Fisher, et al. are moving towards shorter chainstays and a tighter back end, for more kick and better hill-climbing ability. The result is a powerful combination of lively, racing-winning performance and 'get you home' stability.

2. Sport/Freestyle. Narrow, twisting trails with as much climbing as descending, and freestyle stunts like hopping on and off logs, rocks and what-else, have led to lighter, tighter designs. On sport mountain bikes, wheelbase, chainstay length, and fork rake are all slightly more compact than on touring models. Rims are usually 28 mm (1.12-inch) and tyres range from 1.5 to 2 inches wide. As a result, sport mountain bikes are responsive and nimble, and move fairly quickly on-road as well as off-road. Fitted with a carrier rack and mudguards, a sport mountain bike is an excellent touring machine or town bike.

3. Trials. People determined to ride their bikes over or through anything they encounter have evolved designs where the geometry is tight, and the bottom bracket very high. The whole idea with trials is to ride 'clean', without the feet touching the ground, and so the bottom bracket is well up to provide clearance over obstacles. People use these bikes to ride over cars, clamber over 5-foot diameter logs, and other incredible stunts.

4. Competition. The emerging style for competition mountain bikes is akin to cyclo-

cross machines: very light and tight, often with dropped handlebars. Rims are often a slim 22 mm (0.875-inch), mounting 1.4-inch wide tyres, and some riders have gone over to conventional 700C rims and 1.125-inch tyres. The idea is to pare weight to the absolute minimum, sacrificing if necessary some of the strength necessary for gonzo descents. The gains on climbs and over the ground more than make up for the loss of speed downhill.

Selecting a Mountain Bike

The classifications I've given are legitimate, but note that races have been won by every kind of bike you can imagine. Different kinds of bikes suit different kinds of riders. You'll get some people who swear a certain bike is the best thing ever, and others who swear it is the worst in all creation. The only good way to find out about mountain bikes is to try them for yourself and see what you like. A big part of the fun are new horizons and new skills. You're exploring, and one cannot say for sure what you are going to find. This said, here are a few general guidelines.
1. Decide what you want the bike for. Are you going to ride all the time in town? Do you like belting down trails and gravel tracks? How about coming down really super-steep slopes, butt well back off the saddle? Do you want to load up with camping gear and explore country roads and trails? Or do you like to go ripping through rolling terrain, zooming up and down like a roller coaster? Would you like to be able to skate over a 12-inch high log? Do you just want a strong, dependable bike?
2. Buy the quality you need. In Norwich, for example, most of the ground is flat. You don't need much of a hot-shot machine if you just want a mountain bike as transportation. Edinburgh, on the other hand, has plenty of hills, and even a plain transportation mountain bike wants to be of fairly good quality, to keep down weight.
3. Buy a good name. There are a lot of Johnny-Come-Lately firms cashing in on the mountain bike act, and some of them are big guns with lots of advertising muscle. Making a good mountain bike is not just a matter of copying what someone else did, or blithely shoving out a bike with a relaxed frame geometry and fat tyres. Beware the 'hot answer', it may be a lot of hot air. The people who know about mountain bikes are the people who ride them. This is just as true for a London dispatch rider as a Welsh trail blazer. For current information, try a subscription to the new magazine *Mountain Bike*, Emmaus, PA 18099-0096, USA.
4. You will hear a lot of opinions about frame size. As with road bikes, the common tendency is to go too big. When you take a mountain bike Out There and really push to the limit of what you can do (the bike usually still has a lot in reserve), you'll find that you want to be able to move the machine around underneath you quickly and easily. My advice is to ride the smallest frame that you can comfortably use. You'll grow into it.
5. Your comfort will depend very much on the reach of the handlebars. Most mountain bike handlebars are very wide, and this lengthens the reach. If you are stretched out on a bike, often a good solution is to move your hands inboard. If this does the trick, the controls can be relocated and the bars trimmed with a hacksaw.

The Case for Gonzo

If you are a beginner and want to really hare off into the back of beyond, you are well advised to take a conservative approach and pick a bike that will help take care of you. Something rugged, and kind, that holds a line when you are too tired to see small obstacles. Something with nice low, low gears that can just settle down and chew along if need be. For any beginner who has not had a lot of Out There experience, and who intends serious off-road excursions, the classic California Gonzo, touring/downhill basher bike is an excellent choice.

It's also of course the machine to have if you want to blast along trails and tracks at very high speeds. It's really fun to let it all hang out and go to the limit. Again, when your teeth are rattling at 30 mph and the bike is skittering around a corner, just barely in control, it is comforting to know that the machine was made for the job and will pull through if you do.

The Case for Sport

Most people have to use their bikes for transport as well as off-road fun, and performance on properly surfaced roads is important. Sport mountain bikes are reasonably lively on-road, and a lot of fun off-road. Like any performance machine, they demand a certain amount of attentiveness and concentration. What this means, for example, is that if you nose into a ditch on a sport model, the timing of your weight transfer to lighten the front has to be a little more precise than with a touring model.

A sport mountain bike is a lot of fun if you like monkeyshines: zipping in and out of hollows, catching air, and sliding the bike a lot in corners, so that it is sort of like freestyle on skis. The 'get you home' bikes don't always appreciate fooling around, and many just naturally try to keep matters regular, which is what they were built to do. Sport mountain bikes are a little more finely balanced and responsive —and quicker to put you on your mettle.

The Case for Trials

Trials bikes are made for riding through and over obstacles. They are skill-orientated machines, and there's always some new trick one can learn. One nice thing is that riding trials doesn't need a lot of room; you can get a good work-out in a small patch of countryside or bit of urban waste ground. The machines are very stable, and of course very strong, and therefore also good for touring and urban commuting—if you get stuck, and are good enough, you can ride over the cars!

The Case for Competition

Personally, I think competition mountain bikes are where it's at. They are really quick, extremely light, and no slouch whatsoever as road and touring bikes. A model from a top custom builder like Charlie Cunningham can pare down to as little as 21-22 lb. Most good competition models will slip under 25 lb. This is starting to go into the same class as road racing bikes. Minimum weight makes for easier climbing and snappier acceleration. It also makes the bike easier to handle, whatever you are doing, from fording a stream to boarding an aeroplane.

A competition mountain bike is dynamite in urban traffic. It's a racing machine that you can use all the time. Flat-out road racing bikes are faster, but racing mountain bikes are a lot tougher and safer—and at 25 lb or less, with hard, fast tyres, they only give away a few minutes on most urban journeys. Often they arrive first, because they don't have to stay on the road.

Touring is a similar story. A full-up, high-quality touring bike is a little faster on roads, but when it comes to the important part, climbing, a competition mountain bike is just as good and often better. Once you want to go off-road, exploring trails and open country, the mountain bike has it all.

The handling of a hot mountain bike can be quick, but not if you are used to a responsive road bike. Its vitality is a safety feature of sorts, because it commands more of your attention. It's not a cruiser. It's a bike for going flat-out, wherever and whenever you want.

Components

Wheels and Tyres

The original gnarlies (knobby tyres) for off-road use were heavy, and noisy and stiff when used on properly surfaced roads. Modern gnarlies are much lighter, and have tread patterns that grip in sand and mud, but roll fairly easily on hard surfaces. For maximum road performance, however, it is better to use tyres made for the street. These range from fairly heavy-duty models made for durability and grip in wet conditions, through to completely bald, high-performance models. The smooth-tread tyres are very fast, roll into corners like a dream, and have excellent grip in dry conditions. In the wet, grip on tarmac is still excellent, but marginal on slippery surfaces such as paint stripes and metal plates. Bald tyres are also very vulnerable to cuts from glass.

Many production mountain bikes are supplied with combination tyres that have a raised centre bead for low rolling resistance on properly surfaced roads, and knobs on the side for traction in dirt. I prefer a well-inflated proper gnarly; so far at least, the combination models are too prone to go slide out in a corner.

One good trick is to run more than one set of wheels. On Midnight Express, I use 22 mm wide rims and quick-release hubs. The town wheels have 1.4-inch Specialized Nimbus tyres, the dirt wheels have 1.9-inch Ritchey Quad tyres or whatever is the latest in gnarly grip, and the fun wheels have 1.4-inch, 120 psi baldies. Although the Nimbus tyres are intended for urban commuting and touring, they are also quite good off-road; the gnarlies are reserved for mud, snow, or very rough terrain. The baldies are lots of fun to ride, but have honed my puncture-repair skills to the sub-two minute level. They would be fine if you live in an area where the streets and roads are kept clean—not London!

Mudguards

It is a very good idea to keep a mountain bike as simple as possible. If you ride a lot through mud, however, mudguards can save a lot of bike cleaning and washing of clothes. Similarly, for wet urban riding, mudguards will spare you many a filthy soaking. Most mudguards mount with only three bolts, and mounting or removal can be done in a tick. Position the mudguards with as much clearance from the tyre as possible, or else mud, sticks, etc., may pack up and drag on the tyre.

Gearing

Most mountain bikes have triple chainrings and 6-speed freewheels. This gives an even spread of gears over a wide range, and is an excellent way to go. If you get to the point of setting up your own gearing, however, give consideration to the less complex arrangement of double chainrings and a 5-speed freewheel. There is less weight all around, shifting is easier and more certain, a wider, stronger chain can be used, and the rear changer can be more compact and swift.

Toe Clips

I highly recommend the use of toe clips. Stabbing your foot out to maintain balance at a tricky moment is usually the beginning of the end. What happens is the formation of a triangle with two legs: your out-thrust appendage as one and the bike on the other. The more you try to gain control by placing weight on your leg, the less weight on the bike and therefore the less traction—the usual consequence is a rear-wheel skid and a split triangle. What you want to do is stay with the bike and move as a unit—a little scary at first, but ultimately a much better means of staying in control. The way to develop this skill is to shove your feet into toe clips, and keep them there.

Toe clips are very much a safety feature. When you get to tearing around it is important to stay connected with the bike. If you lose a pedal, you lose a lot of your ability to manoeuvre the bike. More than once I've miscalculated, hit a rock or kerb with a pedal and momentarily lost control, and then recovered. So long as you and the bike are moving in the same general direction, you can catch up with each other. Also, one specific hazard of open pedals is a whop on the shin from a jagged pedal, and that one can really hurt. I promise: the risk of injury is much greater with open pedals than with toe clips.

The Great Outdoors

There is a lot of controversy over the use of mountain bikes in the countryside. In some places they are banned. My views on the subject are pretty simple. Anyone riding off the beaten track should have an idea of what is going on, and of how to behave with respect to fields under cultivation (stay off), livestock (stay clear), farm gates (leave as found), and horses and hikers (give wide berth). They should be self-sufficient, and not surprised that it becomes colder at night.

As far as mountain bikes themselves are concerned, they do less damage to terrain than a horse. Of course, if you come down through a mountain meadow with the back wheel locked up and plowing a deep furrow in the earth, then a lot of harm can be done. The furrow becomes a watercourse, erosion takes place, and bang, no more meadow filled with pretty flowers.

Wilderness and the countryside has to be treated with care and respect, but it should be used. I see mountain bikes as a great help for conservation and the environment. The more people who get outdoors and learn to love natural things, the better. Sure there are gonzo riders who headbang down trails, scaring the wits out of hikers and horseback riders. But the majority of mountain bikers enjoy and love the countryside just as much as anyone else, if not more.

Restrictions are a horrible fact of life. Prohibited. Not allowed. No swimming. No skiing. No, no, no. It's really very difficult. I've seen a lot of wonderfully beautiful places ruined and turned into rubbish heaps by thoughtless, wantonly destructive people. It's criminal. The concern with preserving the countryside has good foundations, even if it does seem to attract an awful lot of busybody types who enjoy making up rules for other people.

I think a lot depends on how you go about your business. If you slip along quietly and don't make a lot of fuss, then most times things will be all right. If you are rowdy and toss beer cans all over the place, you're more likely to attract trouble. Talk to people: farmers, foresters, hunters, fishers, hikers. Try to hear what they are saying, whatever it is. Once they feel they are being heard, the process is much more likely to work in reverse, and once they know you have feelings and ideas, too, matters usually get a lot better.

Zzzwwaaaammo!

Air is thick stuff. A cyclist moving at 20 mph displaces some 1,000 pounds of air a minute, a task that consumes about 85 per cent of the rider's total energy output. The idea of improving performance by reducing aerodynamic drag dates from at least 1895, when a man named Challand built a recumbent bicycle in Belgium. In the period 1912-33, conventional upright bicycles fitted with egg-shaped fairings set numerous speed records. But the proofs of performance that influenced history came between 1933 and 1938, when a relatively unknown Frenchman, Francois Faure, riding a fully-faired recumbent bicycle built by Charles Mochet called a Velocar, shattered speed records for the mile and kilometre. These feats provoked, however, a negative reaction: in 1938 the world governing body of cycle racing, the Union Cycliste Internationale (UCI), banned recumbent bicycles and aerodynamic devices from racing.

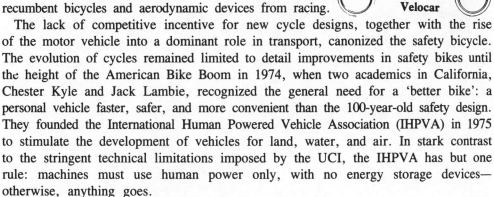

Velocar

The lack of competitive incentive for new cycle designs, together with the rise of the motor vehicle into a dominant role in transport, canonized the safety bicycle. The evolution of cycles remained limited to detail improvements in safety bikes until the height of the American Bike Boom in 1974, when two academics in California, Chester Kyle and Jack Lambie, recognized the general need for a 'better bike': a personal vehicle faster, safer, and more convenient than the 100-year-old safety design. They founded the International Human Powered Vehicle Association (IHPVA) in 1975 to stimulate the development of vehicles for land, water, and air. In stark contrast to the stringent technical limitations imposed by the UCI, the IHPVA has but one rule: machines must use human power only, with no energy storage devices—otherwise, anything goes.

Machines built under IHPVA auspices have rewritten the record books. The age-old dream of human-powered flight is a reality many times over, with perhaps the

Daedalus prototype. Wingspan 102 feet, weight 68 lb.

most spectacular accomplishment the crossing of the English Channel in 1979 by Bryan Allen, pedalling Gossamer Albatross to scoop the £100,000 Kremer Prize. A harder but less acclaimed event was a 72-mile flight from Crete to mainland Greece, by the MIT-backed Daedalus in 1988. An IHPVA machine, Flying Fish, is the first successful human-powered hydrofoil and holds the world record for speed on water. But land vehicles are the most popular and widespread portion of IHPVA activities. For over a decade, speed records have fallen one after the other. Pedalling all on their lonesome over level ground, people have exceeded 65 mph in a sprint, and covered more than 41 miles within an hour. The IHPVA's free rein for innovation has resulted in some very wild and wonderful creations, but recumbent designs are the mainstream. Collectively, they're known as human-powered vehicles, or HPVs for short.

Broadly, an HPV is defined as any human-powered vehicle not allowed to compete in UCI events. Because HPVs are pedal-powered there is an automatic tendency to compare them with bikes. But bikes are—bikes. A wonderful, singular design refined and sharpened for over a century. HPVs are a new class of vehicles with different characteristics, in designs that are varied and very much in evolution.

Quest for Speed

The four central elements in the speed of an object through air are frontal area, smoothness, shape, and power. A recumbent cycle has about 20 per cent less aerodynamic drag than a conventional upright bicycle. This is mostly due to reduced frontal area and a more streamlined shape. Things begin to cook properly when the flow of air is smoothed with a fairing (body shell). In comparison with an upright bike, a fully-faired recumbent has up to 80 per cent less aerodynamic drag, or 70 per cent less energy consumption. It takes 200 Watts (0.26 horsepower) to maintain 20 mph on an upright bike, and only 64 Watts (0.085 horsepower) for the same speed in a fully-faired recumbent.

From this point onward the physics of speed become a good bit more complicated. With the current crop of record-breaking machines, shape is a major consideration that

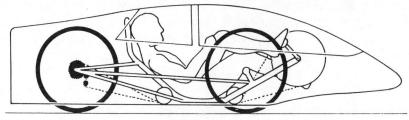

Vector

can overshadow frontal area, which is sometimes large. And then there's engine position; different configurations suit different purposes. But the bottom line is pretty clear: HPVs are the most efficient vehicles in the world. Per distance per weight carried they consume less energy than anything else going. Yes they are very fast. No solo UCI bike will ever see 65 mph on level ground, or more than 40 miles in an hour. But the key asset of HPVs, particularly as transportation, is their efficiency. A cyclist fit enough to be classed as an athlete will usually average around 18-19 mph on a racing safety bike. Riding 25 miles within an hour on such a bike is an accomplishment that rates genuine pride. In a good HPV an ordinary person in reasonable health can average 20 mph. If he or she trains and becomes fit enough to output 0.25 horsepower, which most people can do, average speeds will start climbing toward 30 mph. In other words, in an HPV most people can achieve riding 25 miles within an hour, and on a regular bike most people cannot.

The fundamental requirement for greater efficiency and speed is a fairing that smooths and eases the movement of air. In my book, an HPV is more specific than just non-UCI. It is a vehicle with a fairing that reduces aerodynamic drag. Most HPVs are based on recumbent cycle designs, but not necessarily so. Alex Moulton's AM upright bicycle, for example, has exceeded 50 mph fitted with a full fairing.

Hardware

What is a good HPV? The evolutionary history has two strands: competition and street. The first consistently successful HPV in both speed trials and road races was the Vector, a low-slung recumbent tricycle mounting a smooth, tear-drop-shaped body shell. It looked futuristic and fast—and was. In 1980 it set a world speed record at Ontario Speedway of 58.89 mph that stood unbroken for many years. The Vector was also an able contender on road racing circuits. Demonstration runs on public roads produced point-to-point average speeds that had many people speculating on when they, too, could buzz the highway patrol on their way to work. Judging by media furore, the future had arrived. But although the Vector was offered for sale to the general public it was not a practical street machine. It cost £5,000, rider comfort was poor, both vision and visibility were severely limited, and there was no provision for basics such as lights and signals. It was a racing machine, built to break records and explore new ground in knowledge.

Enter street. Recumbent bicycles were an early line of development for street usable machines that could be produced inexpensively. The configuration is more or less a tandem rearranged to seat one person, and building does not involve untoward problems for anyone familiar with bikes. Designing and building a good recumbent trike, however, is a demanding business that only a few people have accomplished successfully. Essentially, the recumbent bicycle is in-line and does not have to endure any more stress than an ordinary bike. A trike, however, is subject to high lateral forces. The design must be strong, and right: the nuances that give good handling, for example, are more slight and critical than with a recumbent bicycle.

There were a number of people producing recumbent bikes, and yours truly was an early customer for a model designed by David Gordon Wilson, the Avatar 2000. Riding 0012, as she is called after her serial number, I became convinced that the machine could outcorner a Vector on a tight course. Derek Henden designed and built a fairing, the drivetrain was modified with cross-over gearing, and with Tim

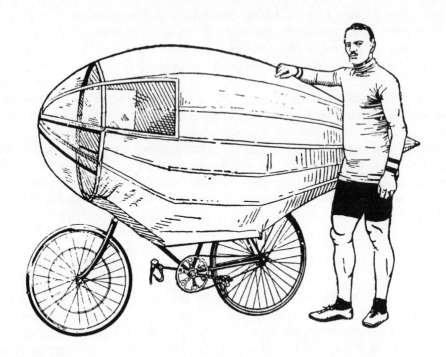

Gartside as engine we were away. At the 1982 IHPVA Championships in California, Tim and the machine christened Bluebell trounced the Vector, setting a world record bicycle speed of 51.9 mph in the process.

The key to Bluebell's success was Derek Henden's fairing, a three-dimensional flow shell shaped like a shark's fin. With a large side area it was a handful in a cross-wind. It was an airfoil: stalled when upright, but given to flight when heeled over in a corner. But the shape was fast and slippery, and the semi-upright riding position good for power.

Bluebell was the first bicycle recumbent to pip the Vector, but other builders had already been working with the design for some time. It wasn't long before Tim Brummer's X-2 Lightning floated by at 57 mph plus. Then the $18,000 DuPont prize for the first HPV to crack 65 mph fell to Gardiner Martin's Easy Racer Gold Rush, ridden by Fast Freddy Markham.

The really fast HPVs tend to have ultra-smooth body shells made from exotic materials like Kevlar and carbon fibre. But a significant advantage of the bicycle recumbent is that the shape takes easily to a fabric fairing. These are inexpensive and of course very lightweight. Such machines are still very quick, and deadly on roads and for circuit racing. Relatively at least, bicycle recumbents are readily available, at prices comparable to ordinary bikes. It's a natural process to start with a bare bike, and then gradually streamline it more and more.

Breaking land speed records has become a specialized activity. The push past 65 mph, for example, took place in the mountains at an altitude of around 8,000 feet, where the air is thinner. Mounting such projects is a lot of hard work, and expensive. The IHPVA has increasingly focused on the development of street machines through practical vehicle competitions, circuit racing, and point-to-point races on open roads held in compliance with traffic laws.

The pattern that has emerged from events in Europe and America is that fully-faired bicycle recumbents have the edge for speed, but only if conditions are good. If the weather becomes dirty, or there are bad cross-winds, the faired tricycles have a much higher survival rate. And there often isn't a lot in the difference. Pete Penseyres rode the Lightning X-2 from Seattle to Portland in 7 hours and 30 minutes, covering 192 miles at an average speed of 25.6 mph. The winner of the 1986 Seattle to Vancouver race was Chico Expresso, a tricycle that covered 166 miles in 7 hours 5 minutes at an average speed of 23.4 mph.

Fourth in the 1986 Seattle to Vancouver race at an average speed of 21 mph was the Windcheetah SL, a recumbent tricycle designed and built by Mike Burrows of Norwich. Popularly known as a Speedy, it was originally made as a practical street vehicle for training riders of record attempt machines. It turned out to be both practical and fast, with exceptional agility and cornering ability. Speedys have garnered many road racing victories, and first and second placings in practical vehicle competitions.

In the immediate future, bicycle recumbents will be the main line of development. They are inexpensive, easy to build, and fast. I think it will be possible to have faired versions that are practical for street use. In the longer term, tricycle HPVs will prove to be the more versatile all-round design for practical vehicles. If you

Bluebell at Eastway

like, the bicycle HPVs will be equivalent to racing safeties, and the tricycle HPVs equivalent to touring safeties.

But Beware! HPV evolution is very much in progress. I know of at least two ultra-low-slung trikes in development that have every chance of busting speed and distance records right, left, and centre. Anyone who says that a trike or a bike is the final answer is just asking to have to eat their words.

What's It Like?

It depends on what you are riding. Broadly, in comparison with safety bikes, recumbent cycles have superior comfort, braking, handling, and speed. Fully-faired HPVs are more like cars.

Comfort

The recumbent position is very relaxed and kind to the body. There's no problem with saddle sores or chafing. In long-wheelbase models the ride is like a tandem bicycle—comfortable. In short wheelbase models, bumps are felt with sharp awareness, but there is no harsh shock rammed up the spine. The chest cavity is open and free to breathe fully. There's no pain in the neck, back, arms, or hands. Riding a supine recumbent is literally relaxing in a comfortable chair.

Weather

On a bare recumbent you've got the same exposure to weather as on a regular bike. In an HPV like the Speedy, the weather is immaterial. I normally wear shorts and a shirt. If the temperature falls to freezing, I add another light shirt. If it gets really cold, say below 20 degrees F, I wear a light jacket and full-length trousers. In the opposite direction, on warm days I open up the convertible top. It can be set in stages: fully closed, half open, or completely open. If it rains I zip up the top and put a little hood over my head. On a hot day this can get you warm, but not as much as you might imagine. Overall, temperatures inside the Speedy seem to be fairly consistent. Like a car, you jump in and go. If you need more air and coolness, you open a vent scoop, and if you want to be warmer, you zip up.

Stability and Accidents

This depends on the vehicle. Long-wheelbase recumbent bicycles tend to be light at the front wheel and to wag back and forth in cross-winds. There's no real problem, just more movement. Shorter wheelbase bikes like the Lightning P-38 are better balanced and don't have this difficulty. In any case, if something goes amiss it is easy to put down both feet. The prototypical example is a stick through the spokes of the front wheel. A safety bike will cartwheel and send the rider to the ground face first. A recumbent bike will just lock up and come to a stop, landing the rider feet first. If a recumbent bike skids in a corner, the rider is already close to the ground and slides rather than falls to the road surface; most recumbent bikes have wide seats, which tend to bear the brunt of the impact.

Trikes such as the Speedy are completely stable, and this is very handy in heavy traffic. It's also great when you want to go: close to the ground on three wheels that can be drifted through a corner, I'm not worried about hitting a pothole, cartwheeling and destroying my face, or skidding on an oil patch and collecting strawberry burns or broken bones. A Speedy can be rolled, but only if you really foul up. If you overcook a corner, then by keeping your body weight properly distributed the Speedy can be made to understeer and scrub off speed. I'm one of those people who prays for snow. Sliding through a corner in a plume of crystals isn't just fun, it's ecstasy.

In a proper crash a bare recumbent is a better bet by far than a safety bike, and an HPV is simply another dimension. I've seen lots of crashes in competition and at record attempts, and only rarely has the rider suffered more than a dusting and minor grazing. I'll never forget watching a bare Speedy crash in a round-the-houses race on London streets. It was an early model that was inclined, in a corner, to suddenly tilt up onto two wheels and arrow off in a straight line. In this incident, the luckless rider careened across the road, bounced off a parked car, mounted a 6-inch high kerb, hit a parked mountain bike, tossing it well into the air, and finished by smashing into a fence of iron railings. Damage to rider: one cut on the shin needing one stitch. Damage to machine: none. Both were off to see the sights of the town within the hour.

An HPV with a body shell is remarkably safe. At San Diego, Tim Gartside in Bluebell hit a steel pole head-on at well over 40 mph. The machine did a mid-air flip and disintegrated; the fairing was made out of a material essentially similar to MacDonald's hamburger boxes. Bluebell came to rest with the forks and head tube torn out by the roots and the fairing shredded to bits. Tim walked away with a few grazes. It's safe bet that on a safety bike, he would have been critically injured or dead. Nor was the incident a fluke. Richard Crane did exactly the same thing in a later edition of Bluebell, when he hit a stout wooden post head-on at 45 mph while going for the hour record. The impact was severe enough to lance strands of carbon fibre deep within the wooden post, but like Tim, Nick walked away with a few grazes.

Visibility

The most common objection to recumbents and HPVs is that they are unsafe in traffic because they are too low to be seen. This simply isn't so. Recumbents and HPVs attract a lot of attention. The Speedy, for example, is far more noticeable than any car, however fancy or expensive. For pulling crowds it can cut a £75,000 Ferrari dead. It's got real spirit. More to the point, in traffic other road users notice and make room for the Speedy far more readily than for a safety bike. It's not just that the Speedy is unusual. To other road users, it is a proper vehicle that looks and behaves like a car, and they give it a lot more respect than a bike. I use the Speedy often in traffic, in no small part because it is the best and safest machine for the job.

There are a few rules. On a bare recumbent you've got more or less the same restrictions as on a regular bike. You don't go snaking through stopped traffic, asking to be caught by an opening door. You're careful when trailing behind a vehicle. On a long-wheelbase machine, you nose out carefully at intersections, as you cannot stand up and have a good look at what's coming. If it is a full HPV that takes time to exit, you watch carefully for any idiot in front who might reverse suddenly. This is the one genuine disadvantage of an HPV in traffic, and going through an Edgar Allen Poe routine just once is enough to make you permanently wary of the problem.

Motorists

Most motorists are charmed by recumbents and HPVs. They think the idea is great and cheer you on. A few cluck mournfully and suggest that you are incredibly foolish. A very few are aggressive. The main factor seems to be status. The cars that feel compelled to blow off the Speedy at a traffic light are usually cheap models with go-faster paint stripes, Porches, and BMWs. They sometimes get a rude surprise on the next corner.

HPVs are new, and most of the people riding them have had experience at racing and mixing it up at close quarters. When a car bullies and tries to shunt them to one side, they usually push right back. It is not perhaps the sensible thing to do, but a machine like the Speedy is a lot better for a paintflake-to-paintflake argument with a car than a safety bike. We've had incidents where HPVs have been deliberately hit from behind by a car and then pushed down the road at high speeds. The amazing thing, so far at least, is that the machines have survived unscathed.

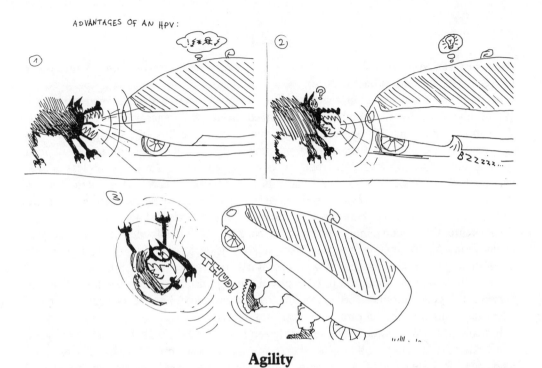

ADVANTAGES OF AN HPV:

Agility

I can't decide which is more fun down a twisting country lane: a recumbent bike or a recumbent trike. Like a regular bike, a recumbent bike banks over. The difference is, you can keep on pedalling, and this gives a completely different dimension of control. On a regular bike, you set up a line for the corner and then ride it out, for better or worse. On a recumbent bike, if you need more bank, you back off the power. If you've room to spare, you screw on the juice.

A trike is stable, and extremely agile. It seems clear that recumbent bikes are awfully fast in corners. I've never seen anything as razor sharp as Fast Freddy Markham whizzing around a road racing circuit on a fabric-faired Easy Racer. But then again, I've never seen anyone as good as Andy Pegg in a Speedy. A lot depends on the rider. This said, more than once I've watched bikes and Speedys go into a corner, and seen a bike go down while the Speedys survived.

Summarily, you have to work hard to overcook a recumbent bike in a corner, but they can go down. A trike with a good centre of gravity is incredibly agile and a great survivor—but beware off-camber corners!

Braking

A recumbent will outstop a safety bike by a wide margin. You can just put out the anchors for all they are worth. And if they are real stoppers, like the twin drum brakes on the Speedy, then you can stop on a penny. It doesn't do to rely on your brakes to get you out of trouble. Nevertheless, the immense, car-class stopping power of recumbents is a great boost to confidence and morale.

Speed

'How fast can you go?' is a question I get at every other traffic light. The answer is: 'Depends on the rider.'

Recumbents are faster than regular bikes. They've been whipping them since the 1930s, and that's why recumbents are banned from UCI sanctioned races. Overall, a recumbent is about 10 per cent faster than a safety bike. But the point of real advantage is not the speed reached at maximum effort, but rather the speed attained for a given effort. Crudely, 20 mph on a recumbent takes 25 per cent less power than 20 mph on a safety bike. Note that this is for higher speeds, where aerodynamics are more significant. In regular traffic, at speeds between 12 and 15 mph, there isn't a lot of difference between a recumbent and a safety bike.

HPVs are like recumbents, only much more so. A lot depends on the machine in question. At 20 mph, a machine like Bluebell is just loafing. I doubt if it needs more than 20 per cent of the power necessary to drive a safety bike at the same speed; 50 Watts, or about 0.06 horsepower should do it. For a machine like the Speedy, I'd guess around 100 Watts or 0.12 horsepower. But it is probably more relevant to answer the question in real life terms.

If I am just going somewhere in the Speedy, it will be at 18-19 mph. Any good club rider on a safety bike—and there are many who are curious—can pull up alongside. If I make a slightly more solid effort, the speed notches up to around 21 mph, a rate that I can keep up comfortably for a fair time. The good club rider is now working, oh, noticeably hard. What happens next depends on the distance, and the people involved. Basically, good club riders can give me an argument—for a while. If there are hills, they have an advantage. But I'll eventually wear them down. In the normal way, I let them get a little tired and then press a bit harder and drift away. They've had enough and since, strictly speaking, there has been no race, honour is intact. It's best not to go for sprints, because you're talking speeds of 30 mph or more—on level ground. I've been pulled over by the police a number of times. Downgrades run 35-45 mph, and I've been clocked at 55 mph on a steep mountain descent.

The thing to appreciate is that as HPV riders go, I'm not very fast. The interesting point of comparison is that riding a good, lightweight safety bike, I can average 15 to 16 mph, sometimes 17 mph, on a regular urban commuting journey. In the Speedy I can do the same trip at an average speed of 20 mph. And watch what happens when I get my hands on a street version of Bluebell!

Power

The foregoing is a frame for the next point. In a recumbent the back is braced, and it is possible to generate much greater thrust and power than with a safety bike. If you want to screw it on for a moment, you can scoot like you wouldn't believe. But the high thrust is strictly momentary. In a recumbent you have none of the advantage of your body weight helping to press down the pedals. It's all down to your legs, and the cadence range for effective power is narrower than with a safety bike. You have to be able to spin, and use gears precisely.

An HPV is a great old man's machine. What you do is ram in the thrust and whiz the thing up to speed, and then jump the gears to a big ratio that you just slowly trundle, taking a rest from the burst that got you going. Hardly any effort is needed to conserve momentum.

Hills are supposed to be the weak point for recumbents and HPVs. Depends on the hill, the conditions, and the technique. There isn't that much difference between a safety and a recumbent of equal weight. With the recumbent you must spin. Beware of recumbents that weigh more than 35 lb, they are just as much hard work as a safety bike of that weight.

With an HPV, there is usually a weight penalty. The works racing Speedy dresses out at 35 lb, complete with fairing. My street Speedy, when equipped with lights, batteries, tools, etc., must go for 55 lb. If the hill is long and steep, I simply settle down and winch my way up. But in the normal course of events the hills are fairly short, or the grade is moderate, and the aerodynamic advantage is still considerable. A short hill can simply be hit with a surge, but a long grade needs consistent delivery of a measured amount of force. What it comes down to is, if I had to climb all through the Alps I'd beg, borrow, or steal the works Speedy. Otherwise, for flat, undulating, or mildly hilly terrain, the aerodynamic efficiency of even a fairly heavy HPV more than offsets the penalty of extra weight.

An HPV for You?

I'm sold many times over on HPVs. Note I didn't say recumbents. You start with a recumbent and learn how it goes before setting it up as an HPV. Machines like the Lightning P-38, Easy Racer, and Windcheetah SL are incredible fun as bare recumbents. But if you're going to get into this business, you might as well go all the way. It's only when you have a full fairing that the performance, weather, and safety advantages really come on stream.

I think perhaps the most basic point to appreciate is that an HPV is not comparable to an ordinary bike. It is a personal vehicle, with utility, performance, and safety standards that no upright bicycle can emulate. If you make any comparison, it should be with cars. You shouldn't run an HPV on public roads, for example, unless you can drive a car or motorcycle with reasonable skill.

If you travel 100 miles to and from work every day, or need to climb 5,000 feet at a clip, an HPV isn't much of a bet as transportation. If you are one of the vast majority who take little journeys here and there at distances of 10 miles or less, usually by yourself, then an HPV is an answer that takes a lot of beating. It's simple, quick, safe, easy to park, weatherproof, and gives you healthy, life-giving exercise. Cheap: it runs on milk and cornflakes or any other bio-digestible substances!

I believe that HPVs transform the whole concept of a personal vehicle. They are good for you, and they don't hurt anybody, or damage the environment. I feel good when I ride the Speedy, and proud that I'm the engine. The Speedy is my Icarus suit. I put it on, and I fly. The bottom line is a kind of fun that is really like sprouting wings. I don't want to overdramatize, or make riding an HPV seem easier than it is. You get out what you put in. But HPVs are the most efficient form of transportation on earth. Within the next three years a human being will ride America coast-to-coast, 3000 miles entirely on pedal power, inside of 5 days. And when we see the twenty-first century, I think HPVs will be all over the place: little and big, solo and tandem, fast and sleek, slow and roomy, each suiting particular people and particular needs—Icarus suits!

Here is a short list of some firms and machines I know about at this writing. No prices, as they are likely to change. If you write for details, enclose a large SAE (with international postal coupon if overseas). For information on events, news-letters, and booklets, contact the British Human Power Club, Sec. John Kingsbury, 22 Oakfield Road, Bourne End, Bucks SL8 5QR, and the International Human Powered Vehicle Association, P.O. Box 51255, Indianapolis, IN 51255, USA.

Machines

Easy Racer and Tour Easy

Long-wheelbase recumbent bicycles in racing and touring models. Upright handlebars. Optional Zzipper fairings in standard and full lengths. Self-build kits, complete bikes, custom framesets, and complete plans. Longest in the business. The full-bore Easy Racer Gold Rush and Fast Freddy Markham hold the world speed record of 65.48 mph. A must see. Easy Racers Inc. P.O. Box 255, 2891 Freedom Boulevard, Freedom, CA 95019, USA.

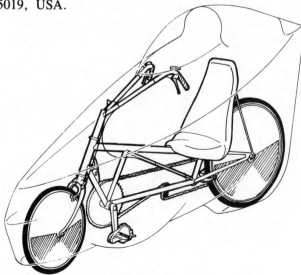

Easy Racer Gold Rush

Infinity

Long-wheelbase recumbent bicycle. Reasonably priced, popular touring and general use machine, available as complete bike or frameset. Ace Tool and Engineering, 292 West Harrison, P.O. Box 326, Mooresville, IN 46158, USA.

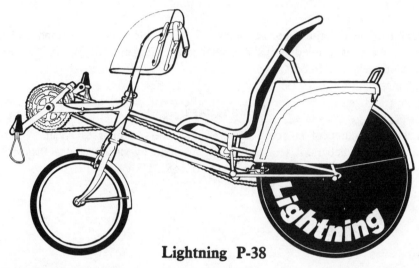

Lightning P-38

Recumbent bicycle, medium wheelbase (chainset above and slightly forward of front wheel axle). Available with a Zzipper windscreen fairing and streamlined panniers. Very able road machine. Brummer Engineering, 1500 E. Chestnut Ct., Lompoc, CA 93436, USA.

Moulton AM-14S

Upright safety bicycle, but 17-inch wheels allow fitting of full-length Zzipper fairing. Very versatile, quick, nimble, and comfortable. One of the great machines—for more information, see the Moulton entry in Chapter 6.

Roulandt

Long-wheelbase bicycle. High, with large frontal area. Not well regarded. Roulandt International B. V., Gildenstraat 23, 7005 BI Doetinchem, the Netherlands.

Trice

Recumbent tricycle. Weight approximately 45 lb. Stable, enjoyable, and (relatively) inexpensive. Fully assembled. Crystal Engineering, Copper Hill Works, Buller Hill, Redruth, Cornwall TR16 6SR.

Vanguard

Long-wheelbase recumbent bicycle. New machine, very similar to Avatar 2000, with underneath seat handlebars. Used as training machine by the Daedalus Project. Ryan Recumbents, 58 Lyle Street, Malden, MA 02148, USA.

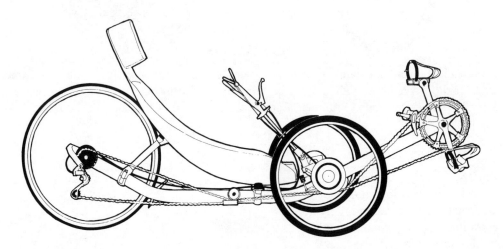

Windcheetah SL

The Speedy! Recumbent tricycle. Weight approximately 35 lb. Very agile and quick, winner of many practical vehicle contests and road races. By my lights, the best all-round street HPV in the world. Currently available only as a basic kit. Skilled metal machining and standard cycle components required to complete. Not a casual project, but within bounds if you are serious. Full body shell in fibreglass, fabric top available. Burrows Engineering, Green Lane West, Rackheath, Norwich NR13 6LW. Another possible source is a co-operative now being formed to produce Speedy machines for members. For information, SAE to Speedy Project, c/o Glen Thompson, Flat 7, Richmond Court, 257 Mare Street, London E8.

Firms

The following firms produce or handle machines that I've not yet personally seen or heard about.

●Alternative Bikestyles, P.O. Box 1344, Bonita, CA 92002, USA. Three long-wheelbase models, one for children.

●Brike International Ltd., 6700 SW 105th Avenue, Beaverton, OR 97005, USA. Lean-steering, front-wheel-drive tricycles, adult and child sizes.

●DeFelice Recumbent Bicycle Corporation., 26 North Depot Street, P.O. Box 321, New Palestine, IN 46163, USA. Two long-wheelbase models.

●H.P.E. Corporation, 7647 South 180th Street, Kent, WA 98032, USA. Corsa recumbent tricycle.

●HUDYN Vehicles, P.O. Box 22444, Indianapolis, IN 46222, USA. Recumbent tricycle.

●Kann Manufacturing Corporation, P.O. Box D, Guttenberg, IA 52052, USA. Long-wheelbase bicycles with folding frames.

●J. G. Leibold, 113 Jailsco Place, Davis, CA 95616, USA. Long-wheelbase bicycle HPV, tricycle HPV.

●Leitra ApS, Box 64 DK-2750, Ballerup, Denmark. HPV commuting tricycle.

● W. L. Lewis, Route 1, Box 128, Arcadia, IN 46030, USA. Tricycle with suspension.

●Not Your Average Bike, 5832 East Camden Street, Tucson, AZ 85712, USA. Long-wheelbase bicycles and framesets.

●Original Car-Cycle Technology Ltd., 2819 Fifth Street, Victoria, BC V8T 4B3, Canada. HPV commuting tricycle.

●RANS, 1104 E. Highway 40 Bypass, Hays, KS 67601, USA. Long-wheelbase bicycles and framesets.

●Thebis America Ltd., 41 Roxborough Street, East Toronto, Ontario M4W 1V5, Canada. Recumbent tricycle.

●Vacuum Velocipede, 307 Del Mar Court, San Luis Obispo, CA 93401, USA. Fully recumbent tricycle with linear drive, front portion (seat, front wheel, and drive system) lean, and hydraulically damped, rear-wheel steering. Basic model 39 lb, aluminium model 31 lb. HPV fairing 23 lb.

"Each flier rode the best machine,
Each man was trained to stay."

Competition

Bicycle racing is quite specialized and involved. Space and my own limited knowledge of the subject permit only the briefest comments and descriptions.

John Forester's *Effective Cycling* (Massachusetts Institute of Technology Press, Boston, USA) contains much information of value to the racer. *The Complete Cycle Sport Guide*, by Peter Konopka (EP Publishing, Wakefield) is detailed and highly regarded. *Bicycle Road Racing*, by Edward Borysewicz with Ed Pavelka (Spingfield Books, Huddersfield) is highly readable and filled with tips from the man who led the United States team to nine medals in the 1984 Olympics. Nearer to home, *Cycle Racing*, by Frank Westell and Ken Evans, (Springfield Books, Huddersfield), is one of the best books ever on road racing, time-trialling, and training.

To race, you will have to join a club, and belong to one or even two organizations, depending on the type of event in which you compete. There are basically four types of events: time trial, road race, track, and cyclo-cross. Here are the addresses of the national organizations:

- British Cycling Federation, 16, Upper Woburn Place, London WC1H 0QE.
- Road Time Trials Council, Dallacre, Mill Road, Yarwell, Peterborough PE8 6PS.
- British Cyclo-cross Association, 8, Wakely Close, Biggin Hill, Kent.

The appropriate national organization above will supply you with the name of a local club to join. To compete in time-trials you need only be a member of a club affiliated to the Road Time Trials Council; to compete in other events you must also take out membership in the British Cycling Federation.

In racing you compete according to age, sex, and ability, so if you are a beginner do not worry about being trounced first time out—most of the riders will be fairly evenly matched. Some of the greatest bike riders in the world are little shrimps. The less weight to lug around, the better. Big people are not excluded either—on downhills they generally have the edge. What counts in the end is fitness—and heart. Bike racing is an extremely rigorous sport. In skiing, running, football, and most other sports, when you are finished you drop. On a bike a lot of weight is supported by the machine and only a small amount of energy is required to maintain balance. It is quite possible to run your body to the finish and beyond, so that when you stop you are unable to stand on your feet. Any serious racer has to keep fit with a year-round physical conditioning programme.

The thing about riding as a racer, or club rider, is that the business is riding, pure and simple. It's all down to you and a bike. You are welcome to start as a raw beginner. The clubs and training programs want as broad a base as possible, as only a very few people will evolve into top level competitors. But you are expected to work hard and develop whatever potential you've got. And as you move up the ladder, one of the many rewards is attaining a level of riding ability that is simply in another class.

The three basic types of races are road, track, and cyclo-cross.

Road

Time Trial

Individual or team rides against the clock over 10-, 25-, 50- and 100-mile courses, or rides for the greatest distance covered in 12 or 24 hours. Pure riding ability and stamina count the most. An increasingly popular variation are point-to-point races over fixed routes where you ride for the best time. Some of these are epic, such as the annual Race Across America (RAAM).

Massed Start

Everybody starts together, first human over the finish line wins. The course can be 10 miles, or 2,600, as in the Tour de France. Most single day events are between 50 and 100 miles for amateurs, and 80-180 miles for professionals. Races lasting 2 days or more are called stage races.

In road racing riders are pitted against each other, and the resulting shenanigans are sometimes incredible. Intelligence, strategy, trickiness, and psychology play an equal role with riding ability and strength. Teams work together to launch a strong teammate ahead of the pack to victory, and block opposition riders. In big races like the Tour de France bicycles collide and pedals jam into spokes. In Europe these races go on despite wars, revolutions, or anything else, and are the subject of intense popular interest.

A type of road race that has increased sharply in popularity because it is easy for TV crews to film is the round-the-houses, or criterium. It is usually held on a closed circuit measuring less than 2 miles around, with sharp and narrow corners, over distances ranging from 25 to 62 miles. Very precise riding is needed to cope with the corners and the dense pack of riders created by the narrowness of the streets or road. Criterium bikes tend to have very stiff frames for quick handling, and a high bottom bracket so that pedalling can continue through the corners.

Cyclo-cross

Cross-country races from point to point or around a course from 1 to 16 miles in length, run either as a time trial or with a massed start. These are typically through steep climbs and descents, mud, thick woods, streams, and hurdles. Some sections are negotiated on foot. It is a rough sport, physically very demanding, with plenty of spills.

Track

The machine common to a wide variety of track events is the greyhound of bikes: an ultra-light frame with a short wheelbase; a fierce position with the saddle high and handlebars low; a single fixed wheel gear, with no brakes; and tyres bonded to the rims with shellac, to withstand the stresses of violent track manoeuvres. There are no quick-release hubs, gears, pumps, cables, etc., making these among the most lovely and functional of bikes.

● Sprint - Usually a 1000 metre course with only the last 200 metres timed. Involves all kinds of tricky tactics and scheming. There are times when racers hold their bikes stock still while jockeying for position. *Behind* the leader and in his slipstream until the final dash is the favoured winning position.

● Pursuit - Two riders or teams start on opposite sides of the track and try to catch each other.

● Time Trials - Against the clock, as in road racing.

● Devil Take the Hindmost - Last human over the line every 2 or 3 laps is out.

● Paced Racing - Motorcycles are used as pacesetters for the riders, who stay as close as possible to the pacer's rear wheel so as to minimize wind resistance. Speeds up to 60 mph.

● Madison - Two-person teams run in relays. Each team member runs one or two laps and then hands over to a teammate, literally throwing him by the seat of his trousers or by a hand-sling. A very spectacular form of racing.

Off-road

Cyclo-cross is formal, and rather like ballet. Mountain bike racing is varied, and while very demanding at the top level, is open to riders of all ability grades. Many 'races' are a wonderful way to see incredible scenery, and even if you come in 545th place it can be an exciting and satisfying accomplishment. For information, contact the Mountain Bike Club, 3, The Shrubbery, Albert Street, St. Georges, Telford, Shropshire TF2 9AS.

THE FINISH OF A RACE

Grandfather's Attic

If you have a little spare space, antique cycles are interesting items to collect and restore. The early models were largely blacksmiths' creations and bringing them up to snuff is a feasible home workshop project. The latter part of the nineteenth century was the heyday of innovation and experimentation in cycles, and many wonderful machines were produced. Some are illustrated in this book. A fascinating read is *King of the Road*, by Andrew Ritchie (Wildwood House, London), which traces cycling history in social terms—for example, how the bicycle changed the role of women. *On Your Bicycle*, by Jim McGurn (John Murray, London) is a lovely book that covers the history of cycling and the significance of the bike in social, economic, political, and even moral terms! Definitive information on hardware and restoration techniques is the forte of *Collecting and Restoring Antique Bicycles*, by G. D. Adams (Tab Books, Blue Ridge, Summit, Pennsylvania, USA). The Veteran Cycle Club, membership secretary Sue Duxbury, 42 Parkside Avenue, Winterbourne, Bristol BS17 1LX, publishes an engaging quarterly with in-depth articles and photographs, *The Boneshaker*, and also *News and Views*, a newsletter with short articles, letters, and for sale/wanted adverts. In America, The Wheelmen, 1708 School House Lane, Ambler, PA 19002, USA, is a similar organization devoted to old bikes.

The best source for veteran bikes is grandfather's attic. Most machines already on the market are expensive. You need to find an old wreck mouldering in a field or root around in the junk shed of great Uncle Fred the bicycle dealer who unexpectedly kicked the bucket decades ago. What you find is usually a disheartening pile of rust, but it is surprising what elbow grease and rust remover can do.

By about 1910 cycle designs had fairly well settled down, and machines from then onwards can be had for reasonable sums. Many are elegant and of very high quality.

American bikes made from around 1930 are now becoming classics. Many were mock motorcycles, with petrol tanks and ornate decorations. In America and Canada there are old bikes just waiting to be discovered in barns, attics, and the like. Paying a lot to an antique shop for a rare classic is nowhere near as exciting as making a 'find'. The book *Introductory Guide To Collecting the Classics*, by James Hurd and Don Hemmings (Antique and Classic Bicycle News, address below), includes information on clubs, shows and sales, and restoration methods. For current periodicals, try the *Antique and Classic Bicycle News*, P.O. Box 1049, Ann Arbor, MI 48106, USA, and John Lannis's newsletter, P.O. Box 5600, Pittsburgh, PA 15207, USA.

SOMETHING FOR THE BACK CARRIER —
SUSSEX COAST

Accessories

In the beginning, cycle accessories were cheap and tinny, and dedicated cyclists avoided them like the plague. Cycle shops are nervous of moving away from selling on price alone, and so toy-like, near-useless accessories still crowd the shop shelves, but the renaissance in cycling and in quality bikes has also fostered the development of accessories that are well-made and truly functional. For many general activities such as touring and commuting, the right selection of extra equipment makes a crucial difference in efficiency, comfort, and pleasure. Choose your accessories with care. Ensure that each item is well-made and will stand up to the job, and expect to pay for it. Fully kitting out a rider and equipping a commuting or touring bike can easily equal the cost of a machine. If you are on a tight budget, don't be lured by cheap equipment, because in the end it will cost you more. Improvise instead, and acquire better when you can afford to do so.

Anti-puncture Products

Punctures are the bane of the cyclist, and not a year passes without the introduction of a new product claimed to eliminate the problem. Here's a brief run-down on the merits and demerits of each type.

● Liquid sealants. These can be used with HPs, and tubulars fitted with a two-piece Presta valve. Sealant adds about 2 oz weight to a tyre, which is then theoretically proofed against direct punctures, as from a nail or thorn, but not against large slashes or cuts, as from glass. If the tyre suffers a major blow-out the sealant can create a thorough mess. It can also put paid to a tyre valve. After six months to a year the solvent evaporates, reducing the effectiveness of the sealant. In most cases, liquid sealants are more trouble than they are worth. But they do work. On trans-Sahara expeditions and other specific occasions, liquid sealants have drastically reduced the number of punctures. If you do high mileages on littered urban streets and are plagued by punctures, and are prepared to replace the inner tube/sealant combination every six months or so, then this type of product may be worth a try.

● Tapes. These are thin ribbons of polymer plastic inserted inside the tyre between the casing and the inner tube. Extraordinarily tough and pliable, they are effective at warding off punctures from ordinary broken glass, nails, and thorns, but cannot withstand a long, needle-sharp carpet tack. In conventional 1.25- and 1.375-inch wide,

55-75 psi tyres, tape has little adverse effect on performance—e.g., ride comfort, rolling resistance, and weight. One difficulty, however, is that in some cases tapes can cause rather than prevent punctures.

This appears to happen when the tape changes position away from the central bead of the tyre. When using tape it is important to deflate the inner tube once a month or so, and ensure that the tape is correctly positioned. It is also important to use the correct size of tape for a given tyre. Problems seem to arise when tape intended for 1.25-inch tyres is used in narrow-section 1- and 1.125-inch wide, 100 psi tyres. In any case, tape in a narrow-section tyre noticeably diminishes performance—so one might as well use a heavier, more durable 1.25-inch wide tyre in the first place.

● Belted tyres. Tyres with a belt of Kevlar or wire mesh embedded in the casing are effective at reducing the number of punctures, and do not have the problems of loose tapes. They seem to be the best way to go. They are expensive, and increase weight and rolling resistance, but they do work.

● Heavy-duty and thorn-proof inner tubes. Very thick tubes with tiny bores, and tubes made of special substances that resist penetration, are effective at reducing the number of punctures. Thick tubes are heavy, however, and noticeably attenuate riding performance. Special substance tubes are something of a gamble; fine so long as they work, but expensive when they don't—which is often sooner rather than later. It's easier and less expensive simply to start with a more robust tyre in the first place.

● Solid inner tubes. No. Fitting a solid inner tube and tyre onto a rim is an event that you will remember, with pain, for the rest of your days. Solid tubes are very heavy and magnify the gyroscopic qualities of the wheel, making it fatally difficult to change direction when riding. Definitely a case of once tried, never again.

● Solid tyres. One hundred per cent puncture proof and also the stuff of a Homeric epic to mount on a rim. Once in place, a solid tyre has such a rough ride that it will destroy the bike, if the rider is not broken first.

Various other anti-puncture nostrums claim to solve the problems of ride, mess, or whatever. I don't believe in any of them. The pneumatic tyre gives a nice ride and is lightweight. The simple route for more muscle against road litter, thorns, and so on is a heftier, stouter tyre. I keep my tyres fresh and inflated very hard, try to stay out of trouble, and carry a puncture kit and spare tube. I'd rather rely on myself than on a product that might or might not work. Most punctures can be mended in minutes. If I am out on the road and it is pouring cats and dogs I use the spare tube and mend later at home, when warm and cosy.

Bells and Horns

Little bells and horns are forever failing or being stolen. Freon horns contribute to noise pollution. Yelling is quick, reliable, and the most expressive.

Car Racks

There are two types of car racks: rear-mounted and top-mounted. Rear-mounted versions are inexpensive, usually quick to attach, and will hold two bikes. The machines tend to scratch each other, and to collect road grit. They are also vulnerable to other cars. Top-mounted versions cost more, attach easily enough, and will hold up to six bikes safely out of harm's way. The LP range of car carriers are sturdily constructed, substantial products that perform efficiently, and include a Universal model for attaching to already existing car racks.

Carrier Racks, Panniers, and Bags

The best sort of carrier depends on your needs. A traditional wicker basket, or a wire basket, is surprisingly versatile and useful. Avoid the type which uses a support rack where part of the rack rests on the head tube. When the handlebars are turned the support rack scratches the head tube.

A cloth slingbag can go with you on and off the bike and will manage books, papers, and the odd container of milk. For bulkier loads use a knapsack or backpack. Most panniers are quick-release, but many have a zillion straps and drawstrings that are a major inconvenience when shopping.

If you like off-road riding, using a backpack keeps the bike limber and versatile. But on-road, and for long distances, it is better to have the bike do the carrying. The possibilities in panniers are numerous: large bags, small bags, itsy-bitsy bags, bags that shrink or grow as required, and even bags that convert to backpacks. There are very neat panniers that double as briefcases when off the bike, and big folding basket panniers that will hold an amazing number of things when open. You really have to go along to a bike shop to see what will meet your requirements.

A bike can be very handy for humping things, for example groceries home, or supplies to a base camp. Fine if you want to take giant watermelons to the beach. But when you want the machine as a bike, resist the temptation to take along the kitchen sink. Boil everything down to the absolute bare minimum, and then discard half of what is left. I like tidy items such as the Eclipse Mini-Wedge, which fits underneath the saddle and holds basics: tools, spare tube, windproof jacket, etc. Their ATB bar bag is another winner. Eclipse are very good on design, quality, and attention to detail. Freedom is another excellent brand. So are many other makes. Some of the equipment is guaranteed for life. The shops are filled with goodies. Whatever you do, avoid the cheap imports. Save up your pennies if need be; better one good, loyal bag than four that fall apart and become none.

Carrier racks can be very useful. For around town use, a lightweight alloy spring clip carrier rack such as the Pletscher will manage briefcases, parcels, and other moderate loads. Steel racks are a bit heavy but are strong, durable, and easily mended. Most people prefer a good-quality alloy rack for both lightness and strength. Look for four-point fixing (drop-outs and seatstays), which is better than three-point (drop-outs and brake bridge). Some models are characterized as 'fast', meaning they are lightweight and therefore weaker. There's no point. The carrier is for loads anyhow, and might as well suffer a few extra ounces to do the job properly. I like the alloy Jim Blackburn racks that started the whole business because they pass a test that the maker would never sanction: carrying a person. The price of one of these will make you dizzy, but on the other hand, they work and they last; I've had a Blackburn rack for many years that has served on several bikes.

If you're going in for a lot of baggage, for example self-contained cycle camping, then use front and rear racks to even out the load. If you are road touring, use a low-rider design front rack that locates the panniers alongside the axle. The improvement this gives for handling is enormous. If you are off-road touring, the traditional design front rack with a loading platform on top may be better, as low-slung panniers tend to catch on branches, rocks, and other obstacles.

New ways and means of carrying things on bikes come along rapidly. It's worth checking out the latest models in a bike shop. I'll repeat: quality counts. If you are short of the ready, bash together a rack from salvaged rubbish (discarded lawn chairs, etc.) and stick on an orange crate. Some people have gone around the world with no more.

Clothing

Cycle clothing makes riding a bike a lot more fun. Take a simple thing like touring shorts. A good pair will have a lined crotch for comfort, and pockets with flaps and buttons so things don't get lost. Or trousers. They'll be lined also, and fit snugly so that nothing flaps in the wind. Chill weather? There are models faced with nylon at the front to break the wind, but with regular fabric at the back for ventilation and ease of movement.

Cycle clothing is very functional, and also very pretty. A lot of people really get off on the designs and bright colours. But judge for yourself. All I want to say is that the stuff is really worth a look.

Catalogues

Catalogues are fun for browsing and seeing what's around. Many are also full of useful tips and information. Bear in mind that while the catalogue firms are reputable and have good merchandise, they pitch hard for a sale. Bike shops usually have a larger selection of goods to choose from, and can give direct advice and answers to questions. No fair to examine and inspect in a shop, and then buy mail order as cheaply as possible! Here are a few (the U.S. ones are for interest; goods from abroad attract carriage, import duties, and VAT on top of the lot, and it is usually easier and cheaper to buy from a U.K. firm):

- Bikecology, P.O. Box 3900, Santa Monica, CA 90403, USA.
- Bike Nashbar, 4111 Simon Road, Youngstown, OH 44512, USA.
- Cycle Goods, 2735 Hennepin Avenue South, Minneapolis, MN 55408, USA.
- Everything Cycling, Ron Kitching, Hookstone Park, Harrogate HG2 7BZ (also available at newsagents).
- Freewheel, P. O. Box 740, London NW2 7JQ (also available at newsagents).
- Mountain Bike Specialists, 1611 S. College Ave., Fort Collins, CO 80525, USA.

●Performance Bicycle Shop, P.O. Box 2741, Chapel Hill, NC 27514, USA.

Child Seats

Carrying a child on a bike is fun. If you are setting out to do this, it is likely to be (a) your child, and (b) something you plan to do for a while. For both fun and safety it is well worth doing the job properly. Rear-mounted moulded plastic seats will manage a child weighing up to 40 lb, and should include a wrap-around spoke guard to prevent feet from tangling in the spokes. These seats will also neatly hold a box of groceries. The mounting hardware for a child seat should be self-contained, and not depend on an existing carrier rack. Models are available that attach and detach in seconds.

Rear-mounted seats should only be used with diamond-frame bikes; without the support of a crossbar (top tube) the extra weight of the child is likely to cause frame whip and unstable handling. For a woman, however, a diamond-frame bike may be impractical, because in most cases the crossbar will high enough to cause awkwardness and a pronounced loss of bike control when mounting and dismounting. (When the rider is off the saddle, the child's weight makes the bike top-heavy and quite unstable—never, never leave a child alone in child seat.) The ideal solution is a small-frame mountain bike with robust tyres and strong brakes. The next best is a touring bike with cantilever brakes.

One way around the handling problem caused by a heavy load at the rear is a seat which attaches directly to the crossbar and places the child between the adult's arms, thus creating a minimal adverse effect on bike handling. I've a really neat wicker model from China that just slips over the crossbar when needed.

Another route is a trailer. I've used the Cannondale Bugger (sorry!) to cart about two hefty children, and it is a wonder. Some people recoil at the idea of placing their nearest and dearest in a 'vulnerable' trailer. I feel that, overall, the detrimental effect on bike handling of a rear-mounted carrier and a older, heavier child creates a greater danger. Further advantages of a trailer are capacity up to one-half the adult rider weight (say 70-80 lb, or two kids), and a quick-release hitch which leaves the bike a proper bike when the trailer is not in use.

Once the child is about age four, he or she can ride the back of a tandem and join the fun via a junior pedalling attachment. Tandems, particularly good ones, can be quite expensive. However, although a child age eight or so can ride a bike on roads in company with adults, no great distances can be contemplated and the adults will have a full-time job in the role of shepherd. Children need to be age 13 or so before they possess a sufficient attention span to be safe when cycling on roads, and the necessary strength to start dusting off the adults. Looked at as a means of family transport for around eight years, a tandem is economically a good investment, and a lot of fun. Plus, if you look after it, you will be able to resell for a tidy sum.

Computers

Cycle computers are interesting, and can be very useful for training. Some models have just a few functions, others more than you can count. Speed, distance, and elapsed time are the basics. Maximum speed reached is a nice function to have, because at the time you are usually too busy to be looking at the computer. Average speed as a computer function that can be called up en route is a handy way of checking pace. Perhaps the most useful function is cadence, the rate at which the cranks are spinning. You can experiment with different cadence rates and gears over known distances and terrain, and learn a lot about maximizing performance.

Cycle computers used to be very expensive, and bulky enough to be an eyesore on a lean bike. You can still pay a lot for a high-tech whizzer that will do everything but dispense your money back, but there are also inexpensive, compact models that can be had for reasonable sums. The constant supply of new cycle computers with ever more features and innovations means that discontinued models are frequently available at attractive discounts. If you are uncertain about the usefulness of a cycle computer, try an inexpensive model first. If you get on with the thing, upgrade to a better model at a later point in time.

Cycle Bags and Cases

Large soft-cloth bags and hard fibreglass cases designed to hold a bike with the wheels off are a great way to fox the anti-bike contingent when travelling by air, rail, or bus. Most will *not* accept a bike with mudguards or a carrier rack. Cloth bags are inexpensive, lightweight, and versatile. You can cram them full of clothes and other gear. At journey's end, once the bike is out, the bag can be folded up and carried on the back of the bike, or for a time, over your shoulder. Cloth bags are convenient, but stripping down and swaddling up a bike so that it has a fighting chance against baggage handlers can take a bit of time. Fibreglass cases are heavier and ruinously expensive, but give much better protection for the bike. Little preparation is necessary. There's usually a set of trundle wheels to help make the case more manageable. At journey's end you need a place where the case can be kept.

Fairings

At 12 mph on a bike the retarding effect of mechanical drag and air resistance is about the same. Past 20 mph overcoming increased air resistance consumes 85-90 per cent of pedalling effort. Put another way, in terms of air resistance 20 mph on a bike takes four times the effort required for 10 mph.

The Zzipper fairing is a clear, bubble-shaped windscreen that mounts to the brake lever hoods in a trice, and claims a 20 per cent improvement in aerodynamic efficiency. The beneficial effect is more pronounced at higher speeds, and works out to the use of a gear 10 inches higher than would otherwise be the case. On long downhills the extra turn of speed is very evident and exciting and, because of the air pressure on the screen, bike handling is actually somewhat steadier. The main drawback is vulnerability to cross-winds, and a large lorry overtaking at speed will put a Zzipper equipped bike out of track by about 12 inches instead of the more usual 6 inches. On a very gusty day you will want to leave it off the bike.

The Zzipper fairing is useful for fending off rain and snow, and helping to keep the rider warm in cold weather. It is most efficient out on the open road; aerodynamics are not of great moment in stop-and-go town riding. If you often carry your bike up and down stairs, having a Zzipper aboard can make matters awkward. However, it really does mount and dismount within seconds, and on long journeys allows greater distances for noticeably less effort. Obtainable from Zzipper, Davenport, CA 95017-0014, USA. Another model I've not personally tried but that looks interesting is the Breeze Cheater by Fairfield Product Engineering Corp., 71 Wildwood Road, Fairfield, CT 06430, USA. It has two parts: a bullet-like lower section made of Kevlar that protects the upper legs, and a clear windshield that can be folded out of the way when climbing hills or when cross-winds are too severe for comfort.

Glasses

For urban riding a pair of glasses will spare grit in the eyes, and at speed in the country eliminate burning of the eyes by the wind. This latter seems to be personal: wind causes eye discomfort in some people, and in others, not. But if your commuting route includes heavily travelled roads, or blustery, dirt-raising weather, then glasses are a definite aid to avoiding discomfort. Plain, untinted glasses are available for those who do not want to jaundice their view of the world. Look for glasses that ride clear of the face, to help minimize condensation problems, or that embody an anti-fog element.

Gloves

Over the years I've come to regard gloves as essential. In the short term, hands can stand a lot of wear and tear. In the long term, gloves help prevent stiff fingers and hands. They are also welcome protection in the event of a fall. Cycling gloves are fingerless, with ventilated mesh backs and padded leather palms. The padding helps to prevent numb hands from pinched nerves. If you are prone to this problem, there are gloves padded with gel-like substances that are particularly effective at insulating against vibration and shock. For winter riding there are full-finger gloves made with Goretex or other materials that are wind- and waterproof, but that allow your hands to breathe. Mittens that allow your fingers to keep each other company are warmest for very cold weather.

Handlebar Tapes

There's quite a dazzling range of handlebar tapes available these days, and if you are at all cosmetically inclined, you should drop by a good bike shop and check out the possibilities. From the functional standpoint of comfort, if your hands numb easily, different tapes offer various degrees of padding to help insulate against road shock. Plastic and cloth tapes are generally cheap and nasty, although they are all that is required on a no-frills racing bike. The exception is Benotto tape, which comes in an outrageous range of colours, and is favoured by many top professional riders. A better grip and a range of colours is to be found with suede and cork type finish tapes. For more padding, Bike Ribbon micro-cell strips in a range of plain and metallic colours, and for the ultimate in comfort, foam sleeve Grab-Ons. These are a popular item, and go for the real McCoy. There are a lot of imitation Grab-Ons around, and most of them are distinctly inferior in performance and durability. The style-minded may favour leather sleeves, which richly deserve the three full pages of instructions on getting them aboard a bike.

Helmet

The Helmets for Cyclists Debate is a topic of increasing interest for the popular press. It's been calculated that some 150-200 lives a year could be saved if all cyclists wore helmets. By this same logic, if all the people who ride in cars were made to wear helmets, perhaps 3,000-4,000 lives a year would be saved!

Abstract ideas and arguments about helmets create false issues and miss the point. Wearing or not wearing a helmet is an utterly personal decision, and there is really only one fact you need to know. In most fatal and serious bicycle accidents the critical injury is to the head. Even a drop of two feet onto a hard surface is enough to fracture the skull. Wear a helmet whenever you cycle. It's inconvenient. So is not being able to think or talk because your head has been pounded into jelly.

The classic cycling 'helmet' consists of a network of padded leather strips, and is great for fresh air but of little use when piling head-first into a brick wall or parked car. There are two kinds of helmets that work: hard-shell, and soft-shell with a fabric cover. Hard-shell models have a shock-absorbing liner or suspension system. Soft-shell models do away with the hard exterior and simply use a liner covered with fabric. You may find it hard to believe that both types work equally well, but they do. The American National Standards Institute (ANSI) and Snell Foundation tests are tough; look for their approval stickers inside any helmet you buy. (There is no comparable British test, or for that matter, British manufacturer of cycle helmets.)

Soft-shell helmets are the latest thing, and are popular because they are well-ventilated and ultra-lightweight, and therefore more comfortable than the hard-shell models. Comfort is vital: in order to protect against impact, a helmet must be on your head in the first place. The easier a helmet is to use, the more readily you will form the habit of always wearing it.

Comfort is a factor that varies from person to person. Helmet weight, feel of fabrics or materials, chin-strap system, and so on all matter, but the main point to watch is ventilation. Cycling is warm work. Even on a temperate day, climbing hills while wearing a heavy, poorly ventilated helmet can leave you awash in perspiration. I cycle very warm and even in mid-winter use a light, well-ventilated helmet. In similar conditions many other people need face masks, hoods, and an extra wool cap. If you do not cycle warm, then a hard-shell helmet will probably be fine. They have worked well for years (all of mine are hard-shell models). A snug fit is essential for effectiveness. A loose helmet can do some nasty work in an accident. Most good models have sizing pads or similar means of customizing fit.

A helmet is itself an aid to comfort. When the sun is baking down with shattering force, a helmet provides a nice bit of shade. When the rains fall, it keeps the wet off your head. Most models come or can be equipped with a visor. This is also useful against the sun, and against rain; by tilting your head down slightly the raindrops are kept out of your eyes, improving both comfort and vision.

Some people object to using a helmet while cycling because they think it looks foolish, or because they want to maintain a spirit of freedom. Somehow, wearing a helmet inhibits having a good time. Hmm. It's true enough that in most cycling accidents it is only the cyclist who is injured or killed; the pleasures of freedom and other helmet-less intangibles need only be weighed against the prospect of death or disablement. However, calculating that prospect is not simple.

Children cycle the fewest miles but have the greatest number of accidents, and cyclists on minor rural roads are in less danger than their urban counterparts. There is a statistical case of sorts, if one wants to make it, for saying that children and urban and racing cyclists are well advised to wear helmets, while adult touring cyclists are at less risk. Statistics have none of the enduring imperishability of a tree or stone kerb with which your head has come into contact. They do not go to the mortuary, bleed, talk funny, or spend six months in hospital. Some of the people that this has happened to were among the most experienced cyclists around. *All too often the accident was in no way their fault.* When you ride a bike without a helmet, you take a chance. Is that what you want to do?

Yes, at first, wearing a helmet is inconvenient, and can make you feel foolishly overcautious. This passes, and when it does, you've gained an extra bit of insurance and help. I've used helmets for years now, and the only time I feel odd is when I ride without one. Like any other good piece of sporting equipment, a helmet increases rather than diminishes my enjoyment of cycling. The idea that wearing a helmet is somehow odious is an assumption made by people who do not use helmets, and it just isn't so.

I hope I never need a helmet to save my life or thinker, and I hope you never need yours. But face facts. There are accidents. In time, some of us will go down, some of us will be hurt, and some of us will die. If we wear helmets our chances of survival are very, very much better. I really hate to think that I might have turned you on to cycling, and then had you go out there without a helmet.

Kickstand

A kickstand adds a lot of weight for very little useful function. There is almost always something against which a bike can be leaned. A lightweight cure for the bike falling over because of front wheel movement is a parking brake, which can be made from a clothes pin or other odd handy bit, and jammed into the brake lever when required. Another way to do this is to snug down the brake lever with an old toe clip strap.

Lights

Adequate cycle lighting presents a whole series of problems for which there is no single perfect answer. The two basic types of lighting systems are battery and dynamo.

Dynamos take power off the wheel, thereby increasing pedalling resistance. There is more hardware, wires can snag and break, and the system is permanently attached to the bike. This can be a problem when locking up on the street; the tin-can dynamo lights of yester-year were of little value, but good-quality modern systems are expensive, and attractive to thieves. In use, dynamo lights are bright and strong, but unless a storage battery is fitted, they go out when you stop the bike. Conversely, at high speeds dynamos produce a lot of juice, which frequently causes bulbs to blow out. This can be cured by fitting a zener diode (voltage regulator)

to bleed off excess current, and better systems have this feature as standard. Dynamo lights are initially expensive, but cheap to run. They are also simple; one click and you have lights.

There are two types of dynamos: bottle, which run by pressing against the tyre side-wall, and bottom bracket, which run by pressing against the tyre centre tread. The bottom bracket models are effective, and have less drag than the bottle type, but get dirty easily and slip in wet weather. No problem if you are a sunshine area cyclist and enjoy the consistent attention needed to keep the dynamo clean and lubricated. If you cycle a lot in wet or dirty conditions then while there are various remedies and incantations that will keep a bottom bracket dynamo going, you are better off with a bottle dynamo. These are noisier and have more resistance than bottom bracket models, but are more reliable. The idea is to have the thing work when required, and these days, dynamo fans are going for bottle models and lights with bright halogen bulbs.

Standard battery lights are generally not as powerful as dynamo lights, but are convenient. They stay on when you stop and have no wires or other bits to snag. They can be got on and off the bike easily. This is handy for map reading and roadside repairs, and when locking up on the street.

Batteries are fairly expensive, but of course you can invest in rechargeable batteries and a charger. Most rechargeable batteries will last for three to four hours per charge, and are good for at least 500 charges or more. It's not as cheap as a dynamo system, but the cost is hardly punitive. The main problem with rechargeable batteries is that when they expire, they do so all at once, without warning. A standard battery dims slowly, and will usually 'get you home' even when on its last legs. (For a last surge, tuck the battery under your armpit and warm it up.) Rechargeable batteries are practical only if you keep track of the number of hours of use, or better, have utterly predictable journeys and a regular charging routine. A good brand is Reflectalite, and they have models for every purpose: complete systems, and batteries and chargers to fit the various special kinds of cycle lights. They also have halogen bulbs that are twice as bright as standard bulbs, although these of course reduce the time period of light per charge.

If you ride mostly in town and do not want to lumber your bike with additional weight when not needed, then battery lights will probably be best. The French WonderLites are not so great for seeing, but are readily visible to other road users, and the mounting brackets are versatile. This allows you to easily get the lights up high, where they are properly visible. Mount the front light on the handlebars and set the beam so that it goes out level, for maximum visibility to motorists. Mounting the front light on the fork blade casts a pool of illumination that is good for seeing the road surface ahead, but not so hot for visibility to other road users. At the back, the reflector should be low, to catch dipped car headlights, and the rear light mounted up high, on the seat post or rear carrier, so that it can be seen from all angles of view. Mounting the rear light on a chainstay or carrier rack strut can make the light invisible to motorists who are in the wrong line of sight. A further danger of mounting on a chainstay or fork blade is that the brackets can loosen and twist the light into the spokes. This has caused some nasty accidents.

One good way to combine the brightness of dynamo lights with the flexibility of battery lights is just that: a home-brewed system using dynamo halogen lamps powered by a single 6-volt lantern battery (the kind used for large hand torches, widely and easily available). The cost of such a battery at this writing is under £3, and it will last for a month or more of regular use. There are a number of options for mounting the battery. If you regularly lock up on the street, the battery can be kept in a briefcase or pannier and simply plugged in when needed. A 6-volt battery will also nest comfortably in a bottle cage (tip: for best weight distribution, mount the bottle cage on the underside of the down tube, just forward of the bottom bracket). If the bike frame size is large enough, the battery may fit tidily in the triangle formed by the seatstays and the seat tube. If you want to leave the battery on the bike and have some protection against thieves, find a small box with a lock (cash box or whatever). Either drill holes in the box and mount it to the bike via the bottle cage bolts, or use endless-band clamps (the kind used on car radiator hoses), positioning the screw heads so that they are inside the box.

If you want lights that will really reach out and illuminate the road, and hang the expense, consider a specialized rechargeable 6- or 12-volt battery system. They are heavy, but with 12-, 18-, and even 40-watts of lighting power, you won't have any problem seeing or being seen. Some systems are able to use optional dynamos as a power source when touring. Here are four American manufacturers:

●Bicycle Lighting Systems, P.O. Box 1457, Falls Church, VA 22041, USA.

●Brite Lite, P.O. Box 1386, Soquel, CA 95073, USA.

●Night Sun, 1104 Mission St., South Pasadena, CA 91030, USA.

●Velo-Lux, 1412 Alice St., Davis, CA 95616, USA.

A trick favoured by mountain bikers is a helmet-mounted light that can be directed exactly where needed: down by the wheel when negotiating tricky sections, up and forward for general information, to the side for sign reading, and so on. Used on its own, however, a helmet light has the peculiar quality of reducing contrast and flattening terrain, so that dips and bumps can catch you unawares. It's best to supplement a helmet light with a conventional bike light. A halogen beam model called the Cycle Ops is offered by Ibis Cycles, P.O. Box 275, Sebastopol, CA 95472, USA.

Any lighting system is capable of failing without notice. A second back-up light of some sort is essential. The French Matex light combines a white front and red rear, weighs only 5 oz, and straps to an arm or leg. Because it is moved around a lot, it is very visible. It's also a handy general light for map reading, camping, etc. It's a sensible complement to a dynamo system that does not have a storage battery to power the lights when the bike is halted. Much more effective as an eye-catcher, however, is a high-intensity flasher light. These blink at a rate of 40-60 flashes per minute and can be attached to your body, or to the bike. The best I've seen so far is the Starlight (R. V. Rutland & Co., Unit D18, Barwell Trading Estate, Leatherhead Road, Chessington, Surrey KT9 2NW), a compact little tube with a Velcro attachment strap and a bright, blue-coloured light. It is lightweight, efficient, and durable; mine has withstood a lot of banging about and bad weather. Another excellent, tried-and-true model is the amber-coloured Belt Beacon (Ampec & Associates, P.O. Box 15461, Phoenix, AZ 85060, USA).

Research has shown that blinking lights are the best means of making cyclists visible to motorists. Some people object to high-intensity lights. One argument is that the need for paying attention rests with the motorist. This is like saying that wars are the problem of people who start them. Another argument is that high-intensity lights can startle a motorist and make them slow down! This is taking low-profile thinking way too far.

As any study of cycling accident statistics will reveal, the problem at night is to survive. Bicycle lights are diminutive. In cities and towns they are easily lost in the welter of traffic lights, street lights, and neon signs. Out in the country the problem is speed: a car coming up from behind may be doing 70 mph to your 10 mph. That's an 88-foot per second speed differential, and if the visible range of your rear lights is 300 feet or less, it is under the distance required for a car to stop (315 feet). In short, if a motorist blinks and rubs an eye just for a fraction of a second at the wrong moment, or turns for a casual quick glance at a passenger, you can be wiped out. A high-intensity flasher light is visible from a good distance and may indeed make a motorist slow down, and this is exactly what you want. The Department of Transport requires that farm machinery and other slow-moving equipment have blinker lights when using fast, dual-lane roads at night. Fine for the farmers and motorists, but what about us slow-moving cyclists? Our risk of a fatal accident is nearly four times greater under conditions of darkness. The reason is that motorists do not see cyclists. Many cyclists think they can be seen when in fact they cannot. They are there, panting away, moving around the place, seemingly well in sight, and cannot understand how anyone could fail to see them. But that is exactly what happens.

A noted cycling author, Fred DeLong, took the trouble to replicate a series of car/bike accidents. He used the actual vehicles, equipment, and clothing involved in the original accident, or duplicates in identical condition, at the same location and times of day. In nearly every instance, and despite the use of regulation cycle lights in some cases, the problem was that the motorist could not see the cyclist, *even knowing that the cyclist was there.* Other experiments of cyclists and motorists approaching each other confirm that cyclists think they are visible long before motorists actually see them.

Cycling at night is dangerous. The many people who ride with no lights at all might act otherwise if they understood how closely they are tempting serious injury or death. A little bit of visibility is not good enough. The only sensible way to cycle at night is looking like a Christmas tree suddenly gone berserk. See also the Reflectors entry in this chapter for more information.

Mudguards

A requirement for tourists and people living in rain forests or at the end of muddy tracks. They do add a lot of air resistance though, and if you want to go like the clappers and don't mind a strip of dirt up your spine once in a while, then leave them off. Mounting or removing mudguards can be done quickly if the bike has drop-outs with separate mounting points (two small bolt-holes), or no carrier in the first place. Short-length mudguards are completely useless. Full-length plastic mudguards are light, but eventually warp and fail. Much better are the chromoplastic models, which will stand years of abuse. Stainless steel and aluminium mudguards are durable, and offer a mounting point for lights and other gear, but tend to be noisy. This can be cured with undersealing paint (motor accessory shops).

Nail Pullers or Flint-catchers

These are small half-loops of wire that ride just above the tyre and brush off shards of broken glass, pebbles, and other nasty things. Most effective with tubular and narrow-section HP tyres, and a significant challenge to fit if you use mudguards.

Odometer

In the economy version these are little mechanical gizmos ticked over by the spokes. Distance is a function also usually included in electronic speedometers/computers (see separate entry).

Pumps

I long ago tired of fending off little urchins who filch equipment, of seeing expensive aluminium-barrel pumps dented and therefore made useless, and of pumps constantly falling about the place while carrying a bike up and down stairs. I keep a large workshop pump at home, which inflates tyres with magnificent efficiency, and carry a short, pocket-size pump that will serve for emergencies. For touring, however, you will need a decent pump. One of the very best is the Zefal Preset, with a self-contained pressure regulator.

A workshop pump will include a pressure gauge, but its read-out is likely to have only a passing affinity with reality. For accurate work with modern high-pressure tyres—essential for peak performance—use a separate tyre pressure gauge.

You may also want to possess a tiny Presta/Schrader adaptor, which allows a Presta tyre valve to be inflated with a petrol station air line. If you use this, be very careful; cycle tyre pressures are high, but the volume of air is small, and only a moment's inattention is required for the whole thing to blow to smithereens.

Rain Gear

The different kinds of rain gear are essentially a matter of degree of protection, convenience in use, and conditions. Weathering a shower or drizzle on a short journey to work is one thing, riding all day in a torrential downpour is quite another. If you only need a bit of protection, more to ward off chill than to stay strictly dry, then a light nylon windbreaker will fit tidily under the saddle and always be available if needed. If it is raining hard and you want to stay dry, one lightweight emergency trick is to use a large plastic rubbish bag, tearing holes for your head and arms. Ordinary shopping bags will do as covers for your head and feet.

The classic cycling cape drapes over the shoulders, back, and handlebars, allowing air to circulate up from underneath. Also circulated is road spray from your tyres, and from other vehicles. This kind of garment is outmoded, although for reasons of simple economy, capes still have many adherents.

The problem when cycling in the rain is to keep away wet from both without and within. Conventional waterproofs that seal out the rain also seal in body perspiration, and of the two types of drenching, the former is preferable. The answer is to use clothing made from a breathable fabric such as Goretex that prevents large water molecules from coming in, but lets out the smaller molecules of perspiration vapour. If function is paramount, then be sure to buy garments made for cycling. Those made for hiking are baggy and flap noisily, and are long and short in the wrong places.

A cycling jacket should be fairly trim, have long sleeves with adjustable wrist cuffs, and a long back. Cycling jackets tend to go for sporty colours and patterns, and while this is good from the standpoint of safety, a general purpose jacket in a subdued colour is something you can use all the time, even with a suit or other spiffy garment. When cycling, colour can be added by wearing a Sam Brown belt or reflective vest (see Reflectors entry). A good jacket lasts for years and years and I have no compunction about owning two: an all-round model for normal daily use, and an expedition model for long off-road tours, yachting, and other pursuits where performance is important.

A hood is a great asset. The kind that hang loosely at the back are always flapping about, and detachable hoods that in theory should be in a pocket are always missing when you need them. I much prefer the kind that live in a little pouch, ready at the moment. Make sure the hood is compact enough so that your vision is not impaired when you turn your head, but large enough to cover a helmet. A hood-covered helmet is very effective. The helmet keeps the hood from touching your skin and becoming all clammy. If the helmet has a visor, you can tilt your head so the visor keeps the rain out of your eyes. Relatively, at least, you'll be quite comfy. Another solution that gives your head even more freedom of movement is to use a lightweight shower cap. It weighs next to nothing and can be a permanent part of your kit.

Trousers need to be cut with room for knee movement, and be large enough to fit over other clothes. I prefer those that have a full front held up with shoulder straps.

A full-size cycling rainsuit is a fairly substantial item. It's fine when touring but something of a pain when riding around in town or off on a tear. Around town I usually leave it at a plain Goretex fabric jacket. Off on a tear it may be a specialized shirt and trousers with waterproof panels at the front to keep off the worst of any rain and wind. There are many interim points between a full suit and a converted rubbish bag; to case them out, call by a good bike shop.

Rear-view Mirror

Little mirrors that mount to the back of the wrist or attach to eyeglasses have a small field of vision, and are not good enough for certain knowledge of what is going on behind. Infinitely superior for drop handlebar bikes is the Mirrycle mirror, which mounts on the brake lever hood, leaves the handlebars clear and unobstructed, and provides excellent visibility to the rear. The information provided not only serves as a warning of impending danger, but is also a great aid to faster, safer riding in traffic. The Mirrycle mirror is easily one of the best aids to cycling comfort to come along in years.

Reflectors

Good lights are your main defence system at night, but do not always identify you as a cyclist to the motorist. It is difficult to judge distance to a single rear light, and the dazzle of the light itself may obscure clear sight of the cyclist. Plus, lights can fail. Reflectors provide a good back-up that always works, and with proper use will help identify you as a cyclist.

Rear, front, wheel spoke, and pedal reflectors are a legal requirement for any bike sold after 1985. A big, red rear reflector is very useful. Mount it as low as possible, so that car headlights catch it easily. An alternative or supplement is a reflectorized rear mudguard flap. White front reflectors are useless. They are stipulated because many cyclists are too dim to use proper lights. Also useless are spoke reflectors, which are visible only when the cyclist is already broadside-on to the motorist. Wheel reflectors unbalance the wheel. When setting up a bike I throw them away. Tyres with reflective side-walls are very eye-catching, but again, only when the cyclist is actually crossing a motorist's path. At close quarters there isn't enough time for extra visibility to be much help.

Pedal reflectors are very good. Their low position is readily picked up by headlights, and their distinctive pattern of movement readily identifies the presence of a cyclist. Active, moving reflectors and lights are four times more eye-catching than static reflectors and lights.

Most reflectors are limited in mechanical effectiveness. Far better are retro-reflective materials, which will reflect light back to a source regardless of the angle of incidence. Millions of microscopic prisms per square inch do the trick. They must be sealed under plastic or other clear covering for effectiveness when wet. An excellent product when made of retro-reflective material is the Sam Brown belt, a lightweight combined belt and shoulder slash that can be used with whatever you are wearing. Another good item are retro-reflective trouser/arm bands, which, like pedal reflectors, are very eye-catching. Panniers, jackets, gloves, shoes, and so on can all be highlighted with retro-reflective tape, dots, and stickers. These all help to tell the motorist who and what you are—the more, the better.

The complete night-time cyclist wants both active and static lights and reflectors. Front and rear lights, and a moving or blinking light that can serve as a back-up if one of the static lights fails. A big rear reflector, and pedal reflectors or trouser bands that move around.

Shoes, Toe Clips, and Cleats

Ordinary street shoes do not provide sufficient support for the foot unless used with rubber or metal platform pedals. Cycling shoes have reinforced soles to distribute the impact of the thin edges of the commonly used cage type pedals. Shoes for racing have no heels, and are not intended for walking. Shoes for touring have heels, and will stand casual walking about. Dual-purpose shoes with partially stiffened soles are designed for both cycling and walking, and for many people, excel at both functions. You can now have a cycling shoe which can stand a 2,000-mile tour and yet looks perfectly in order with formal clothes.

Toe clips and straps elevate cycling into a new dimension, and ensure that your feet will remain on the pedals in the event of a mis-shifted gear or unexpected bump. Many ordinary shoes and most cycling/walking shoes have soles with sufficient texture to grip the pedals when snugged down with straps, but still can be slipped out with ease when required. Some dual-purpose shoes have ridges moulded into the soles to help grip the pedal. Fine if the alignment is in accord with that of your foot, but if not, a slight twist of your foot can damage your leg.

Cleats attach to the sole of the shoe and then in turn lock to the pedal. They give tremendous get up and go and are a must for racing and fast riding, but can be inconvenient on a tour when you want to stop and stroll around (you'll have to change shoes or go barefoot), and can be dangerous in traffic. Traditional cleats are nailed to the shoe. Modern cycling shoes have adjustable cleats mounted to the shoe with screws. These allow you to set up the cleat exactly as you like, and to change the setting if you switch to another machine with different pedals.

Even with cleats on, a healthy yank will usually get the foot off the pedal. For safety and effectiveness toe straps have to be quite snug. This can lead to chafing and foot pains. A very good answer for this problem are system pedals and cleats, such as made by Look, Adidas, and others. These are special design pedals and cleats that mate and lock together, like step-in ski bindings. They're wonderful. So long as the pedalling forces are in the plane of crank rotation, it is difficult or impossible to lose the pedal. But when you do need to detach, a lateral roll of the foot does the trick at once. It's a lighter, safer, and more effective method than regular cleats and toe straps. An important bonus is greater comfort. There is more stress on the shoe, which must be a good fit. I particularly like shoes that fasten with Velcro straps, because they are easy to adjust. System pedals are the current rage and you should see what new offerings are in the shops. At this writing the most popular make is Look, and many other brands are Look-compatible.

There are practical difficulties in specific recommendations for shoes. The first is that shoes, like saddles, are personal. Bliss for one person may be agony for another. The second is that there are too many for anyone to have tried them all. These points noted, a popular general purpose cycling shoe for use without cleats is the Sidi Comfort. The sole is thick and hard and comfortable for long hours in the saddle. I've also used it often for mountainbiking, but only with toe clips and straps. The hard sole is slippery and unsafe on open pedals. In cleated shoes the Sidi Performance with Velcro straps is a popular model often seen at race meetings. For a general purpose shoe good for walking and safe on open pedals, I'm quite happy with the Adidas Tourmalet. The Specialized Touring model is slightly bulkier but gives stronger support for the foot.

For winter riding lined cycling boots are available, and for wet weather there are slip-on booties that will go over regular shoes. One can also fit toe warmers over the toe clips.

Speedometer

Tyre drive models are generally inaccurate and increase drag. See the Computers entry for information on electronic models

Spoke Guard

This is a thin plate mounted on the rear wheel that prevents the rear derailleur from catching in the spokes. With a properly adjusted derailleur this should never happen, but should the derailleur malfunction or break (as has happened to me), then down you go, and with the back of the bike twisted into spaghetti.

Trailers

Trailers are absolutely super for hauling around groceries, laundry, children, and all manner of heavy gear. Most models attach and detach from the bike in seconds and can free you of the need for racks and panniers—very nice if you are running a high performance machine.

Despite the obvious advantages of trailers, only a few bike shops stock them, and firms producing trailers have a tendency to come and go. If you can find a unit called the Bike-Hod, consider it carefully. It's built along the lines of a golf cart and yet will manage a full-size cello or 4 × 8 sheet of plywood. A more recent model is the Pelican (Design Works, Birchwood, Cock Clarks, Chelmsford CM3 6RF), a handy-looking, bin-like affair with a capacity of 90 litres and a locking lid.

When using a trailer, all-up trailer and load weight should not exceed one-half bike rider body weight. Best machine for the job is a mountain bike. Be cautious when descending hills and over rough ground. It is difficult to overturn a properly designed and loaded trailer, but it can be done.

Turn Signals

The kind that mount on a bike are silly. There isn't enough distance between the lights to clearly indicate direction. Hand signals are more definite and effective. What can be very useful at night is a strip of retro-reflective material around the wrist or on the back of a glove. Often when cyclists signal a turn at night, their arm is lifted above the range of dipped car headlights and absorbed by the general ink of night. The signal is literally invisible.

Water Bottle

Don't ignore this common item. Vigorous cycling dehydrates the body, and a drink may not be readily to hand unless carried on the bike. Drink before you get thirsty. There are any number of patent concoctions available that variously contain glucose and/or salts. Personally, I find that a little honey in plain water is just the ticket for a lift when nearing the end of a long ride. Caffeine will also give a momentary blast. Thermal bottles are also available for a warm drink of soup.

Wheel Discs

In HPV racing wheel discs—smooth covers over the spokes—are SOP. Everyone knows that spokes churn air like an eggbeater, increasing turbulence and drag. If you want to go fast, you use discs. In UCI sanctioned races for conventional safety bikes, wheel discs are allowed only if the disc is an integral part of the wheel structure. This means heavy weight and ruinous cost. In UCI races, you don't go fast unless you have big money.

In the everyday world there are cheaper options. Many a time I've used light cardboard or plastic and tape to create temporary discs for an event. Leave a hole for the valve and cover it with tape. There are also pre-formed plastic discs available, but all the ones I've seen so far are heavy and crude.

The best discs I know of are the Quick Disc made by MSR, Box 3978 Terminal Station, Seattle, WA 98124, USA. They use adjustable aluminium rings and a stretch fabric. This makes them very light and easy to work with. The fabric can be put on or removed in a twinkling. Perhaps more importantly, the fabric is semi-porous. In practical terms, air flows over stretched fabric nearly as efficiently as over a smooth, polished surface. But cross-wind forces are reduced because they are able to partially pass through the fabric. You'll appreciate just how important this is the first time you ride a safety bike with wheel discs. It's not so bad at the rear wheel, but at the front wheel a sudden gust of wind from the side can have a major effect on steering and course. The problem is worse if the bike is a criterium racer with a steep head tube angle. Some people feel that a front disc is too dangerous for general use. I think it is more a question of getting used to very different handling, and developing the appropriate reflexes. With time and experience you learn where and when gusts are likely to come. In any case, if conditions become too difficult it is literally a snap to remove the fabric and eliminate the problem.

Summary

The right selection of accessories can make a vital difference to your cycling efficiency, comfort, and safety. Do not be afraid to spend a healthy wad of money on equipment, as the return on investment will probably be excellent. But be aware also that there are many people who have climbed aboard some beat-up old bike outfitted catch-as-catch-can, and traversed entire continents. You can always improvise; the virtue of purpose-designed equipment is usually that it is very much better.

BOOK TWO

Bike Care

Bike Care

Working on bikes is fun, a part and parcel of riding. How the bike works and responds is very much a function of maintenance. Ideally, you are going to work on your own bike because you want a together, tight machine under you, i.e., you will do it because you want to.

As with all things, you get back in proportion to what you put in. It is essentially a question of fineness. The nature of bikes is that they are at their best when well-lubricated and carefully adjusted. A sensitivity to this sort of refinement does not happen the instant you mount a bike. Give it time. As you ride you will become increasingly aware of your bike's characteristics. A well set-up bike fits you like a suit of clothes, and you will soon develop an 'ear' for the sound of bearings and a 'feel' for other parts, such as the brakes. The development of this sensitivity—the result of personal and direct participation—is part of the reason for owning a bike in the first place. Eventually, you will find that increased riding pleasure is not just a reward for doing your own maintenance, the mechanical sensitivity itself becomes part of the riding pleasure.

As I say, this is all something that you should grow into. The idea of having a bike is to have fun. A fair amount of latitude is possible in servicing bikes and you have hopefully chosen a machine suited to your level of interest. So you can minimize or maximize maintenance as per your own inclinations. Bear in mind, however, that most machines, and certainly bicycles, need a certain amount of lubrication and adjustment if they are to function at all. Without it, they rust away, and because the parts are dry and out of kilter, they slowly chew themselves to bits when ridden. I have seen 'old dependables' that have been left out in the rain for years and have never seen an oil can or a mechanic. They make it for years—and then snap a chain in the middle of a tour or a brake cable at the start of a long hill. Or eventually the rust destroys them. There is no need for this. A properly maintained bike will easily last a lifetime (one of mine was made in 1920 and has seen plenty of hard service to boot). For reasons of simple economy and safety, if you can't be bothered to do routine maintenance then take your machine to a bike shop for servicing at least twice a year.

You should of course have an ongoing relationship with a bike shop, as a source of components and bits and pieces, advice, and servicing. If you are really determined, you can do every job on the bike yourself. But many jobs are far better done with specialized, expensive tools, while others (such as wheel truing) come more easily to people who do them often. A good bike shop is a professional outfit.

It can be great fun to hand a bike over for servicing and get it back in apple pie order, but you'll find that this is more successful if you look after your bike by keeping it clean, lubricated, and properly adjusted. Shops dread ill-looked after, rusty bikes, because they are difficult and time-consuming to work on. This sends the labour charge zooming upwards, when often the bike is not worth much. A machine that has been regularly looked after is much easier and quicker to work on, and this helps keep cost down. It also leads to better work. Mechanics greatly prefer to work on sound, clean bikes, and tend to give short shift to machines that have been neglected.

The conventional starting point for work to be done by a bike shop is an examination of the machine and then a written estimate specifying the agreed work, parts, and cost. This is for the shop's protection as much as yours. When the relationship is more established you can leave matters on a more open basis, so that if the shop sees something that needs doing, they know they can go ahead and do it. Get to this stage as soon as you can; it's a right pain to collect your bike just before a dream tour or important event and then discover that something vital was not done because it was not covered in the estimate.

Minor adjustments and fine points are best carried out by you. Only you know exactly where you like the brake lever to engage, for example. Also, it is kind of silly to leave your bike at the shop for three days for a job that takes ten minutes to do.

The most important reason for doing at least some of your own work, however, is that this makes preventive maintenance almost automatic. Preventive maintenance is replacing parts before they wear out and break, usually at an inopportune time and miles from any bike shop. If you pay hands-on attention to the various parts of your bike and keep it in tune, preventive maintenance will happen pretty much as a matter of course. In turn, breakdowns and roadside repairs will be rare. This is the easiest and most efficient approach to maintaining a bike. It's more fun to work on a bike at the moment and place of your choosing, and more fun to ride a bike in which you have complete confidence.

Here is my approach to this manual: each major component system of the bicycle such as brakes, wheels, gears, etc., is broken down into four areas:

How It Works

Adjustment

Disassembly

Trouble-shooting

The idea is to give you a basic understanding of what is happening—and make you a mechanic! How It Works for each section is required reading. It does no good for you to diddle with this or adjust that if you have no idea of how it works. And if something is broken it is impossible for you to fix it unless you know how it works in the first place. It will help a lot if, while reading the How It Works sections, you look at and handle the corresponding parts of your bike.

I don't cover everything. There are many different specific products and covering them all would require a voluminous, proper shop manual. On the other hand, in mainstream models, one wheel is pretty much the same as another. I have tried to include representative types of equipment currently in use but there are bound to be exceptions. If this happens to you, try to find the item in this book which most closely resembles the part you are servicing or fixing. Pay particular attention to *function* and then analyse your own part the same way. This should get you through almost anything.

There are also some tasks which are just not worth doing. Getting into the innards of a coaster brake multi-speed hub is one of these. It takes a long, long time and isn't fun at all. Even most bike shops refuse to overhaul these units and simply replace them—it's actually cheaper this way. If you insist on doing this sort of work (some people say it has therapeutic value) detailed instructions are available from the bicycle manufacturer or from the hub manufacturer.

Tools

You can get by with amazingly little in the way of tools. However, for some kinds of work there are a few you will just have to get. Also, what you need depends on what kind of bike you have.

Before going into particulars a word on quality: do yourself a favour and buy good tools. The cheap tools sold by chain stores, supermarkets, and even hardware stores are a false economy, for they are made of inferior metals that will break or bend under stress, or made so poorly that they don't even work. In the long run good tools are well worth the investment.

I suggest that you differentiate between workshop tools that you will use for maintenance and servicing, and tools that you carry on the bike as a contingency measure for road repairs. The workshop tools should of course be good; the road-side tools can be lightweight, and in the manner of one-time razors, at least somewhat disposable. Many bike shops sell pre-assembled tool kits. Some have tools of good quality, others (such as the Mafac) are made for lightness and compactness above all else. When buying a kit make sure that the tools in it are relevant to your particular bike. Many components can only be serviced with special tools supplied by the manufacturer. The following list is necessarily rather general:

Tyre levers (plastic ones are light and smooth).
Tube patches and glue.
8″ or 6″ adjustable end spanner.
Pliers.
¼″ tip, 4-5″ shank screwdriver.
⅛″ tip, 2-3″ shank screwdriver.
Phillips (×-tip) 2-3″ shank screwdriver.
Set of metric spanners.
Set of hex (Allen) keys.
Cable cutters/wire snips.
6″ mill bastard (metal) file.
Thin hub spanners, 13 mm × 14 mm and 15 mm × 16 mm.
Spoke key.
Pedal wingnut spanner (for pedals with outside dust cap only).
Chain rivet remover.
For cotterless cranks, crank remover as per brand of crank.
Headset spanners, as per make and and type of headset.
Freewheel remover. Each make of freewheel has its own pattern of remover; make sure you have the right one for your freewheel. If you have a cassette freewheel

then you don't need a remover, but make sure you have any special tool required
to remove the locknut.

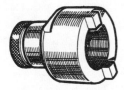 

Freewheel removers

There are many other tools and gadgets that can be handy to have. Channel-lock
pliers or Vise-grips are perennial favourites. So is a big (12″ or so) adjustable spanner
for really having a go at things. A small portable vise is very useful. A hammer
will be needed sometimes. However, as you can see, many of the tools listed are
for specialized jobs and you do have to acquire them all at once. At the very
minimum, have a small 'essential' tool kit, with tyre levers and either a patch kit
or a spare tube.

You will need some means of holding the bike steady. One method is to simply
turn the bike upside down. With dropped handlebars use a narrow cardboard or wood
box with slots cut in the side to support the handlebars and keep the brake cables
from being bent against the ground. It's better if the bike is upright. A nail driven
into a beam with a rope to hang the bike by will suffice, but best by far is a
proper work stand. These cost a little bit but are very worthwhile. Make sure the
one you buy can handle bikes with large tubing (mountain bikes, aluminium bikes).
For inflating tyres I highly recommend a track pump that stands on the floor and
has a handle for both hands. Frame pumps carried on bikes have a job to reach
the high pressures required by modern tyres, and a track pump makes life a whole
lot easier.

Lubrication

This is a general discussion of lubrication. For details look under the part in question, e.g., brakes, hubs, gears, etc. There are a number of different types and forms
of lubricants. Each has advantages and drawbacks depending on the kind of machinery
and riding involved.

Oil is the old stand-by. Be sure to use a good grade such as motorist's SAE
30, or Sturmey-Archer cycle oil. Do not use ordinary household oils, many of them
leave behind a sticky residue that gums up the works.

Grease is used for bearings. Ordinary grease from a motorist's shop will work
well enough. Lithium greases such as Filtrate and Cycle Pro are less likely to be
washed away by water. Also good in this respect is Bardahl Multi-purpose grease.
Red S waterproof grease comes in a tube with a nozzle that makes it easy to use
exactly the right amount of lubricant. The best waterproof grease of all is green
Phil Wood Waterproof Bicycle Grease. Campagnolo grease is quite expensive and
while no-one is quite sure if the stuff is truly superior, it is popular for use with
very fine components.

Generally, white lithium greases such as Filtrate or Cycle Pro are lightweight and run more freely than heavy, stiff water-resistant greases such as Phil Wood or LPS-100. You'll find that many racing people favour the lighter greases, and often brew up exotic mixtures of their own design. Remember, though, that these folk usually think little of stripping down and lubricating a bike for nearly every race. The tourist, commuter, and recreational rider will usually prefer the longer interval between services provided by the stiffer waterproof greases.

Your bicycle has upwards of 200 ball-bearings held in place by cups and cones. The cone remains stationary while the cup, and whatever part is attached to it—in this example it would be a wheel—rides on the ball-bearings and spins around. The distance between the cone and the cup is adjustable and must not be too tight or too loose. Sometimes the ball-bearings are held in a clip called a *race*. Typically, this is positioned so that the balls are against the cup.

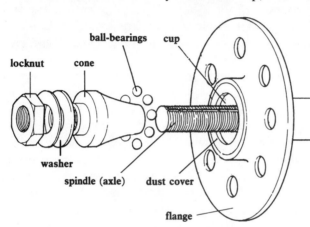

Another type of bearing is a sealed unit known as a cassette or cartridge. These are held in place in various ways: press fit, glue, and with bearing retainers that serve the same function as a cone. Mechanisms that use cartridge bearings are sometimes adjustable, and sometimes not. In general, cartridge bearings are intended to be left alone until they need replacement. Traditional ball-bearings and cones are designed for servicing

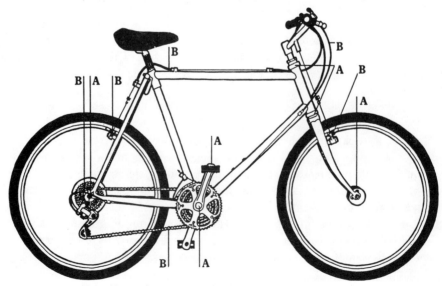

and lubricating, but cartridge bearings are usually sealed against dirt and water, and designed for the minimum of servicing, if any. As you might imagine, the difference cuts both ways: ball-bearings and cones are usually more vulnerable to dirt and water, but can be cleaned and lubricated without much difficulty; cartridge bearings are the most resistant to contamination, but are usually replaced rather than serviced, and the work frequently calls for special tools.

You will find bearings at the headset, bottom bracket, wheels, and pedals (A). When lubricated with a lightweight, oil-based grease these bearings are usually disassembled, cleaned thoroughly in solvent, packed with grease, and reassembled every

Pouring in the " Little Oil Bath."

six months. (See under relevant section for disassembly technique.) With a good waterproof grease the job can be left for three years if the bike is in moderate service (2,000 miles a year or less). High mileage bikes (5,000+ miles a year), bikes with heavy or hard riders, and bikes used regularly in wet, dirty conditions will need servicing annually. Any bearing which runs rough or tight requires immediate attention.

Some bearings are both greased and oiled, in particular, 2- and 3-speed hubs,

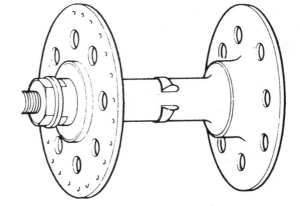

and old-fashioned ultra-fancy racing bike hubs. You can tell these by the fact that the hub has a small oil cap or a clip that seals a small oil hole.

These need lubricating once a month: multi-speed internal gear hubs a tablespoonful, regular hubs about half a teaspoonful, and coaster brake hubs 2 tablespoonfuls. Some bottom brackets are set up to use fluid as well as grease. A teaspoonful once a month. Use fluid

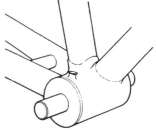

wherever you find oil caps or clips. Too little is better than too much. If fluid leaks out of the sides of the bearings and dribbles all over your crankset or wheels, you are using too much.

I prefer the use of a dry lubricant for the chain, freewheel, derailleur, brake pivot bolts, cables, and any other parts which do not have to use grease (B). Dry lubricants usually come in spray form and contain an exotic and sometimes secret blend of ingredients. The important thing is that after the solvent evaporates, the lubricants are dry. The trouble with oil is that it attracts dirt which then mixes with the oil and forms a gooey, abrasive mess, greatly increasing mechanical wear. Everything gets dirty, including you. In the case of the chain, for example, this means that once a month you have to break and remove it, soak it clean in a solvent, dry it, oil it, and then remount it. It's time consuming and messy. If you use a dry lubricant you need do this job only once every two or three months. You must lubricate more often—bi-weekly in normal service, weekly in hard service—but with a spray this job takes only a few seconds. The same rationale applies for the freewheel and derailleur. The spray is particularly useful for the brake pivots and all cables. Oil has a tendency to leak out onto the brake levers and handlebars, and brake shoes. Once a month is sufficient.

One excellent dry lubricant is called Superspray. It's incredible stuff, with a very high load tolerance that gives it good resistance to abrasion and wear. Another thing I like is that the aerosol is air-powered and thus does no harm to the environment. I've also had good results with Tri-Flo products, which include both a waterproof grease and a general spray lubricant. An important point to note is that some dry lubricants do not mix well with oil or grease. If you want to use a dry lubricant on a chain for example, first clean off the old grease and grunge.

Another extremely good, very cheap dry lubricant that does not attract dirt is paraffin wax (the kind used for sealing homemade preserves), available in grocery shops. It must be renewed fairly frequently, every 800-1,000 miles or so, but this is easy to do, and the chain will have a long life. To use paraffin wax, first clean your chain in the conventional manner with solvent. Melt the paraffin in a coffee can or old aluminium container over the stove. Dump the chain in, let it soak for a while, and then hang it up so that the paraffin drippings fall back into the can. Save the old paraffin, and when you need to lubricate the chain again, just heat up the paraffin and toss in the chain. The dirt will come off the chain and rise to the surface of the paraffin, where it can be skimmed away. Use oil or spray for the brake pivot points, freewheel, and derailleur. Paraffin will not work well on these parts because it cools and hardens too quickly on contact with the metal to penetrate effectively. It is excellent for brake cables, however. Just run the cable through a block of paraffin a few times until it is well impregnated.

NOTE: A new bike or a bike that has been standing around for a long time may be dry as a bone. OIL EVAPORATES! Be sure to lubricate the bike before using.

General Words

There are a number of things to keep in mind when servicing bikes.

1. Do not use a great deal of force when assembling or disassembling parts. Bicycle components are frequently made of alloys for light weight. These are not as strong as steel and it is not hard to strip threads or otherwise damage parts. Always be sure that things fit. Be careful and delicate. Snug down bolts, nuts, and screws firmly, not with all your might.

2. Most parts tighten *clockwise* and come apart turning *anti-clockwise*. This is called a right-hand thread. A left-hand thread tightens *anti-clockwise* and loosens *clockwise*. Left-hand threads are not often used. The left side pedal and the right side bottom bracket cup and locknut are usually left-hand threads.

3. When fitting together threaded parts hold them as perfectly aligned as you can, and turn one backwards (loosen) until you hear and feel a slight click. Then reverse and tighten. If this is new to you, practise on a nut and bolt until you have the feel of it perfectly.

4. If you get stuck with a rust-frozen bolt or nut, soak it in penetrating oil, give it a few taps to help the oil work in, and then try to undo it again with a tool that fits exactly. If this fails try a cold chisel and hammer. Go at this carefully since if you slip you may gouge a chunk out of your bicycle. If this method fails, hacksaw or file the nut or bolt off, or drill it out. How did it get this rusty in the first place?

5. Be neat and organized when working on a bike. Lay parts out in the order in which they came apart or go together. Put tiny parts in boxes or jars. You might have to break for a meal or a visit to the shop, the cat might scatter your ball-bearings—anything could, and often does, happen. If the job is organized and secure, you can come back to it much more easily.

6. Allow time for working. One thing often leads to another, especially if the bike hasn't been tended to for a while. A simple brake shoe adjustment, for example, may also see you overhauling the brake mechanism and installing a new cable.

7. There are a number of little nuts and bolts on your bike for racks, brake lever mounts, gear-shift lever mounts, and the like. These tend to get loose and need to be checked about once a month. One way to meet this problem is to let the nuts and bolts bed in first, and then fix them in place with a product such as Loctite.

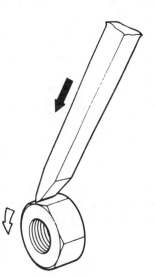

8. The left side of the bike is on your left when you and the bike both point forward.

9. Bearing adjustments are a matter of measurement, feel, and circumstances. For example, when adjusting the bearings on a quick-release hub, allowance must be made for the fact that when mounting the wheel onto the bike, closing the lever will also tighten the bearings. It's always a good idea to check bearing adjustment after all parts are in place. Generally, new bearings are set up tight, so that they wear into proper adjustment as they bed in. Bearings that are already broken-in should be carefully set to the correct tolerance; too tight a setting risks damage.

For any given bearing there is an optimum or best adjustment, and it is up to you to find it. Basically, bearings should be adjusted as precisely as possible while still running smoothly. If the instructions say: 'Screw cone home finger tight, reverse

one-eighth to one-quarter turn, and lock in place with locknut', and the component still runs rough, then try widening the adjustment a little more. If, in order for the component to run smoothly, the bearing adjustment has to be so wide that there is pronounced side-to-side play, then something is wrong.

10. Solvents. Although petrol is to be found sloshing around at a zillion car service stations, no-one will ever tell you to use it as a solvent. The reason is that every once in a while someone gets blown to kingdom come. The petrol itself is not so bad, but the vapour it gives off is very volatile. Because petrol vapour is heavier than air, it settles and pools on the ground, where it can then seep along to some unexpected spot to meet a careless match or appliance pilot light—Boom! It happens fairly often, and this is why there are 'No charging' signs in most car parks.

Paraffin can be used as a solvent, but it contains water. On a part that you can clean and wipe dry with a rag, no problem. A component such as a chain with lots of fiddly bits is likely to be damaged, however, unless it is dried out in an oven. There are also degreasers such as Spray Away or Gunk, though these once again involve water.

11. Finish: a good quality auto-paste wax will preserve your paint job and make

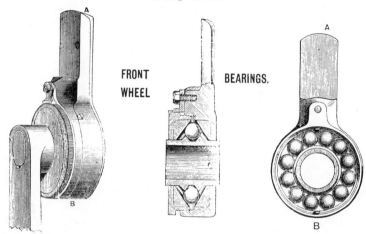
it easier to keep the bike clean. Do not wax wheel rims where the brake shoes make contact! If the rim sides need cleaning, use fine steel wool.

It is a good idea to wipe the bike clean once a week. A high-pressure hose can be used to clean a very dirty machine, such as a mud-encrusted mountain bike, but be sure to re-lubricate the bike at once. Before storing away a bike that has got very wet, ride it for a mile or two (or put it on a work stand and spin the various parts) to help drive water out of the bearings and other bits.

12. Wire cable is used for brake and gear controls. If you need to trim a new cable to size, do so with wire snips for a clean cut. Pliers will fray the cable end so that it will not pass through the cable housing. After snipping, solder the cable end to prevent fraying, or alternatively, dip it in epoxy glue. File away excess solder or glue. In a pinch, wrap the cable end with a little tape.

13. Last but by no means least, do not be afraid! The whole idea of mechanical things is that they go together and come apart. A feeling that something is delicate and might break if you mess with it is a symptom of uncertainty. Get with it, get greasy, and stay with it until you *know* you've got it together.

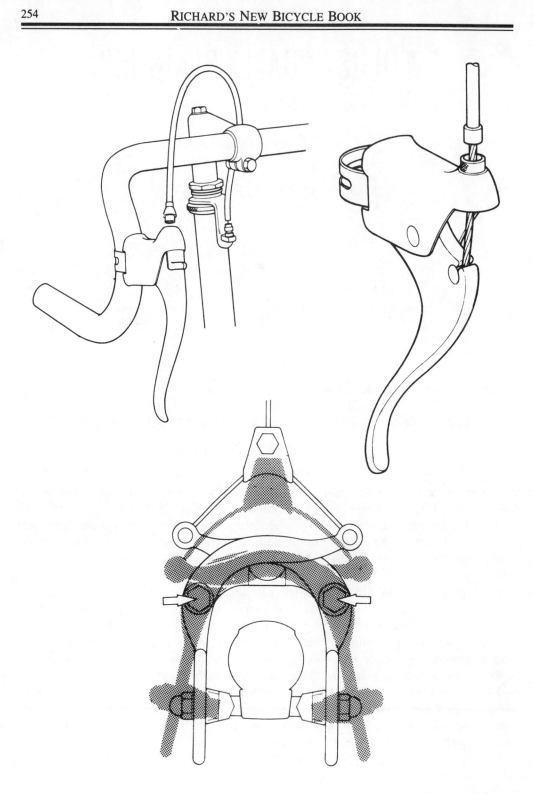

Brakes

Bicycle brakes come in three basic types: hub, disc, and calliper. A hub coaster brake is inferior on several counts. Under conditions requiring a quick stop it tends to lock up the rear wheel, causing the bike to skid rather than slow down. It has poor heat dissipating qualities and can burn out on a long downhill. It is difficult to service. It is for the rear wheel only, cutting braking efficiency below 50 per cent, as it is the front wheel that gives the greatest braking power. In fact, on dry roads it is difficult if not impossible to lock up a front wheel. This is because braking throws weight forward, increasing traction for the front wheel. If your bike has only a coaster brake, for safety's sake equip it with a calliper brake at the front. Only children whose hands are not strong enough to operate calliper brakes should have a coaster brake, and they should not ride in any situation requiring quick stops or sustained braking. If something goes wrong with your coaster brake, simply remove the entire rear wheel and take it to a bicycle shop for overhaul or replacement. It is complicated to fix.

Hand-operated hub drum brakes are sensitive and powerful, but not in the models so far offered by mainstream cycle manufacturers. Disc brakes give good stopping power in both wet and dry conditions, but are heavy, and tend to be mechanically sensitive.

Calliper brakes offer a good balance between weight and stopping power. Modern brake shoes give reasonable performance under wet conditions and very good performance under dry conditions. Calliper brakes are relatively simple to service.

How Calliper Brakes Work

Calliper brake systems all work on the same basic principle. There is a hollow, flexible tube called a cable housing between the brake lever mount and the cable hanger, or a cable stop on the frame. The cable housing is flexible so that the handlebars can turn back and forth. Through the cable housing passes a cable, attached to the brake lever at one end, and to the brake mechanism at the other. The brake mechanism is attached to the bicycle frame and functions like a pair of ice tongs. When the brake lever is operated, it pulls the cable through the cable housing and pulls together the arms (or *yokes*) of the brake mechanism, causing the two brake shoes attached to the yokes to press against the wheel rim and stop the wheel.

When the lever is released, a spring forces the yoke arms away from the wheel rim, and returns the brake lever to the off position. The illustrations on the opening page of this chapter are for a centre-pull brake with two yoke arms, each rotating on a separate pivot point.

The side-pull brake uses only one pivot point, with the cable housing attached directly to one yoke, and the cable to the other. The effect is the same.

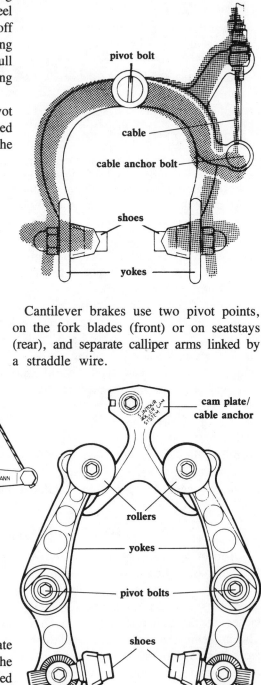

Cantilever brakes use two pivot points, on the fork blades (front) or on seatstays (rear), and separate calliper arms linked by a straddle wire.

Roller-cam brakes also use two separate arms and pivot points, but instead of the arms being pulled together, a wedge-shaped metal plate or similar device pushes them apart.

All calliper brake systems
have a cable adjusting bolt for
changing the relationship of the
cable housing and the brake
cable. On a side-pull brake it
is usually on the yoke to which
the cable housing is attached
(A), while on centre-pull and
cantilever brakes it is usually at
the brake lever (B) or the cable

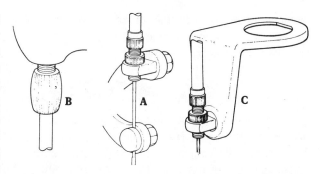

hanger (C). In most cases properly adjusted brake shoes are close enough to the
rim so that the tyre will not
slide between them when
removing the wheel. Accordingly, many brake systems have a
means for creating a little extra slack in the brake cable.
This can be a small button
which allows the brake lever to
open more, or a cam plate
device on the cable hanger or

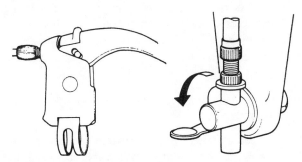

the brake mechanism. Cantilever and roller-cam brakes are easily opened apart by
disconnecting the yoke cable or cam plate.

The basics of calliper brake systems are: a brake lever, a brake cable and housing with an adjusting bolt, a cable hanger or frame stop eyelet for centre-pull and

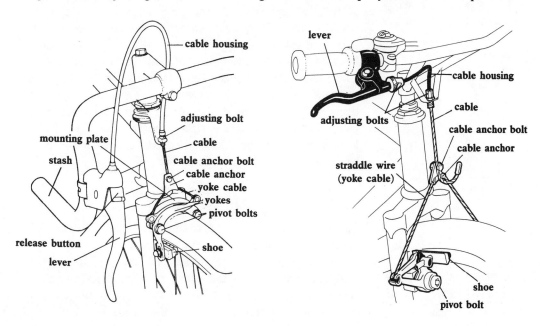

cantilever systems, and the brake mechanism, including yokes, springs, and brake shoes. Some designs include either a button or cam to provide extra slack in the cable when removing the wheel or servicing the brakes.

Lubrication

Avoid oil. At the brake levers it works out over everything and gets your hands dirty every time you ride. At the brake mechanism it dribbles down to the brake shoes, cutting braking power. A better product is a dry lubricant such as Superspray, which displaces water and does not attract dirt. Use the little plastic nozzle which comes with the can for pin-point accuracy, and spray pivot bolts, all exposed cable (use a piece of paper or cardboard as a backstop to prevent the spray from going all over your bike), yoke cable anchor points, brake lever pivots, and inside the cable housings. Machines used once or twice a week need lubrication every two months, those in daily use, monthly. More often on tours, or if your bike is fond of swims.

Adjustment

There are two basic adjustments for calliper systems: (1) seeing that the brake shoe hits the wheel rim properly, and (2) keeping slack out of the cable between the

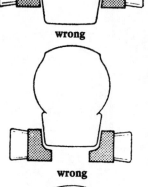

wrong

wrong

right

brake lever and mechanism, so that the brakes engage before the movement of the lever is stopped by the handlebar.

First check that the wheel is true by spinning it and seeing that the rim, not the tyre, stays about the same distance from the brake shoe all the way around. If play is greater than approximately ⅛" the wheel should be trued before any brake adjustments are attempted. Check also that the wheel is reasonably centred between the fork arms or stays, and that the rim is free of major dents and scratches. If the wheel is out of track (not in the same plane as the other wheel), take the bike to a shop to have the frame checked, and if the rim is badly banged up, get a new one.

Brake Shoes

These need to be aligned so that the shoe hits the rim squarely. An important point to note with cantilever brakes is that they arc down and not up like other calliper brakes. Keep the shoes positioned so that they strike high on the rim, close to the tyre. If the contact point is low on the rim, toward the inside of the wheel,

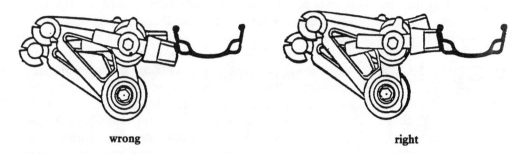

wrong   right

then under heavy braking the shoe can compress slightly and slip off the rim—surprise, no brakes. Brake shoes wear out steadily, and are also sometimes put out of adjustment by a chance knock; make a habit of checking them often.

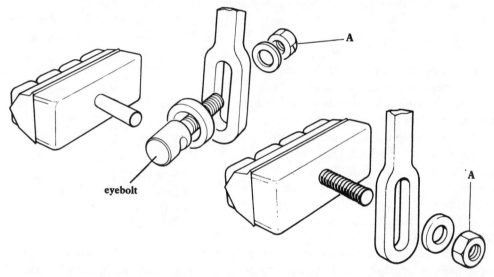

Brake shoes are held on by a conventional bolt or an eyebolt. Loosen nut A, adjust brake shoes to meet rim, and tighten. One method is to loosen nut A just a little bit and gently tap the shoe into proper position with the spanner handle. With conventional bolts you'll find that the brake shoe twists slightly when you tighten the nut back down. A good trick is to set the shoe high (or askew, as the case may be), so that the final tightening of the bolt brings it perfectly into position. Do not use too much force. Brake bolt screws strip easily.

Eyebolt type shoes are easy to adjust so that the face of the shoe is flush with the rim. Achieving this effect with a conventional bolt brake shoe sometimes requires bending the yoke. CAUTION: alloy fatigues easily. Slight, gentle bending is usually all right, but hard bending can make the alloy brittle and prone to break. It is better to position and face a brake block by shaving it with a razor or sandpaper, or by using a tapered washer to tilt it in the right direction. Note also that new brake shoes frequently wear into correct alignment after a few days.

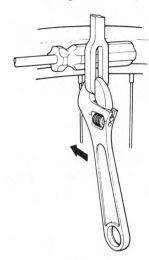

If bending is the only way, remove the brake shoe altogether and fit an adjustable end spanner snugly over the end of the yoke. If the yoke needs to be bent outward, simply pull on the handle of the spanner. If the yoke needs to be bent inward, provide a pivot point by wedging another spanner, screwdriver handle, or other object between the yoke and tyre, and push in the spanner handle.

If you are replacing the brake shoes consider using the synthetic type, as they are much better for all-around performance and sensitivity than the shoes supplied by brake manufacturers. Do so only if you have good quality brakes in crisp, firm condition. Synthetic shoes are very quick, and will snatch and grab if the brake mechanism is loose and sloppy.

Brake shoes must be toed-in, so that the front of the shoe contacts the rim before the back of the shoe. Because of twist and play in the brake mechanism, under actual braking the shoe is flush with the rim. Synthetic shoes and extra long shoes need more toe-in than rubber shoes and short shoes. The gap can be as large as ¼"; try ⅛" to start and adjust as needed.

Most if not all synthetic shoes are supplied with bevelled washers that allow you to adjust the toe-in. The feature is also an integral part of many brake mechanisms. Loosen fixing nut A and rotate control washer B to adjust toe-in.

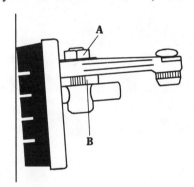

When the brake shoe mounts with a straight bolt and no bevelled washer is provided, use an adjustable end spanner to twist the yoke arm itself. Be delicate.

Cables

Once the brake shoes have been properly aligned they should be placed as close to the rim as possible without rubbing when the wheel is spun, ⅛" or less. This is done via the cable adjusting bolt and locknut, and the cable anchor bolt.

anchor bolt

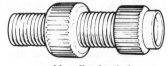

cable adjusting bolt

The idea is to screw in the cable adjusting bolt, take up as much slack as possible at the anchor nut, and then use the cable adjusting bolt to take up slack as required. When the cable adjusting bolt reaches the limit of its travel, the process is repeated. There are a number of different methods for doing this job, depending on the type of tools that you have. A very handy gadget is called a third hand and is a spring-like affair for compressing brake shoes together. Bike shops have them. The reason for this tool, or substitute (an old toe clip strap does nicely), is that otherwise, when you loosen the anchor cable bolt, spring tension from the brake yoke arms will pull the cable through the small hole in the bolt, and you will have a hard time putting it back in.

Undo locknut and screw cable adjusting bolt all the way home. If there is a brake release button or cam, check that it is set for normal operation. If you have a third hand, mount it. Or use a C-clamp. Or even string. If you have none of these things, squeeze the brake yoke arms together with your hand. With the other hand, pull the cable at the brake mechanism out so the brake lever is fully home, as it would be if the brakes were not on. Make sure the cable housing has not caught on the outside lip of the cable adjusting bolt. Now look at the amount of slack in the cable. For centre-pull and

cantilever brakes this is the distance between the yoke cable and the cable anchor A. For side-pull systems, it is the amount of new cable protruding beneath the yoke A.

Estimate the amount of slack to be taken up with a ruler, tool handle, or finger. Disengage the yoke cable from the cable anchor (centre-pulls/cantilevers). Eliminate this step if you have a third hand or similar device. Use two spanners to slacken the cable

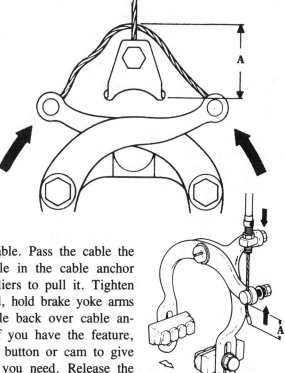

anchor nut. Avoid twisting the cable. Pass the cable the required distance through the hole in the cable anchor bolt. If it sticks, use a pair of pliers to pull it. Tighten cable anchor bolt. If no third hand, hold brake yoke arms together again and slip yoke cable back over cable anchor, or cable back into yoke. If you have the feature, now is the time to use the brake button or cam to give you that little bit of extra slack you need. Release the second or third hand, as the case may be. Only one or two turns of the cable adjusting bolt should bring the brake shoes as close as possible to the wheel rim without actually touching when the wheel is spun. If you have gotten it right (it usually takes a couple of tries), use wire cutters to snip off the excess cable for a neat job. Cover the cable end with a cap (bike shops), dip it in glue or solder, or tape it. Frayed cable ends have a habit of snagging fingers and clothing.

Straddle Wires and Cam Plates

With a centre-pull brake the yoke cable is usually fixed in length, which means adjusting shoe and rim clearance as per above. With a cantilever brake the yoke cable (often called a straddle wire) is adjustable for length. Together with the eyebolt mounting for the brake shoe, and the cable anchor bolt for the brake cable, there

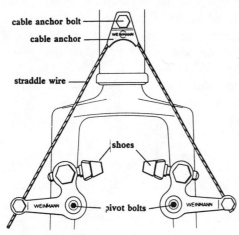

are three means of adjusting shoe and rim clearance. Each has a fair bit of latitude, but try to keep the whole thing in balance.

Use a fairly generous length of straddle wire. There are various ideas about the best length. One school of thought is that, when the brake shoes are pressing against the wheel rim, the straddle wire should form a 90° with the yoke arm. Another is that the straddle wire should be as short as possible, for maximum mechanical advantage. In the real world, if the straddle wire is long, and breaks, you may then have enough wire left to get the brake going again. More importantly, if the straddle wire is short and the cable anchor bolt loses its grip, the straddle wire can be drawn into the tyre—instant flight for the rider. See that the end of the brake cable protrudes 2-3″ out of the cable anchor bolt, and crimp the end 90°. If the bolt loosens and slides down the wire it will hopefully catch on the crimp and still keep the straddle wire clear of the tyre. Keep your cable anchor bolts tight!

With a roller-cam brake, the cable anchor bolt and the cable adjusting bolt are there to keep the cam plate properly positioned. The cam plate is Y-shaped. Each arm of the Y has (or should have) a slight bump or rise. The moment of maximum mechanical advantage is when the brake arm rollers meet the slight bump or rise

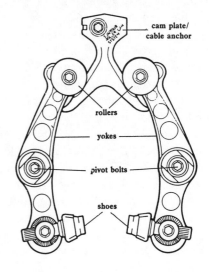

on the cam plate, and this is when the brake shoes should strike the wheel rim. Thus, adjusting a roller-cam brake is a two-stage affair. Start by screwing home the cable adjusting bolt. Then loosen the cable anchor bolt and position the cam plate so that the two rollers on each brake arm nest into the indents in the cam plate. Slightly tighten the cable anchor bolt and then see if, when the brake lever is compressed to the point where you would like the brakes to engage, the brake arm rollers have moved up the cam plate to where the sides have a bump or rise. If a few turns of the cable adjusting bolt won't do the trick, reset the position of the cable anchor bolt. When all is well, use the eyebolt adjustment to position the brake shoes ⅛" from the rim.

At this point you may well discover that the spring tension for the brake arms is inadequate, or out of balance. The brake returns to the off position too slowly, or one shoe drags on the rim. The crude way to deal with this is to just bend the spring arms until they do what you want, but if this is done too often the spring may weaken and break. Better to loosen the pivot bolt, rotate the spring mount with a thin cone spanner until the spring tension is correct, and then lock the mount in place with the pivot bolt.

Roller-cam brakes are a fair job to get just right, but persevere; the results are worth the trouble.

Pivot Bolt(s)

Side-pull brakes: make sure nut A is tight. Turn in locknut C one-half turn while holding acorn adjusting nut B still with another spanner. Turn both B and C in flush against brake yoke arm. Back B off one-half turn, hold in place and lock locknut C against it.

Centre-pull brakes: see under Trouble-shooting. The pivot bolts on cantilever and roller-cam brakes do not need adjustment as such, but should be periodically cleaned and lubricated; see under Disassembly.

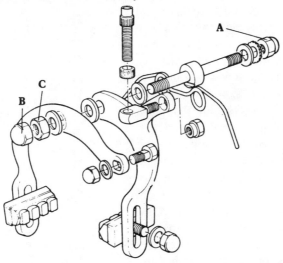

Levers

Brake levers for dropped handlebars are rarely adjustable; mountain bike brake levers usually are. Undo the locknut N for the brake lever bolt A (see page 267), tighten or loosen the latter as required, and then fix it in place with the locknut. Some brake levers have a travel adjustment screw C which enables fine-tuning of the brake lever position; screwing it in will move the lever closer to the handlebar—a good option for people with small hands, or if you frequently ride on steep slopes and need to have two fingers on the handlebar grip and two fingers on the brake lever.

Disassembly

Cables

The frequency with which you will need to replace brake (and other) cables depends on how you use your bike. Machines consistently left out in the rain, or used hard

every day, are going to need new cables sooner than well cared for or average use machines. There is no hard and fast rule. Any obvious defect, such as a frayed cable, is immediate grounds for replacement, as is stickiness in the motion of the cable through the cable housing (see Trouble-shooting). It is a good idea to replace both brake cables at the same time. They are cheap, and if one has run its course, it is likely that the other has, too. The inconvenience of a broken cable is not worth the gain of a month's extra use. If you have purchased a used bike I would replace cables all around unless you know they are relatively new and obviously in good condition. Good condition means they are clean, have no kinks or frayed spots, and pass easily through the cable housings.

Unless you can specify the brand and model of brake, take your bike or old cable to the store. Cables come in different shapes, lengths, and thicknesses. It is very irritating to discover in the middle of things that you have the wrong part. If you can, use thick cable as supplied on better mountain bikes. Thick cables are stronger and less prone to stretch, and

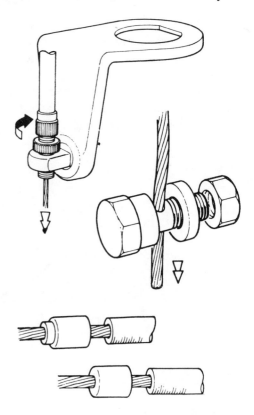

make brake control positive and definite; by comparison, thin cables are more elastic, and tend to make brakes feel spongy and indefinite. Mountain bikes should be able to use thick cable without difficulty, other bikes may need a little adjustment, such as enlarging the hole in the cable anchor bolt, or alternatively, replacement parts that are correctly sized—in particular, the cable housings. Changing to thick brake cable may involve a bit of bother, but the benefit to performance is very noticeable.

Use the left-hand brake lever for the rear brake. Since the rear brake is usually favoured for routine braking, the right hand is free for signalling cross-traffic turns. This is, of course, a function of Britain's unique system of travelling on the left side of the road; elsewhere in the world people travel on the right side of the road, and bikes are wired with the right-hand lever for the rear brake. Left to rear does have an advantage in that the more powerful and sensitive front brake is easier to control with the dominant, right hand. Even if you are a left-handed southpaw, go left-rear, right-front, or some unhappy day your reflexes will betray you when riding another bike, or a friend will have a rude surprise when riding your bike.

For any calliper brake system, first screw home the cable adjusting bolt. With a centre-pull or cantilever, push together the brake yoke arms (use a third hand or similar device if you have it) and slip the yoke cable off the cable anchor. Undo cable anchor bolt and nut and slide same off cable. With a front brake, slide the cable housing off the cable. If there are ferrules (little caps over the ends of the cable housing), keep track of where they go. With a rear brake, if the housing is held to the bike with clips, then slide the cable out of the housing.

Fully depress the brake lever. Most have a provision for disconnecting the cable by sliding it through a slot. If not, simply thread the cable back out of the brake lever.

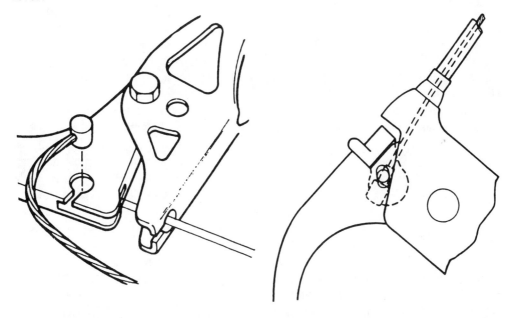

Before installing new cable, check the cable housings to see if they need replacement. Are they kinked or broken?

Are the ends free from burrs? You can eliminate a burr by:

(1) snipping off the cable housing end with a strong pair of wire cutters (pliers are not good enough);

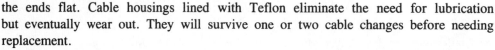

(2) clamping the cable housing end in a vise and filing it down; or

burr   **clean**

(3) using a tool called a taper ream, which you insert in the cable housing end and twist until the burr has gone.

If you use wire cutters be sure to get the cutting edges in between the coils of the housing or else you will mash the ends flat. Cable housings lined with Teflon eliminate the need for lubrication but eventually wear out. They will survive one or two cable changes before needing replacement.

When installing new cable, save any cutting for last. Unless the wire cutters are first-class, cutting invariably frays the cable end and makes it hard to slide through the housing and cable anchor bolt. However, some cables are made with a brake nipple at one end, and a gear nipple at the other end, and have to be cut—be as neat as possible. One help if you don't have a good pair of wire cutters is to wrap the cable with tape and

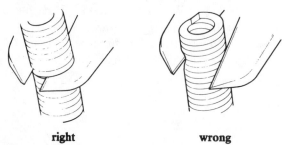

right   **wrong**

then cut through the tape. Another trick is to coat the area where you will make the cut with a little quick-setting glue.

Installation is the reverse of removal, and for clarification look at the illustrations for that section. For unlined cable housings, lubricate the cable. I like to use a fairly stiff grease that will last for a while, but most anything slippery will do. Slip cable through brake lever mount and attach to brake lever. Thread cable into housing, or housing onto cable. Whichever way you do it, twist the cable or housing as you go, and be sure to do it in the right direction or the cable will unravel.

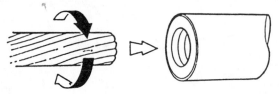

Push free cable end through cable hanger or frame stop eyelet (centre-pulls, cantilevers, and roller-cams), or through cable adjusting bolt at yoke (side-pulls), and then through cable anchor bolt hole. To adjust see Adjustment, this section.

Levers

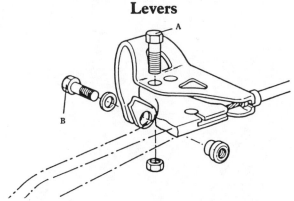

To adjust lever position, slacken A and move. To remove lever, take off bolt B. An old-fashioned lever may have to be slid off the handlebar, in which case the grip must be removed. If the grip is stuck in place, a little soap and water will do the trick.

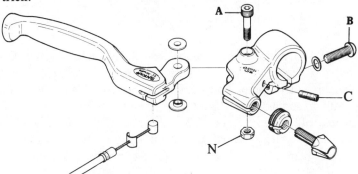

A is the bolt for the lever, and B is the mounting bolt.

Drop handlebar brake levers vary, but most use a band and bolt as below. Fully depress brake lever (you may have to disconnect the cable for enough room) and use a screwdriver or socket spanner on bolt A.

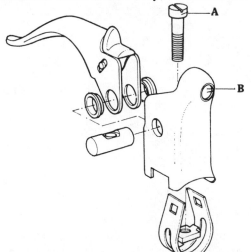

Brake Mechanism

Side-pull

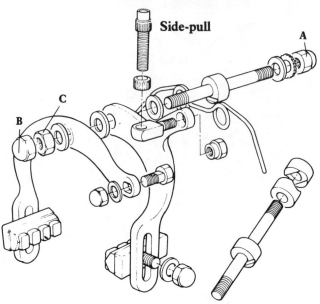

Disconnect brake cable. To remove entire brake from bike, undo nut A. Disassembly should be done only to replace a specific part if it won't work. Start with brake mechanism on bike, or end of pivot bolt clamped in a vise. Undo the brake spring by prying it off with a screwdriver. Careful of fingers. Separate nut B from nut C, and take them both off the pivot bolt. Then the rest of the stuff. Keep the parts lined up in the order in which you remove them. If you are replacing the pivot bolt, undo nut A and take off bolt. Reverse procedure for reassembly.

Centre-pull

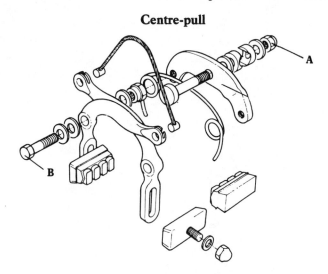

Disconnect brake cable. To remove unit from bike, undo nut A, remove washers and seating pads, and then brake mechanism. Full disassembly varies considerably from model to model and is covered for three types in Trouble-shooting, below.

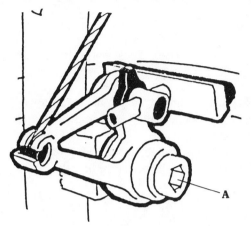

Cantilever

Disconnect brake cable. Undo pivot bolt A, and be meticulous about keeping track of the bits and pieces as they come off. Each marque and model has a different assortment, but there is a reason for every part. Know which way is right side up, and don't mix the parts from one side to the other. The right and left springs, for example, are different.

Roller-cam

Disconnect brake cable by compressing the brake arms and lifting the cam plate away from the brake arm rollers. Free the two springs S from the tabs on the brake arms. Undo the nut A on the pivot bolts and lift off the arms. The brake arm rollers undo with a hex key. Clean everything up, replace any worn or defective parts, and lubricate.

Note that the mounts for the springs rotate, and have two small slots sized for a thin cone spanner. When you replace the brake arm, it is likely that you will need to adjust spring tension with a cone spanner. When it is right, lock the arm and spring in place with the pivot bolt nut.

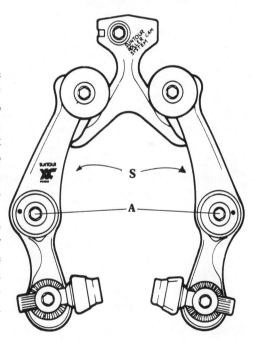

Trouble-shooting

Before using this section please read How It Works and Adjustment. You have to know how it works in the first place in order to figure out what's wrong. Brake problems come in three broad categories. In each category there are three possible areas in which the trouble may be: brake lever, cable, or mechanism. The first thing is to find in which of these the problem originates, and this is done by isolating and activating each unit separately.

Category 1 — No or very weak brakes

●Is rim oily?

●Are shoes striking rim?

●Will brake mechanism compress when you squeeze it with your hand? If no, go to Category 3, below. If yes,

●Does lever move freely? Yes? Broken cable. Replace.

●Lever will not move. Disconnect cable at brake mechanism end. Will cable housing slide off cable? No? Cable is frozen inside housing. Get it off somehow and replace. If cable and housing separate easily then,

●Lever is frozen. First see if your unit has an adjustable bolt for the lever (B), and if so give it a try. No? A major bash may have pinched together the sides of the brake lever mount housing. Examine it carefully and bend out dented parts with a big screwdriver.

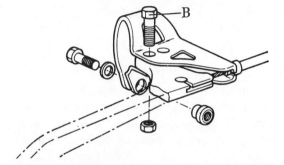

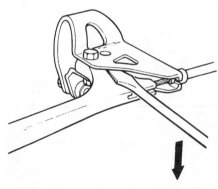

Or the lever itself may be bent. If the damage is slight, bend it back. If the damage is severe, replace the lever or unit. Metal which has been bent a lot may look perfectly OK but be fatigued and weak, and snap under the pressure of a hard stop.

Category 2 — Brakes work, but unevenly or make noises

●Juddering. Can be caused by a loose brake mechanism, uneven rims, or sometimes by a loose headset. If it is the brake mechanism, tighten up the pivot bolt(s) A. With a side-pull, undo locknut C from acorn adjusting nut B and screw both in flush against brake yoke arm. Back off B one half turn and lock into place with locknut C.

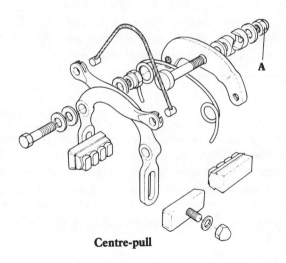

Centre-pull

●Squealing. Brake shoes may be old and hard. Sometimes rubber from shoes has streaked rim. Clean with fine steel wool and/or strong solvent like benzene or cleaning fluid in a WELL-VENTILATED AREA. Squealing brakes can sometimes be fixed by toeing in the brake shoes (see Adjustments) and sometimes this problem just can't be eliminated.

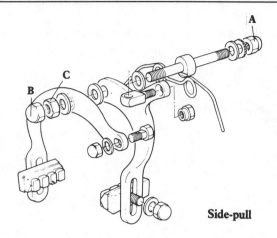

Side-pull

Category 3 — Sticky or dragging brakes

This is the most common problem. First determine whether it is the lever, cable, or mechanism which is at fault.

●If it is the lever, see Frozen lever (above).

●If it is the cable, replace it (Replacement, above).

●Brake mechanism.

Side-pull

First make sure everything is there and properly hooked up. This sounds simple-minded, but there is a reason for each of the parts and the mechanism won't work without them. Is the spring complete and attached to both yoke arms? Make sure nut A is tight. Undo locknut C from acorn adjusting nut B and screw both flush against yoke arm. Back B off one-half turn and lock it with C. Check pivot bolt D is straight and replace if necessary. Lubricate.

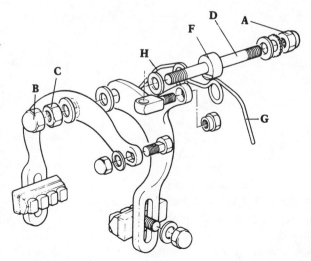

If one shoe drags against rim: loosen the mounting nut A, hold brake yokes in correct position, and tighten nut A. No soap? Examine brake seating pad F. If it has a slot for the spring you will have to try bending the spring. There are two ways to do this. One is to pry the spring arm off the brake yoke which is dragging and bend it outward using pliers or a similar tool. The second is to take a big screwdriver and poise it against G or H, whichever is OPPOSITE the

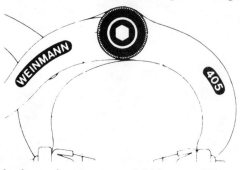

dragging shoe, and give it a sharp bash with a hammer. This second method is quicker, but of course a little riskier.

Many Weinmann brakes have a little recessed hex bolt for making this adjustment. Clever, but the tool to fit the hex bolt is usually tinny and more likely to break than not. Better to just slacken pivot mounting nut A.

Still no soap? Check to see that the brake yokes are not rubbing against each other. If so, bend them apart with a screwdriver, or slide in a piece of fine emery cloth (sandpaper for metal) and file it down.

If this is not the problem and you have tried everything else, a complete disassembly (see previous page) is necessary. Study each part to see if it obviously needs replacing (like a washer bent out of shape). It may be that the yoke cannot rotate on the pivot bolt. File down and polish the bolt, or enlarge the holes in the yokes (with a taper ream, or emery cloth wrapped around a nail). If none of these things work, get a new brake mechanism.

Centre-pull

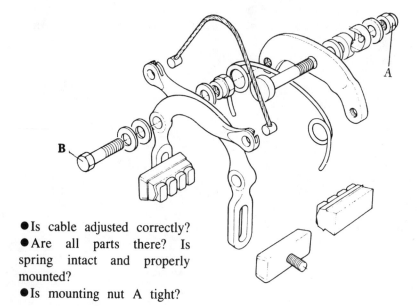

● Is cable adjusted correctly?
● Are all parts there? Is spring intact and properly mounted?
● Is mounting nut A tight?

If one shoe is dragging against rim, slack off A, centre the brake mechanism, and tighten A.

If both shoes stick, try lubricating the pivot bolts B while wiggling the yokes back and forth. No? You will have to get into the pivot bolts.

First disconnect the spring. Study the bolts to see whether they are type 1, where the pivot bolt screws into the brake arm bridge H; type 2, where the pivot bolt screws into a post which comes off the brake arm bridge and on which the yoke rotates; or type 3, where the pivot bolt simply goes through the brake arm bridge and the yoke rotates on a bushing (metal or plastic sleeve.

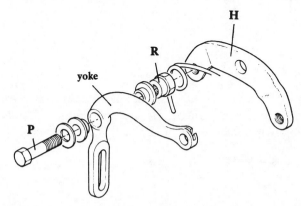

Type 1

First try slacking off the locknut R and undoing the pivot bolt P one quarter to one half turn. On some models the locknut R is on the other side of the brake arm bridge H. If yoke will now pivot, tighten locknut R. If not, remove pivot bolt P altogether. Keep track of all the washers. Is the pivot bolt P straight? Look for dirt or scarred surfaces on the pivot bolt P and inside the yoke. Clean and polish. If yoke will not turn freely on pivot bolt, enlarge yoke hole with a taper file or ream, drill, or emery cloth wrapped around a nail. Or sand down the pivot bolt. Lubricate and reassemble.

Type 2

Undo spring and remove pivot bolt P. Remove yoke and keep track of washers. Check for grit and clean. Is post R scarred? Polish with fine sandpaper or steel wool until yoke will rotate freely on it. Lubricate and reassemble.

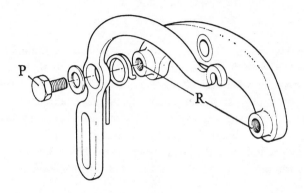

Type 3

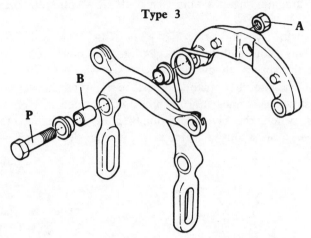

Undo nut A and remove pivot bolt P. Keep track of bushings and washers. Is pivot bolt straight? Is bushing B in good condition? Check for grit and clean. If yoke still sticks, try polishing pivot bolt with steel wool. Lubricate and reassemble.

Cantilever

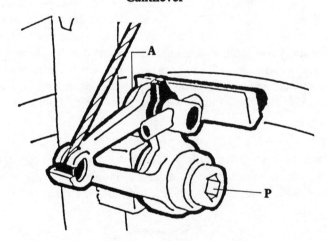

First check that the cables are all OK and properly adjusted. Sometimes dirt in the straddle wire anchor, or a kink in the straddle wire, will cause uneven pull on the arms. Disconnect the straddle wire and check the movement of each arm. If rough, then the pivot bolt is probably dirty and needs cleaning. Undo pivot bolt P, take apart in orderly sequence, clean and lubricate, and reassemble. If spring tension is weak, then unwind the arm and bend the spring until it has more moxie, or replace the spring. If the springs won't pull the arms away, see if you can move the brake shoes away from the rim (eyebolt nut A) so that the springs engage sooner when the arms are compressed.

Roller-cam

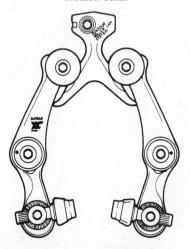

Roller-cam brakes are sensitive but oddly straightforward. The most common cause of a malfunction is dirt, and the first thing to do is take the unit apart (see Disassembly), clean and lubricate it, and then check that the various parts work. Any problem will be quite self-evident: a sticking roller, a brake arm catching on the pivot bolt, or a broken or fatigued spring. A bad spring must, of course, be replaced, do both to keep tension even. Parts that stick must be worked on until they free up, and be delicate, because the tolerances are fairly exact. If you can't get a part to go with a good cleaning and a bit of fiddling, then replace it.

SWITCHBACK

Position
and
Direction

Saddles

Saddle design balances two functions: supporting weight and reducing friction between the legs. The more active the riding style, the narrower the saddle. Thus, roadster bikes with an upright riding position have wide, pillow-like saddles, while racing bikes have sparse, lean saddles that are sometimes little more than rails. Between these two extremes are a galaxy of saddle designs in varying widths and materials, many with padding or other insulation.

Saddles are very personal. I don't know you, how you ride, and least of all anything about your behind. Generally, the narrower a saddle you can use, the better, but if you are just starting out, then an anatomic design saddle with some padding is probably the safest bet. Later on you can slim things down. If you are female, be sure to get a women's model.

The greatest saddle story of all belongs to the American off-road champion Cindy Whitehead, who was a mile along in a punishing 50-mile race through the Sierra Nevada Mountains when her saddle fell off. She rode standing up for the remaining 49 miles, climbing and then descending 7,500 feet—and won the race.

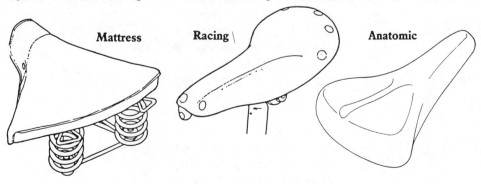

Mattress   Racing   Anatomic

Adjustment

Saddles with a plastic base rarely have any provision for adjusting cover tension. Good leather saddles do, at nut A.

To raise or lower the saddle, loosen the binder bolt D. Be sure to use a tool that fits the nut precisely. It has to be tight, and the wrong tool can tear up the

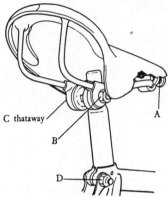

C thataway

B

A

D—

nut. On a mountain bike there will often be a quick-release lever. If it is not tight enough, open the lever, hold the opposite side nut still, and wind the lever on until it is tight enough when closed. The seat post should be lightly greased to prevent corrosion and ensure that you can get it back out.

The seat post above is the most basic kind. To remove the saddle from the seat post, or to adjust it backward, forward, or to tilt it, loosen nuts B and C. More sophisticated seat posts have micro-adjusting bolts (M). Loosen bolt or screw on end to be raised, tighten bolt or screw on end to be

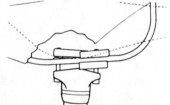

lowered. Loosen both an identical number of turns to slide saddle forward or backward. For proper saddle position refer to Fitting.

Leather saddles need a bit of care. Try to avoid getting them wet, and form the habit of covering the saddle (any old plastic bag will do) when parking the bike outdoors.

At least once a year nourish the saddle with a dressing—Brooks Proofide is good stuff. If you want to speed up the breaking-in process for a new leather saddle, saturate it with neatsfoot oil from UNDERNEATH. Do this only once, or else the saddle may become too soft.

Trouble-shooting

If the seat post keeps sinking slowly into the frame as you ride, no matter how

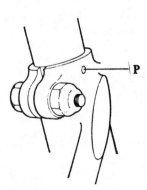

P

tightly you draw up the binder bolt, then the post is almost certainly too small in diameter for the seat tube. Pop around to a bike shop and see what can be done.

Some bikes just want to be kept going at zero expense. You can stop a seat post from sinking by fixing a thin bolt through the frame and seat post at point P.

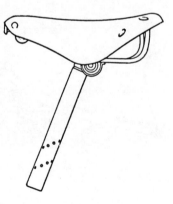

Turn the bike upside down while drilling the hole, or metal shavings will fall down the seat tube and make hash of the bottom bracket bearings. Make more than one hole in the seat post if you want height to be adjustable, and make them in a spiral pattern if you want to be fancy.

Handlebars

Adjustment

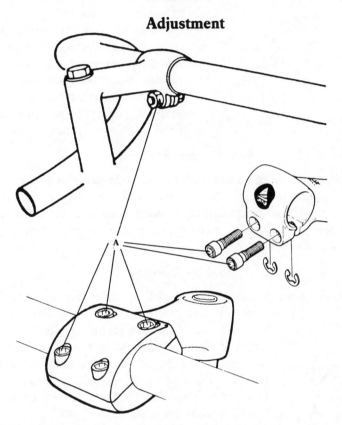

To change handlebar position loosen binder bolt(s) A on stem and reset bars. Height adjustments are made with the stem (next section).

Taping

I prefer non-adhesive tapes. Adhesive tapes gum everything up with a sticky residue which ultimately leaks out all over the place. There are many options in tapes, see Accessories for information.

Be sure that the brakes are in the position you want. Start about 2″ from the stem. Use a small piece of sticky tape to hold down the end of the tape where you start. Work directly from the roll to minimize confusion, and maintain a continuous light tension as you apply the tape. First take a couple of turns at the starting

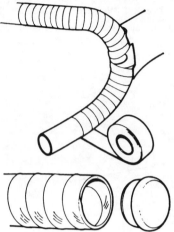

point and then start down the bar, overlapping each turn with about one-third of the tape width. At the bends you will have to overlap more on the inside than the outside. For a neat job, loosen the brake lever mount, tape underneath, and retighten. Have 2-3″ of tape left when you reach the end of the bar. Fold this over and push it inside the handlebar.

Finish off with a bar plug (bike shops) to hold tape securely. If plug is difficult to insert, rub some soap on it and tap it in with a hammer. Bar plugs can also be made from champagne corks. Use something—if you spill, an open bar end can make a hole in you.

Grips and Sleeves

A little soap and water usually makes it easy to slide grips and sleeves on or off handlebars. An old grip or sleeve that is stuck fast can just be cut away. If you want to save the thing, use a hypodermic to inject soap and water into the middle. To prolong the life of foam sleeves or grips, add a layer of tape at the points of greatest wear.

Trouble-shooting

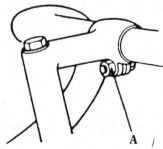

●Bar spins around on stem: tighten binder bolt A. If binder bolt spins uselessly, remove it and see if the little protrusion on it has been worn off, or if the corresponding slot on the stem into which it fits has been damaged. If the problem is the bolt, get a new one. If it is the stem, get a proper bolt with a nut that you can grip with a spanner or hex key. In a pinch, you can use pliers or vise-grips to hold the round part of the old bolt.

If the binder bolt is in working order check and see that the lips of the stem do not meet. If they do, it's either a new stem or new bars (expensive) or a shim (cheap). Shimming: find a small piece of flat metal slightly longer than the width of the stem lips. Something that won't rust, such as aluminium, is preferable (hardware shops, machine shop litter, junk lying around), but part of a tin can or a finishing nail will do. Remove binder bolt. Use a screwdriver to pry apart

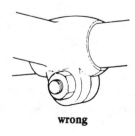

wrong

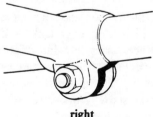

right

the lips of the stem, slip the shim into the gap between the handlebar and the stem, and replace binder bolt.

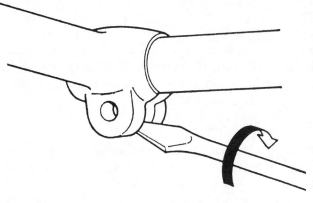

● Bent bars. Steel bars can be bent back into shape. Bent aluminium bars should be used for sculpture. Bending them back into shape risks fatigue and an unexpected failure that could kill you. It's obviously very tempting to bend expensive aluminium bars back into shape. I'm telling you on the basis of experience that you should not.

Stem

How It Works

One end of the stem has a clamp which holds the handlebars in position. The other end of the stem is attached to the fork tube. One type of stem fits over the fork tube and is held in place with a clamp and pinch bolt. It is most often used on mountain bikes. The other type of stem has a tube which fits inside the fork tube. Down the length of the stem tube runs an expander bolt, which is attached to a wedge nut (A).

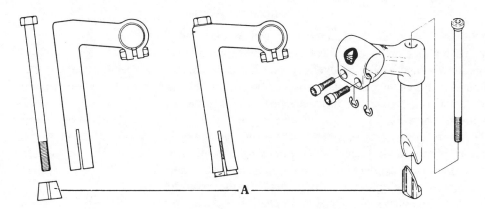

A

When the expander bolt is tightened, it draws the wedge nut into the tube, and this in turn forces apart the split sides of the stem, pressing them against the sides of the fork tube and thereby holding everything in place. Another type of design uses a slanting washer to force the wedge nut against the fork tube. The basic idea is the same.

Adjust or Remove

Pinch Bolt

Simply undo the pinch bolt and move or lift off the stem. If it balks, gently tap it back and forth until it works loose. If this doesn't work, drive a wedge between the lips of the clamp and also squirt in some penetrating oil.

Expander Bolt

Undo expander bolt two turns. Using a wooden block or piece of cardboard held

against the expander bolt to protect the finish, tap it with a hammer or heavy object. Repeat as necessary to get stem loose. Adjust height or remove. If you remove altogether and reassemble, note that some wedge nuts have a dog guide which must fit into a corresponding slot on the stem. KEEP AT LEAST 2½" OF STEM IN THE HEAD TUBE.

Tighten expander bolt so that when you stand in front of the bike with the wheel clasped between your legs you can twist the handlebar and stem in the fork tube. This way, if you take a spill the bars will give instead of bending or breaking.

Trouble-shooting

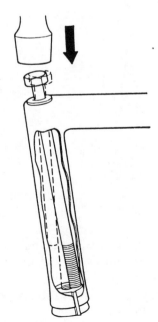

● Stem is loose and expander bolt comes out freely: wedge nut has come off. Take out stem, turn bike upside down, and shake wedge nut out. Reassemble.

● Stem is frozen in place and expander bolt spins uselessly: threads on wedge nut have stripped (1), or expander bolt has snapped (2).

(1) Separate expander bolt from wedge nut by grasping it with pliers or vise-grips and maintaining a continuous upward pressure while twisting it. If it is obstinate, help it along by wedging a screwdriver between the expander bolt head and the stem. Once the expander bolt is free of wedge nut leave it inside the stem.

(2) Remove top half of snapped expander bolt. Find a rod or bolt which will fit inside stem and touch wedge nut while still protruding an inch or two above the stem. (1) and (2): Lightly tap the expander bolt or rod, working the end inside the stem around the edges of the

wedge nut. Work firmly but gently; too hard a blow will jam the whole thing. When stem comes loose, turn bike upside down and shake out wedge nut.

● Stem tube cracked. Replace it.

Headset

How It Works

The headset connects the fork tube to the head tube of the bicycle frame. The fork tube is held solidly to the bicycle but is allowed to turn freely by using ball-bearing sets at the top and bottom of the head tube. Starting at the bottom, the crown of the fork has a fork crown bearing race (A), then come the ball-bearings (B), and next is the bottom set race (C), screwed or force-fitted into the head tube.

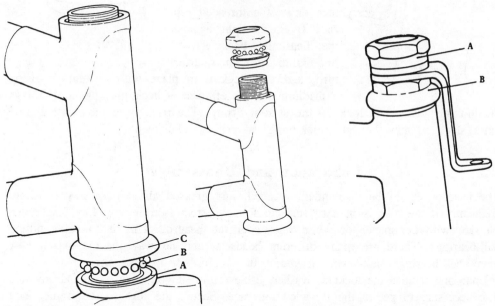

To keep the forks inside the head tube and evenly positioned, a second set of races is used at the top of the head tube. There is a top set race, screwed or force-fitted into the head tube, more ball-bearings, and, the key to whole business, the top race, which is threaded onto the fork tube. This is capped by a washer, the cable hanger and/or other accessory mounts, if used, and a locknut to keep the top threaded race exactly in place.

Adjustment

Forks should turn freely but with no up-and-down play. A simple test for looseness is to lock the front brake and rock the bike forward and backward. A clicking noise from the headset indicates loose bearings. Get after them; a slack headset can easily bend the races and ruin the headset, particularly if it is made of alloy. To adjust, loosen locknut A. Sometimes this locknut is designed with notches. If you haven't got the right tool to fit, it can be loosened with a hammer and centre punch or screwdriver.

There are also all too many headsets with unique design locknuts that can only be shifted with special tools made by the clever manufacturers of the headsets. It

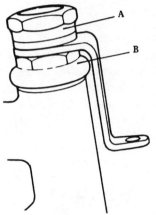

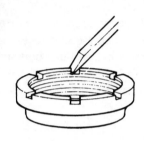

is unfortunately worth having the right tool for the job. If instead you go in for big spanners borrowed from a plumber's tool-box, be very careful not to bend the nuts or races.

Once the locknut is loose, turn down the threaded top race B finger tight against the bearings, back it off one-eighth to one-quarter turn, and then lock it in place with locknut A, using a medium amount of force. Check play again. If things are looking good, then lock up the system firmly. The trick is to have just a little extra slack so that the final lock-up gives perfect adjustment.

Lubrication and Disassembly

The headset should be dismantled, cleaned, and greased about once a year, more frequently if the bike is in hard service. Remove stem (see above). Lay bike down on side with newspaper or white rag under the headset. This is to catch falling ball-bearings. There are many different headsets, and no way for me to tell how many ball-bearings should be in yours; be careful not to lose any.

Undo and remove the locknut, washer, cable clamp (if you have one), and anything else necessary to get to the threaded top race. Secure the fork to the frame. You can do this with rubber bands, elastic carrier straps, shoelaces, etc., but the simplest way is to hold it with your hand. Be sure to do something, or what you do next will cause the fork to fall out along with a rain of ball-bearings. Next: undo the threaded top race A. You will either have loose ball-bearings and are to follow instructions for (1), or bearings in a clip, in which case follow (2).

(1) A few ball-bearings may stick to the threaded race, a few may fall on the newspaper, and most will probably stay in the top set race. Gather them together, count them, and put bearings and race into box or jar. Next: make sure head tube is positioned over newspaper or rag. Slowly draw out fork tube. Ball-bearings will fall out. Gather and count them, including any that are still stuck to the bottom set race, the fork tube, or whatever, and put them in a jar.

(2) Clipped bearings: Lucky you. Remove clip, noting carefully which side goes down against the top set race, and put in a jar or box. Now draw out fork tube and lift out clip for bottom race. Further disassembly for routine lubrication is not necessary.

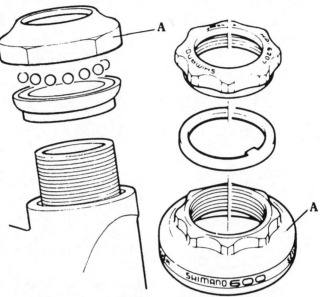

(1) & (2) Soak and clean thoroughly all parts in solvent. Use a rag to clean out the top and bottom set races, and the fork crown race. Ball-bearings should be smooth and unpitted. Clipped bearings should be securely in place. Races should be evenly coloured all the way around where the balls run. Place them on a glass surface to see if they are bent or warped. Replace any defective parts.

Reassembly: pack fresh grease in the top and bottom set races. Just fill the grooves; excessive grease will attract dirt.

(1) Push ball-bearings into grease on bottom set race. Grease will hold them in place.

(2) Put some grease inside the clip. Slip it down over the fork tube to rest on the fork crown race.

(1) & (2) Carefully insert fork tube into head tube. Keeping it snug against the bearings, check that it turns freely. Hang onto fork so that it does not fall back out.

(1) Stick ball-bearings into grease of top set race.

(2) Grease and slip on clipped bearings.

(1) & (2) Screw down top threaded race. These threads are fine, so do it carefully (see General Notes for best technique). Set it finger tight, and then back it off one-eighth to one-quarter turn. Pile on washer, cable anchor mount, etc., and locknut. Be careful to keep threaded top race in position when tightening locknut. Check for play.

If the bike has been in a smash-up or if rust has got to the bearings, it may be necessary to do a complete disassembly. This is a job better left to a bike shop, because the head tube itself should be checked and faced with a special (quite expensive) tool to ensure that everything is correctly sized and positioned. If the frame is new, this work is essential before installing a headset.

Take fork and ball-bearings out as per for lubrication. Remove crown fork race from fork. If it is stuck, pry it up *gently* with a screwdriver, working around the edges a little at a time. Be careful, it is easy to bend. Remove top and bottom

space for screwdriver in levering bearing race diagram

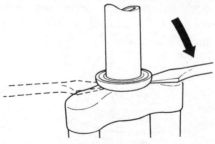

set races. You may possibly have threaded set races, in which case simply unscrew
them. For force set races, insert a large screwdriver,
piece of pipe, or stiff rod into the head tube and tap
around the edges of the race. Clean all parts with solvent. Test that race are uniform by seeing if they lie
flat on glass or other smooth
surface.

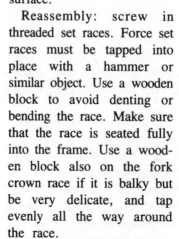

    Reassembly: screw in
threaded set races. Force set
races must be tapped into
place with a hammer or
similar object. Use a wooden
block to avoid denting or
bending the race. Make sure
that the race is seated fully
into the frame. Use a wood-
en block also on the fork
crown race if it is balky but
be very delicate, and tap
evenly all the way around
the race.

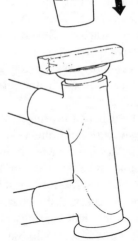

Trouble-shooting

● Fork tube is extremely loose in the head tube. May just need adjustment, but
if things have come to this pass I suggest dismantling and checking condition of parts.
● Adjustment does not work: top threaded race or fork is stripped. Dismantle and
see. It is unlikely that this is the result of excessive tightening, and likely that the
top threaded race was screwed down off-centre. When you have your new parts
review General Notes, Threading, before starting.
● Fork binds or catches, makes grating and rasping noises when you turn handlebars,
or prefers a particular position. Something is broken or bent, completely worn out,
or there are too many or too few ball-bearings. Review the possibilities. Has fork
or headset been severely whacked recently? A couple of months ago? Did you or
someone else service the headset and lose a bearing or two, or place too many

in one race and not enough in the other? Perhaps the bike is simply ancient, and needs new races? In any case, disassemble, clean, and check all parts. Are ball-bearings evenly distributed (ask your bike shop how many should be in your headset), and free of dents, cracks, and pitting? Are races unpitted, flat, and perfectly round? Replace defective parts and reassemble. If problems persist, take the thing down to your bike shop and see what they say.

Forks

How They Work

The fork holds the front wheel in place and allows the bike to be steered. The fork arms are curved, raking the axle drop-outs away from a line drawn through the fork tube. The amount of rake varies according to the purpose of the bike. Broadly, touring bikes and mountain bikes have more rake, racing bikes have less. The more rake, the more stable the handling, although this is also a function of head tube angle.

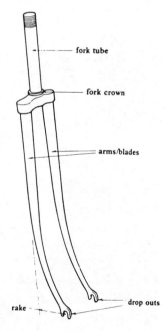

The main problem that can arise with forks is if they are bent in an crash. The best thing is to replace them. Bending fatigues metal and makes it weak. The weakness does not show. What happens is that the fork suddenly gives up while you are tearing along at 30 mph. This does not happen very often, but once is enough.

On the other hand, bike shops do have special tools for straightening bent forks and if the bend in yours is slight, you may want to try it. Go by the advice of the shop. Be aware that you are taking a calculated risk, however small.

Tests for bent forks: the bike will ride funny. If forks are bent to one side, the bike will always want to turn to the left or right. Test by taking your hands off the handlebars. Any decently set-up bike can be ridden hands off for miles. Forks which have been bent in, usually through a head-on collision, make the bike's ride choppy and harsh, and make it feel like it wants to dive in the corners. A sure sign of bent-in forks is wrinkled paint on the upper fork arms, or at the join of the fork tube and fork crown. Forks which have been bent out (rare) manifest themselves in a sloppy, mushy ride, and curious, wide arcing turns. Again, there will probably be paint wrinkles at the bend point.

Wheels

Wheel Removal

Wheels need to be removed often, for a variety of reasons, and sometimes on the road. So you can and will do this with a free-standing bike, but it is easier if the bike is hung up. Alternatively, most bikes can simply be turned upside down on handlebars and seat, as long as cables or shift selectors are not damaged. Once you know the drill, you can also just hold the bike with one hand while removing the wheel, and then lay the bike down on the ground. Bikes with calliper brakes in proper adjustment should require some slacking of the brakes so that the tyre will pass between the brake shoes.

Front Wheel

Wheel will be held to fork by hex nuts, wing nuts, or a quick-release lever.

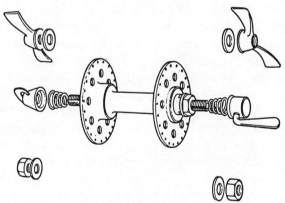

For nuts, undo both simultaneously (anti-clockwise) and unwind a turn or two. Levers, pull open, rotate slightly to loosen if necessary. Remove wheel. Note washers go outside fork drop-outs.

Rear Wheel

Derailleur Gear

Run chain to outside (smallest) freewheel sprocket. Undo nuts or lever as for front wheel, and push wheel down and out. If you have a free hand hold back the derailleur so that the freewheel clears it easily, otherwise just gently wiggle it past.

Hub Gear

Shift to 3rd gear. Disconnect shift cable at rear hub by undoing locknut A and unscrewing adjusting sleeve B from pole. Undo nuts simultaneously (anti-clockwise). Remove wheel, and note washers are outside drop-outs.

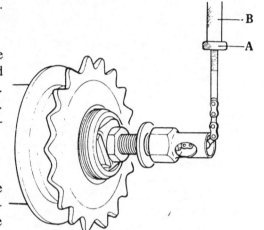

Coaster Brake

Disconnect coaster brake bracket from bike frame (metal arm at left end of rear axle), undo nuts (anti-clockwise), and remove wheel.

Replacing Wheels

Front Wheel

Axle with nuts: back off nuts a few turns and slip axle onto drop-outs. Washers go outside drop-outs. Set nuts finger tight and check that rim is centred between fork arms before tightening nuts firmly down. Reset calliper brakes if you have them.

    Levers: slip axle onto drop-outs with lever on left side of bike. If this is difficult, hold knurled cone with one hand and unwind lever a couple of turns with the other. Slip axle on drop-outs and wind lever down just short of finger tight. Check that wheel rim is centred between fork arms, and close lever so that it points upwards and backwards. Closing should take a firm amount of force, but not all your might. (Make a habit of using the same amount of force, as too much could tighten the bearings out of adjustment.) Reset calliper brakes.

Rear Wheel

Derailleur Gear

Work axle into drop-outs, slipping chain over smallest sprocket on freewheel. Set nuts or lever for light tension. Pull wheel toward rear of bike until right end of

axle hits the back of the drop-out. Use this as a pivot point to centre the rim between the chain stays, and tighten nuts or lever. Reset calliper brake.

Hub Gear

Work axle into drop-outs, slipping chain over sprocket. Lightly tighten nuts (washers
are outside drop-outs), and pull back wheel so chain has ½″ play up and down.

Check that this remains consistent through a full rotation
of the chainring. If it doesn't
(common with cheap chain-
sets), compromise as best you
can. Centre rim between chain
stays and tighten down nuts.
Check chain tension again.

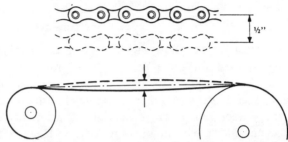

If coaster brake, connect
brake bracket to frame. If hub gears, move gear selector to 3rd (H), connect barrel
sleeve o hub gear chain, and set locknut with cable slightly slack. Test gears and
adjust if necessary. Reset calliper brake.

Tyres

How They Work

A pneumatic cycle tyre works by supporting a casing, the part touching the road,
with an inside tube which is filled with air like a balloon. With tubular tyres the

tube is fully encased by the casing; with
wire-on tyres the tube is held in place by
two wire or Kevlar beads which run
around the outside edges of the tyre and
press against the rim sides.

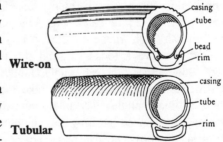

Air is pumped into the tube through a
valve which comes in three types. Many
wire-on tubes have Schraeder valves, the
kind typically found on cars. Some wire-
ons and all tubulars have Presta type valves, which require either a bicycle pump,
or a special adaptor for petrol station air pumps. On a Presta, undo the locknut
A in order to add or remove air. Increasingly rare, and thankfully so, is the Woods

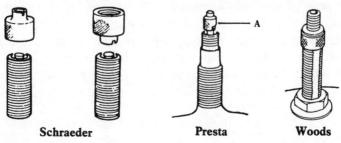

Schraeder   Presta   Woods

valve. This is a two-piece affair where the valve is inserted and held in place with a locknut. The valve itself is a small tube closed at the inner end, with a hole in the side that is covered and sealed with a rubber sleeve. The sleeve permits air to pass into the tube, but not out. The design is particularly rich in possibilities for malfunction, and while Woods valves are easily serviced or replaced, avoid them if you can.

Pressure

Tyre pressure is the most important element in bike performance and comfort. It's got to be right for the tyre, weight of rider and baggage if any, and conditions of use. A variation of as little as 5 psi can make a big difference, and for accuracy, a tyre pressure gauge is essential. The easiest and best way to inflate tyres is with a track pump (the kind with handles, that stands on the floor), and better models include a built-in pressure gauge. These are not always perfectly accurate, and I still prefer to have a separate tyre pressure gauge. A foot-operated pump will do, but is generally more awkward than a track pump. Avoid using petrol station air pumps; the proper pressure for your tyre may be as high as 120 psi, but the total volume of air is small, and it takes only seconds to blow a tyre out. If you are stuck and must use a petrol station air pump, jab the hose down on the valve for just a second, then release and test.

Know the recommended pressure for your tyres (often printed on tyre sidewall), it can vary from 30 to 110 psi depending on tyre size and model. Increase pressure for heavy riders and/or heavy touring loads, bad conditions, and riotous living. The best protection for a tyre is plenty of air. A 200 lb weight rider will need 15-20 psi more than a 125 lb rider with low to medium range 40-70 psi tyres, and 5-10 psi more with high range 90-120 psi tyres. Keep an eye on matters. Sometimes a rim and tyre are a loose fit, and the tyre can blow off the rim if grossly over-inflated. Other times you can safely double the manufacturer's recommended pressure. It all depends—try and see. If you take the trouble to experiment with tyre pressures, you'll soon find that there is an optimum psi for the balance of ride comfort (shock absorption) and speed (rolling resistance) that you prefer.

Hot weather above 80 °F may require that you bleed some air from the tyre to avoid over-inflation and a possible blow-out. In very slippery conditions some people reduce pressure in an effort to obtain better traction. This trick is of limited effectiveness with narrow road tyres, but works well with wide mountain bike tyres. The drawback is a greater risk of banging the tyre casing against the wheel rim, thereby pinching the tube and puncturing it in a distinctive pattern called 'snakebite'. In the opposite direction, mountain bike tyres rated at around 45 psi can usually stand 80 psi or more, which greatly reduces rolling resistance for on-road use. It is important to adjust for conditions, however; off-road, a hard tyre will skitter and dance, and make the bike feel uncertain.

Pumping

Track and frame fit pumps are sized differently for Schraeder, Presta, and Woods valves. Presta and Woods valves are roughly the same size, and a pump for one type can usually be bodged into working for the other. Schraeder valves are a different size and design. Bike shops sell converters that allow a Schraeder valve pump to be used with other types of valves, and vice versa, and it is worth having one of these in your tool kit.

Schraeder or Woods valve: if your pump has a hose fitting, first screw the hose into the pump and then onto the valve. Periodically check tightness of hose as you pump. Alternatively, the pump may just fit over the valve and lock in place with a lever.

Presta valve: undo valve locknut, push pump on valve, close lever if the pump has one, hold pump and tyre together firmly with one hand, and pump with the other. Keep pump perpendicular to valve. If all you get is a lot of hissing, tighten down the cap that holds the pump rubber washer in place. When finished, disengage the pump with a sharp downward knock of the hand; wiggling the pump off will lose air and possibly bend valve. Close valve locknut.

Trick: if you have a Presta valve, a Schraeder pump, and no converter, cut the top off of the Presta valve cap. The tube thus formed will serve as a crude converter.

Riding

Some people are more puncture-prone than others. Most tyre problems are the result of picked-up debris working into the casing as you ride. Going over rocks, through potholes, and on and off kerbs will cause ruptures. Cultivate an eye for these hazards, and if you are forced to go through a patch of broken glass, for example, check and see that the tyre has not picked any up. Be aware of your tyres and—the fates willing—you will have less trouble. A useful gadget for tubular tyres is a nail-catcher (bike shops) which rides lightly over the tyre and brushes off particles before they can cause damage.

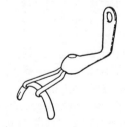

Keep oil away from tyres. It rots rubber. Grease, do not oil, bicycle pumps. Oiled bicycle pumps can vaporize the oil and blow it inside the tube. Check cement on tubulars about once a week.

Care and Storage

Keep spare tyres in a dry place, away from direct sunlight. Tubular spares should be carried folded so the tread is on the outside and not folded back on itself. Under the seat is a dandy place. Secure with straps or rubber bands. Every two weeks or so inflate a folded spare and let it stand for a while. Refold in the opposite direction.

Flats

Flats take the form of violent blow-outs (rare), or punctures (common) which leak air with varying degrees of speed. Blow-outs are usually terminal, doing so much damage that the tube and sometimes the tyre must be replaced. Punctures which are not gaping wounds can be repaired. Some people patch a tube until it looks like calico. Others, myself included, assign a tube to spare status once it has had a few punctures.

Wire-on Tyres

You will need a tube patch kit containing patches, glue, a piece of abrasive material, tyre levers (the kind which hook onto spokes are handiest), and chalk.

First check valve by inflating tyre slightly and placing a drop of spit on the end of the valve stem. A leaky valve will bubble or spit back. If it is a Schraeder valve, tighten the valve core with the valve cap (if it is shaped to do so) or suitable part of a pressure gauge.

Hooray if the problem was a loose or defective valve. If not, spin the wheel and look for an obvious cause like a nail or piece of glass. Yes? Dig it out and mark the spot.

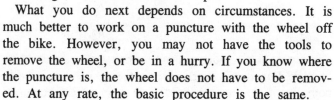

What you do next depends on circumstances. It is much better to work on a puncture with the wheel off the bike. However, you may not have the tools to remove the wheel, or be in a hurry. If you know where the puncture is, the wheel does not have to be removed. At any rate, the basic procedure is the same.

Deflate tyre and remove valve stem locknut if you have one. Work the tyre back and forth with your hands to get the bead free of the rim. If the tyre is a loose fit on the rim you may be able to get it off with your hands. This is best, because tyre levers may pinch the tube and cause additional punctures. The trick is to work the casing with your fingers, moving it away from the rim sides and down into the deeper groove where the spokes are held. When everything is loosened up, take a healthy grip on the tyre with both hands and pull it up so that one bead comes over the rim. Then go around the rim working the bead completely off.

You will probably need to use tyre levers. Use tyre levers, not screwdrivers, as these are likely to cut the tube. An

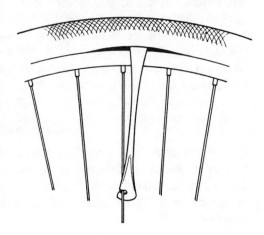

alternative are small ring spanners, so long as they are smooth and free from burrs.

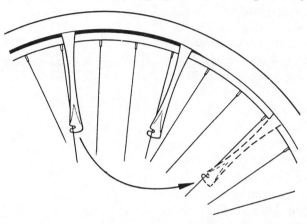

Free bead from rim, as per above. Insert tyre lever under bead, being careful not to pinch the tube, and lever it over the side.

Insert second lever 2″ or 3″ away from first lever, and past where bead is over side of rim. Lever lever. For most tyres this will do the job. No? A third lever. If this doesn't work, use the now ′ free 2nd lever for a fourth attempt, repeating process as often as necessary. If you don't have tyre levers which hook onto the spokes, then you will need to use elbows, knees, etc., to hold down the levers as you work away. Be careful not to inadvertently crush a spoke, and keep your face away in case something slips and tyre levers start jumping about.

If you have only two tyre levers and need a third, scrounge something up. In the country a flat rock or a stick. In the city a pencil, a beer can opener, or something from the rubbish. Look around. At any hour there will be something. Pry up bead with a tyre lever. Insert foraged tool between bead and rim and wiggle lever out. Use tyre levers to pry up bead on either side of foraged tool.

When one bead is off the rim, push valve stem up into tyre, and remove tube. Use chalk or eidetic memory to make note of which way tube was in the tyre. Inflate tube and rotate it past your ear. If you can locate the puncture through the hiss of escaping air, mark it with chalk. No? Try moving it past your lips. Still no? Find a container and water (or a puddle), immerse tube in water and look for escaping air bubbles. Dry tube with a rag while holding finger over puncture, then mark with chalk.

Use sandpaper or rough metal supplied with patch kit and abrade the tube at the puncture point over an area slightly larger than the patch size. Spread a layer of cement over this area and let dry tacky—this is important, all the solvent must evaporate. Peel the paper backing off a patch without touching the surface thus exposed, and press it firmly on the puncture. Set tube aside to dry while you find and cure what caused the puncture.

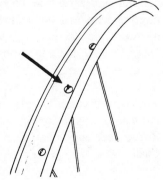

If puncture was on inside of tube, a protruding spoke probably caused it. File the spoke flush with the rim. Check other spokes.

If the puncture was on the outside of the tube, find what caused it by rubbing your fingers around inside the casing. Check the rest of the casing for embedded particles, and for ruptures or breaks. Replace the tyre at the first opportunity if it has these. If there is nothing inside the casing, check the tread for a glass cut—a common cause of puncture. A small cut is nothing much to worry about; a large cut is—you can buy a filler/glue that will probably mend the cut, but the end of the tyre's life is in sight.

To install the repaired tube, first inflate it slightly to prevent it from folding and pinching itself. (I like to inflate the tube generously for placement into the casing, then bleed off air for enough room to mount the casing on the rim.) Push the part of the tube with the valve stem into the tyre, and the valve stem through its hole on the rim. Fit valve stem locknut loosely. Stuff rest of tube into tyre being careful not to pinch or tear it. Check that valve stem is still straight.

Push valve stem partially out, and slip bead of tyre at that point back over the rim. It is important that you hold the base of the valve stem clear of the rim as you do this, or the bead may catch on it, creating a bulge in the tyre.

Work around the rim replacing the bead and always taking care not to pinch the tube. Ideally you can do the entire job with your hands. Check that the valve stem is still straight. The last bit will be hard. Just keep working at it with your thumbs, first from one side, then from the other. Make sure that the portion of tyre which is already over the rim edge is well down in the central groove of the rim. When about 2″ of bead remain give it the grand mal effort. Don't wonder if it will go over; decide it will. If you have to use a tyre lever, be very careful not to pinch the tube. When the tyre is fully aboard, work it around with your hands, checking that it is even on all sides. Inflate the tyre lightly, and check again that all is true, square, and upright. Sometimes a bead will catch on the central groove of

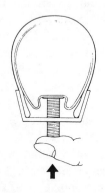

the rim and refuse to take its rightful place at the side of the rim. Try inflating the tyre hard and bouncing it (the tyre, not the wheel!) on the ground. If this does not work, let the air out, work everything around with your hands, and try again. Once you've done the job enough times (sigh), you'll have the touch.

Tubular Tyres

You will need:

Patches	Needle	Thread
Rubber cement	Sandpaper	Talcum powder
Chalk	Screwdriver	Sharp knife or razor blade.

Remove wheel. Deflate tyre completely by opening locknut A on valve and holding down. Remove tyre from rim with your hands. Inflate and immerse in water a little at a time. Do not be misled by air bubbles coming out by the valve. Since the tyre is sewn, the valve hole and puncture hole are the only places air can escape. Hold finger over puncture when located, dry tyre, and mark puncture with chalk.

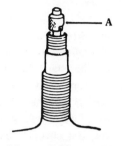

With a screwdriver or similar implement pry away about 5″ to 6″ of the tape on the inner side of the tyre at the puncture area. Next, cut two of the stitches, each

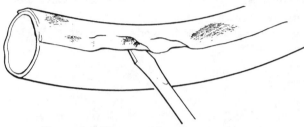

about 2″ to either side of puncture. Make only two cuts to avoid having to pick out numerous bits of thread, and cut up and out to miss tyre.

Gently remove tube and locate leak. A mixture of soap and water will pin-point elusive ones. Dry tube if wet. Abrade area around puncture with sandpaper. Apply cement and let dry tacky. Peel protective paper from patch without touching surface thus exposed and apply to puncture. Dust with talc to prevent tube from sticking to casing. Get whatever caused puncture out of casing. Insert tube, inflate, and check for leaks. Do this carefully. You are going to be mad if you get it all back together only to discover it still leaks.

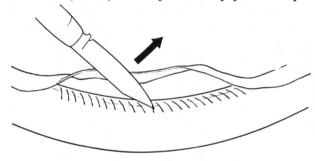

Thread the needle and knot the two loose ends of thread. In a pinch 12 lb linen thread or silk fishing line will do. Using the old holes, start with an overlap of about ½″ past where thread was cut. Pinch the sides of the casing between thumb and forefinger to keep the tube out of the way. Pull stitches firm, but not so tight as to cut casing. Finish with a ½″ overlap into original stitches. Layer cement on casing and inside of peeled-away tape and keep apart until dry. Position carefully and press together firmly.

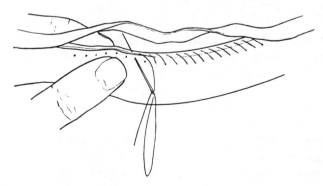

Mounting a Tubular

Oh fun. Stretch a new tyre by inflating it off the rim, and then on the rim. If the rim cement is old and grungy, clean it off with shellac thinner or solvent (bike shops). There are two methods for mounting a tubular: double-sided rim tape, and cement. Cement is doubtless stronger, but I've had no problems with double-sided tape, which has the advantage in convenience. Whichever product is used, there are two basic ways of doing the job.

(1) Slow but sure. If using tape, apply one side to rim and leave protective paper on other side. Deflate tyre. Insert valve. Stand rim on soft surface with valve stem up, and working from above, work tyre down over rim. Be careful to distribute tyre evenly around rim. Finish by grabbing with both hands and getting the last bit over by main force.

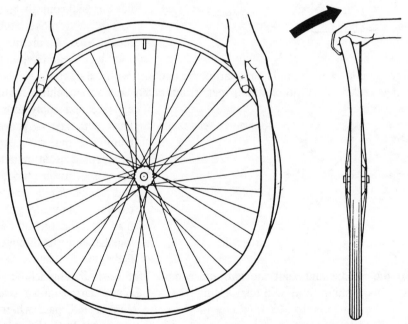

Inflate tyre and check that it is evenly distributed and centred on rim. Deflate. If tape, pull away protective paper wrapping, feeding tyre into place as you go. If cement, roll back a portion of the tyre and brush glue on rim and lining. Repeat all the way around and from both sides. Check again for evenness. Inflate hard. Allow half a day to dry before using or tyre may creep (bunch up in spots) or simply come off the rim in a corner.

(2) Fast method. Wear old clothes. Apply glue to rim and tyre and allow to dry tacky. Or the tape. Assemble as above.

Road repairs: use the old cement on the rim and don't lean hard into corners going home. Or, double-sided tape.

Rims and Spokes

How They Work

The rim which supports the tyre is held in place by the spokes, which hook onto the hub at one end, and at the other, attach to the rim via threaded nuts called nipples. The nipples stay in place on the rim, and when turned, regulate the tension of the spokes.

Adjustment

The tension on the spokes relative to each other determines both the strength and the position of the rim. Positioning the rim correctly, both up and down, and side-to-side, is a job requiring lots of patience and skill. Some people develop more skill than others, a few become masters of the art. The work of a really good wheelbuilder is truly superior, and many good bike mechanics who can themselves build creditable wheels, have their own wheels built by a master. A talented wheelbuilder is well worth using, but nevertheless, one should still be able to do up a wheel if need be, and make minor adjustments without much fuss.

Have a spoke key. Emergency repairs can be made with a small adjustable spanner, but a spoke key is far superior. Madison's Spokey is excellent. Hang up the bike or place the wheel in a jig. Spin the wheel holding a pencil or some-such at a fixed point like the fork arm or a seatstay with the point near the rim to see how bad the wobble is. If it is over ½ " pack up the entire project and take the wheel to a bike shop. If they think they can save the wheel, fine, otherwise get a new wheel.

With less than ½ " wobble: deflate tyre. If job looks to be major, it will be easier if you just remove the tyre altogether. Pluck the spokes with your fingers—they should all 'ping'—and tighten any that are slack so that they all have an even tension. Spokes are tightened by turning the nipple (the part that holds the spoke to the rim) anti-clockwise. Frozen nipples that cannot be moved must be replaced (see below). If more than three or four spokes have frozen nipples I once again suggest resorting to your friendly bike shop.

Hold a chalk or pencil at the outer edge of the rim while you spin the wheel so that the high spots are marked. (Up and down, not sideways.) Working one-half to one turn at a time, tighten the spokes at the chalk mark (anti-clockwise) and loosen them opposite the chalk mark. Continue until wheel is round. This may not be easy, as the rim has to be an even circle in the first place. If you get stuck it may be because the rim is damaged . . . friendly bike shop.

Hold pencil or chalk at side of rim and spin wheel so that side-to-side wobbles are marked. Working one-half to one turn at a time, and in groups of four to six spokes, tighten up the spokes opposite each chalk mark and loosen the ones next to it. Tighten or loosen the spokes which are in the centre of the chalk marks a

little more than the ones at the edges of the marks. When you have finally succeeded, or compromised, run your finger around the rim and check for protruding
spoke ends. File protruders down.

Replacing Spokes

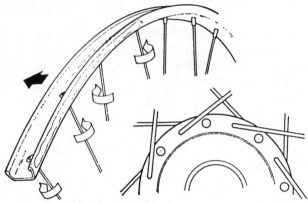

Remove tyre. If you are dealing with spokes on the
freewheel side of a rear wheel,
the freewheel will have to be
removed. Take broken spokes
out of hub and rim. Get
replacements which are exactly the same; many different
kinds are available.

New spokes should go into
hub so that head is on the opposite side of hub from
adjoining spokes and spoke is pointed in opposite direction. Be sure that spokes are correctly positioned in the
hub with respect to the bevels in the holes. On almost
all bikes the spokes touch where they cross. Weave new
spokes through old as per other spokes on wheel. Place
nipples on spokes and tighten. True wheel (see above),
file down any protruding spokes which might puncture
the tube, and remount tyre.

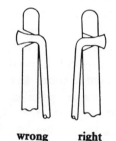

wrong   right

Trouble-shooting

● For side-to-side wobbles and elliptical wheels, see above.
● For straightening bulges in the rim caused by piling into kerbs, stones, etc., you
will need Vise-grips, Channel-lock pliers, a C-clamp, a small vise, or similar. If

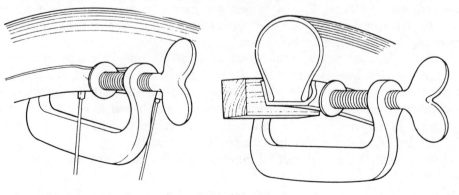

bulge is equal on both sides of rim, place implement over bulge and squeeze gently until the rim is even again. If the bulge is on the side of the rim, distribute
the pinching force of your implement on the non-bulge side with a block of wood
or some-such. Fixing bulges almost invariably leaves a slight dimple because the
metal itself was stretched, but the wheel will probably be usable. Rims that have
been dented are almost impossible to mend.

Wheelbuilding

You may want to go the whole route and build your own wheels. This is at once
straightforward, and an art. A good book on the subject is *Building Bicycle Wheels*,
by Robert Wright (World Publications). *The Bicycle Wheel* by Jobst Brandt (Avocet,
Inc.) is an engaging general scientific appraisal of the wheel, and has excellent building
and repair instructions.

Hubs

How They Work

A hub consists of an axle (spindle), two sets of bearings, and a casing or shell.
The spindle is attached to the frame drop-outs, and the hub shell, to which the
spokes are attached, spins around the spindle by riding on the bearings. The method
of dealing with the bearings gives two broad types of hubs: loose ball-bearing and
cassette (cartridge) bearing. Loose or caged bearings ride around in a cup that is part

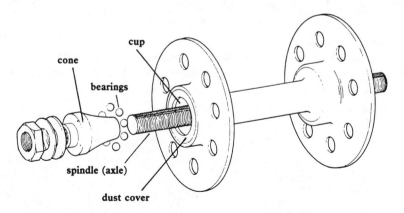

of the hub shell, and are held in place by an adjustable cone. Cassette bearings
are self-contained in a mechanism that includes the cup and cone functions. The
cassette is pressed into the hub shell, and the axle rides on the inner part of the
cassette. In most cases the design includes seals to keep out water and dirt.

Adjustment

You need thin hub spanners (bike shops). Hubs with loose ball-bearings and adjustable cones are simple and easy to service. Some cassette bearing hubs are adjustable, and others are not. Many that are adjustable, such as SunTour hubs, need a special tool or a bit of ingenuity for the job. If you've got a sealed, cassette bearing hub—a likely possibility—check with a bike shop for instructions and any special tools.

Wheel bearings are out of adjustment if, with the axle held firmly in place, the wheel can be wiggled from side to side (usually with a clicking noise), or if the wheel will not turn easily.

Loose Bearings

Remove wheel. Undo locknut A from cone B. Holding axle with a spanner at locknut C screw cone B fully home and then back off one-eighth to one-quarter turn. Lock in place with locknut A. Test for side-to-side play. Wheel should spin freely, and on good hubs the weight of the tyre valve will pull the wheel around so that the valve rests in the six o'clock position. NOTE: tightening the skewer on a quick-release hub compresses the axle and tightens the bear- 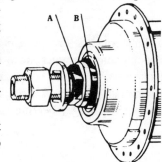 ing adjustment too tight. Always give a hub bearing adjustment a final check with the wheel mounted in place.

On a 3-speed hub the bearing adjustment is made on the side opposite the hub gear chain and sprocket. Loosen locknut A, turn cone B fully home, back off one-quarter turn, reset locknut A.

On a Sturmey-Archer SC coaster hub loosen locknut B, then turn C clockwise to tighten, anti-clockwise to loosen. Reset locknut B.

Odd information department: front wheel 'dynohubs' are adjusted at the left side, away from the dynamo, while rear 'dynohubs' are adjusted at the left side, next to the dynamo. In both cases, loosen locknut A, turn slotted washer B fully home, back off one-quarter turn, and reset locknut A.

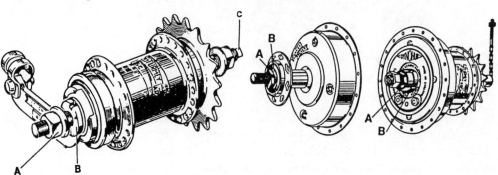

Cassette Bearings

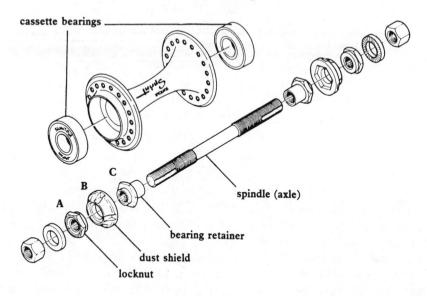

cassette bearings

C

B

A

spindle (axle)

bearing retainer

dust shield

locknut

Remove wheel. Undo and remove quick-release skewer or axle nuts. Remove locknut A while holding dust shield B still with special SunTour tool, or a pin tool. Undo dust shield B; the bearing retainer C will come with it. The bearings should stay in place. Screw in C and B finger tight against bearing. Hold B still and tighten locknut A against it.

Lubrication

How you lubricate a hub depends on how it is set up in the first place, and on what you want. Many hubs are fully sealed and do not need any lubrication at all. They run until they drop and are then discarded or rebuilt. At the other extreme are hubs set up for regular lubrication with oil or grease. Some old-fashioned models have oil clips or grease nipples. The most common of this type of hub is Ye Olde Faithful Hub Gear, which can use about a teaspoonful a month of good quality cycle or motor oil. (Don't use household oils.) Coaster brake hubs are thirstier and 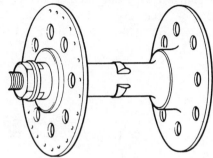 can go for a tablespoonful or more a month. Hubs for derailleur gear bikes are sparing: a few drops to half a teaspoonful. You're not likely to find these except on classics, and hubs customized for racing.

The majority of hubs just use grease. There are a few oddball hubs with grease

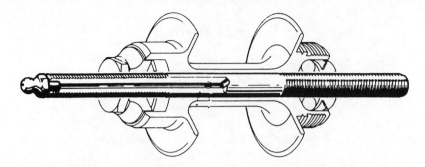

nipples (ram the stuff in until it bleeds out the sides, hopefully carrying away any dirt in the bearings), but most must be taken apart. As you might imagine, the racing crowd like thinner greases and don't mind whipping a hub apart and back together fairly frequently. Off-road and utility riders generally prefer a thick, waterproof grease that endures for a long time. The frequency of lubrication depends on many variables: mileage, conditions of use, rider weight, etc. Broadly, if you use a thin grease you should know when you plan to take the hub apart again, not often beyond six months. With a good-quality, thick waterproof grease (like Phil Wood), you can more or less forget about it until the idea returns from atavistic memory. I don't want you to be too casual about this, but many hubs run for two, three and more years without a hitch. Especially with fixed cassette bearings, many mechanics regard bearing wear and lubrication as synonymous: when the bearing starts to run loose and rough, it's time for a new cassette and fresh packing of grease.

Disassembly and Replacement

Loose or Caged Bearings

Remove wheel from bike. Derailleur gear rear wheels, remove freewheel. Lay wheel down on rags or newspaper to catch ball-bearings. Undo locknut A from cone B and remove both while holding on to axle at C. Remove dust cover D. To do this it may be necessary to let the axle drop in just a little way so you can pry the dust cover off with a screwdriver. Pry out the loose or clipped ball-bearings (or

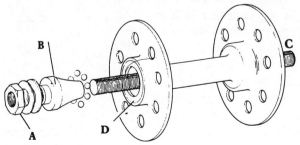

turn the wheel over and dump them out), count, and place in jar. Now slide axle all the way out and dump out remaining ball-bearings. Garner and count. Undo remaining locknut and cone and remove from axle. Clean all parts in solvent. Examine ball-bearings to see that they are not cracked or pitted. Clipped bearings should be secure in clip. Cups and cones should be even in colour all around where bearings run and free of pitting. Test axle for straightness by rolling on a glass surface. Replace any defective parts.

Reassembly: pack cups with grease. If ordinary grease, then not too much as excess will attract grit. If a waterproof grease then really pack it in so that grease seals out water (which it will do until it gets dirty). Lock a cone and locknut on axle. Slip dust cover on axle. Pack ball-bearings into cup on one side of wheel. The grease will hold them in place. Gracefully insert axle and turn wheel over. Pack ball-bearings into cup, replace dust cover, screw on cone and locknut, and adjust as per above.

Cassette Bearings

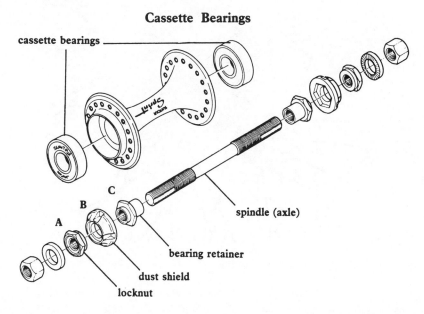

cassette bearings

spindle (axle)

bearing retainer

dust shield

locknut

A B C

Undo and remove the locknut, dust shield, and bearing retainer (see SunTour above), and draw axle out of hub shell. The bearing cassettes can be flushed clean with solvent and re-packed with grease, but this is a tedious job and the fresh grease may not reach into every nook and cranny. Most manufacturers advise against removing the bearings, citing need for special tools, precise alignment, and experience. It is indeed easier and usually more practical to leave this job to a bike shop, but it is still within bounds for a home mechanic. The basic technique is to expose the cassette, get something behind it, and tap it out. Specialized make a cassette bearing removal tool that works very well. Of course if you go this far, you might want simply to install new bearings.

Trouble-shooting

If something goes wrong it is usually because a cone and locknut have come adrift, or a part has cracked, broken or bent, or there has been an invasion of grit. In all instances if routine adjustment will not solve the problem, completely disassemble hub and replace broken or defective parts as per above.

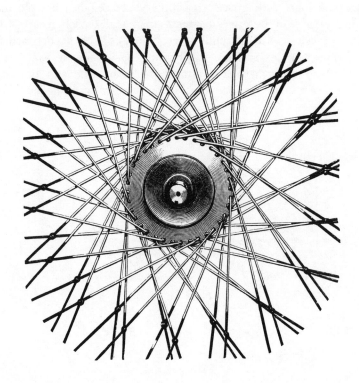

Transmission

Pedals

How They Work

A pedal consists of a pedal body and platform for the shoe, or an attachment point for a platform that is part of the shoe, an axle (called a spindle) which screws into the crank, and bearings on which the pedal body rides as it rotates around the spindle. In design, pedals fall into three broad categories: one-piece platform or cage; cage with removable sides; and step-in, where a special cleat on the shoe mates with a clamping mechanism on the pedal, like a ski binding. The bearings are of two designs. In one type, loose ball-bearings are held in place with an adjustable cone. In the other, ball- or needle-bearings are in a self-contained cassette (cartridge), press-fitted into place within the pedal body. Sometimes a press-fit cartridge is also held with glue. Some pedals with cartridge bearings can be adjusted for play, others cannot.

Adjustment

Pedals need attention if they are either (a) dragging and squeaking, or (b) can be wiggled back and forth on the spindle with a clicking sound.

Ball-bearing and Cone

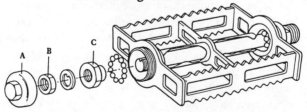

Remove dustcap A. Some threaded dustcaps can be undone with an ordinary spanner; others require a special tool. If you don't have the appropriate tool and instead use large pliers, be careful not to damage the dustcap. One trick is to tie a length of string to the shaft of a screwdriver, wind the string tightly around the dustcap, and then use the screwdriver as a lever to unscrew the dustcap. If the dustcap is the wedge type (press-fit), pry it off with a screwdriver.

Undo locknut B from cone C. Screw cone C fully home and back off one-eighth to one-quarter turn. Tighten locknut B firmly, but not hard, and check for play and that pedal spins easily. Adjust as necessary, each time tightening locknut B firmly but not hard, until the play is just a little more than you would like. A final hard tightening of locknut B should then bring the bearings into perfect adjustment. Replace dustcap A.

Cartridge Bearings

Pedals with cartridge bearings tend to vary in design, and in method for adjustment and disassembly. The instructions here are for the popular Look and Mavic 645 LS models, and at least in basics, will cover most pedals with cartridge bearings. However, if the pedals you want to service are a different make, it would be good insurance to first check with a bike shop for any particular servicing instructions or tips. In some cases, using the wrong technique or tool can cause irreversible damage.

Remove spindle cup A. This cup also serves as a retainer for the outer bearing OB. If the pedal has been loose and rattling, tightening the spindle cup may solve the problem. No? Use an 11 mm socket spanner to check the spindle nut N. NOTE: the spindle nut for the left-side pedal has a left-hand thread and unscrews clockwise. The nut has a nylon bushing to hold it in place and you should be able to feel resistance when screwing it in or out. If it is worn and moves very easily, replace it. If it feels OK, turn it in or out as necessary to adjust the pedal. Replace spindle cup A, making sure that it is firmly in place.

Step-in pedals often have a screw or bolt (T) for setting the tension of the release mechanism. Tension is increased by tightening the screw, and as a rule of thumb the amount of tension can be high; in an emergency or a crash the mechanism will still release. When first using a step-in pedal you will probably want a low tension setting until you are proficient at engaging and releasing the pedal. Take care when adjusting bolt T, as the plate it threads into is thin. If lowering the tension setting, do not unscrew bolt T more than 2½ turns from the fully home position.

Lubrication and Disassembly

Ball-bearings and Cones

Pedals lead a hard, dissolute life, and pedals with loose ball-bearings and cones need cleaning and lubricating every six months, more often if you ride a lot or often in wet weather. The outside end of the pedal is well-protected and therefore usually has a creditable amount of grease when inspected by removing the dustcap, but the inside end of the pedal near the crank arm is more vulnerable, and the bearings there usually go dry before the outside bearings. You have to take apart the pedal in order to check the inside bearings and therefore, if you are going to bother with the pedal at all, it's best to just give it the works: disassemble, clean, grease, and reassemble. Then you know it's right.

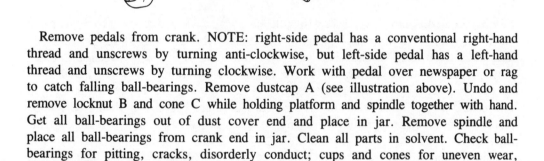

Remove pedals from crank. NOTE: right-side pedal has a conventional right-hand thread and unscrews by turning anti-clockwise, but left-side pedal has a left-hand thread and unscrews by turning clockwise. Work with pedal over newspaper or rag to catch falling ball-bearings. Remove dustcap A (see illustration above). Undo and remove locknut B and cone C while holding platform and spindle together with hand. Get all ball-bearings out of dust cover end and place in jar. Remove spindle and place all ball-bearings from crank end in jar. Clean all parts in solvent. Check ball-bearings for pitting, cracks, disorderly conduct; cups and cones for uneven wear, pitting, spindle for straightness.

Reassembly: pack grease into cups on platform. Pack ball-bearings into cup on crank side of platform (grease will hold them in place), and slide on spindle. Pack ball-bearings into dust cap side cup. Screw down cone C finger tight and spin pedal a few times to nest everything in place. Check that cone C is fully home and then back it off one-eighth to one-quarter turn. Secure with locknut B. Check for play and that pedal spins easily. Replace dustcap.

NOTE: When replacing pedals on bike be sure that left-side pedal, stamped 'L' on end of spindle shaft, goes on the left-side crank. It screws on anti-clockwise. The right-side pedal is stamped 'R' (surprise!) and screws on clockwise.

Cartridge Bearings

Pedals with cartridge bearings vary in durability, even in a particular model. Many people find that pedals of this type work without complaint for two or more years, and regard them as disposable. When the old pedals are worn out, they are replaced with pedals of a newer, more attractive design. Other people find that their pedals start squeaking or rattling after less than a year of use, and service them. Cartridge bearings that are merely dirty can be cleaned and lubricated, but so long as you have the right tool, it is easier to just replace them. The snag is possession of the tool, an expander-type bearing remover. Some well-equipped bike shops have this tool, but most do not. If you cannot find one, it can be ordered (reference CV28) from The Third Hand, P.O. Box 212, Mt. Shasta, CA 96067, USA.

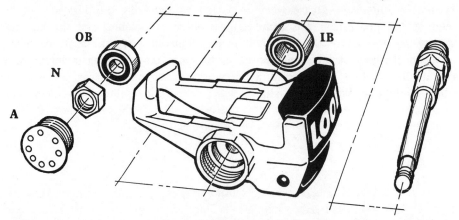

Remove spindle cup A. Unscrew spindle nut N until it stands proud of the pedal body, but still has 3-4 threads gripping the spindle. NOTE: nut N for the left-side pedal has a left-hand thread and unscrews clockwise. Tap nut N against a block of wood or with a plastic mallet to free the spindle. Remove nut N and pull spindle out of pedal. The outer bearing OB is a slip-fit; remove by gently pushing it from behind with a screwdriver or drift punch. The inner bearing IB should be removed only with a bearing remover; trying to drift it out will probably damage the pedal body.

Clean all parts with solvent. If the inner bearing IB is inside the pedal body, ensuring that all of the old grease is removed is a bit tricky. Use a small brush to help work the solvent into the bearings, and be careful not to dislodge any of them. When the bearings are clean, make sure that all the solvent evaporates by blowing the parts dry with an air hose, or placing them in warm place such as on top of a boiler. (See why it is easier to just replace them?)

Work fresh grease into the bearings IB and OB. If you have done a complete disassembly, tap inner bearing IB into place with a bearing installation tool, or a ½" or 14 mm socket. Lightly grease spindle. Insert spindle into pedal. NOTE: make sure you have the left-hand thread spindle mated with the left-side pedal body! Slide outer bearing OB into pedal body. The spindle threads should protrude through the centre of bearing OB. Thread on correct spindle nut N—again, a left-hand thread for the left-side pedal (tighten anti-clockwise)—and tighten it firmly but not hard. The spindle end should be only slightly proud of the nut N, and the spindle should rotate freely within the pedal body. Screw on spindle cup A firmly, but not too hard.

NOTE: if you try to put a right-side step-in pedal onto the left-side crank it will be obvious that something is amiss. One more time: the left-side pedal goes to the left-side crank and screws on anti-clockwise. The right-side pedal goes to the only crank left (hah!), and screws on clockwise.

Trouble-shooting

● Pedal is tight to crank but askew. Bent spindle. Replace immediately, bent pedals can play havoc with your knees.

● Grinding noises, hard to turn pedal. Try routine adjustment as above. No? Something is probably broken. Disassemble as above and replace defective parts. Check that the number of ball-bearings on each side is correct, it is easy to have too many or too few, or for one to have gone rollabout.

● Loose pedal. Check that it is tight to crank. Left pedal tightens anti-clockwise, right pedal tightens clockwise. No? Check the crank (see below) for tightness. No? It's got to be loose, worn, or missing ball-bearings.

Cranks

Cranks support the pedals and transmit pedalling power to the chainrings. They are attached to a bottom bracket axle (spindle) which rides on bearings inside the bottom bracket shell. There are three types of cranks: one-piece; cottered three-piece; and cotterless three-piece.

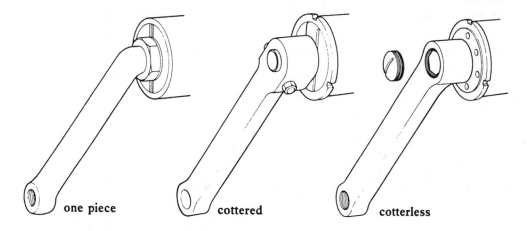

one piece   cottered   cotterless

One-piece cranks include the bottom bracket axle and are covered under Bottom Brackets. To test a cottered or cotterless crank for tightness, position the pedals equidistant from the ground (three o'clock/nine o'clock). Press firmly on both pedals with hands and release. Rotate crankset one-half turn and press pedals again. (You can also do this with your feet, while riding.) If something gives, one of the cranks is loose.

Adjustment and Disassembly

Cottered Cranks

Support the crank with a block of wood which has a hole or V-notch into which the cotter pin A fits. Alternatively, use a short length of pipe that fits over the cotter pin at one end, and braces against the floor at the other. Be sure that the support block or pipe touches only the crank and is firmly in place. Otherwise what you do next will damage your bearings by driving the balls into the sides of the cup and scoring it (called brinelling). Next: if you are tightening, give the head of the cotter pin two or three moderate blows with a wooden mallet, or hammer and wooden block combination. Then snug down nut firmly, but not with all your might or you will strip it. If you are removing the crank, undo cotter pin nut two or three turns so that nut is slightly proud of the pin to protect the threads, and then tap the threaded end of cotter pin. Repeat if necessary. Be careful not to damage the threads as you will want to use the pin again. If the pin absolutely will not move, take the bike to a shop and see if they can get it out 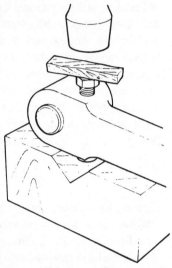 with a cotter press. If no, and you don't want to leave the problem to them, you can drill the pin out. It will take a while. To avoid damaging the axle, drill a small pilot hole to start, then progressively increase the diameter of the hole. If you use a new pin and it does not fit, file down the flat side until it does.

Cotterless Cranks

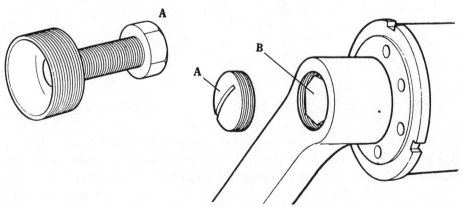

You will need a crank installer and extractor which fits your particular brand of crank. Cotterless cranks are made of alloy and must not be tightened with the same force as steel parts. To tighten or loosen, first remove the dust cover A. To tighten, apply socket spanner or installer tool to nut B and turn down, wiggling and lightly tapping the crank arm to make sure it is seated all the way. Check tightness of new cranks every 25 miles for the first 200 miles of use. To remove crank, undo and remove nut B and washer, if there is one. Back inner bolt A of extractor all the way out. Screw extractor into crank, being careful not to cross-thread it, and then tighten down inner bolt A. Do not do this with all of your might or you may strip the threads. If, as is likely, the crank does not come loose with a firm tightening on the extractor bolt, give it two or three taps with a hammer, and tighten the extractor bolt one-eighth of a turn. Repeat until crank comes free. When replacing crank, lightly grease axle. Wiggle crank back and forth and make sure it is fully home before you give it the final firm tightening. After a few miles of riding, check the crank; it is almost sure to need tightening again.

Trouble-shooting

●There is a 'click' as you bring the pedal around on the upstroke and then a momentary dead spot and another 'click' as you push it down. It may be a loose pedal, bottom bracket, or crank. If it looks to be the crank, test and tighten if necessary as per above.

●Stripped holding bolt on a cotterless crank. Get a new bottom bracket axle. If this is impossible, a machine shop may be able to re-thread the axle to accept a larger bolt. Be sure that the head of the larger bolt is small enough so that you can still use an extractor.

●Stripped thread for the extractor on a cotterless crank. A bike shop should be able to solve the problem. You may be able to find a substitute tool which will do the job. I have one which probably has to do with flywheels or plumbing. Anyway, the arms A will hook onto the crank or sprocket while the bolt passes against the bottom bracket axle.

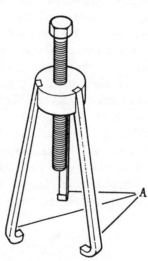

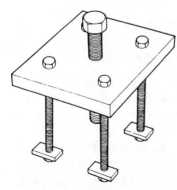

If you can't find a substitute tool a machine shop may be able to make an extractor. Explain that you want a steel plate or bar threaded in the centre for an extractor bolt, and with holes drilled so that other bolts can be slid through and in turn be attached to metal plates which will hook behind the chainset.

This example of whizzing up a Back Yard Special is mostly for fun, because any good bike shop should be able to deal with a stuck crank. The point is that you can get these things together yourself. I still remember with affection managing an emergency bottom bracket overhaul with a beer can opener, rock, and piece of string.

If the crank will not shift no matter what, or will have to be replaced anyhow, you can burn or hacksaw it off. Aluminium expands much more rapidly than steel, so if you give the crank a fast scorch, you may be able to get it off with a hammer and punch. If you hacksaw it off, be careful not to damage the axle.

● Bent crank. Could be dangerous, cranks do break every once in a while, and the fatigue created by a bend and subsequent repair is no help. Check with a bike shop, which will also have the right special tool for the job.

Bottom Bracket

How It Works

The bottom bracket axle (spindle) rotates on bearings inside the bottom bracket shell, and holds the cranks. On the Ashtabula type one-piece crankset, the two cranks and spindle are one unit. Three-piece cranksets (cottered and cotterless) consist of two cranks and a separate spindle. The bearings may be loose and run in adjustable cups and cones threaded into the bottom bracket shell itself, or be in non-adjustable cassettes that are fixed in place. A popular type of bottom bracket is a fully

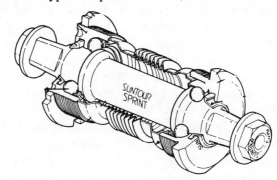

self-contained, maintenance-free unit that slides into the bottom bracketshell and is held in place with lockrings. This is an easy solution for the problem of crossed or stripped bottom bracket threads. When the unit wears out after two or three years it is simply replaced, often at less cost than overhauling a conventional bottom bracket.

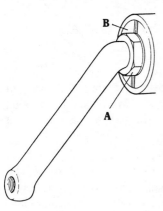

Adjustment

Ashtabula One-piece

If axle is hard to turn, or moves from side to side in bottom bracket shell with a clicking sound, first lift chain off chainwheel, and then loosen locknut A by turning it clockwise (left-hand thread). Use a pin tool or screwdriver in slots of cone B to turn it fully home (clockwise), and then back it off one-eighth turn. Tighten locknut A (anti-clockwise), and check that cranks spin freely without side-to-side play.

Three-piece

Bottom bracket axle (spindle) should be free from side-to-side play and spin easily. To adjust, first disconnect chain from chainwheel. Loosen notched lockring C on

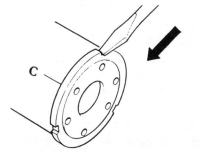

left side of bracket with a C spanner (bike stores) or hammer and punch (anti-clockwise).

Then tighten (clockwise) adjustable cup D fully home with a pin tool, or light taps of a hammer on a punch inserted in hole or slot.

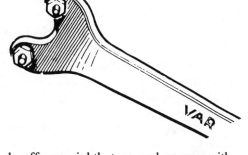

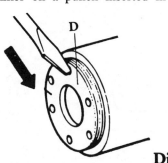

Back off one-eighth turn and secure with lockring C. Check that spindle spins freely and has no side-to-side play.

Disassembly

Bottom brackets with adjustable cones should be disassembled, cleaned, and greased once a year.

Ashtabula One-piece

Bearings for one-piece cranksets are held in clips so don't worry about losing them. Remove left pedal (clockwise) and chain from chainring. Undo locknut A (clockwise), remove keyed washer, and unscrew cone B (anti-clockwise). Remove bearing clip. Slide all parts off crank and place in a jar. Now move axle to right and tilt to

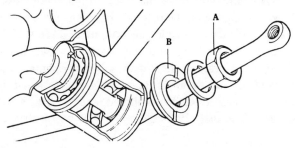

slide whole unit through bottom bracket and out of frame. Take right-hand bearing clip off axle. Clean everything thoroughly with solvent. See that ball-bearings are secure in clips and free from pitting or cracks; cups and cones should be even in colour where ball-bearings run and free from pitting or scoring. If cups are deeply grooved replace them. Remove with hammer and steel rod or screwdriver. Seat new cups by tapping them into place with a hammer and wooden block.

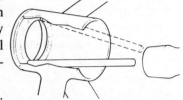

Reassembly: pack grease into bearing clips and cups.

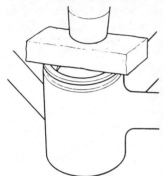

Slide one clip on axle with solid side against right cone. Gracefully insert crankset through bottom shell from right side. Slide on bearing clips with balls in, solid side out. Screw on cone (clockwise) handtight. Spin cranks to bed everything in, turn cone home and then reverse one-eighth turn, replace washer, and secure the whole business with the locknut (anti-clockwise). Check that crankset spins freely without side-to-side play. Replace pedal (anti-clockwise) and chain.

Three-piece, Standard

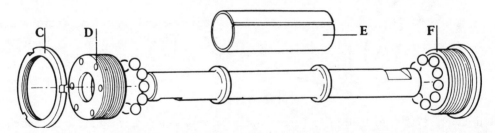

Disconnect chain and remove cranks (see Cranks). Place the bike on a work stand, or lay it on the floor right side down over newspaper or rags to catch loose ball-bearings. Undo lockring C with C-spanner or hammer and punch and remove. Hold axle in place against right-side bearings and remove adjustable cup D with a pin tool or anything that will fit into one of the holes in the cup. Look out for the ball-bearings! Some will fall out, others will stick to various parts. Gather, count, and place in jar. Make sure you have them all. If your bearings are clipped, lucky you. Now pull spindle straight out. Garner all the right-side ball-bearings and jar 'em.

There may be a plastic tube E inside the bottom bracket shell. This is to prevent grit in the frame tubes from falling into the bearings. Take it out and clean it off. Clean out inside of bottom bracket shell with solvent. Examine the fixed cup F with a torch. If it is unpitted and wear is reasonably even, leave it alone. Otherwise unscrew and replace. It has a left-hand thread and unscrews clockwise. Clean all other parts in solvent. See that: ball-bearings have no pits or cracks, and if clipped, are secure in retainers; inside of adjustable cup and cones on spindle also have no pits and wear is even; spindle is straight. Replace defective parts.

Reassembly: pack cups with grease. If ball-bearings are clipped, pack retainers. Replace plastic sleeve. Pack ball-bearings into cups. Grease will hold in place. Clipped bearings go with solid side on cone (balls face out). Carefully insert spindle, long end to chainwheel side of bottom bracket shell. Without jarring loose the ball-bearings, fit on adjustable cup and screw home. Rotate spindle as you do this to make sure it goes in all the way. Back off one-eighth turn and secure with lockring. Be careful threading this on as it is easy to strip. Check that spindle spins easily with no side-to-side play. Replace cranks and chain.

Three-piece, Sealed

Undo left-side lock ring A (anti-clockwise). Ditto right-side lock ring B, which has left-hand thread and unscrews clockwise. Next the left cup C (anti-clockwise) and right cup D (another clockwise). Remove spindle unit—if you can. Many units, such as the justly popular FAG, can only be extracted with a special tool. If the bearings in the unit are replaceable, the job should be done by a bike shop. A special tool is again required; bodging stands an excellent chance of ruining the bearings.

Replacement: mount right-side cup D (anti-clockwise). Insert spindle unit. If it is a SunTour as illustrated, the letter R side of the brand name is the end that goes against the right cup D. Set the chainline by moving cup D in or out as required. Remember, it is a left-hand thread, and tightens by rotating anti-clockwise. Onward: tighten left cup C (clockwise) until it is snug, but not tight. Fix right cup D in place with lock ring (anti-clockwise), and left cup C also with lock ring (clockwise). Check that spindle rotates freely.

Trouble-shooting

● Tight or loose crankset, grinding noises. Try adjustment as above. No? Disassemble and replace defective parts as above.

● 'Click' on pedal upstroke followed by dead spot and second 'click' on downstroke. Could be a loose bottom bracket spindle, but more probably the cause is a loose crank or pedal.

Chainring(s)

Adjustment

Check periodically for bent or chipped teeth. Remove chain. With a strong light behind the chainwheel, rotate it, looking from the side for chipped teeth, and from above or in front for bent teeth. If teeth are chipped, replace chainring (see below). If bent, take an adjustable spanner, snug it down over the

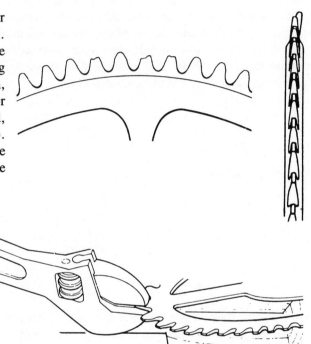

bent tooth, brace the chainring on a block of wood or table edge, and bend the errant tooth back into line.

Disassembly

It's replacement time when the chainring teeth start sharpening up and looking like waves. Do them all at the same time. This is a good moment to review your gearing options (see the chapter Bike Set-up). One-piece crank and chainring units have to be  replaced completely. Good chainsets have detachable chainrings held with bolts. Simply undo the bolts (most need a hex key). Keep track of all the washers and spacers. When you mount the new chainring(s), snug down the bolts, use the bike for a few miles, and then check the bolts again. Chainring bolts are animate: they are fond of sneaking up on you, springing a surprise, and then running away and hiding in a deep drain. I like to break in and seat the chainring bolts, and then fix them in place for sure with a product like Loctite.

Trouble-shooting

● There is a clunk sound every time you bring the chainwheel around. One possible cause is a bent tooth. Check by hanging bike up and slowly running chainset. If chain suddenly jumps up where it meets the chainring—bent tooth. Fix as above.
● Chainset wobbles from side-to-side, hitting front derailleur cage or rubbing chain stays. If this is not due to incredibly loose bottom bracket bearings, loose chainring bolts, or a bent spindle, the chainring is warped. Fixing is a job requiring both great delicacy and considerable force. Techniques vary so much according to the exact problem that I strongly suggest you leave it to a bike shop.

Chain

The chain is that innocent and simple looking business which transmits power to the rear wheel. There are two kinds: one is used on non-derailleur bikes, is ⅛" wide, and held together with a master link which can be taken apart without special tools; the other for derailleur equipped bikes, is 3/32" wide, and has no master link (it would catch in the rear gear cluster), so that a special chain riveting tool is needed to take it apart or put it together.

Lubrication

Dry film lubricants such as Superspray are clean, do not attract dirt, and go on in a flash. A lot of people just pile on the stuff every time they think of it, or after an especially wet or muddy ride, and don't bother to remove the chain until it needs replacement.

Oil is the traditional lubricant and is cheap (free if scrounged from a petrol station wastebin). The problem with oil is that it attracts grit and the solution is to add more oil in the hope that it will float the grit away—messy. Oil every link once a week, and remove and soak clean the chain in solvent once a month.

The most economical lubricant is paraffin wax, available in grocery shops. Remove and clean chain. Melt wax in coffee can or similar grade container, toss in the chain, and then hang it to dry so that drippings fall back into can. Save the can as is. One beauty of this method is that you only have to clean the chain with solvent the first time. Thereafter you can just toss it in the wax. The dirt will rise to the surface where it can be skimmed off. Every 800-900 miles.

Disassembly

Chains on bikes that see constant use will probably need replacement every two years, and on bikes in average service, every three years. It depends on how hard the chain is worked, and on how well it is lubricated. Although the chain may look perfectly sound, the tiny bit of wear on each rivet and plate adds up to a considerable

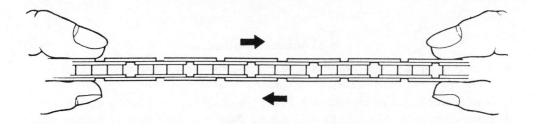

alteration in size. A worn chain will chip teeth on gear sprockets and in general be a pain. To test for wear, remove chain (see below) and lay on table with rollers parallel to surface. Hold chain with both hands about 4-5″ apart. Push hands together, and then pull apart. If you can feel slack, replace chain.

Another simple test for chain wear is to lift the chain 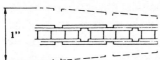 away from the front chainring. If the chain will clear the teeth it is more than time for replacement.

Test also for side-to-side deflection. It should not be more than 1″.

To remove and replace a master link chain find the master link and pry it off with a screwdriver.

To remove a derailleur chain you need to drive out a rivet with a chain tool. It is an excellent idea to learn the techniques of breaking and joining with some old bit of chain. It's an easy knack once you've done it a few times.

Nest the chain over the two pegs that are the most distant from the side of the tool where the pin emerges—the chain link plate must be braced or else it and not the

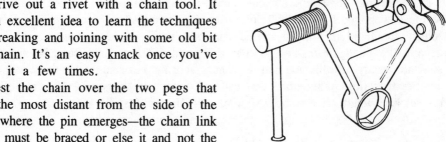

rivet will move. Be sure that the point of the chain tool centres exactly on the rivet. The usual number of turns for the handle is 6½, or 13 half-turns, but in any case, DO NOT DRIVE THE RIVET ALL THE WAY OUT. Go only as far as the outside plate. Stop frequently to check progress. Once rivet is near chain plate, free the link by slightly twisting the chain.

To replace the rivet, reverse chain in tool. Again, be careful how far you go. Stop when the rivet stands proud of the outside plate by the same amount as on the other plates. On the inside, where the point of the chain tool is pressing, the rivet will still be too high, and the link will be tight. Loosen the link by moving the chain to the spreader slot on the chain tool (the two posts nearest to where the pin emerges) and driving in the rivet just

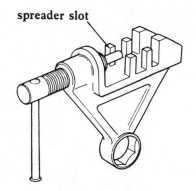

spreader slot

a little more—a quarter to one-half turn should do it. Check that everything is in place; if a rivet end sticks out too far it may cause problems in shifting and in chain feed.

Fitting

Most new chains need to be shortened in order to fit properly. On a non-derailleur bike it should be set so that there is ½" up-and-down play in the chain with the rear wheel in proper position.

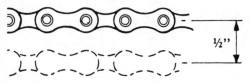

½"

On a derailleur bike, strictly speaking the chain should be long enough to fit on the large front chainring and large back cog, and short enough to fit on the small front chainring and small rear cog. Sometimes this is asking an awful lot, especially with widely spaced triple chainrings. You should never go big to big or little to little anyhow. Personally, I set the chain up so that it moves across the chainrings and cogs as a unit: little chainring to big cog, medium chainring to medium cog, and big chainring to little cog. This way, the derailleur has less chain to wrap, and can be slightly more compact and efficient.

If you have an indexed derailleur system (the kind with click stops for each gear ratio), it is likely to require a quite specific length of chain. If you are putting on a new chain, you'll have the old chain as a template. If you are mounting a new changer, there will be specific instructions with it.

If you just want to check how you are going, thread the chain through everything and over the big chainring and big rear cog. Pull it to a length that, at maximum, has the derailleur arm pointing at the ground. Keeping the chain at the same length, put it over the small chainring and small cog. If the derailleur does not wrap up and bite itself, you've no problem. If it does, shorten the chain, and never shift big to big.

Trouble-shooting

●Jammed link. Use chain tool to free tight links by working the rivet back and forth a quarter-turn on the chain tool at a time. If your chain tool has a spreader slot, use it.

●'Clunk' sounds and/or chain jumping sprockets. Test chain for excessive wear as per above. May also be a bent tooth.
●Chain squeals or creaks. Lubricate it!

Freewheel

How It Works

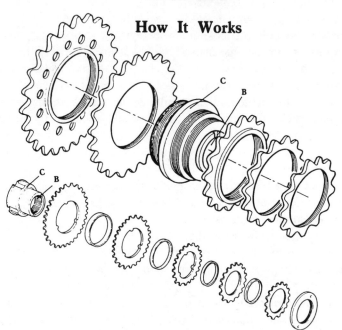

The sprockets (also called cogs) are threaded and/or slide onto the freewheel body. The exact combination varies from model to model. The freewheel body itself is in two main parts. The inside part B threads or slides onto the hub. The sprockets go on the outside part C. The freewheel is ratcheted so that when the outside part C is moved clockwise by the chain, the inside part B (and hence the wheel) also moves. But when the chain is stationary, part C holds still while part B rolls merrily along. The ratcheting is accomplished through the use of a clever maze of ball-bearings, pins, springs, and other minute parts inside the freewheel.

Freewheels come in 5-, 6-, and 7-speed models. Five-speed freewheels have standard spacing between each sprocket. Six-speed freewheels are of two types: standard or compact spacing. A standard 6-speed is slightly wider than a 5-speed, a compact 6-speed is the same width as a 5-speed. Seven-speed freewheels use compact

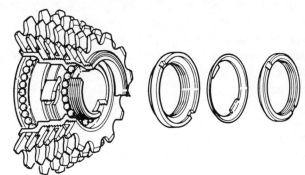

spacing, and are just slightly wider than a standard 6-speed. Freewheels with com-pact spacing need to use a chain that is slightly narrower than standard chain.

If you look at the wheel from behind the bike, you'll see that the hub is offset to the left, with the left-side spokes and hub flange farther away from the rim than the right-side spokes and hub flange. This insetting of the right-side hub flange is called dishing, and is done to make room for the freewheel, so that when everything is put together, the axle ends are equidistant to either side, and the wheel is cen-tred between the stays. Seven-speed freewheels need more dish than 5-speed freewheels, and while, technically speaking, standard space 6-speed freewheels also need a little more wheel dish, they can often be shoe-horned into place. Thus, if you have a wheel sized for a standard 5-speed freewheel and want to change to a 6-speed freewheel, the alteration is easy enough so long as you use a compact 6-speed model, and of course change the chain as well. It's equally straightforward to change from a standard space 6-speed to a compact 7-speed. If you want to change from a 5-speed to a 7-speed, however, the wheel will have to be re-dished for a deeper inset (thereby slightly weakening the wheel), and the chain stays spread apart slightly more—very much a job for a well-qualified bike shop. The only really good reason for going to a 7-speed is to be able to fit a final drive 12T sprocket, for maximum speed on descents. Fine for competition or if you are a speed freak, but otherwise much bother for little useful gain. Basically, unless you want to re-vamp the entire range of gear ratios, and possibly the transmission as well, stick with what you've got.

Adjustment

Tooth Care

Periodically clean the sprockets with an old toothbrush and solvent, and check them for chipped or bent teeth by looking at them in profile. Replace sprockets that have chipped or broken teeth, or uneven gaps between teeth. If things have come to this pass it is best to replace all the sprockets, and the chain as well. A stretched chain will kick up on new sprockets. If it's the odd bent tooth, straighten it by removing the sprocket (see below), gripping the bent tooth with an adjustable end spanner, and bending it upright.

Chainline

When standing in front of the bike and sighting between the two front sprockets (double) or in line with the middle ring (triple), you should see the centre sprocket of a 5- or 7-speed back gear cluster, or between the 3rd and 4th sprockets of a 6-speed cluster. One way to adjust the chainline is at the front, with longer or shorter bottom bracket axles, or with adjustments of the bottom bracket unit if it is the type that can be moved. Other problems may arise, though, such as a crank arm fouling a chain stay, and the front changer will need resetting.

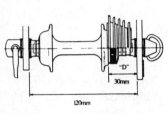

At the back, the freewheel can be moved out with spacers (in, if spacers are already there). Ah, but then another spacer will probably be needed on the other side of the hub, to keep everything in balance, and then perhaps the wheel won't fit into the drop-outs. I don't want to make you give up entirely, but it usually better to let a bike shop deal with problems of this sort.

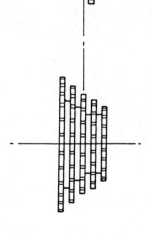

Lubrication

There's no adjustment for the freewheel as such. Keep it clean and lubricated. Some models like the SunTour Winner have an oil hole. Use oil or a liquid lubricant, and not grease, which may lock up the pawls and prevent the freewheel from freewheeling. About once a year remove the freewheel and soak it clean in solvent.

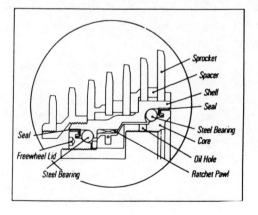

Disassembly

There are two kinds of freewheels: threaded and splined, or cassette. With the latter type you invariably need a special tool to undo the locknut holding the freewheel body on the spline. Undo the locknut and the rest is easy.

With a conventional threaded freewheel you must have a freewheel remover that fits your particular make and model of freewheel. It's no good trying to improvise. Freewheels can be tough to remove and a tool that doesn't quite fit is sure to tear everything to bits.

Remove wheel from bike. Bolt-on hubs: remove nut and washers from freewheel side of axle. Quick-release hubs: remove conical nut and spring from shaft of skewer and place spring in a jar. Leave axle or skewer in hub. Fit freewheel remover. If it won't go on, you may have a spacer nut. Remove with a spanner while holding axle stationary with another spanner on the left-side cone or locknut. Fit freewheel remover into slots or splines, and check that the fit is exact. Replace nut on axle or skewer and screw down finger tight, but firmly. Use a large spanner on the freewheel remover to break the freewheel loose. If it won't go, put the freewheel remover in a vise and turn the wheel. The moment the freewheel breaks loose, stop turning and slack the nut on the axle or skewer, and then spin the freewheel off by hand.

When mounting a freewheel first put a little grease or Superspray on the hub threads. Screw the freewheel on by hand, and be very, very careful not to cross-thread it, or to strip the threads. Snug the freewheel down with the remover but don't worry about tightening hard; this happens automatically as you ride.

To change sprockets you need a couple of sprocket removers, and if you are removing all the sprockets, a freewheel vise. The technique varies with the design of tool. Follow the instructions given with your particular tools. It's not hard, but this is another one of those jobs that, unless you know exactly which sprockets are threaded and which are not, is best left to a bike shop. A good way to find out about a particular freewheel is to handle a new one of the same type; you can usually get the sprockets off using just your hands.

One tip: if you have a new freewheel with sprockets that screw onto the block, then on your first ride, use the chain to tighten the sprockets systematically in the order with which they are mounted. If you tighten them out of order, there may be unexpected gaps.

Dismantle freewheel. Nah. If you want to do it for fun sometime, all right. It's logical enough inside, but there are a lot of tiny ball-bearings and such-like. Getting them all to stay in place while you reassemble the freewheel can be quite a trick. If you want an education, by all means. If you need a freewheel and yours doesn't work after a cleaning with solvent, buy another one.

Trouble-shooting

● A 'clunk' two or three times per complete revolution of the front chainring. May be a bent tooth on a freewheel sprocket. Check as per above.

•Freewheel won't freewheel. Try soaking in solvent to free up innards. No? Replace it.

•Freewheel turns but hub doesn't. Spin cranks while holding bike stationary and look at freewheel. If both parts spin around the hub, threads on hub are stripped. Ohh. New hub. If outside part of freewheel spins around inside part, freewheel is clogged up so that the pawls won't engage, or the pawls are broken. Try soaking in solvent. No? Replace. If you are afield and cannot replace, remove wheel from bike, and undo the the freewheel cover plate with a hammer and punch, pin-tool, or rock and nail. Inside there will be pawls and springs, and one or another of these parts will be stuck or broken. If the problem is clogging, clean the thing (flush by peeing on it, if you have nothing else) until it works. If something is broken you may be able to improvise a replacement part. At worst, just jam whatever you can find into the freewheel (old nuts, pebbles, hard-rock candy) until it locks up and works. It won't freewheel any more—be sure to keep pedalling whenever the bike is moving—but the bodge will get you home

Hub Gears

How They Work

Hub gears come in 2-, 3-, and 5-speed versions, with planetary or sun gears inside the hub. I consider these units too complicated to be worth disassembling, and so does any bike shop I have asked about doing such work—consider the exploded view of a 3-speed hub. There are some precious 8-year-old kids who routinely defeat chess

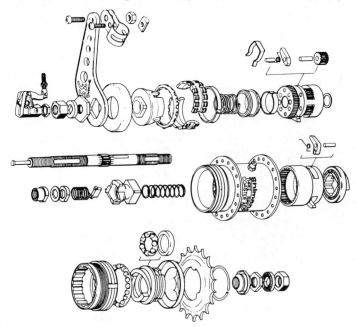

Grand Masters while simultaneously whipping apart and
reassembling 3-speed hubs, but
believe me, if you run into
trouble with your hub and can't
solve it with routine adjustment
or trouble-shooting (below), the
best thing to do is remove the
wheel and take it to a bike
shop. The chance of problems
arising is quite small. A
regularly lubricated hub should
last the life of your bike.

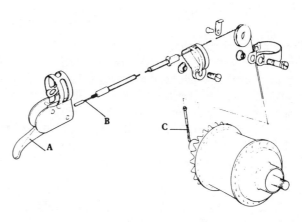

There are several brands of hub gears. Most are essentially similar to the original,
the Sturmey-Archer discussed here. Shift trigger A connects to cable B, which in
turn connects to toggle chain C on hub. Position of trigger determines gear.

Adjustment

Three-speed Hubs

First move the shift lever to 3rd or H.
Then take up slack in cable by loosening
locknut A and screwing down barrel sleeve
B. Leave cable very slightly slack. If barrel sleeve cannot do job, move the fulcrum
clip which holds the cable housing on the
bike frame forward.

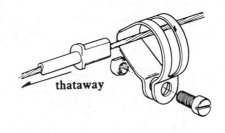

thataway

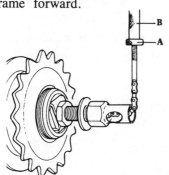

Test gears. No? Check position of indicator rod by looking through the hole in
the side of the right hub nut. With the
shift lever in 2nd or N position it should
be exactly even with the end of the axle.

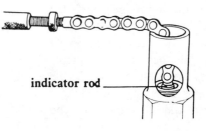

indicator rod

Adjust if necessary with barrel sleeve.
Test gears. No? Remove barrel sleeve
altogether. Check that indicator rod is
screwed finger tight fully into hub.
Reassemble and adjust as above. No? Turn
to Trouble-shooting, this section.

Five-speed Hubs

There are two shift levers. For the right-hand lever, follow procedure for 3-speed hub as above. For left-hand shift lever, set it all the way forward and screw cable connector to bellcrank B two or three turns. Then run shift lever all the way back, take slack out of cable with cable connector, and secure with locknut C.

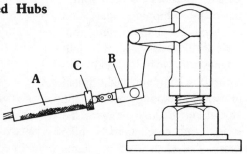

Lubrication

A teaspoonful to a tablespoonful of oil inside hub once a month. Less for a little used bike, more for a much used bike. If it starts dribbling around the place, less. Use a quality cycle oil, or motorist's SAE 30 oil. Some household and other cheap oils leave behind a sticky residue when the oil evaporates. This is the last thing in the world you want. Once a month use a spray like Superspray or a few drops of oil on the trigger control, cable, and inside the cable housing.

Disassembly

Hub: Remove wheel and take it to a bike shop.
Cable: It needs replacement when it becomes frayed, the housing kinked or broken, or there is evidence of suspicious political tendencies.

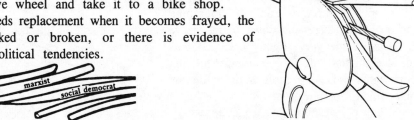

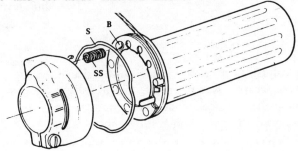

Move shift selector to 3rd or H. Disconnect barrel sleeve from indicator and loosen fulcrum clip (for illustration, see above). The method for freeing the cable depends on the type of shift lever.

Trigger: shift to 1st or L, pry up holding plate A with a small screwdriver, and push cable in until nipple clears ratchet plate. Pull cable out. Remove entire cable and housing assembly from bike and set aside fulcrum sleeve.

Twist grip: first take off the spring S with a screwdriver. Slide the twist grip off the handlebar and catch the ball-bearing B and spring SS if they fall out. Release nipple from slot and remove cable housing assembly from bike.

Take the old cable with you

to the shop when obtaining a replacement. This kind of cable comes in a variety of lengths.

Trigger: place the fulcrum sleeve on cable housing and thread through fulcrum clip. Pry up trigger control plate, insert cable through hole in trigger casing, and slip nipple into slot on ratchet. Run cable over pulley wheel if you have one, and attach to toggle chain. Shift to 3rd or H. Position fulcrum clip so cable is just slightly slack and tighten. Adjust if necessary as per above.

Twist grip: insert nipple into slot. Grease and replace spring and ball-bearing. Slide twist grip on handlebar and secure with spring clip. Use a small screwdriver to work the spring clip in. Run cable over pulley wheel if you have one, and attach to toggle chain. Shift selector to 3rd or H and adjust as per above.

Shift Lever

If you have a bashed or recalcitrant shift control the best thing is to replace it. They are not expensive.

Trigger: disconnect cable (see above) and undo bolt B.

Twist grip: I recommend replacing with a standard handlebar trigger, which is a much better mechanical design and more reliable. To remove old unit disconnect cable (see above) and undo bolt B.

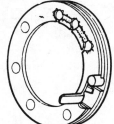

Trouble-shooting

No gear at all (pedals spin freely) or slips in and out of gear.
● Is gear in proper adjustment?
● Is cable binding? Check by disconnecting barrel sleeve at hub and working cable back and forth through housing. Replace if it binds.
● Is shift mechanism together and functioning? Twist grip models are especially prone to slippage after the track for the ball-bearing becomes worn.
● Insides of hubs may have gotten gunked up through the use of heavy or household oils so that pawls are stuck. Try putting in solvent or penetrating oil and jiggling everything around. No?
● Remove wheel and take it to a bike shop.

Derailleur Gears

Consists of a shift lever connected via a cable to a front or rear gear changer (derailleur) through which the chain passes. When the shift lever is actuated, the derailleur moves sideways and forces the chain onto a different chainring (front) or sprocket (rear). Although we are dealing here with a system, it will simplify everything to take it piece by piece first, and then deal with it as a whole.

Shift Levers
How They Work

The function of the shift lever is to position the derailleur in line with the selected sprocket or chainring. There are four kinds: down tube lever, stem or head tube lever, bar-end, and thumb-shift. All but the down tube type use both a cable and a cable housing. Down tube levers go either way; some use only cable, others use both cable and housing—it depends on how the bike is set up, and on the type of derailleur.

Although the external shape of a lever differs according to mounting point, the inside works are one of three basic mechanisms: friction, ratchet or clutch, and indexed. Friction levers are stopless, and hold the derailleur in place with simple force (tension). Ratchet and clutch levers have a little gear or clutch to hold the derailleur, and usually make a rapid click-click-click sound when operated. Indexed levers have stops for each position, and the lever moves with a single loud click for each change of gear ratio.

Adjustment and Disassembly

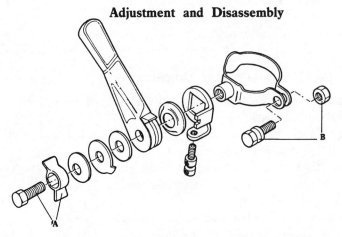

Friction type levers have a tension screw (A), with a slot for a screwdriver or coin, or a wing nut, or a wire loop—they all work the same way. The shift lever needs to be loose enough so that you can move it without undue effort, yet stiff enough to hold fast against spring pressure from the derailleur. Just loosen or tighten A

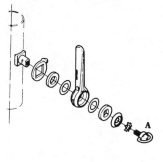

until it works OK. Take apart the unit for cleaning by removing A, being sure to keep everything in order, as there can be a fair number of bits. Periodically clean the mechanism, but don't lubricate it.

Ratchet and clutch type levers are frictionless, but there is still a bolt (A) for the lever to rotate on, and this also serves as a tension screw. If the lever is slipping,

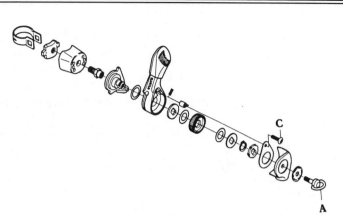

or hard to move, adjust the tension screw. To get the lever off entirely, remove bolt A and and cover screw B. For the Bar-Con, the expander bolt C has to be undone (clockwise) with a hex key.

Ratchet and clutch levers need occasional cleaning, and lubrication with grease or a spray like Superspray. Frequency depends on how hard the bike is used, and in what kind of weather—once a year will probably suffice. There are a lot of little bits, washers, springs, and whatnot, and if you prefer, the whole unit can be sloshed in solvent, dried, and lubricated. Or you can take it all apart, keeping careful track of the order of parts. One trick is to hammer a finishing nail part-way into a board; as you disassemble the lever, place each part in sequence over the nail. Another is to just thread the parts on a length of string. Do something: there are literally hundreds of different models of levers, and no way to show them all. The job is simple enough (do watch out for the spring) so long as you're careful.

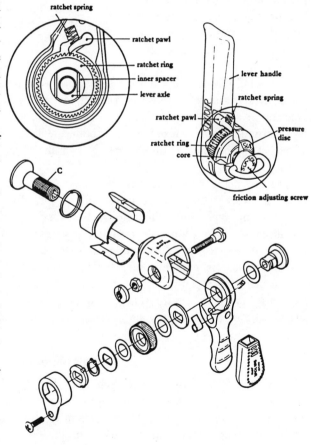

Indexed shift levers have pre-set stops for each gear ratio position. The lever and derailleur are synchronized via the cable adjusting bolt, and there are usually two: one at the derailleur, the other at the shift lever. If the derailleur shifts easily from a larger to a

mounting boss
right lever stop
serrated spacer
seal
washer
right lever
index/selection
ring cartridge
mounting bolt

smaller sprocket, but only with difficult in the opposite direction, tighten a cable adjusting bolt. If the problem is the reverse, loosen a cable adjusting bolt.

In servicing terms, indexed shift levers are a no-go area. They have internal works similar in appearance to those of ratchet levers, because the non-indexed mode uses a ratchet or friction mechanism. Life should therefore be simple, but to date, factory instructions for indexed levers abound with strict injunctions against removing the ratchet mechanism, or disassembling it or the index mechanism, on pain of voiding warranty.

There are many pre-conditions that must be met in order for an indexed shifting system to work well: correct frame alignment, drop-out configuration, cable type, cable housing type, hub dimensions, freewheel spacing, and chain, among others. Tolerances are tight: 'Variance from these measurements by as little as 1 mm (1/25th of an inch) can disrupt adjustment and performance,' relates one leaflet. One twenty-fifth of an inch is not very far. Indexed systems are sensitive, and in calling for maintenance and repair work to be done by a qualified bike shop, the manufacturers are trying to ensure that the things work as they should. At any rate, at least for the time being, if your indexed shift lever packs in, take it to a bike shop.

Trouble-shooting

Basically, the lever has a simple job: pull the derailleur into position, and hold it there. Shifting problems therefore often have their source elsewhere in the system, with the cable or derailleur. If the difficulty looks to be of this type, consult the Trouble-shooting section for the part in question.

Unexpected shifts to smaller sprockets.

●Is shift lever tension screw tight enough? If yes, cable may be catching in housing and then releasing when the bike hits a bump. Check by disconnecting the cable anchor bolt and ensuring that cable can move freely within housing.

● Is the derailleur unit itself adjusted properly? On a rear mech, sometimes the jockey wheel is too close to the freewheel sprocket, and the chain does not have enough clearance when moving from one sprocket to another. The shift lever and cable have enough power to pull the mech from a smaller to a larger sprocket, but in the other direction, when the mech is powered only by spring tension, it may hang up or move in fits and starts. See Rear Changers, Adjustment.

● Is the derailleur able to move back and forth easily? Check by pressing the shift lever fully home to release the derailleur spring, and then holding the chain clear of the sprockets while pushing the mech in and out. If it moves jerkily, there may be dirt in the works.

● If the lever is indexed, try it in non-indexed mode. If it works OK, 'the index adjustment needs tightening.

Shift lever cannot move derailleur to largest or smallest sprocket or chainring.

● Is cable too tight or slack? (Sometimes when a bike has had a new component or accessory added to it, the cable has inadvertently been fouled.)

● Are derailleur travel stop screws correctly adjusted?

Shift lever moves, but nothing happens, or response is fitful.

● Is cable anchor bolt tight?

● Is cable broken?

Shift lever won't move.

● Is tension screw too tight?

● Is cable or derailleur frozen? Check by isolating each part and seeing if it can move. If one is stuck, consult Trouble-shooting entry for that part.

Cables
Adjustment

Derailleur cables are thin and prone to wear. Check them often for fraying. Adjust-

ment is needed when the shift lever has to be pulled or pushed all the way back to engage the large sprocket. Set the shift lever so that the chain is on the smallest sprocket. Most systems have a cable ad-justing bolt, either at the derailleur or at the shift lever, and some systems have both. Undo the locknut A and move the cable adjusting bolt up un-til slack is removed from cable. If this will not do the job, turn it back down fully home, and reset the cable anchor bolt.

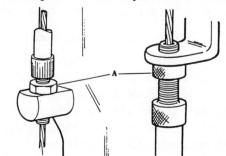

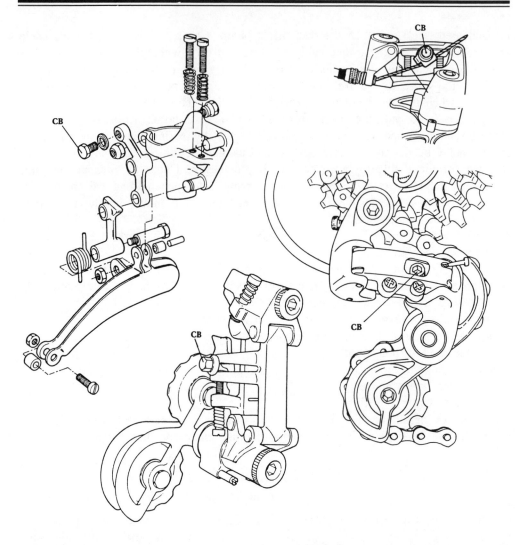

All derailleurs, front and back, use a cable anchor bolt or screw to hold the cable (CB).Sometimes the location is devious, well inside the derailleur body. Just trace the cable run and you'll find it. Loosen the cable an-chor bolt, pull the cable through until slack is removed (use pliers if necessary), and tighten cable anchor bolt.

Removal and Replacement

Move chain to smallest sprocket. Screw home cable ad-justing bolt. Undo cable anchor bolt and thread cable out of derailleur. Check cable housings (not on all models) for kinks and breaks. Remove cable from lever by threading it out—exact procedure varies from lever to lever, but the basic idea is the same.

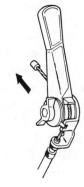

Do not cut new cable to size until after it is installed or it may fray and jam when going into cable housing. If you are replacing the cable housing as well and

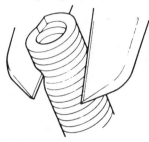

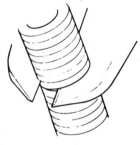

must cut it to size, be sure to get the jaws of the cutter between the wire coils of the housing, or else it will be squashed. Thread the new cable through the shift lever, and then through down tube tunnel, cable stops, cable housings, and whatever else is in your particular system. As you pass the cable through cable housings, twist it so that the strands at the end do not fray apart. Finish at derailleur. Move shift

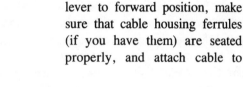

lever to forward position, make sure that cable housing ferrules (if you have them) are seated properly, and attach cable to cable anchor bolt. Work the mechanism a few times to take any stretch out of the cable, and reset the cable anchor bolt if necessary.

Trouble-shooting

Cable problems are evinced by delayed shifts, or no shifts at all. In any case, the procedure is the same: undo the cable anchor bolt and slide the cable around by hand, looking for sticky spots. Check carefully for fraying, and for kinks in the cable housing.

Front Changers

How They Work

There is a metal cage through which the chain passes as it feeds onto the chainrings. The cage can be moved from side to side, and, by pressing on the side of the chain, shifts it from chainring to chainring.

Virtually all derailleurs are built as a parallelogram. Heh.

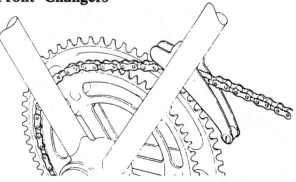

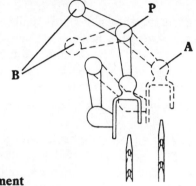

This design is used to keep the sides of the cage A straight up and down as the cage is moved from side to side on the pivot bolt P. The cage is moved by pulling with a cable at point B, and when the cable is released, spring tension pushes it back. Details may vary, but this is the basic concept.

Adjustment

The changer as a whole must be properly positioned, with the outer side of the cage about ¼″ above the sprocket. There are many nuances for this setting. For example, some front changers are designed to be used with triple chainsets where the difference between chainrings is at least six teeth or more. If the difference is less, say four teeth, then raising the changer a little higher may do the trick. Move the changer by loosening the mounting bolt B.

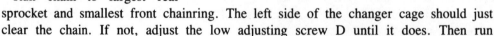

Side-to-side travel of the cage must be set. First check that cable is properly adjusted. Then locate the high and low stop adjusting screws. Sometimes they are cleverly hidden, but they can't go far—push the changer back and forth and see what things go bump.

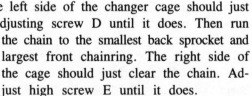

Run chain to largest rear sprocket and smallest front chainring. The left side of the changer cage should just clear the chain. If not, adjust the low adjusting screw D until it does. Then run

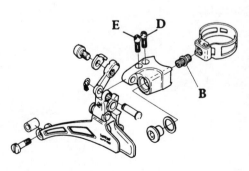

the chain to the smallest back sprocket and largest front chainring. The right side of the cage should just clear the chain. Adjust high screw E until it does.

Test operation of gears. If you don't have the bike up on a work stand, get a friend to hold the rear wheel off the ground while you turn the cranks and run through the gears. This is an important safety check. If you take the bike out on the road and something tangles, both you and the bike can be badly hurt.

You're almost certain to find that the changer needs further adjustment and diddling of one kind or another, for example to stay clear of a crank. It is also frequently necessary to over-set the travel of the changer in order to get the chain to move over, and this can have the chain rubbing the cage unless you remember to reverse the shift lever slightly after making a shift. When you get to the sometimes-it-shifts/sometimes-it-doesn't stage, move the adjusting screw only one-quarter turn a time.

Lubrication

A little Superspray or a few drops of oil on the pivot bolts once a month. If the unit becomes dirty, take it off and soak it clean in solvent.

Removal and Replacement

The vast majority of front (and rear) changers are pinned together with rivets, as opposed to bolts, and cannot be disassembled. When the unit becomes worn and sloppy, replace it. Remove chain or bolt at end of cage, if there is one. Undo cable anchor bolt and slip off cable. Undo mounting bolt(s) B and remove unit.

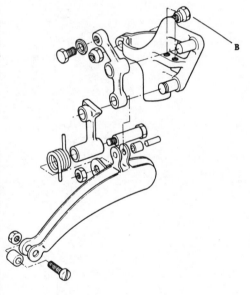

Trouble-shooting

Most of the difficulties experienced with the front changer are actually caused by problems elsewhere in the power train. I am assuming that you have already set your changer as per Adjustment, above.

Chain rubs side of cage.
● Is shift lever tight?
● Can you stop the rubbing by diddling with shift lever? For example, the amount of travel necessary to shift the chain from the small chainring to the large chainring may leave the cage too far to the right when the chain is on the large back sprocket, and cause the chain to rub the left side of the cage. It is common with front changers to move the cage back just a trifle after a shift has been completed.
● Is the chainset warped or loose?

Chain throws off sprocket.
● Is shift lever tight?
● Cage travel may be set too far out. Adjust it slightly.
● Is chain old? Is a link frozen?
● Are sprocket teeth bent?
● Are front and rear sprockets in alignment?

●If chain continually overrides big front sprocket, take an adjustable spanner and bend the leading tip of the outside cage in very slightly—about 1/16".

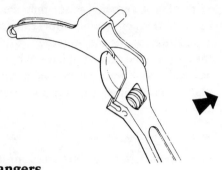

Delayed shifts or no shifts at all.

●Are pivot bolts clean? Try a little spray or oil.

●Is spring intact and in place?

●Is cable sticking or broken?

Rear Changers
How They Work

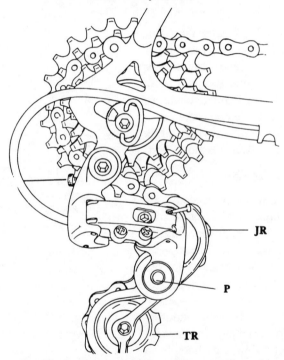

As the chain comes off the underside of the front chainring it passes through the rear derailleur riding over two pulleys, the tension roller (TR) and the jockey roller (JR). The cage holding the rollers is fastened to the main body of the changer by a pivot bolt P, and is under spring tension so that the chain remains taut. The cage position, and hence that of the chain on a particular freewheel sprocket, is determined by the changer body, which is also under spring tension in the direction of the smallest freewheel sprocket. A shift lever and cable are used to position the changer body over each of the inner sprockets; the shift lever draws the changer inward, and when the shift lever is released, spring tension carries the changer back outward.

Derailleurs come in an assortment of designs. Some are simple, others have compound articulation points. The more complex models are usually designed with the intention of keeping the jockey roller an equal distance away from each sprocket, on freewheels where the range of sprocket sizes is large (say, 14-30T or more). The best way to see and understand what is happening is to put the bike up on a work stand and watch how the derailleur moves while you rotate the cranks and run the chain through the various gears.

Adjustment

Changer Body

Most modern derailleurs are set on the frame so that the main body of the changer is parallel with the chainstay. Often there is an angle adjusting screw A. Basically, you adjust the angle of the derailleur to suit the size of the largest freewheel sprocket, more for larger, less for smaller. Thus, if you replace a 14-28T freewheel with a 14-32T model, you'll almost certainly need to increase the angle of the derailleur to clear the larger sprocket. Why not just set all derailleurs so that they clear anything? Because the closer and more compact everything can be, the more efficiently and crisply the derailleur will perform.

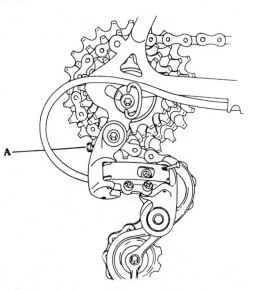

Some derailleurs are quite sophisticated with regard to adjustment of inclination and angle. The Campagnolo Chorus has two changer arm positions, marked A and B at either end of the changer body. Position A places the parallelogram at an angle of 5°, for optimum performance with freewheels with sprockets up to 27T (30 for LG touring model). Position B increases the angle to 30°, for use with sprockets up to 32T (34 for LG). To make the switch, loosen the bolts F and G, move body to new position, and tighten F and G. Fine-tune with angle adjusting screw A.

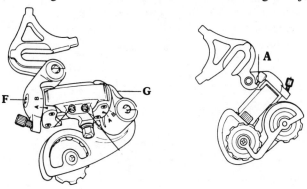

High Gear/Low Gear

The derailleur must be adjusted so that when the shift lever is released, spring tension moves the derailleur to the smallest freewheel sprocket (high gear), and when the shift lever is fully drawn back, the derailleur is over the largest sprocket (low gear).

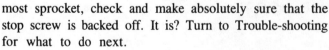

Run the chain to small rear sprocket and large front chainring, fully release the rear derailleur shift lever, and check that the cable is just slightly slack. Use the cable adjusting bolt (CAB) and/or the cable anchor bolt (CB) to adjust as necessary.

Side-to-side travel of the derailleur is regulated with two stop screws, high (E) and low (D).

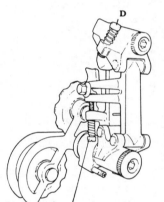

If derailleur moves too far, throwing the chain off the outermost or innermost sprocket, use the shift lever to position the derailleur so that the jockey wheel lines up with the sprocket on the side you are working on, and turn in appropriate adjusting screw until resistance is felt. Stop. Test shifting operation. If derailleur now does not go far enough, back the stop screw off until it does. It will take a bit of fiddling, and when you reach the sometimes-it-works stage, rotate the stop screw only one-quarter turn a time. If you cannot get the derailleur to move far enough to engage an innermost or outer-most sprocket, check and make absolutely sure that the stop screw is backed off. It is? Turn to Trouble-shooting for what to do next.

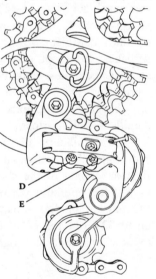

Indexed Stops

The stops on an indexed lever are pre-set. After you've got the side to side travel of the derailleur adjusted (above), use the cable adjusting bolt(s) to ensure that lever stop and derailleur position are synchronized. This adjustment can be fiddly, and the best method is to set it crudely with the bike on a work stand, and then fine-tune it as you ride.

Cage Spring Tension

On the majority of modern derailleurs the spring tension of the roller cage cannot be adjusted. Many use a spring of the spiral type, which has a wide range of even pressure and should not need attention. Other changers use coil or lever springs, and these often can be adjusted. Spring tension on the roller cage should be sufficient to keep the chain taut when in high gear. Excess tension will cause unnecessary drag and rapid wear. On the other hand, too loose a chain will skip and/or whip. If your chain is skipping and the tension seems OK, check the chain itself for wear. Worn chains skip. Check also the condition of the freewheel sprockets; if the teeth are worn and look like pointed fangs rather than square-ended incisors, head for new freewheel sprockets and chain.

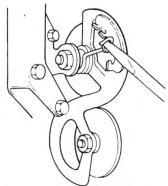

Cage spring tension adjustment procedure varies according to type of derailleur. Some old models have an external spring set on a hook on the cage. Move it with pliers or a screwdriver.

A popular way of tensioning the roller cage is with the use of a coil spring around the pivot bolt, and a series of holes in the cage for the spring end, as on the old Campagnolo Record and current Campagnolo Chorus and Croce d'Aune models.

Record: remove tension roller by undoing bolt G. Use one hand to hang onto the

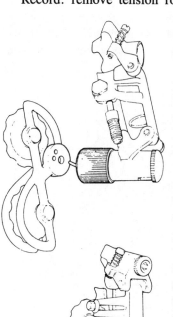

chain roller cage and prevent it from spinning, and unscrew the cage stop bolt SB. Now let the cage unwind (about one-half to three-quarters of a turn). Remove cage pivot bolt with hex key and lift off cage. Note that protruding spring end engages one of a series of small holes in the cage. Rotate cage forward until spring fits into next hole. Replace pivot bolt. Wind cage back one-half to three-quarters of a turn and replace cage stop bolt. Replace tension roller and go back to the races.

Chorus and Croce d'Aune: hang onto cage to prevent it from spinning, and unscrew the pivot bolt P. When there is enough clearance over the cage stop knob K, gently allow the cage to unwind until the spring is slack. Undo the pivot bolt, and the cage will lift away to reveal the holes for the spring end. Choose another hole (or not, as the case may be), slip in the spring end, and reassemble, winding the cage up against the spring before finally tightening the pivot bolt.

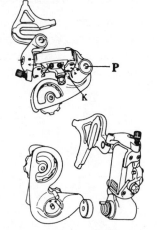

A fair number of changers use a coil spring held with a serrated nut that gives different tension settings. The basic technique is to undo the cage stop bolt, let the cage unwind, undo the pivot bolt, and change the slot in which the spring nests.

Lubrication

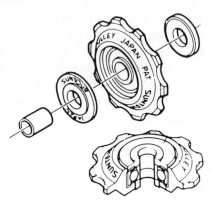

Pivot points on the changer body should be kept clean, and lightly lubricated with a spray like Superspray, or a tiny amount of oil. The main pivot bolts are usually greased, although Superspray can also be used. Treatment for the roller wheels is something of a personal decision. On most changers the makers claim that the wheels are self-lubricating. You can just leave them. But those poor roller wheels really get a lot of grit and wet, and I like to clean and juice them up often. Superspray is good. Grease is good. Anything clean and slippery is good. Another alternative is to use replacement pulley wheels with sealed bearings. These work well, but removing, cleaning, and lubricating a standard roller is easily and quickly done, and then you know the thing is in good shape.

Removal

Disconnect cable from anchor bolt. Remove tension roller or slip off chain, if you have a half cage. Undo the frame mounting bolt B and you're done.

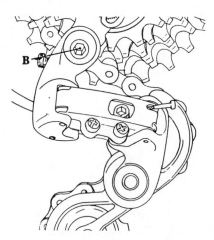

Disassembly

The parts that need regular attention are the chain rollers and the pivot bolts. Chain rollers are of two types: washers and bushing, and hub and ball-bearing. Most

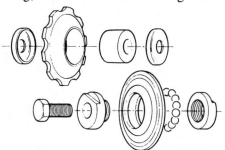

are straightforward and come apart by undoing the roller axle bolt. With a few others the cage arm pivot bolt and the roller axle bolt are a combined unit, and the former must be undone in order to undo the latter. You in any case need to periodically remove, clean, and lubricate the pivot bolt(s), so if you have a combined pivot/roller bolt, take it as a bonus rather than a hardship, and for instructions, go back to Adjustment, Cage Spring Tension.

One nice thing about a derailleur is that once you have it off the bike, you can sit down in a comfortable chair and examine the thing at your leisure. After the pivot and roller bolts, however, scope for disassembly is usually limited. Most derailleur main bodies are assembled with rivet pins and when these become worn, the unit is retired. (The cleaner you keep your mech, particularly the pins, the longer it will last.) Just the same, it may be helpful to go through all the paces, and here they are for three: the museum Campagnolo Record, the archtypical SunTour ARX, and the spiffy Campagnolo Chorus.

Campagnolo Record

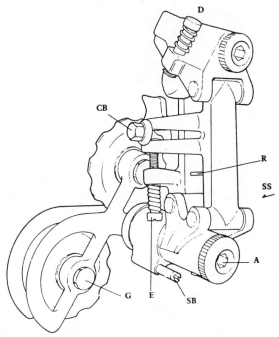

Hold chain roller cage to prevent it spinning and remove cage stop bolt SB. Let cage unwind (about one-half to three-quarters of a turn). Undo cage pivot bolt locknut and lift off cage. Slide out pivot bolt A and spring. Back off high gear adjusting screw E to minimize changer body spring tension, and undo spring bolt SS. Clean all parts with solvent and lubricate. Reassembly: screw in spring bolt SS while holding changer body spring R in position. Replace cage spring and slide in pivot bolt. Put cage on changer with two half-moon sides next to changer. Put nut on pivot bolt. Rotate cage back one-half to three-quarters of a turn and screw in cage stop bolt SB. Replace jockey roller. Mount derailleur on frame. Replace tension roller, cable. Adjust side-to-side travel.

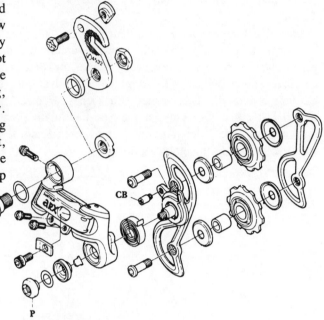

Wind up cage and body, hold tight, remove cage stop screw CB, and allow cage and body to unwind. Undo cage pivot bolt nut P and separate cage and body. Clean everything, replacing spring if necessary. Rejoin body and cage, fitting spring into slot on pivot bolt, and replace nut P. Wind cage up clockwise and fit cage stop screw CB.

Campagnolo Chorus

Hold cage body tight, slightly undo pivot bolt P until cage will clear stop, and allow cage to unwind. Detach roller bolt R from pivot bolt, lift off cage, and draw pivot bolt P out of body. Note position of cage spring end in cage. Clean everything (including other roller wheel), lubricate, and reassemble.

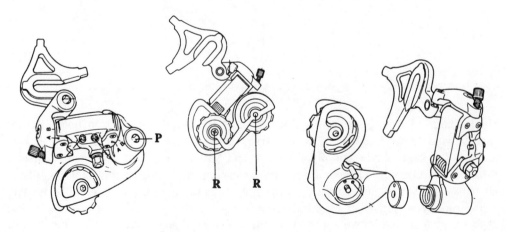

Trouble-shooting

Derailleur is sticky, won't shift, sometimes shifts unexpectedly.

●Is shift lever working smoothly but with enough friction to hold derailleur in place?
●Are cables sticking?
●Are pivot bolts lubricated and clean? On a very few models these bolts can be adjusted.

Derailleur will not go far enough.

●Is cable slightly slack when shift lever is fully released?
●Are adjusting screws properly set?
●Does cable slide easily?
●Is pivot or main changer spring broken?
●Are chain rollers lined up with chain?
●Try to wiggle the derailleur unit by hand. Can you push it to the desired position? If yes, the works are gummed up. Clean in solvent and lubricate with spray or oil. Adjust (not possible with all models) by undoing pivot bolts one-eighth of a turn and resetting.

If you cannot push the derailleur into line with the big rear sprocket and the adjusting screw is backed off, go to a bike shop. If the derailleur won't reach the little rear sprocket and the adjusting screw is backed off, a spacer washer at the mounting bolt may help.

Chain throws off sprockets:

●Are adjusting screws set properly?
●Are any teeth worn or bent?
●Is chain good?
●If chain is skipping, is spring tension for roller cage sufficient?
●Is roller cage aligned with chain?

Power Train—Trouble-shooting Index

Noises

First make sure that noise is coming from power train by coasting bike. If noise continues it is probably a brake or hub problem. If noise persists, try to determine if it comes from the front (crankset), the chain, or the rear (freewheel or derailleur). Do this by disconnecting the chain and spinning the various parts.

Grinding

Front -
- Bottom bracket bearings OK?
- Pedal bearings OK?
- Chain rubbing derailleur?
- Front chainring rubbing cage or chain stay?

Back -
- Wheel bearings OK?
- Freewheel OK?

Clicks or Clunks

One for every revolution of crankset -
- Pedal tight?
- Crank(s) tight?
- Bottom bracket bearings OK?
- Are teeth on chainring(s) bent?

  Two or three for every revolution of the crankset -
- Are teeth on rear sprocket(s) bent?
- Is chain worn or frozen?

Movement, but No Power

- Is chain there?
- Is freewheel OK? If it spins without moving wheel, the pawls are stuck or the pawl springs are broken. See Freewheel.

No Movement

Find out which part is stuck: bottom bracket, chain, freewheel, or hub, and turn to Trouble-shooting section for particular part.

Ride On!

Everybody has dreams and here is one of mine: motor vehicles exist only in memory and museums. Cycles are used for local personal transport and light goods carriage, and mass transit systems are used for long journeys and bulk loads.

The efficiency of such an arrangement in terms of money and energy expenditure is tremendous. A cycle factory is a low-technology operation that is far easier to initiate and maintain than an automobile factory. Cycle production and use does not necessitate vast support industries in petroleum, metals, rubbers, plastics, and textiles. Road requirements are minimal. There is no need for traffic regulation, licensing, courts, solicitors, and expensive insurance. There are no 6,000 loved and cherished people dead and gone each year, and no hundreds of thousands of maimed people requiring expensive hospital, emergency, and other medical services.

A dream? In China, there are about 25,000 people for each motor vehicle, as against three people per motor vehicle in Britain and the United States. People cycle or use public transportation. A direct comparison would of course be misguided. China is culturally very different, and is a developing country that is austere by Western standards. Much work is done by hand, including crop irrigation, waste disposal, and movement of goods up to several hundred pounds in weight. A bicycle is a serious piece of equipment that can cost up to two years' wages, and requires a government permit to purchase. At the moment there is about one bike for every five people in China, but production has been increasing at about 15 per cent annually and by now is pointing toward 50 million bikes a year. In terms of sheer transportation efficiency China has got it right.

In Britain, the government has at last conceded that cycles ought to be a recognized feature of the transportation system. Fine, but the cancer of motor vehicles is already terminal. British Rail has the lowest subsidy of any nation-wide rail system in Europe, and is headed the way of the dodo. Railway route closures have been a steady feature for many years, and in turn, motor vehicles and roads have proliferated; one prediction is that the end of the century will find 27 million cars in use (*Instead of Cars*, T. Bendixson, Penguin Books, London). Cyclists and pedestrians will continue to slug it out with motorists, motorists will slug it out with each other, and with more cars in use than ever before, the price in human suffering over the next decade will be even greater than that of the last: killed—62,000; seriously injured—800,000; slightly injured—2,500,000.

The cancer responsible for this carnage is carried by an agent known as the road lobby, made up of organizations and people who make money out of motor vehicles: principally, the petroleum, motor vehicle, and road building industries, and their hand-maiden, the government and the Department of Transport. The road lobby is an ugly phenomenon, well documented and described in *Wheels Within Wheels*, by Mick Hamer (Routledge and Kegan Paul, London). Briefly, the road lobby has money, while the population at large is armed only with the force of public opinion. The power of money is constant, that of public opinion is variable, and at the end of the day money usually triumphs.

Is there any hope? The answer depends very much on where you chew the stick. So far as mass transport and long journeys are concerned, forget it. The die is cast. The Department of Transport has over 10,000 employees involved in highway licensing (vehicle testing and taxation), another 2,500-odd employees involved in road pro-grammes, and less than 100 employees concerned with the railways. So far as per-sonal transport and short journeys are concerned, however, there is hope. The ma-jority of journeys are short, 74 per cent are under 5 miles and a staggering 86 per cent are under 10 miles, and for these distances the formula more cars, more roads simply doesn't work. Indeed, the formula produces yet even greater conges-tion, bettering the climate for the ideal instrument of guerrilla transport warfare— the bicycle.

Little more than a decade ago, bikes were toys. If you started talking about the importance of bikes, people thought you were touched. Harmless, but not all there. Today things are very different. You can earn a respectable living working in the area of cycling, and cycle transportation engineering is a movement of growing force and intensity. Provisions for cyclists in Britain are embryonic, undernourished, and sparse, but the roots and strands are there—in the wasteland of cars, fumes, noise, destruction, and death, that distant, barely perceptible glimmer of motion is the bike slipping through!

Take for example the conversion of disused railways into cycle paths. This scheme originated with the Bristol group Cyclebag, who in the summer of 1979 built a cy-cle path along 5 miles of disused railway between Bath and Bitton, using limestone grit rolled over the existing railway ballast. The route passes through pretty coun-tryside, was originally graded for trains and is therefore easy to cycle, and immediate-ly found a high level of use by both cyclists and pedestrians. The success sparked more work by Cyclebag and other groups, and helped the commissioning by the Department of Transport of John Grimshaw & Associates, to produce *Study of Disused Railways in England and Wales - Potential Cycle Routes* (HMSO).

According to this study, since 1923 at least 7,000 miles of railway has become disused in England and Wales, and a good proportion of this is readily convertible into cycle paths without major expense. Over 200 miles of railway cycle path can be built for less than the cost of one mile of motorway, and construction is labour-intensive, giving local employment and demand for materials. Railway cycle paths are lovely: tarmac ribbons meandering through countryside and farmlands with nary a petrol station or other rancid commercial enterprise in sight, yet of course linking

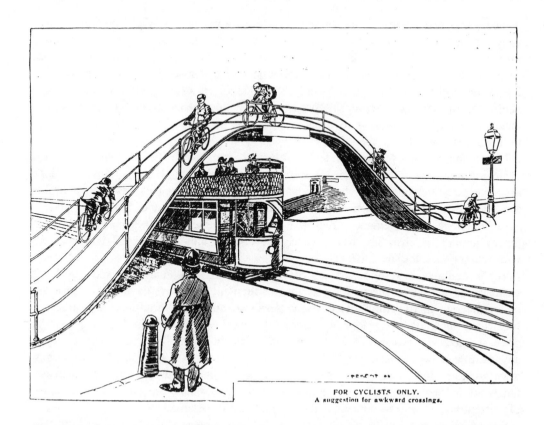

FOR CYCLISTS ONLY.
A suggestion for awkward crossings.

urban locations and other logical journey points. No cars: safe for children, elderly people, and the rest of us, too! A nation-wide network of railway cycle paths is a fabulous idea, and while attaining this goal is still a long way off, many regional routes are now under construction, and more are in sight. For particular information, ask of your local Cycle Campaign group.

Railway cycle paths are utopian; providing for cyclists in the context of already extant transportation systems is a lot more difficult. The easiest way is to start from scratch, and the classic example of building an entire town with provision for cyclists is Stevenage, England. Stevenage has a population density greater than that of Central London, and yet there is not one single traffic, cycle, or pedestrian light in the entire town. Even at rush hour the flow of traffic is so even and smooth that there does not appear to be anybody around. The reason is that there are no conflict points and no impediment to movement whether you are driving a car, riding a bike, or walking. There are independent roads for motor vehicles, cyclists, and pedestrians. Use of one particular type of road is not obligatory; the charm of the system is that it works so well that most road users prefer to use the road designed for them.

You can cycle or walk anywhere you wish in Stevenage and never encounter a motor vehicle. The offical cycleways system is shared by all types of cycles, small mopeds, and pedestrians. Some of the cycleways are completely independent routes. Others frequently run alongside main roads but are separated by grass verges and trees from both the roads and footpaths. Conflict at cross points is resolved by the generous use of underpasses. These are a study in sensitive design. An overpass for cycles has to rise at least 16 feet, which involves steep gradients and a lot of hardware. An underpass for cycles only needs 7½ feet of clearance and in Stevenage they are made by excavating to a depth of 6 feet, and using the excavation material to raise the road by 3 feet.

In addition to the cycleway system, cycles are free to use the footpaths, and most cycle journeys are door-to-door. Despite mixing cyclists and pedestrians, accidents are very rare, and minor. So far as I know, the worst in decades has been a broken arm. There are no rules and regulations for the cycleways and footpaths, and no need for police involvement. There's no silly business about bikes having to use the cycleways. Cyclists are free to use the roads if they prefer, and that's exactly what racers and the odd HPVs do.

The benefits of a system such as Stevenage's are often intangible and not easily reckoned on a balance sheet. What is the worth of never, ever, having an obstruction or aggravation in travelling? That whole series of abrasions, conflicts, and problems for which most of us armour up each day just doesn't exist in Stevenage. What price a mother's peace of mind, knowing that her children can walk or cycle anywhere and never encounter a motor vehicle? Sixty per cent of the workers in town go home for lunch. How do you measure the value and effect of this increased family life? These alterations in the quality of living resemble the pastoral peacefulness of 'primitive' societies—but with full technological benefits!

Stevenage started with a clean slate. In the vast majority of places, providing for cyclists must be done in the teeth of already established transport systems and distribution of real estate. It's rarely easy, and blunders are common. All too often the provision of a cycle facility is just an excuse for clearing bicycles off the roads, and some cycle paths are more dangerous than the roads they have replaced. Equally, cycle planners and activists have scored many successes. Cycle transportation engineering is a complex and technical subject; a good, brief guide is *The Bicycle Planning Book*, by Mike Hudson (Friends of the Earth, London). Read also *Getting There*, by Don Mathew, and *Pro-Bike*, by Andy Clarke (both Friends of the Earth, London). If you want to know the score on today's roads, read *Danger on the Road: The Needless Scourge*, by Mayer Hillman and Stephen Plowden (Policy Studies Institute, London). Further afield, *Bicycle Transportation*, by the American John Forester (MIT Press, Cambridge, Massachusetts, USA) is highly useful. Forester is an original, at times dogmatic, but a fighting crusader who has laid down many important guidelines in cycle transportation engineering. Another useful book is *A Handbook for Cycle Activists*, by Ernest Del (Stanford Law School, Stanford, Connecticut, USA). *Energy and Equity* and *Tools for Conviviality*, by Ivan Illich (Penguin, London) are wonderful books for relating philosophy to nuts and bolts.

The organizations to contact are the Cycle Campaign Network, c/o London Cycling Campaign, Tress House, 3 Stamford Street, London SE1, and Friends of the Earth,

26-28 Underwood Street, London N1 7JQ. If you are stateside or want American publications, try Bikecentennial, P.O. Box 8308, Missoula, MT 59807-9988, USA, and Bicycle USA, Suite 209, 6707 Whitestone Rd., Baltimore, MD 21207, USA.

In the Netherlands the idea that people come first is well advanced. They've of course got cycleways like you wouldn't believe. You can get anywhere on a bike. They've also got residential districts called *woonerfs* that are designed primarily for people. Cars can gain access, but only very slowly and not in numbers. Landspace in a woonerf belongs to the people, and is safe for children to play in. Such an arrangement gives a far wider dimension to the concept of home. It's definitely the sort of thing we should work towards. Woonerfs demonstrate the key concept in planning for people—territory. Fully half the space in our cities is given over to motor vehicles. People are secondary to routing cars around the place. For example, zebra pedestrian crossings are often provided only after a certain number of people die at the location. How crazy can you get?

Will we see a world in which cars are just a memory? Will we see an end to the bomb? The idea of vaporizing the planet many times over also does not make a lot of sense. Like the road lobby. the war establishment is vast, wealthy, and solidly entrenched; it seems inevitable that one day, in the name of security and protection, the world will go bang. But you don't give up. You don't quit living just because living might end. Cars as a transportation necessity are as much of a hoax as bombs for peace. The ten largest companies in the world all produce oil or cars. They routinely buy and sell governments. The vested interest in cars is colossal. And nowhere is the car more important, more a fundamental cornerstone of transport, than in Britain and America. You still don't quit. In fact, sometimes you win a few—like by riding a bike.

People do want to live. To be themselves. And that's my vision of the future. I keep seeing people in personal vehicles (PVs) that are essentially extensions of their bodies. Icarus suits. Transportation not just as something that happens, but a conscious activity that people do, each in their own way and for their own purposes. In my mind's eye it looks like many fish swimming in the sea: little and big, slow and fast, all orbiting and moving—and open. That's the most important feature. Not people wrapped in metal shells, but people part of their environment, moving with it and using it.

That's my faith, and I live it a lot in a world of bikes and HPVs and all the adventures large and small that can be devised. It has a richness and a texture that I am mortally convinced is right for people. I've loved bikes for most of my life simply because they are fun, rewarding, and kind. They go with human life, human contact, loving relationships—and even worthwhile work!

And it is also a war. Every day out might be the last. The dead passing through our cemeteries and crematoriums and the maimed and injured in our hospitals are embraced with glee by the road lobby. Haven't you known someone, perhaps someone close, who was killed or seriously injured in a road crash? Do you imagine that you will live the rest of your life without losing someone you love in a road crash? Was it necessary? Is it necessary? What would the answers be if we were talking about trains? Few ask such questions, and still fewer put the financial support behind alternative schemes necessary to create a choice. It is very difficult to find a workable perspective for this kind of situation, but in the end one fact is stark: my life, and yours, is on the line.

Some crazy comes running down the street, shooting people dead left, right, and centre, and unless he runs out of ammunition there isn't much choice—you blow him away. Like a mad dog. Now Hymie Dunderhead comes along driving a 140-mph Turbo-Fuel-Injected Special. Hymie has worked hard to get his idiot crate. From day one he's listened to his parents, to the telly, to his school masters, to his employers—Hymie has co-operated with his society, however insane, and now he wants his reward, some kind of evidence of his co-operation as a sop to a malformed ego—and that just happens to be a 140-mph Turbo-Fuel-Injected Special that in Hymie's hands is far more dangerous and indiscriminate than a gun. What do you do with Hymie—shoot him like a mad dog? According to his lights he's playing by the rules, however crazy. If you do something drastic to him, he'll come back for more, inflamed by the angry knowledge deep in his heart that basically, he's wrong.

So what? A lot of people are wrong in the head. We've got a long history of wars, genocides, and other destructive madnesses. Self-preservation has to come into effect at some point. Make it early. You're on your bike and a motorist endangers your life? Go for their throat. The cars ignore a 15 mph speed limit past the local school? Mine the road with bricks. Blow up the road. Too dangerous? You might go to jail? Then that is the price you place on your child's life. And yours.

The right to live is a birthright—but you must fight for it. There's no matter of right or wrong, good guys or bad guys. It is a very simple situation: motor vehicles are filling the air with deadly fumes and noise, recklessly wasting a dwindling supply of natural resources, *and killing and injuring people.* Four out of every ten cars in Britain will someday kill or injure a human being, or have already done so.

Where you pick up on the situation is up to you. When cars pull a rat-run race through a residential neighbourhood some people respond by lobbing plastic bags filled with brake fluid at the cars. Other people try speaking nicely to the motorists. Most effective are speed bumps that force the cars to slow down—but do what you have to do. There are many fronts and strategies. Each moment of opportunity is a matter of individual assessment and decision. It might be fun, it might be hard, it might be little, it might be great—the only rule, I think, is to honestly do it for yourself. Do it because you want to, because you must, not because you think you should. Sometimes the moment is right to move, other times there's something else to do. Life is dynamic; we develop, change, and grow every day. We move according to our best understanding of the moment, act as we are best able, and are responsible for the consequences—that's how we learn. Right and wrong are relative; the important thing is, if a chance to move comes your way, take it.

RENDEZVOUS
WHEN HITLER'S LITTLE GAME IS FINISHED!

Index

Useful addresses

You can write to various national tourist offices and cycling organizations for information:

Albania—Federata Sportive Shgiptare-Bruga, Abdi Toptani 3, Tirana.

Austria—Arbeitsgemeinschaft umweltfrreundlicher Stadtverkehr, Frankenberggasse 11/2, A-1040 Vienna. Also: Osterreichischer Radsport-Verband, Prinz Eugenstrasse 12, 1040 Vienna.

Australia—Bicycle Australia, PO Box K499, Haymarket, New South Wales 2000.

Belgium—GRACQ, 28, rue Ernest Gossart, B-1180 Brussels. Also: Ligue Velocipedique Belge, 49 Avenue du Globe, 1190 Brussels.

Bulgaria—Federation Bulgare de Cyclisme, Boulevard Tolboukhine 18, Sofia.

Czechoslovakia—Ceskoslovenska Sekce Cyklistiky, Na Porici 12, 115 30 Prague 1, CSSR.

Denmark—Dansk Cyklist Forbund, Kjield Langes Gade 14, DK-1367 Copenhagen K.

Eire—Irish Cycling Federation, 5 St Christopher's Road, Montemotte, Cork.

Finland—HePo, Valpurintie 6 A17, SF-00270 Helsinki 27.

France—FUBICY, 4 rue Brulee, F-67000 Strasbourg. Also: Federation Francaise de Cyclotourisme, 8 rue Jean-Marie Jego, 75013 Paris.

Hungary—Hungarian Cyclists' Federation, Budapest 1146.

Luxembourg—Letzebuerger Velos Initiativ, 135 Ave de la Faienciere, L-1551 Luxembourg.

Netherlands—ANWB, Wassenaarseweg 220, 2596 EC Den Haag. Also: Echte Nederlandse Fietserbond, Postbus 2150, NL-3440 BH Woerden. Also: Netherlands Cycletouring Union, P.O. Box 240, 2700AE, Zoetermeer.

Italy-Bici e Dintormi, Via Morosini 3, I-10128 Torino.

New Zealand—Bicycle Association of New Zealand, PO Box 2454, Wellington.

Northern Ireland—Northern Ireland Cycling Federation, 9a Great Northern Street, Belfast.

Norway—Norges Cykleforbund, Hauger Skolevei 1, 1351-Rud, Oslo. Also: Syklistenes Landsforening, Majorstuveien 20, N-0367 Oslo 3.

Poland—Brenard Rzeczynski, ul Engla 14 m 5, 60-232 Pozan. Also: Polska Zwiazek Kolarska, 1 Plac Xelaznej, 00136 Warsaw.

Portugal—Federacao Portuguesa de Ciclismo, Rua Barros Queiroz 39-10, Lisbon.

Spain—Amics de la Bici, Agrupacio d'Usaris Barcelona, Apartat de Correus 10012, 08080-Barcelona. Also: Federacion Espianola de Ciclismo, Calle Ferraz 16-50, Madrid 8. Also: Pedalibre, Calle Campomanes 13, E-28013 Madrid.

Sweden—Cykelframjandet, P.O. Box 3070, S-103 61 Stockholm 2.

Switzerland—Comite National du Cyclisme, P.O. Box 930, 1211 Geneva 3. Also: IG Velo beider Basel, Frobergstrasse 43, CH-4052 Basel. Also: Verkehrs Club der Schweiz, Spitalgasse 5, CH-8001 Zurich.

West Germany—ADFC, Postfach 107744, D-2800 Bremen 1.

USSR—USSR Cycling Federation, Lougenetskay Naberognay 8, Sportcomite, 119270 Moscow.